Lecture Notes in Computer Science 15736

The series Lecture Notes in Computer Science (LNCS), including its subseries Lecture Notes in Artificial Intelligence (LNAI) and Lecture Notes in Bioinformatics (LNBI), has established itself as a medium for the publication of new developments in computer science and information technology research, teaching, and education.

LNCS enjoys close cooperation with the computer science R & D community, the series counts many renowned academics among its volume editors and paper authors, and collaborates with prestigious societies. Its mission is to serve this international community by providing an invaluable service, mainly focused on the publication of conference and workshop proceedings and postproceedings. LNCS commenced publication in 1973.

Salem Lahlou · Madhavan Mukund
Editors

Networked Systems

13th International Conference, NETYS 2025
Rabat, Morocco, May 21–23, 2025
Proceedings

Springer

Editors
Salem Lahlou
Mohamed bin Zayed University of Artificial Intelligence
Abu Dhabi, United Arab Emirates

Madhavan Mukund
Chennai Mathematical Institute
Chennai, Tamil Nadu, India

ISSN 0302-9743 ISSN 1611-3349 (electronic)
Lecture Notes in Computer Science
ISBN 978-3-032-00346-1 ISBN 978-3-032-00347-8 (eBook)
https://doi.org/10.1007/978-3-032-00347-8

This Springer imprint is published by the registered company Springer Nature Switzerland AG
The registered company address is: Gewerbestrasse 11, 6330 Cham, Switzerland

Preface

This volume contains the papers accepted at the 13th edition of the International Conference on Networked Systems (NETYS), which was held from May 21–23, 2025 in Rabat (Morocco). NETYS aims to bring together researchers and engineers from the theory and practice of distributed and networked systems. The scope of the conference covers all aspects related to the design and development of these systems. Additionally, this year, NETYS also featured works on various research areas of machine learning, including large language model applications.

For this edition, we received 45 submissions. Each submission was reviewed by at least 3, and on average by 3.12, members of the Program Committee, which consisted of 28 international experts spanning all relevant fields related to networked & distributed computing and to machine learning. Following a discussion by the Program Committee, 16 regular papers and 1 short paper were selected based on their originality and quality for publication in this volume.

In addition to the presentation of these contributed papers, the conference program included keynotes by the following renowned researchers:

Swarat Chaudhuri
Marc Shapiro
Sanjit Seshia
Praneeth Vepakomma
Mohamed El Amine Seddik

As Program Co-Chairs of NETYS 2025, we extend our sincere appreciation to all who made this conference a success. We are particularly grateful to the authors for their outstanding submissions and to the keynote speakers for their illuminating presentations. The Program Committee members and external reviewers deserve special recognition for their thorough evaluations and valuable input during the selection process.

We would also like to express our heartfelt thanks to everyone involved in organizing NETYS 2025, especially the dedicated Organizing Committee and webmaster, Bilal Taghdouti. We are indebted to our General Co-Chairs: Ahmed Bouajjani (Université Paris Cité, France), Mohammed Erradi (ENSIAS, UM5R, Morocco), and Rachid Guerraoui (EPFL, Switzerland) for their visionary leadership and continuous support throughout the preparation of this conference.

We are grateful to our partners and sponsors: UM6P, UM6P College of Computing, ENSIAS, Université Mohammed V de Rabat, CID, and Association Al Khawarizmi de Génie Informatique.

Lastly, we would like to thank Microsoft CMT, which helped us manage and organize the submission of papers, the review process, and the preparation of the conference proceedings.

May 2025

Salem Lahlou
Madhavan Mukund

Organization

General Co-chairs

Ahmed Bouajjani	Université Paris Cité, France
Mohammed Erradi	ENSIAS, UM5R, Morocco
Rachid Guerraoui	EPFL, Switzerland

Program Co-chairs

Salem Lahlou	MBZUAI, UAE
Madhavan Mukund	Chennai Mathematical Institute, India

Program Committee

Achour, El Mehdi	RWTH Aachen University, Germany
Akshay, S.	IIT Bombay, India
Alami, Reda	Technology Innovation Institute, UAE
Basmadjian, Robert	UM6P, Morocco
Benkaouz, Yahya	Mohammed V University, Rabat, Morocco
El Hamlaoui, Mahmoud	ENSIAS, Morocco
Freisleben, Bernd	Philipps-Universität Marburg, Germany
Gorbunov, Eduard	MBZUAI, UAE
Hélouët, Loïc	University of Rennes, Inria, CNRS, IRISA, France
Hernandez-Garcia, Alex	University of Montreal and Mila, Canada
Jarir, Zahi	Cadi Ayyad University, Morocco
Jmaiel, Mohamed	University of Sfax, Tunisia
Koulali, Mohamed Amine	ENSAO, Morocco
Lahlou, Salem (Co-chair)	MBZUAI, UAE
Liu, Tongliang	University of Sydney, Australia
Lukas, Nils	MBZUAI, UAE
Molla, Anisur Rahaman	Indian Statistical Institute, Kolkata, India
Mukund, Madhavan (Co-chair)	Chennai Mathematical Institute, India
Podelski, Andreas	University of Freiburg, Germany
Potop-Butucaru, Maria	LIP6, Sorbonne University, France
Rajsbaum, Sergio	UNAM, Mexico

Seddik, Mohamed El Amine	Technology Innovation Institute, UAE
Sharma, Pradeep	ServiceNow, USA
Srivathsan, B.	Chennai Mathematical Institute, India
Taik, Afaf	University of Montreal and Mila, Canada
Tixeuil, Sebastien	LIP6, Sorbonne University, France
Touati, Ahmed	Meta AI, France
Viswanathan, Mahesh	University of Illinois Urbana-Champaign, USA

Additional Reviewers

Azize, Achraf	ENSAE, France
Benomar, Ziyad	ENSAE, France
Bourassi, Jihad	BRGM, France
Chandramouli, Y.	CMI, India
Cherrat, El Amine	Quantum Signals, France
Dahmani, Safae	INPT, Morocco
Ennadir, Sofiane	KTH, Sweden
Gupta, Aditya	Amazon, USA
Kumar, Rajendra	IIT Delhi, India
Mannava, Mohan Krishna	Walmart, USA
Menghnani, Mohit	Twilio, USA
Misra, Pranabendu	CMI, India
Muhammad, Sajan	MBZUAI, UAE
Polepalli, Shashidhar Reddy	Fortinet, USA
Srivastava, Piyush	TIFR, India
Suresh, S. P.	CMI, India
Tengali, Sandeep Ravindra	Atlassian, USA

Contents

Verification

Reachability and Verification of Assertions for IoT Applications 3
S. R. Nagalakshmi and Meenakshi D'Souza

Enhancing Numerical Invariants Learning with Bounded Reachability Analysis 19
Ahmed Bouajjani, Wael-Amine Boutglay, and Peter Habermehl

Distributed Systems

Distributed Computation of Temporal Twins in Periodic Undirected Time-Varying Graphs 39
Massinissa Tighilt, Lina Azerouk, Camille Palisoc, Binh-Minh Bui-Xuan, and Maria Potop-Butucaru

Verifying Parameterized Networks Specified by Vertex-Replacement Graph Grammars 57
Radu Iosif, Arnaud Sangnier, and Neven Villani

Secure Lineage Storage on Public and Private Blockchains 81
Bilel Zaghdoudi and Maria Potop-Butucaru

Byzantine Fault-Tolerant Distributed Set Intersection with Redundancy and Its Relationship with Byzantine Optimization 97
Shuo Liu and Nitin H. Vaidya

Pattern Formation of Mobile Agents in Dynamic Grids 114
Masahiro Shibata, Sayaka Kamei, Fukuhito Ooshita, and Hirotsugu Kakugawa

An Automaton Model to Succinctly Represent Suffix-Based Specifications of a Concurrent System 129
R Keerthan, B Srivathsan, and R Venkatesh

SmartShards: Churn-Tolerant Continuously Available Distributed Ledger 146
Joseph Oglio, Mikhail Nesterenko, and Gokarna Sharma

On Restricting Separator Problems in the OBLOT Computational Landscape 163
Quentin Bramas and Sébastien Tixeuil

Machine Learning

Going Forward-Forward in Distributed Deep Learning 171
Ege Aktemur, Ege Zorlutuna, Kaan Bilgili, Tacettin Emre Bök, Berrin Yanikoglu, and Süha Orhun Mutluergil

An Ensemble Model for 30-Minute Blood Glucose Prediction in Type 1 Diabetes: Balancing Accuracy and Simplicity 187
Khadija Tlemçani, Kebira Azbeg, Wafaa Wakrim, Laila Fetjah, Ouail Ouchetto, and Said Jai Andaloussi

Networked LLM Agents: Toward Autonomous LLMs for Querying Heterogeneous Databases 202
Khadija Baddouj, Mohammed Erradi, Mohammed Ali Essabri, Hanae Kolone, Nour Oulad Moussa, and Rebii Jamal

Plant Diseases Detection with Retrieval-Augmented Generation 214
Outhmane Bourkoukou and Khadija Ghommat

Impact of Sparsification and Quantization on Energy Consumption in Federated Learning 230
Ouiame Marnissi, Karim Boubouh, Hajar EL Hammouti, El Houcine Bergou, and Robert Basmadjian

Vgg-ViT: A Framework for Deepfakes Images Detection 241
Achraf Ibnouzaher and Noureddine Moumkine

Heterogeneous Graph Neural Network Based Arabic Coreference Resolution 253
Rihab EL Yousfi, Mounir Ourekouch, and Mohammed Erradi

Author Index 271

Verification

Reachability and Verification of Assertions for IoT Applications

S. R. Nagalakshmi(✉) and Meenakshi D'Souza

International Institute of Information Technology, Bangalore, India
{nagalakshmi,meenakshi}@iiitb.ac.in

Abstract. IoT applications are typically developed on serverless platforms and deployed for use with an underlying cloud service provider. Such applications typically use JSON files to represent sensor data and communicate with the IoT core using protocols like MQTT, MQTT-SN, AMQP, HTTP, etc. The main functionality of an IoT application is implemented on the serverless platform including synchronous and asynchronous computations on the sensor data, notification services, accessing databases, data streaming, etc. We provide a framework to verify the requirements of these IoT applications specified as assertions. Our framework extends the notion of asynchronous call graphs of serverless applications to IoT applications by including notations for communication protocols, their QoS features, and message-passing properties, modeling both synchronous and asynchronous computations and services that support notifications, sensor actuation, etc. We then use this framework to verify assertions corresponding to correctness properties of the IoT applications.

Keywords: IoT Applications · Asynchronous Call Graphs · Control Flow Graphs · Assertions

1 Introduction

Large-scale IoT applications are ubiquitous and there are numerous application development platforms available that facilitate developing applications to manage data from several thousands of devices [1]. Popular IoT development platforms AWS [2,3], Samsung [5], Google Cloud IoT [4] are NodeJS serverless platforms that provide support for writing functionality and provide features to model sensor data (as JSON files), support many communication protocols for device connectivity (like MQTT [18], HTTP, AMQP etc.), provide API endpoints for actuating devices, sending notifications, storing in databases etc. An IoT application created in the cloud platform can be deployed on the devices seamlessly and the same functionality can be retained with guaranteed performance and other quality parameters.

Industrial IoT and health care IoT applications are safety-critical in nature, rigorous testing and verification are useful to verify the correctness requirements of these applications. Such IoT applications also deal with a lot of sensor

S. Lahlou and M. Mukund (Eds.): NETYS 2025, LNCS 15736, pp. 3–18, 2026.
https://doi.org/10.1007/978-3-032-00347-8_1

data, making testing and verification of the requirements challenging. Verification efforts have concentrated on security and privacy requirements [6] and on properties of IoT protocols [7]. On the testing side, specific problems like cross-app interference have been handled [14] and recently, a coverage criteria-based white-box testing framework has been proposed [15].

Control flow graphs and call graphs have been traditional abstract models of applications that have been used for testing simple reachability properties and the associated assertions. For IoT applications, these graphs and the assertions on the handler functions constitute a rich source of information that can be used for testing and verification. Given the fact that IoT applications are developed on the NodeJS serverless platform, a simple solution will be to use the corresponding graphs for NodeJS to reason about IoT applications too. Unfortunately, they cannot be directly used for IoT applications.

Research on generating control flow graphs and call graphs for NodeJS applications have evolved for the past few years [9,10,21,22] mostly along with evolving features of NodeJS. While they are now considered robust for reasoning about NodeJS applications, they do not directly cater to reasoning about IoT applications on the NodeJS platform. For generating call graphs, the papers either consider only synchronous communication or cater to asynchronous communication exclusively. For control flow graphs, the tools are evolving continuously with evolving features of NodeJS. IoT applications deal with sensor data, communication protocols exclusive to the IoT domain (like MQTT, XMPP, AMQP, HTTP etc.), and also use both synchronous and asynchronous execution modes within one application. None of the above work can smoothly generate call graphs and control flow graphs that support all these features of an IoT application.

We address this gap in this paper and provide definitions for call graphs and control flow graphs specific to IoT applications, we call them IoTCG and IoTCFG respectively. These graphs include notations specific to the IoT domain as detailed above and can support both synchronous and asynchronous executions. In addition, the two graphs can be 'combined' (superimposed) to get one holistic view of the control flow, across emitters, callbacks and handlers, and within a particular handler function. We also write assertions that describe the correctness properties of IoT applications and use the IoTCG and IoTCFG to 'reach' the assertions by appropriately configuring the Mocha testing framework [24]. The experiments on in-house examples illustrate the successful application of our framework on verifying IoT applications against assertions.

The paper is organized as follows. A motivating example is presented in the next section. Section 3.1 describes the architectural and the design components of an IoT application. The call and control flow graphs for IoT applications are discussed in Sects. 4.1, 4.2 and finally Sect. 4.3 details our verification framework, additional examples, and their assertions.

2 Overview Example

We present an example that clearly highlights the need for an IoT call graph and control flow graph that support all the features unique to the domain. The complete code, followed by its graphs and the verification of an appropriate assertion is provided in the authors' git-page[1].

The application highlights the delivery guarantee property of the MQTT protocol using the Last Will and Testament (LWT) feature [18]. The LWT is a message that a client uses to notify the broker during the connection phase. This message is stored by the broker and upon the unexpected disconnection of a particular device, the LWT message on "Device Disconnection" is delivered on the specified topic, to all its subscribers. Such a guarantee is critical to the correctness of an IoT application and this example illustrates the successful verification of the associated assertion.

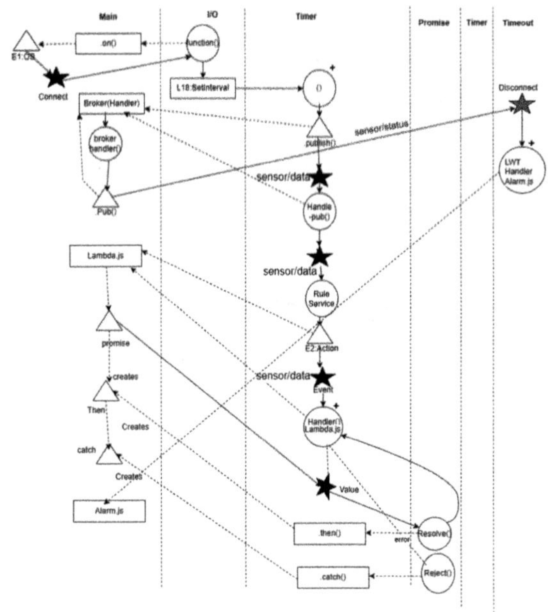

Fig. 1. IoTCG: MQTT-LWT Delivery Application.

A code snippet of the application is given below, along with the corresponding IoTCG in Fig. 1. The generation of LWT is simulated as an explicit abort and results in the execution of the handler that has subscribed for the LWT topic. The handler, in turn, triggers an alarm. LWT event emission indicating device failure can be identified in the IoTCG explicitly (a red-colored star node).

```
const MQTTBroker = require('./Mqtt');
class Sensor {
  .......
connect() {
```

[1] https://github.com/NagalakshmiAthreya/IoT-App-Graph-Generation.

```
  this.broker.connect(this.sensorId, {
  LWT: { topic: 'sensor/status',
  message: JSON.stringify({ sensorId: this.sensorId,
  status: 'dead' }) },});
  this.startPublishing(); }
startPublishing() {
     this.interval = setInterval(() => {
    .....
      this.broker.publish('sensor/data', JSON.stringify(data));
    }, 3000); }
stop() {
    ........
    this.broker.publish('sensor/status',
    JSON.stringify({ sensorId: this.sensorId, status: 'dead' }));
    this.broker.disconnect(this.sensorId);
  } }


class LambdaHandler {
.....
  start() {
    this.broker.on('message', (clientId, topic, message) => {
      if (topic === 'sensor/data') {
        .......
  }
}
class AlarmHandler {
  ...
  start() {
    const clientId = 'alarm-handler';
    this.broker.subscribe(clientId, 'sensor/status');
    this.broker.on('message', (clientId, topic, message) => {
      if (topic === 'sensor/status') {
       .....
        if (status.status === 'dead') {
          console.log(ALERT! Sensor  is dead. Triggering alarm!');
  }
}
```

In the IoTCG, we can see two distinct paths— one from MQTT to the data handler function `lambda.js` on the "connect" event which further publishes sensor data and another path from MQTT to the function `alarm.js` that triggers an alarm on the sensor "disconnect" event. Such a graph cannot be generated using existing tools and help us to verify an assertion that ensures that the LWT message is handled appropriately, i.e., For every LWT message published on the sensor/status topic, the alarm handler must receive and process it, ensuring guaranteed delivery. This assertion that is defined with the help of the paths of the IoTCG is then verified using the tool Mocha [24].

3 IoT Applications on Serverless Platforms

A large-scale IoT application is typically developed on a cloud platform and has capabilities of modeling the data sent by sensors, communication protocols used by the IoT application, IoT core, the computing base that uses the sensor data to implement the functionalities of the application and to send back actuator commands. In addition, applications also have access to a database to persist data, support for data analytics, SQS (Simple Queuing Service), API end-points, HTTP communication and other related services. Popular IoT platform service providers like AWS IoT [2], Microsoft Azure IoT [3], and other platforms provided by PTC ThingWorx, Siemens, Oracle etc. [1] use a serverless framework, usually, NodeJS [8], to bundle together all the tools and features necessary for the design, deployment, and development of large-scale IoT applications.

3.1 IoT Architecture

Figure 2 gives the high-level architecture of a large-scale IoT application. It is derived from the AWS [2] but several other IoT platforms follow a near similar architecture structure with the names of the services being possibly different [3–5]. We identify and list the common features below, together they constitute an IoT applications architecture [15].

- IoT devices, *things*, (sensor, sensor-embedded devices, actuators) connect using *communication protocols* (like MQTT, AMQP, XMPP or HTTP) to send and/or receive data. The protocol helps to connect and communicate the device data throughout the IoT architecture for providing basic functionality including storage and handling through user-defined rules.
- *Data* in an IoT application is the information generated by interconnected devices as they interact with their surroundings. Data is typically represented using the JSON format.
- An *event* refers to a significant occurrence or happening that takes place within the system. Events are used to represent changes in the state of a device, environment, or system, and they trigger specific actions or responses. The data values measured provide context about the event and are transmitted as JSON objects.
- Security of data is managed through Identity and Access Management (IAM) policies and through standard SSL/TLS X.509 certificates.
- The platform is typically serverless, supports a variety of programming languages for developing the functionality of an IoT application.

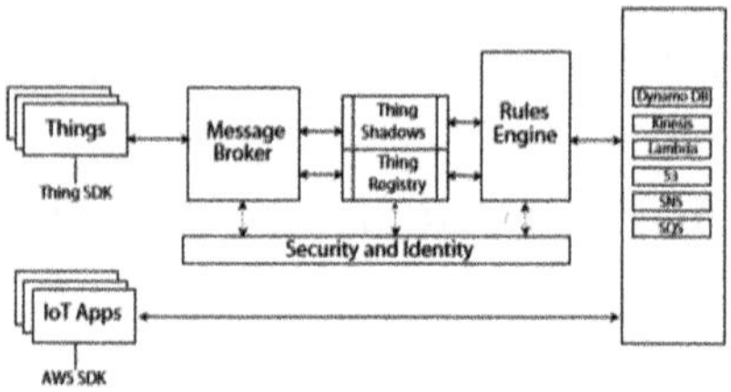

Fig. 2. AWS IoT Generic Architecture [2]

An *IoT applications architecture*, or IoT architecture, in short, is one framework that includes all the above components and depicts several details regarding their interactions encompassing the functionality of the application. Two views of the architecture can be considered: one that focuses on components and connectors and another one that focuses on the events and their generation and flow across an application [15]. We consider the components of the architecture in this paper and elaborate on the design aspects of the components. The design caters to the underlying functionality of the application and for each (λ) function, a control flow graph captures the functionality coded by the function. The various function calls that represent a path through the IoT architecture are captured by the call graph with events flowing through the graph to reach the various API endpoints.

4 IoT Applications: Call Graph and Control Flow Graph

As mentioned earlier, even though algorithms for generating control flow and call graphs for JavaScript applications running on NodeJS have been proposed [9,11,12], IoT applications involve libraries and packages that are unique to the domain and also support communication using both synchronous and asynchronous mechanisms by using specific SDKs for these platforms as highlighted in Fig. 2. Data exchanged in an IoT application is transmitted by the 'things' and are represented using the JSON notation and abstracted as events. Several unique properties can be verified for an IoT application using the underlying call graph and the control flow graph. For example, sensors tend to break or run out of battery and the LWT feature of MQTT illustrated in Sect. 3 comes in handy to notify operators. Such properties are critical to the correctness of an IoT application and cannot be modeled using existing frameworks.

The main contribution of this paper is a framework for defining and generating call graphs and control flow graphs that are unique to IoT applications. We extend the notations used in [9,11] to add call graph nodes and edges that are specific to IoT applications including but not limited to the MQTT protocol and its message broker, SQS services, rule engines etc. Our extension can support other IoT protocols like AMQP, XMPP etc., making it generic.

4.1 IoT Application Call Graph

An IoT Application Call Graph (IoTCG) has all the nodes and edges corresponding to a serverless application [9] and in addition, several nodes that are unique to an IoT application. We explain the notions that are unique to the IoTCG and justify the reasons behind the categorization of these nodes.

To re-cap the standard call graph notations for asynchronous serverless applications [9], there are nodes that correspond to callback registration (API uses that register one or more callbacks to be executed, represented by a □ symbol), callback execution (a call graph node that corresponds to actual execution of a callback, represented by a ◯), a callback trigger (which is a node that leads to the actual execution of a callback, represented by a ★), and finally a node that represents the creation of a promise or an emitter object (represented by a △). All of these notations continue to exist in IoTCG.

As IoT applications are event-driven, the 'event (JSON data)' connects the components through event rules or through MQTT's `publish()`/`subscribe()` or HTTP's `request`/`response` or platforms device SDK methods. Thus, event sources are emitter objects, event destinations are listeners/consumers. As the sensor/device publishes data, it will reach the IoT core, which internally contains a message broker, a device registry (containing device shadows), and rules filtering services (like a rule engine in the case of AWS). Our IoT application call graph IoTCG includes a node representing each of these components as they play a critical role in deciding the path of an application through the underlying architecture. A particular handler function gets executed only when the corresponding rule condition evaluates to true. Similarly, IoT applications write updated status of the devices to shadows to reach actuators event during connectivity issues, again these updates can also trigger some event handlers. To track these paths of the application, a node representing a shadow needs to be added (similar to a data store node of [10]).

Event emitter node (E) emits an 'Event' (trigger node) that causes the execution (F) of the registered listener (L). This is the pattern through which we establish connections among the components in the IoT application call graph. Figure 3 presents this pattern in the IoTCG and identifies the kind of node by labeling it explicitly as an emitter or an execution node or a listener node, within the call graph node types.

The `publish()` method of MQTT is treated as an emitter object as its emission causes the execution of the registered function. The data that it carries in the topic names is considered to be an event (trigger) for the execution, The `subscribe()` method of the destination is a listener. The rule action is another emitter object that triggers the execution of handlers/destination logic by routing (emitting) the event to destinations as per the rule condition.

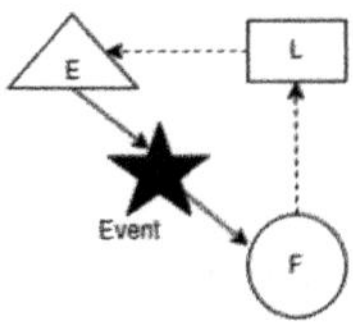

Fig. 3. Event-Emitter-Listener relationships

We also capture information related to the underlying sensor data that is transmitted as an event. In specific cases, the actual data parameters need to be captured, to verify a particular assertion related to the IoT application. One such entity is the message broker component of MQTT. A device node on receiving a 'connect' event after successful connection establishment, executes the registered listener and emits the data to the intended destination (IoT core- MQTT broker). Message broker has a series of handler functions that listen to the MQTT client (device,) requests to handle data, LWT (Last Will and Testament) messages, publishing, subscribing tasks, errors, connections, and disconnections [17]. Data that is transmitted across these functions through the call graph is captured for use in verifying important assertions about the functionality of the application.

All of the above can be generated using the NodeProf tool [19] and by augmenting the already available asynchronous call graph generator for NodeJS applications [9]. The complete workflow of the proposed framework is given in Fig. 4. In addition, as noted earlier, IoT applications have functionality that also needs synchronous communication at times. We extend the notations proposed in [10] to include API end-points, object stores and certain stateless services. These features are modeled within our IoTCG directly, using the respective categories of nodes.

4.2 IoT Application: Call Graph to Control Flow Graph

Like in all applications, certain nodes of the control flow graph also occur in the call graph, specifically, the nodes that correspond to the statements that execute procedure calls. For IoT applications, we highlight the nodes that are common to the call graph and the control flow graph, and the transfer of control that facilitates the same. An IoT Control Flow Graph (IoTCFG) is a graph that represents all the paths that might be traversed through a particular serverless function that gets invoked by a call in the IoTCG. While there have been tools to generate the control flow graph from serverless applications [20–22], updated features of the JavaScript programming language are not supported by many tools. Moreover, the SDKs specific to IoT applications (HiveMQTT [18], for example) are not supported by the available tools. Tools that are based on static analysis are not sufficient for generating the control flow and call graphs exhaustively and soundness of these tools has been a topic of study [20,22].

We provide a customized algorithm for generating the IoTCFG that includes all the IoT specific components. SDK libraries for MQTT are usually available without the source code, so we consider a corresponding abstraction for MQTT. Algorithm 1 describes the generation of IoTCFG using the logs of the NodeProf tool along with the customization. The algorithm is dynamic and hence does not guarantee completeness. This CFG suffices to instrument the Mocha tool for verifying assertions. If a particular assertion is not reachable, we can augment the CFG algorithm with additional logs, but our experiments indicate that this is usually not necessary. GraphViz is used to visualize the graphs.

The execution of a given IoT application starts with the arrival of events (sensor data) from the `publish()` method of an MQTT client (sensor or device) or from the HTTP `post()` method. The event handlers for each of these events are the entry nodes of the IoTCG and the IoTCFG. For each identified event source, an edge to the corresponding handler is added in the IoTCG. We also include the nodes corresponding to the MQTT broker in the IoTCG but these nodes are considered as it is, to be used as APIs.

As mentioned in Sect. 4.1, the asynchronous call graph is generated using the same algorithm as that of [9]. Such a call graph generates only the asynchronous flow of events, split across the event loop, based on the time slots. The asynchronous call graph is then superimposed with the control flow corresponding to synchronous execution within a particular time slot. The exit nodes from the IoTCFG can also act as call nodes as a part of the IoTCG. Specifically, in IoT applications that are developed on serverless frameworks, the handler functions (Lambda functions) always return a promise after their execution. The promise, in turn, is either resolved or rejected. In the former case, the lambda function typically handles new events. Such nodes are common to both the IoTCFG and the IoTCG.

In the IoTCG, we also create additional nodes that provide the functionality of interactions with external services (like sensors, device shadows, actuators etc.) and nodes corresponding to the various triggers, then add edges to the corresponding handlers (both synchronous and asynchronous) Using NodeProf logs and configuration information. Some of these nodes are also a part of the IoTCFG. Typical examples are the read APIs (`get`, `publish()`), write APIs (`put`, `publish()`). We annotate the specific nodes with a + superscript to indicate that it will expand into a function having its own IoTCFG. Algorithm 2 gives the details.

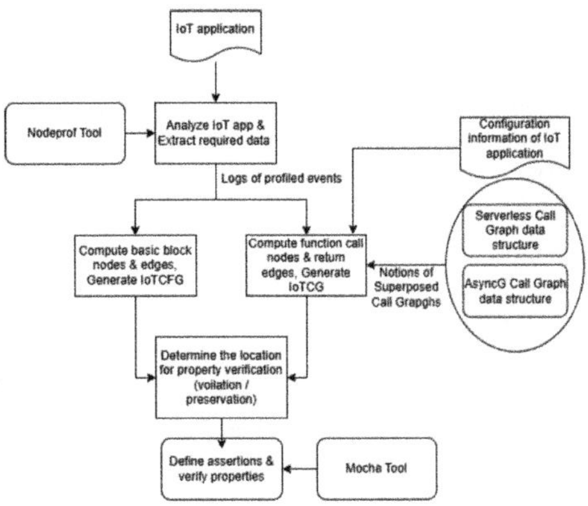

Fig. 4. Framework for generating IoTCG and IoTCFG and assertion verification.

The overall framework for generating the IoTCG, followed by the IoTCFG, that handles both synchronous and asynchronous functions, components unique to IoT like MQTT, device shadows etc., is presented in Fig. 4. Once such graphs are generated, we can use them to visually determine the locations where the IoT properties can be verified through the user-defined assertions. Mocha [24] is a JavaScript testing framework that supports all the constructs needed for

Algorithm 1 Construct IoTCFG

Require: Nodeprof Logs of IoT application $L\{log_1, log_2, \ldots, log_n\}$ for each profiled events.

Ensure: IoTCFG $G = (V, E)$

```
Initialize graph G = (V, E), stack S_f ← ∅, stack S_a ← ∅
Initialize maps R_c, R_p ← ∅, prevNode ← ∅
for each log ℓ ∈ L do
    Extract (type, value, location) ← ℓ
    currNode ← CreateNode(type, value, location)
    if prevNode ≠ ∅ then
        switch type do
            case "function-enter" or "async-enter"
                AddEdge(G, prevNode → currNode, "call")
                Push(type = "function-enter"?S_f : S_a, currNode)
            end case
            case "function-exit" or "async-exit"
                last ← Pop(type = "function-exit"?S_f : S_a)
                AddEdge(G, last → currNode, "return")
            end case
            case "conditional"
                AddEdge(G, prevNode → currNode, "branch")
            end case
            case "Callback Registered" or "Callback Executed"
                if type is "Callback Registered" then
                    R_c[value] ← currNode
                    AddEdge(G, prevNode → currNode, "registers")
                else
                    if value ∈ R_c then
                        AddEdge(G, R_c[value] → currNode, "invoked")
                    end if
                end if
            end case
        end switch
    end if
    prevNode ← currNode
end for
return G
```

testing IoT applications, specifically all the functions that constitute the nodes of the IoTCG and the IoTCFG. Mocha tool is configured to reach the assertions through appropriate paths in the IoTCG and IoTCFG. Automatic execution by the Mocha tool is used to collect the test results and analyze the truth or falsity of assertions. In this way, we can test an IoT application for several useful properties.

Algorithm 2 Construct IoTCG

```
Require: Logs L = {log_1, log_2, ..., log_n}
Ensure: IoTCFG G = (V, E)
Initialize graph G = (V, E), stack S_f ← ∅, stack S_a ← ∅
Initialize maps R_c, R_p ← ∅, prevFuncNode ← ∅
for each log ℓ ∈ L do
    Extract (type, value, location) ← ℓ
    switch type do
        case "function-enter" or "async-enter"
            AddEdge(G, prevFuncNode → currNode, "calls")
            Push(type = "function-enter"?S_f : S_a, currNode)
        end case
        case "function-exit" or "async-exit"
            last ← Pop(type = "function-exit"?S_f : S_a)
            AddEdge(G, last → prevFuncNode, "returns")
        end case
        case "Callback Registered" or "Callback Executed"
            if type is "Callback Registered" then
                R_c[value] ← currNode
                AddEdge(G, prevFuncNode → currNode, "registers")
            else
                if value ∈ R_c then
                    AddEdge(G, R_c[value] → currNode, "invoked")
                end if
            end if
        end case
    end switch
    prevFuncNode ← currNode
end for
return G
```

4.3 Results

The proposed framework was applied on a few real-life examples [13] and in-house boilerplate applications illustrating specific features unique to IoT applications. The details are available here[2]. Apart from the MQTT assertion involving LWT, we elaborate on two more examples in this section.

The second application has two functionalities: (1) publishing sensor data and (2)handling fire detection events. Since publishing triggers the handler of MQTT, `publish()` is an emitter node. The function `handleFireDetection()` checks if the data exceeds the thresholds and if it does, the handlers `createBundle()` and `uploadStr()` are invoked asynchronously. The order in which they finish execution is non-deterministic [16], through one of the two different possible paths of execution. Figure 5 gives the IoTCG for this application. The edges from two nodes corresponding to Async functions reaching the common node seen in its IoTCFG given in git-page[3] reflect the unpredictable

[2] https://github.com/NagalakshmiAthreya/IoT-App-Graph-Generation.
[3] https://github.com/NagalakshmiAthreya/IoT-App-Graph-Generation.

Sl. No.	IoT Applications	Assertion Properties
1	LWT-IoT application	Delivery Guarantee
2	Order Conflict Async IoT app.	Order Preservation
3	Chain-Action IoT app.	Trigger Condition Verification
4	Conflicting Actions IoT	Simultaneous actions
5	End-to-End IoT application	Destination Reachability
6	Home-safety System IoT	Delivery Guarantee
7	Multi-Sensor-IoT	Order Preservation
8	Sync Async -IoT-1&2	Order Preservation
9	Temperature Monitoring System IoT	Delivery Guarantee

execution order of the asynchronous functions. Thus, the target for verifying property is the location in the graph where two the paths gets merged (inside `handleFireDetection()`), after the two asynchronous function calls. We define the assertion as, ***assert(createBundle-done-before-uploadStr, "Assertion Failed: createBundle must complete before uploadStr!");***. This specifies to always check if `createBundle()` has completed before executing `uploadStr()`, preserving the intended order.

```
async function createBundle(data) {
 return new Promise((resolve) => {
   setTimeout(() => {
     console.log('Bundle created');
     ...
  }, Math.random() * 3000); // Delay up to 3 seconds
 });
}
async function uploadStr(data) {
 return new Promise((resolve) => {
   setTimeout(() => { console.log('Data uploaded );
   ...
   }, Math.random() * 3000); // Delay up to 3 seconds
 });
}
async function handleFireDetection(data) {
  try {
    if (data.temp>TEMP_THRESHOLD || data.smoke>SMOKE_THRESHOLD){
      const createPromise = createBundle(data);
      const uploadPromise = uploadStr(data);
      await Promise.all([createPromise, uploadPromise]);}
    handleFireDetection(data);
 });
```

The third application is inspired by one of the examples in [14] and contains a temperature sensor that publishes data on an MQTT topic. There are

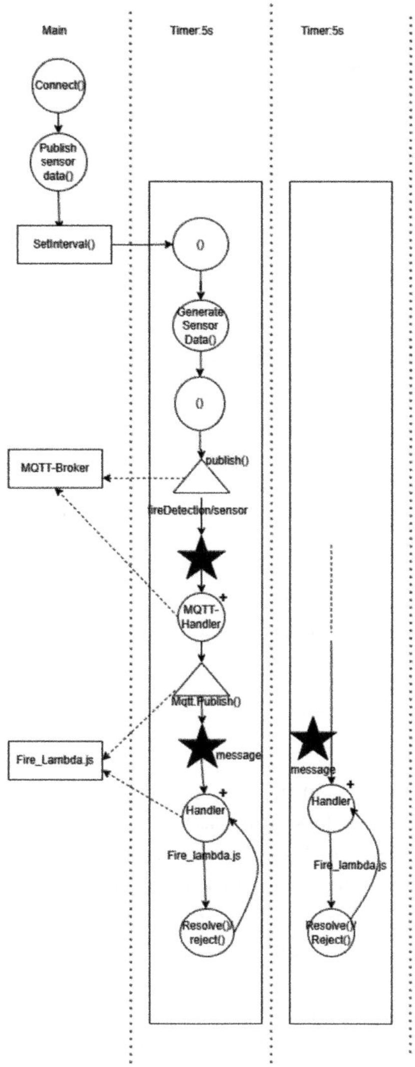

Fig. 5. IoTCG: Order-Conflict-App.

two rules that are coded: (1) The publishing of the data triggers `tempHandler`, which checks the temperature and publishes the AC status, and (2) The change in AC status triggers another `windowHandler` which then performs a window action, which is not intended, this is due to event propagation. The corresponding IoTCG is given in Fig. 6 and the path connecting multiple handler functions depicts this functionality. If a subsequent handler is associated with a trigger from a different source, then it reveals the conflict of chaining action. An assertion checks that the intended action trigger happens and at the same time unintended action does not happen.

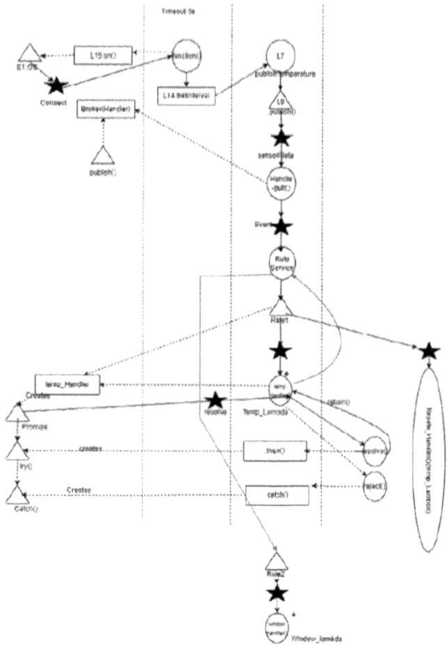

Fig. 6. IoTCG: Chaining-Action-App.

5 Related Work

There have been several attempts to generate the call graphs and control flow graphs for (NodeJS) serverless applications. The "Async Graph" model of [9] helps to understand runtime behavior of NodeJS applications, several kinds of errors specific to asynchronous execution are detected. In [10], the authors propose an "extended service call graph" for serverless applications. This method enhances traditional call graphs by integrating information about the relationships between serverless functions and platform services, particularly in JavaScript-based AWS Lambda applications. The approach captures event declarations and method calls, providing a comprehensive view of serverless applications. [11] introduces a "service call graph" that extends traditional call graphs by including nodes representing platform services. This model captures control flow through service interactions, transforming individual serverless functions into a unified application and offering insights into the data flow between functions. A study on NodeJS concurrency bugs [16] highlights various concurrency issues that can arise in these applications. They are particularly relevant in IoT, as IoT applications rely on NodeJS for handling asynchronous operations and event-driven programming. Our work extends [9,10] to define an IoT application call graph and control flow graph that supports both synchronous and asynchronous communications, along with SDKs specific to the domain of IoT. We can detect all the errors from these papers, and in addition, IoT specific errors.

On the testing and verification of IoT applications, [15] considers a coverage-criteria based white-box testing focusing on IoT architecture paths. The proposed coverage criteria are useful in detecting several errors, but do not consider errors that could arise due to asynchronous control flows. An elementary notion of data flow testing for serverless applications is proposed in [23] but the proposed criteria do not extent smoothly to IoT applications.

6 Conclusion and Future Work

We provide a comprehensive call graph and control flow graph notations for IoT applications hosted on serverless platforms along with the algorithms that can generate these graphs using a combination of static parsing and dynamic execution. Our algorithms extend already available algorithms to cater to the notations specific to IoT applications. These graphs are useful to verify assertions by explicitly coding the paths that reach these assertions in the graph. In addition to assertions, the graphs could potentially be used to verify other requirements like safety etc.

We plan to use these graphs for a fuzz testing framework for IoT applications. Such a framework will use these graphs and augment additional data flow information to automatically generate fuzz test cases.

An inherent limitation of the proposed framework is that the call graphs might not be complete, they are generated by analyzing the logs of the underlying application. Moving forward, working on a static analysis framework for generating these graphs will yield sound analysis results.

References

1. Gartner Magic Quadrant for Global Industrial IoT Platforms, Gartner Research, 29 April 2024. Available from https://www.gartner.com/en/documents/5389163. Accessed Apr 2025
2. AWS IoT Core Documentation. Available from https://docs.aws.amazon.com/iot/latest/developerguide/aws-iot-how-it-works.html. Accessed April 2025
3. Azure IoT Documentation. https://azure.microsoft.com/en-in/solutions/iot. Accessed April 2025
4. Google Cloud IoT Documentation. https://cloud.google.com/iot/docs. Accessed April 2025
5. Samsung SmartThings Developers Documentation. https://developer.smartthings.com/docs/getting-started/architecture-of-smartthings. Accessed April 2025
6. Celik, Z.B., McDaniel, P., Tan, G.: SOTERIA: automated IoT safety and security analysis. In: Proceedings of the 2018 USENIX Annual Technical Conference, pp. 147–158 (2018)
7. Diwan, M., D'Souza, M.: A framework for modeling and verifying Iot communication protocols. In: Larsen, K.G., Sokolsky, O., Wang, J. (eds.) SETTA 2017. LNCS, vol. 10606, pp. 266–280. Springer, Cham (2017). https://doi.org/10.1007/978-3-319-69483-2_16
8. NodeJS© JavaScript run-time environment, OpenJS Foundation (2024). https://nodejs.org/en. Accessed Aug 2024

9. Sun, H., Bonetta, D., Schiavio, F., Binder, W.: Reasoning about the Node.js event loop using async graphs. In: Proceeidngs of the IEEE/ACM Intl. Symposium on Code Generation and Optimization (CGO 2019), IEEE Press, pp. 61–72, (2019)
10. Obetz, M., Patterson, S., Milanova, A.: Static call graph construction in AWS Lambda serverless applications. In: Proceeidngs of the 11th USENIX Conference on Hot Topics in Cloud Computing (HotCloud'19) (2019). https://dl.acm.org/doi/10.5555/3357034.3357059
11. Obetz, M., Das, A., Castiglia, T., Patterson, S., Milanova, A.: Formalizing Event-Driven Behavior of Serverless Applications, Service-Oriented and Cloud Computing. ESOCC 2020, LNCS, vol 12054. Springer, Cham. https://doi.org/10.1007/978-3-030-44769-4_2
12. Winzinger, S., Wirtz, G.: Model-based analysis of serverless applications. In: IEEE/ACM 11th International Workshop on Modelling in Software Engineering (MiSE), 2019, pp. 82–88 (2019). https://doi.org/10.1109/MiSE.2019.00020
13. Serverless Examples, Serverless Inc., (2024). https://github.com/serverless/examples/?tab=readme-ov-file. Accessed Feb 2025
14. Chi, H., Zeng, Q., Du, X., Yu, J.: Cross-app interference threats in smart homes: categorization, detection and handling. In: Annual IEEE/IFIP International Conference on Dependable Systems and Networks (DSN),2020, pp. 411–423 (2020). https://doi.org/10.1109/DSN48063.2020.00056
15. Nagalakshmi, S.R., D'Souza, M.,:Testing, C.C.B., of IoT Applications, in Distributed Computing and Intelligent Technology ICDCIT,: LNCS Vol 14501. Springer, Cham. (2024). https://doi.org/10.1007/978-3-031-50583
16. Wang, J., et al.: A comprehensive study on real world concurrency bugs in Node.js. In: 32nd IEEE/ACM International Conference on Automated Software Engineering (ASE), 2017, pp. 520–531 (2017). https://doi.org/10.1109/ASE.2017.8115663
17. MQTT Last Will and Testament. https://www.hivemq.com/blog/mqtt-essentials-part-9-last-will-and-testament/
18. HiveMQ User Guide. https://docs.hivemq.com/hivemq/latest/user-guide/index.html. Accessed April 2025
19. Sun, H., Bonetta, D.: Christian Humer, pp. 196–206. Efficient Dynamic Analysis for Node.js. in Proc. CC, Walter Binder (2018)
20. Antal, G., Hegedus, P., Tóth, Z., Ferenc, R., Gyimóthy, T.: Static JavaScript call graphs: a comparative study. In: IEEE 18th International Working Conference on Source Code Analysis and Manipulation (SCAM), 2018, pp. 177–186 (2018). https://doi.org/10.1109/SCAM.2018.00028
21. Jensen, S.H., Moller, A., Thiemann, P.: Type Analysis for JavaScript, Proc. 16th Intl. Static Analysis Symposium (SAS), LNCS 5673, Springer-Verlag, August (2009)
22. Esben Sparre Andreasen and Anders Møller and Benjamin Barslev Nielsen, Systematic Approaches for Increasing Soundness and Precision of Static Analyzers, Proc. 6th Intl. Workshop on the State Of the Art in Program Analysis (SOAP), June 2017
23. Winzinger, S., Wirtz, G.: Applicability of coverage criteria for serverless applications. In: IEEE International Conference on Service Oriented Systems Engineering (SOSE) **2020**, pp. 49–56 (2020). https://doi.org/10.1109/SOSE49046.2020.00013
24. Mocha - The fun, simple, flexible JavaScript test framework. https://mochajs.org
25. ECMAScript parsing infrastructure for multipurpose analysis. https://esprima.org/doc/index.html. Accessed Feb 2025

Enhancing Numerical Invariants Learning with Bounded Reachability Analysis

Ahmed Bouajjani[1], Wael-Amine Boutglay[1,2(✉)], and Peter Habermehl[1]

[1] Université Paris Cité, IRIF, Paris, France
{abou,boutglay,haberm}@irif.fr
[2] Mohammed VI Polytechnic University, Ben Guerir, Morocco

Abstract. We address the problem of verifying safety properties for iterative numerical programs. This problem amounts in, given a program and its specification (a pair of pre and post conditions), to find a strong enough inductive invariant allowing to establish correctness. The verification problem being undecidable in general, our aim is to provide a powerful invariant synthesis method allowing to handle automatically a large number of programs in practice. We propose such a method based on a data-driven approach that is enhanced with symbolic bounded reachability analysis. Our method builds on prior work we published in CAV'22 [6] where we defined an invariant learning procedure based on a new technique for generating relevant decision-tree attributes extracted from convex separators of samples (sets of program states seen as vectors of integers). In this work, we show that by coupling the previous method with a symbolic bounded model checker it is possible to improve significantly performances both in terms of running time and in the number of solved cases. The model checker can help in two ways: it might prove faster that a program is unsafe (by hitting error states), or more interestingly, it can provide interpolants (showing unreachability of error states) which can be used as attributes to speed-up the convergence of the learning procedure. We have implemented our new algorithm and shown that it is quite competitive with state-of-the-art tools such as Spacer, CVC4/5, solving globally more cases than these tools on the SyGuS and SV-COMP benchmarks.

Keywords: Formal verification · Invariant synthesis · Data-driven program verification · Bounded model checking

1 Introduction

Invariant synthesis is fundamental to automated program verification. Given a specific loop with a predefined precondition and a target postcondition, the challenge is to derive a property that both entails the postcondition and serves as an over-approximation of the set of states reachable through iterative loop execution from the initial precondition. Various approaches have been developed over

S. Lahlou and M. Mukund (Eds.): NETYS 2025, LNCS 15736, pp. 19–36, 2026.
https://doi.org/10.1007/978-3-032-00347-8_2

the years, including abstract interpretation, counter-example guided abstraction refinement (CEGAR), property-directed reachability (PDR), and syntax-guided and data-driven methods, etc. [7,9,10,13,15,19,22,24,27]. Despite these advancements, invariant synthesis continues to face challenges related to scalability and expressiveness.

In recent years, invariant synthesis for numerical programs has been increasingly dominated by PDR-based methods, syntax-guided synthesis techniques, and data-driven approaches. PDR-based techniques [7,11,17] and their extension, Spacer [19], iteratively refine inductive invariants through counterexample-guided abstraction refinement. Unlike traditional approaches, they perform model checking without explicit unrolling of the transition relation, instead relying on quantifier elimination or model-based projection to compute under-approximations of the predecessors of bad states. Additionally, they use interpolation to systematically exclude these states from candidate invariants. Syntax-guided synthesis approaches [1,22–24] constrain the search space by imposing predefined syntactic templates on invariants, making them particularly effective for generating structured invariants. Data-driven methods [27,30] are based on classifying a sample of *positive* states, i.e. program states reachable from the initial ones, and *negative* states, which include bad states or those that reach bad states. The resulting classifier can be seen as candidate invariant, which can be automatically checked using an SMT solver which either proves it or provides a counterexample. A notable example of data-driven methods is the ICE framework [15] where the learning sample in ICE includes not only positive and negative states but also implication constraints of the form $p \rightarrow q$. These constraints enforce that if p is included in the invariant, then q must also be included, reflecting program transitions.

One instantiation of the ICE framework is ICE-DT [16], which demonstrated very promising results. This approach uses decision trees as its learning component, showing strong potential for synthesizing disjunctive invariants compared to existing techniques. However, the method requires a predefined pool of attributes, i.e. atomic constraints over program variables, that the decision tree uses to classify the sample. This pool of attributes must be sufficiently expressive to correctly classify the sample and at the same time, for efficiency, the pool size should remain relatively small to prevent excessive complexity. In the original ICE-DT [16], the pool of attributes is constructed by enumerating candidates based on predefined templates, similar to syntax-guided approaches. For instance, in numerical programs, the selected patterns are specific types of linear constraints (like intervals, octagons or polyhedra), and candidate attributes are obtained by exhaustively enumerating all possible coefficient values within a predefined bound. While this brute-force approach can be effective in many cases, it often limits scalability and makes it challenging to discover inductive invariants for complex programs.

In [6], we introduced a data-driven invariant learning method based on ICE-DT with a novel technique for automatic attribute discovery for numerical programs to avoid this brute-force enumeration. This technique is purely data-driven, as it constructs a separator—a set of convex sets—that consistently covers the sample. The separator ensures that all positive states are included, negative states are excluded, and implications are saturated (i.e., for each implication $p \rightarrow q$ in the sample, if p is included in the separator, then q must also be included). The approach is guided by two key requirements: (1) minimizing the size of the attribute pool to reduce the complexity of invariant construction, and (2) ensuring that the pool does not contain unnecessary constraints, such as those that separate positive examples in regions without negative ones. To satisfy these requirements, we consider separators that, whenever they contain two convex sets, cannot form their convex union (the smallest convex set containing both) without including a negative example. The set of constraints describing the convex sets in the separator are then taken as attributes for the decision tree learning algorithm. The proposed method was implemented in a tool called NIS, which was competitive with state-of-the-art tools LoopInvGen [23], CVC4 [4,24] and Spacer [19] and even outperformed them in terms of the number of solved cases on the SyGuS-Comp'19 benchmark set. The tool is parameterized by the abstract domain used to describe the convex sets, supporting intervals, octagons, and polyhedra.

The performance of these state-of-the-art tools has improved significantly since then. CVC4 was succeeded by cvc5 [3], and Spacer has been enhanced with an alternative model-based projection implementation and a quantifier reduction technique based on the approximation of quantifier alternations [14].

In this work, we also introduce an improvement over the approach in [6] with a bounded model checker (BMC). ICE learning gathers reachability information through implication counterexamples, which can arise arbitrarily in the program's state space without systematically progressing toward violations. To address this, we run NIS concurrently with a BMC instance. If the program is unsafe, the BMC is likely to find a counterexample before NIS, enabling early termination with an unsafe verdict. If the program is safe, the BMC does not produce counterexamples, allowing NIS to continue searching for an inductive invariant. Additionally, the BMC generates interpolants that over-approximate reachable states within the unrolling depth, extracting atomic constraints from them and communicating these as additional attributes to NIS. NIS then constructs candidate invariants using both separator-based attributes and those obtained from the BMC. This collaboration terminates when either the BMC finds a counterexample to safety or NIS, with its enhanced attribute pool, successfully discovers an inductive invariant.

Our experimental evaluation shows that the proposed method is very effective for invariant synthesis of numerical programs. Its implementation, NIS+, achieves state-of-the-art performance, solving with competitive performance more instances than existing tools, including CVC4 [4,24], cvc5 [3], Spacer [19] and NIS, on the LIA benchmarks from both SyGuS-Comp [2] and SV-COMP [5]. Overall, across both benchmark sets, the proposed method using polyhedra verifies 64 more programs than CVC4, 54 more than cvc5, 21 more than Spacer and 13 more than NIS (also with polyhedra). On commonly solved instances, using polyhedra, NIS+ reduces execution time by 146 s compared to NIS.

Related Work. Numerous learning-based approaches have been developed for the verification of numerical programs. One of the earliest methods, Daikon [12], infers likely invariants from program tests using a predefined pool of formulas. Later approaches synthsize sound invariants by iteratively classifying reachable and bad states [26,27]. LoopInvGen [23] dynamically enumerate predicates on demand using a hybrid enumeration strategy [22]. The ICE framework [15] introduced implication counterexamples as fundamental reachability information for invariant learning. Its first instantiation was based on constraint solving, later extended to decision tree learning [16], where predicates were enumerated from fixed templates. Interval counterexamples, which allow the teacher to provide regions of states rather than single states, were later introduced [29]. Horn-ICE [13] and HoICE [8] generalized ICE learning to solving Constrained Horn Clauses (CHC). An other CHC-solving method employ decision trees and SVM [30]. Deep learning was explored in CLN2INV [25] (continuous logic networks) and Code2Inv [28] (graph neural networks with reinforcement learning).

2 Preliminaries

In this section, we briefly define the problem we tackle and recall the ICE framework [15] and its instantiation ICE-DT [16] using decision trees.

2.1 Safety Verification

Let $\mathcal{X}$ be a set of variables of integer sort $\mathbb{Z}$. The set of primed variables is defined as $\mathcal{X}' = \{x' \mid x \in \mathcal{X}\}$. For each $i \in \mathbb{N}$, we also define a set of copies of $\mathcal{X}$ as $\mathcal{X}^i = \{x^i \mid x \in \mathcal{X}\}$. We define $\mathcal{E}(X)$ as the set of expressions which can be built by applying operations to variables and constants. Let $\mathcal{F}(\mathcal{X})$ be the set of (first-order) formulas with free variables $\mathcal{X}$ constructed by applying (relational) predicates to expressions of $\mathcal{E}(\mathcal{X})$ and combining them using the standard Boolean operations. The definition of $\mathcal{F}(\mathcal{X})$ is intentionally general. The concretely used operations and predicates depend on the applications. A valuation σ is a function which maps each variable from $\mathcal{X}$ to an integer value. Then, the satisfaction relation $\sigma \models F$ with $F \in \mathcal{F}(\mathcal{X})$ is defined in the usual way.

Given a formula $F \in \mathcal{F}(\mathcal{X})$, we use in the following a function $\textsc{isSat}(F)$ returning $\bot$ if F is not satisfiable and an valuation of the free variables $\mathcal{X}$ if it is satisfiable.

The problem we address is the safety verification of programs (we consider programs like the one shown in Fig. 1). To formulate it generally, we use *transition systems*, as defined below. Given a program written in a language with assertions that must

```
int i, j, n, sn, k ← 0;
assume(i ≥ 0 ∧ j ≥ 0 ∧ n ≥ 0 ∧ sn ≥ 0);
assume(i = j);
while i < n do
    if * then
        k ←*;
        sn ← sn + 2k;
        i ← i + k;
        assume(i ≤ n);
    else
        sn ← sn + 2;
        i ← i + 1;
assert(sn = 2(n − j) ∨ sn = 0);
```

Fig. 1. Example program

hold for all executions, a corresponding transition system can be derived in a standard manner.

Definition 1. *A (symbolic linear)* transition system $\mathcal{T}$ *over the variables in* $\mathcal{X}$ *is a tuple* $(\mathcal{X}, Init, Tr, Bad)$ *where* $\mathcal{X}$ *is the set of variables,* $Init \in \mathcal{F}(\mathcal{X})$ *denotes the set of initial states,* $Bad \in \mathcal{F}(\mathcal{X})$ *denotes the set of bad states, and* $Tr \in \mathcal{F}(\mathcal{X} \cup \mathcal{X}')$ *is the transition relation.*

A state $s \in \mathbb{Z}^{\mathcal{X}}$ in the transition system is a full valuation of values to the variables in $\mathcal{X}$, where $\mathbb{Z}^{\mathcal{X}}$ represents the set of all possible states of the transition system. Alternatively, if the variables are ordered, i.e., $\mathcal{X} = \{x_1, \dots, x_k\}$, we can represent s as a vector $\langle \sigma(x_1), \dots, \sigma(x_k) \rangle$, where $\sigma(x_i)$ denotes the valuation of variable x_i. We write $Tr(\mathcal{X}^i, \mathcal{X}^j)$ to denote the formula Tr with all variables in $\mathcal{X}$ (respectively, $\mathcal{X}'$) replaced by their counterparts in $\mathcal{X}^i$ (respectively, $\mathcal{X}^j$).

A transition system $\mathcal{T}$ is *unsafe* if and only if there exists a state satisfying Bad that is reachable from $Init$. Formally, using the definitions introduced above, $\mathcal{T}$ is unsafe if and only if there exists some $N \in \mathbb{N}$ such that the formula $Reach_N^{\mathcal{T}}$ is satisfiable, where:

$$Reach_N^{\mathcal{T}} := Init(\mathcal{X}^0) \wedge Tr(\mathcal{X}^0, \mathcal{X}^1) \wedge \cdots \wedge Tr(\mathcal{X}^{N-1}, \mathcal{X}^N) \wedge Bad(\mathcal{X}^N) \quad (1)$$

A transition system $\mathcal{T}$ is *safe* if and only if no state satisfying Bad is reachable from any initial state. Given a transition system $\mathcal{T}$, the *safety verification* task is to determine whether $\mathcal{T}$ is safe or unsafe. In general, this problem is undecidable.

To prove that a transition system is safe, one approach is to find an appropriate *inductive invariant* $\mathcal{I} \in \mathcal{F}(\mathcal{X})$ that satisfies the following conditions:

$$\forall s.\, Init(s) \implies \mathcal{I}(s) \quad (2)$$

$$\forall s.\, \mathcal{I}(s) \wedge Bad(s) \implies \bot \quad (3)$$

$$\forall s, s'.\, \mathcal{I}(s) \wedge Tr(s, s') \implies \mathcal{I}(s') \quad (4)$$

These conditions ensure that the invariant holds initially, it excludes all bad states, and it is preserved across transitions, guaranteeing safety for all reachable states.

2.2 The ICE Framework

ICE [15] adopts the active learning paradigm where a learner and a teacher interact to iteratively infer an inductive invariant for the given transition system $\mathcal{T}$. ICE is depicted in Fig. 2.

In each iteration, the learner infers a candidate invariant J based on the *ICE sample* $\mathcal{S} = (D, C)$, which consists of counterexamples collected from previous iterations. We first define formally the *ICE sample*.

Input : A transition system T.
Output: A safe inductive invariant for T or UNSAFE
Initialize ICE sample $\mathcal{S} = (D, C) \leftarrow (\emptyset, \emptyset)$;
while *true* **do**
  $J \leftarrow$ LEARNER.LEARN($\mathcal{S}$);
  $ce \leftarrow$ TEACHER.ISVALID(J);
  if $ce = \bot$ **then**
    return J;
  else
    $\mathcal{S} \leftarrow$ ADD($\mathcal{S}, ce$);
    if $\neg$CONSISTENT($\mathcal{S}$) **then**
      return UNSAFE;

Fig. 2. The ICE framework.

Definition 2. *An* ICE sample $\mathcal{S}$ *over the variables* $\mathcal{X}$ *of a transition system* T *is a tuple* (D, C) *where* $D \subseteq \mathbb{Z}^{\mathcal{X}}$ *is a set of states and* C *is a set of classification constraints over the states in* D*. A classification constraint* $c \in C$ *has one of the following forms:*

1. $\top \rightarrow s$*, where* $s \in D$*, indicating that* s *must be included in the invariant (classified as positive);*
2. $s \rightarrow \bot$*, where* $s \in D$*, indicating that* s *must be excluded from the invariant (classified as negative);*
3. $s_1 \rightarrow s_2$*, where* $s_1, s_2 \in D$*, indicating that if* s_1 *is included in the invariant then* s_2 *must also be included in the invariant, and if* s_2 *is excluded from the invariant then* s_2 *must also be excluded form the invariant.*

Given an ICE sample $\mathcal{S} = (D, C)$, we inductively define $\mathcal{S}^+$ and $\mathcal{S}^-$ as the sets of states that must be included in or excluded from the invariant, respectively:

$$\forall (\top \rightarrow x) \in C.\, x \in \mathcal{S}^+ \tag{5}$$

$$\forall (x \rightarrow \bot) \in C.\, x \in \mathcal{S}^- \tag{6}$$

$$\forall (x_1 \rightarrow x_2) \in C.\, x_1 \in \mathcal{S}^+ \implies x_2 \in \mathcal{S}^+ \tag{7}$$

$$\forall (x_1 \rightarrow x_2) \in C.\, x_2 \in \mathcal{S}^- \implies x_1 \in \mathcal{S}^- \tag{8}$$

Once $\mathcal{S}^+$ and $\mathcal{S}^-$ are computed we also define $\mathcal{S}^{\rightarrow}$:

$$\forall s_1 \rightarrow s_2 \in C.\, s_1, s_2 \notin \mathcal{S}^+ \cup \mathcal{S}^- \implies s_1 \rightarrow s_2 \in \mathcal{S}^{\rightarrow} \tag{9}$$

An ICE sample is said to be *consistent* if and only if $\mathcal{S}^+ \cap \mathcal{S}^- = \emptyset$.

The candidate invariant J inferred by the learner must be consistent with the ICE sample, in the sense that it respects all the constraints in C. The teacher then verifies whether the proposed candidate is a valid inductive invariant for the transition system. If the candidate invariant is valid, the process terminates, concluding that the transition system is safe. If it is not valid, the teacher provides a counterexample ce to guide the learner in refining its hypothesis. The counterexample ce is a classification constraint that is added to C, and any states it involves are included in D if they are not already present. When the teacher verifies the validity of the candidate invariant J and the check fails, ce takes the form $\top \rightarrow s$, if an initial state s is excluded from J despite satisfying $Init$ ($s \models Init \wedge s \not\models J$), indicating that future candidate invariants must include s. If the failure occurs because a bad state s is incorrectly included in J ($s \models Bad \wedge s \models J$), then ce is assigned the form $s \rightarrow \bot$, requiring future candidates to exclude s. If the failure is due to a lack of inductiveness, meaning that $s_1 \models J$ but its successor s_2 is not included in J ($s_2 \not\models J$), then ce is set to $s_1 \rightarrow s_2$, meaning that J does not satisfy the inductiveness condition and that the learner must ensure consistency with this reachability information in subsequent iterations.

2.3 Learning Invariants Using Decision Trees

In [16], the ICE learning framework (Fig. 2) is instantiated with a learner that extends classical decision tree learning algorithms by incorporating the handling of implications. In the context of invariant synthesis, decision trees are used to classify program states. These trees are binary, where the internal nodes are labeled by predicates selected from a set of attributes, $Attributes \subseteq \mathcal{F}(\mathcal{X})$, and the leaves are labeled as either positive (+) or negative (-). The attributes are typically simple quantifier-free formulas without Boolean operators, depending on the underlying abstract domain. Consequently, a decision tree can be naturally interpreted as a formula in $\mathcal{F}(\mathcal{X})$.

Classical decision tree learning algorithms construct a decision tree from a given sample of positive and negative examples and a predefined set of attributes. The construction process iteratively selects an attribute using a heuristic, typically based on information gain, and splits the sample into two subsets: one containing points satisfying the attribute and the other containing the remaining points. The process continues recursively until each subset is almost homogeneous, meaning it contains mostly positive or mostly negative points. However, in the context of verification, the goal is exact classification, requiring every point in a leaf to be classified consistently with the sample.

The ICE-DT learner extends this classical approach by incorporating implication constraints into the decision tree construction. The ICE-DT learner (Algorithm 3) takes as input an ICE sample $\mathcal{S} = (D, C)$ and a set of attributes, and constructs a decision tree that is consistent with the sample. To correctly handle implications, the learner considers states appearing as endpoints in the implications but not explicitly labeled in S^+ or S^-. Initially, these states are treated as unclassified, and their classification is determined dynamically. If, during tree construction, a subsample contains only positive (or only negative) points along with unclassified points, all unclassified points in that subsample are classified accordingly. To maintain consistency with implications, an implication closure is computed and stored in a global mapping G, which associates states in $\mathcal{S}^{\rightarrow}$ with classifications (Positive or Negative). The closure enforces that if a state s is classified as Positive, all states reachable from s via implications are also

```
Input  : An ICE sample S = (D, C) and a set of Attributes.
Output: A tree (formula) or fail
Initialize G (a partial mapping of end-points of implications to
  {POSITIVE, NEGATIVE} to empty ;
Let Unclass be the set of all end-points of implications in S⇒;
Compute the implication closure of G wrt. S.;
return DECISIONTREEICE(⟨Pos, Neg, Unclass⟩, Attributes);
```

```
Proc DECISIONTREEICE(Examples = ⟨Pos, Neg, Unclass⟩, Attributes)
    Move all points from Unclass classified as POSITIVE (resp. NEGATIVE) to
      Pos (resp. Neg);
    if Neg = ∅ then
        Mark all points of Unclass in G as POSITIVE;
        Compute the implication closure of G wrt. S;
        return Leaf(+);
    else if Pos = ∅ then
        Mark all points of Unclass in G as NEGATIVE;
        Compute the implication closure of G wrt. S;
        return Leaf(−);
    else
        if Attributes = ∅ then return fail;
        a ← CHOOSE(Attributes, Examples);
        Divide Examples into two: Examples_a with all points satisfying a and
          Examples_¬a the others;
        T_left ← DECISIONTREEICE(Examples_a, Attributes \ {a});
        T_right ← DECISIONTREEICE(Examples_¬a, Attributes \ {a});
        return Tree(a, T_left, T_right);
```

Fig. 3. LEARN-DECISION-TREE($\mathcal{S}$, *Attributes*).

classified as Positive. Similarly, if a state s' is classified as Negative, all states leading to s' via implications are also classified as Negative.

The function CHOOSE(Attributes, Examples) selects the attribute with the highest information gain, ensuring that the most discriminating predicate is used at each step. Several gain functions have been proposed in [16], including one that penalizes decision splits that cut across implication constraints.

Figure 3 ensures that the decision tree remains consistent with the ICE sample while also allowing the learning process to adaptively refine the attribute set. It guarantees that a valid decision tree can always be constructed if a sufficiently expressive attribute set is available.

In [16], this method is further extended to an ICE learning algorithm that starts with an initial set of attributes (e.g., octagonal constraints of the form $\pm x \pm y \leq c$, where $x, y \in \mathcal{X}$ are program variables and c is a bounded constant). If the attributes are insufficient to classify the sample, additional attributes are introduced by increasing the bound on constants.

The syntactic enumeration in ICE-DT is a performance bottleneck; it becomes impractical for invariants with large constants or constraints from expressive domains like polyhedra. Additionally, retaining irrelevant attributes increases selection overhead as the sample grows, further slowing the learning process.

3 Relevant Attribute Discovery

To address the attribute enumeration issue in ICE-DT, we build on our previous work [6], which discovers attributes through separator construction. This data-driven approach eliminates syntactic enumeration by constructing a separator from the current ICE sample and extracting its defining constraints as attributes. We enhance this method to extract additional relevant attributes from interpolants produced in a bounded model checking process.

Figure 4 presents the learner algorithm of the proposed method. The learner takes as input a consistent ICE sample $\mathcal{S}$ and produces a classifier J, which serves as a candidate invariant. The lines highlighted in green indicate the modifications introduced to the learner from [6] to enable collaboration with the bounded model checker (BMC). The BMC that sends attributes to the learner is introduced later in Sect. 3.2.

```
   Input  : A consistent ICE sample S.
   Output: A classifier J of S
1  InitAttributes ← Initial set of attributes;
2  ItpAttributes ← ∅;
3  Attributes ← InitAttributes;
4  Proc LEARNER.LEARN(S)
5      if ¬SUFFICIENT(Attributes, S) then
           /* Attributes discovery by separator construction   */
6          𝕊 ← CONSTRUCTSEPARATOR(S, A_X);
7          SepAttributes ← ⋃_{d∈𝕊} Const(d);
8          /* Receive all pending attributes from the BMC      */
9          pending ← RECEIVEALL(BMC);
10         ItpAttributes ← ItpAttributes ∪ pending;
11         Attributes ← InitAttributes ∪ SepAttributes ∪ ItpAttributes;
12     J ← LEARN-DECISION-TREE(S, Attributes);
13     return J;
```

Fig. 4. A Learner with separator-based and interpolant-based attributes.

The algorithm starts by initializing a set of attributes. Initially, this includes a predefined set of attributes (*InitAttributes*), mainly extracted from the program and the specifications. Additionally, a separate set *ItpAttributes* is maintained to store attributes received asynchronously from the BMC. The working attribute pool (*Attributes*) is then initialized with *InitAttributes*.

The main learning procedure LEARNER.LEARN checks if the current working attribute pool is sufficient to classify the sample $\mathcal{S}$ (Line 5). If it is not the case, the algorithm expands the attribute set. To achieve this, it first constructs a separator using CONSTRUCTSEPARATOR($\mathcal{S}, A_{\mathcal{X}}$), which identifies constraints distinguishing positive and negative examples. The constraints defining the separator (*SepAttributes*) are then extracted (Line 7) and added to the attribute pool (Line 11). The details of the separator construction are provided in Sect. 3.1.

In parallel, the BMC component running asynchronously extracts and sends attributes from interpolants that witness the unsatisfiability of bounded reachability checks. These attributes are received using the function RECEIVEALL(BMC) (Line 9), which retrieves all pending attributes sent by the BMC. The learner updates *ItpAttributes* with these new attributes (Line 10) and adds them into the main attribute pool (Line 11).

Once the attribute set is updated, the algorithm constructs a decision tree using the current sample and attributes (Line 12) as described in Sect. 2.3. The resulting classifier J is then returned as the output.

3.1 Attribute Discovery with Separator Construction

We present here how attributes are discovered using separator construction as in [6].

A *separator* of a sample $\mathcal{S}$ is a set of convex sets that satisfies the following conditions:

1. Every state in $\mathcal{S}^+$ must be included in at least one convex set;
2. No state in $\mathcal{S}^-$ should be contained within any convex set;
3. If a state s_1 belongs to a convex set and there exists an implication $s_1 \rightarrow s_2$, then s_2 must also be covered.

The attribute generation method relies on computing a specific type of separator known as a *join-maximal separator*. A separator $\mathbb{S}$, constructed in an abstract domain $A_{\mathcal{X}}$, is considered join-maximal if no two of its elements can be merged without including a negative state:

$$\forall d_1, d_2 \in \mathbb{S}, \quad d_1 \neq d_2 \implies \exists n \in \mathcal{S}^-, \; n \in d_1 \sqcup d_2. \tag{10}$$

This condition ensure that the separator maintains a small sufficient set of convex sets that separate positive and negative states while respecting the implication constraints.

We construct join-maximal separators iteratively using an abstract domain $A_{\mathcal{X}}$, such as intervals, octagons, or polyhedra, and use join ($\sqcup$) operations to merge convex sets while ensuring that no negative states are included. The process is outlined in algorithm in Fig. 5.

The algorithm begins by initializing each positive state in $\mathcal{S}^+$ as a separate convex set, forming the initial separator (Line 2). The main loop iteratively merges convex sets using the abstract domain's join operator($\sqcup$), provided that the merged set does not contain any negative states from $\mathcal{S}^-$ (Line 4). After each merge operation, the algorithm verifies that all implications in $\mathcal{S}^{\rightarrow}$ are respected. If an implication $s_1 \rightarrow s_2$ exists and s_1 is already included in a convex set while s_2

Input : Consistent ICE sample $\mathcal{S} = (D, C)$, abstract domain $A_{\mathcal{X}}$.
Output: A separator $\mathbb{S}$ consistent with $\mathcal{S}$.

1 **Proc** CONSTRUCTSEPARATOR($\mathcal{S}, A_{\mathcal{X}}$)
2    $\mathbb{S} \leftarrow \{\{s\} \mid s \in \mathcal{S}^+\}$; `// Initialize each positive state as a separate convex set`
3   **while** $\exists d_1, d_2 \in \mathbb{S}$ *s.t.* $d_1 \neq d_2$ *and* $\forall s \in \mathcal{S}^-.\ s \notin d_1 \sqcup d_2$ **do**
4       $\mathbb{S} \leftarrow (\mathbb{S} \setminus \{d_1, d_2\}) \cup \{d_1 \sqcup d_2\}$; `// Merge convex sets`
5   **foreach** $s_1 \rightarrow s_2 \in \mathcal{S}^{\rightarrow}$ **do**
6   **if** $\exists d \in \mathbb{S}.\ s_1 \in d$ *and* $\forall d \in \mathbb{S}.\ s_2 \notin d$ **then**
7             $\mathbb{S} \leftarrow \mathbb{S} \cup \{\{s_2\}\}$; `// Ensure consistency with implications`
8   **return** $\mathbb{S}$

Fig. 5. Constructing a Join-Maximal Separator.

is not, a new singleton set containing s_2 is added to maintain consistency (Line 7). The process continues until no further merges can be performed without violating constraints. Once the iterations complete, the final separator $\mathbb{S}$ is returned.

In the implementation, we actually use an incremental version of the algorithm in Fig. 5 (see [6]).

3.2 Bounded Model Checking and Additional Attribute Discovery

The algorithm for the bounded model checker, which runs in parallel with the previously instantiated ICE framework, is presented in Fig. 6.

A key ingredient of many approaches for invariant synthesis is to be able to overapproximate sets of reachable states without overapproximating too much and including bad states. These approaches, for this purpose, use interpolation [11,17,19,20], which we recall below.

Interpolation and Interpolation-Sequence. Let $A \in \mathcal{F}(\mathcal{X})$ and $B \in \mathcal{F}(\mathcal{Y})$. For an inconsistent pair of formulas (A, B), i.e. $A \wedge B$ is unsatisfiable, an interpolant for A and B is a formula $Itp = \text{ITP}(A, B) \in \mathcal{F}(\mathcal{X} \cap \mathcal{Y})$ defined over the common variables of A and B, satisfying the conditions:

$$A \implies Itp \text{ and } Itp \implies \neg B. \tag{11}$$

This ensures that Itp captures information from A while remaining disjoint from B.

The notion of interpolant can be generalized to sequences of formulas. Consider an inconsistent sequence of formulas $A = [A_1, ..., A_N]$ with $A_i \in \mathcal{F}(\mathcal{X}_i)$ for all $1 \leq i \leq N$, meaning that:

$$\bigwedge_{i=1}^{N} A_i \text{ is unsatisfiable.} \tag{12}$$

An interpolation sequence $Itp = \text{SEQITP}(A)$ is a sequence of formulas $Itp = [Itp_1, ..., Itp_{N-1}]$ such that:

$$\forall 1 \leq i \leq N-1 \quad Itp_i \in \mathcal{F}\left(\left(\bigcup_{k=1}^{i} \mathcal{X}_k\right) \cap \left(\bigcup_{k=i+1}^{N} \mathcal{X}_k\right)\right) \tag{13}$$

$$A_1 \implies Itp_1 \tag{14}$$

$$\forall 1 < i < N, \quad A_i \wedge Itp_{i-1} \implies Itp_i \tag{15}$$

$$Itp_{N-1} \implies \neg A_N \tag{16}$$

This sequence ensures a stepwise separation of the unsatisfiable sequence into intermediate interpolants that preserve information across adjacent formulas.

For example, in interpolation-based model checking [20], when the satisfiability check of the formula $Reach_N^T$ which defines states reachable in N steps (see (1) in Sect. 2.1) fails, a sequence of interpolants is constructed. Each interpolant I_i overapproximates the set of states reachable from $Init$ in i steps while ensuring separation from states that can reach Bad in $(N - i)$ steps. The algorithm attempts to generalize these interpolants to construct an inductive invariant.

```
Input : A transition system T.
1 N ← 0;
2 while true do // loop forever
3     if isSat(Reach_N^T) then
4         Terminate UNSAFE;
5     itps ← seqItp(Reach_N^T);
6     attrs ← ⋃_{itp∈itps} atomics(itp);
7     asyncSend(attrs, Learner);
8     N ← N + 1;
```

Fig. 6. Bounded Model Checking with attribute extraction from interpolants.

Integration into the invariant Learning Process. The algorithm of Fig. 6 iteratively checks the satisfiability of the reachability formula $Reach_N^T$ (see (1) in Sect. 2.1) for an increasing bound N (Line 3). If a counterexample is found, the algorithm terminates immediately and the program is deemed unsafe (Line 4). Otherwise, the algorithm proceeds to extract a sequence of interpolants by calling SEQITP on $Reach_N^T$ (Line 5), which computes a sequence of interpolants over the unrolling of the transition relation up to depth N. The atomic constraints extracted from the interpolants are collected (Line 6) and sent asynchronously to the learner (Line 7), which add them as additional attributes for decision tree learning. This interaction ensures that the learner benefits from relevant constraints derived from bounded model checking, enhancing its ability to infer inductive invariants.

4 Experiments

We have implemented the proposed method by extending NIS, we refer to it as NIS+, hence it is also written in C++ and is configurable with an abstract domain for handling abstract objects. It relies on Z3 [21] for SMT queries and APRON's abstract domains [18].

We denote by NIS(`I`) and NIS+(`I`) the respective tools configured with `I` as the abstract domain. The abstract domain `I` can be the abstract domain of intervals (`int`), octagons (`oct`), or polyhedra (`poly`).

The evaluations below were conducted on linear integer arithmetic (LIA) programs, comprising 164 program from SyGuS-Comp'19 [2] and 132 from SV-Comp'24 [5]. Each experiment was run with a timeout of 300 s (5 min) per program on a machine with an 8-core 3.2 GHz CPU and 16 GB of RAM.

Before comparing NIS+ with state-of-the-art tools, we first evaluate its performance against NIS for each abstract domain to assess the benefits and overhead of running an interpolating BMC in parallel, as well as the impact of including attributes extracted from interpolants in addition to those discovered by NIS in decision tree learning.

Table 1. Number of programs solved by NIS and NIS+ per abstract domain.

Benchmark	NIS (`int`)	NIS+ (`int`)	Δ	NIS (`oct`)	NIS+ (`oct`)	Δ	NIS (`poly`)	NIS+ (`poly`)	Δ
SyGuS-Comp	122	131	+9	136	140	+4	151	156	+5
SV-Comp	89	91	+2	92	95	+3	99	107	+8
Total	211	222	+11	228	235	+7	250	263	+13

Table 1 shows the number of verified program per instances of NIS and NIS+ using different abstract domains. For each benchmark set, NIS+ solves more instances than its corresponding NIS variant. This improvement is observed across all domains, demonstrating the benefit of integrating interpolant-based attribute discovery. Overall, NIS+ achieves a total increase of +11 solved instances in the interval domain, +7 in the octagon domain, and +13 in the polyhedra domain.

Table 2 compares the total solving time for programs commonly verified by both NIS and NIS+ across different abstract domains. In each configuration, NIS+ demonstrates a reduction in total solving time compared to its corresponding NIS variant. The results clearly demonstrate that NIS+ consistently

Table 2. Total time in seconds on commonly solved programs by NIS and NIS+.

Benchmark	NIS (int)	NIS+ (int)	Δ(s)	NIS (oct)	NIS+ (oct)	Δ(s)	NIS (poly)	NIS+ (poly)	Δ(s)
SyGuS-Comp	517.2	369.0	-148.2	854.0	553.1	-300.9	167.0	87.3	-79.7
SV-Comp	598.9	234.7	-364.2	247.8	103.6	-144.2	305.3	238.2	-67.1
Total	1116.1	603.7	-512.4	1101.8	656.7	-445.1	472.3	325.5	-146.8

outperforms NIS in terms of efficiency, significantly reducing the total computation time. Overall, the total solving time across all benchmarks is significantly reduced: NIS+ achieves an improvement of 512.4 s for intervals, 445.1 s for octagons, and 146.8 s for polyhedra. These results confirm that incorporating BMC and attributes from interpolants not only improves the number of solved instances (as shown in Table 1) but also enhances efficiency.

We now compare NIS+ with CVC4, its successor cvc5, and Spacer. CVC4 and it successor cvc5 are SMT solvers from the *cooperating validity checker* (CVC) family, using an enumerative refutation-based approach [3,4,24] for syntax-guided synthesis. Spacer is a PDR-based CHC solver that uses model-based projection and a fast approximation of quantifier elimination [14,19], integrated into Z3. All these tools are implemented in C++.

Table 3. Benchmark results of NIS+(`poly`) vs. NIS(`poly`), Spacer, cvc5 and CVC4.

Tool	SyGuS-Comp		SV-Comp		Total		
	Safe	Unsafe	Safe	Unsafe	Safe	Unsafe	All
NIS+(`poly`)	**138**	**18**	**85**	22	**223**	40	**263**
NIS(`poly`)	133	**18**	81	18	214	36	250
Spacer	122	**18**	79	**23**	201	**41**	242
cvc5	132	0	77	0	209	0	209
CVC4	129	0	70	0	199	0	199

Table 3 presents a comparison of NIS+(`poly`) against NIS(`poly`), Spacer, cvc5, and CVC4 on the two benchmark sets. The results demonstrate that NIS+(`poly`) achieves the highest overall number of solved instances, successfully verifying 263 programs, outperforming all other tools. Compared to NIS(`poly`), the integration of interpolant-based attribute discovery results in 13 additional solved instances, demonstrating the effectiveness of the proposed enhancements. Additionally, NIS+(`poly`) outperforms Spacer by solving 21 more programs. For example, the program in Fig. 1 is only solved by NIS+(`poly`).

The performance of the proposed method and NIS depends on the quality and quantity of attributes in the pool and the representativeness of the sample.

Well-chosen attributes improve generalization, but a large pool increases selection overhead, reducing efficiency. CVC4 and cvc5 rely on enumerative refutation, often testing irrelevant formulas before concluding, and cannot handle unsafe programs. SPACER generalizes predecessors using quantifier elimination, model-based projection, and interpolants in the IC3/PDR framework. While generally effective, it may fail to construct an inductive invariant. In contrast, our method improves efficiency by selecting a minimal set of sufficient attributes, leveraging separator construction and interpolants to refine classification.

Overall, these results indicate that NIS+(`poly`) provides state-of-the-art performance, achieving the best results in terms of total verified programs.

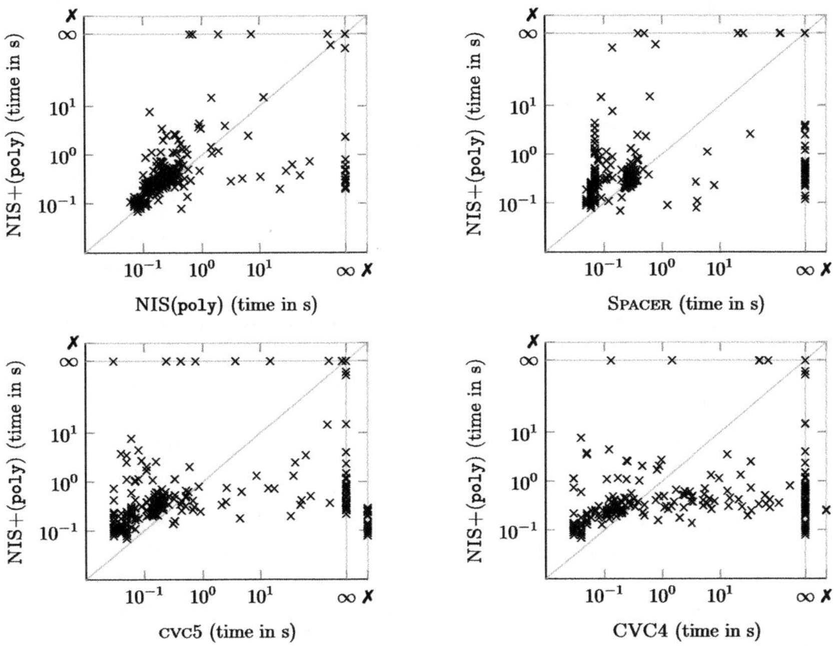

Fig. 7. Runtime of NIS+(`poly`) vs. NIS(`poly`), SPACER, cvc5 and CVC4.

The plots in Fig. 7 compare the execution times of NIS+(`poly`), against NIS(`poly`) SPACER, cvc5 and CVC4. The results indicate that NIS+(`poly`) is generally faster than both cvc5 and CVC4, while exhibiting comparable performance to NIS(`poly`) and SPACER in terms of execution time.

5 Conclusion

We proposed a method to improve the performance of a data-driven approach for invariant synthesis based on ICE, which utilizes decision tree learning and automatic attribute discovery from the sample. The key enhancement introduced in this work involves running a bounded model checker in parallel and extracting atomic predicates from interpolants to use as additional relevant attributes. The implementation of this approach demonstrates competitive results with state-of-the-art tools, solving more instances overall on the SyGuS and SV-COMP benchmarks.

References

1. Alur, R., et al.: Syntax-guided Synthesis. In: Formal Methods in Computer-Aided Design, FMCAD 2013, Portland, OR, USA, October 20–23, 2013, pp. 1–8. IEEE (2013)
2. Alur, R., Fisman, D., Padhi, S., Singh, R., Udupa, A.: SyGuS-Comp 2018: results and analysis. CoRR **abs/1904.07146** (2019)
3. Barbosa, H., et al.: cvc5: a versatile and industrial-strength SMT solver. In: Fisman, D., Rosu, G. (eds.) Tools and Algorithms for the Construction and Analysis of Systems - 28th International Conference, TACAS 2022, Held as Part of the European Joint Conferences on Theory and Practice of Software, ETAPS 2022, Munich, Germany, April 2–7, 2022, Proceedings, Part I. Lecture Notes in Computer Science, vol. 13243, pp. 415–442. Springer (2022)
4. Barrett, C., et al.: CVC4. In: Gopalakrishnan, G., Qadeer, S. (eds.) CAV 2011. LNCS, vol. 6806, pp. 171–177. Springer, Heidelberg (2011). https://doi.org/10.1007/978-3-642-22110-1_14
5. Beyer, D.: State of the art in software verification and witness validation: SV-COMP 2024. In: Finkbeiner, B., Kovács, L. (eds.) Tools and Algorithms for the Construction and Analysis of Systems - 30th International Conference, TACAS 2024, Held as Part of the European Joint Conferences on Theory and Practice of Software, ETAPS 2024, Luxembourg City, Luxembourg, April 6–11, 2024, Proceedings, Part III. Lecture Notes in Computer Science, vol. 14572, pp. 299–329. Springer (2024)
6. Bouajjani, A., Boutglay, W., Habermehl, P.: Data-driven numerical invariant synthesis with automatic generation of attributes. In: Shoham, S., Vizel, Y. (eds.) Computer Aided Verification - 34th International Conference, CAV 2022, Haifa, Israel, August 7-10, 2022, Proceedings, Part I. Lecture Notes in Computer Science, vol. 13371, pp. 282–303. Springer (2022)
7. Bradley, A.R.: SAT-based model checking without unrolling. In: Jhala, R., Schmidt, D.A. (eds.) Verification, Model Checking, and Abstract Interpretation - 12th International Conference, VMCAI 2011, Austin, TX, USA, January 23–25, 2011. Proceedings. Lecture Notes in Computer Science, vol. 6538, pp. 70–87. Springer (2011)
8. Champion, A., Kobayashi, N., Sato, R.: HoIce: an ICE-based non-linear horn clause solver. In: Ryu, S. (ed.) APLAS 2018. LNCS, vol. 11275, pp. 146–156. Springer, Cham (2018). https://doi.org/10.1007/978-3-030-02768-1_8
9. Clarke, E.M., Grumberg, O., Jha, S., Lu, Y., Veith, H.: Counterexample-guided abstraction refinement for symbolic model checking. J. ACM **50**(5), 752–794 (2003)
10. Cousot, P., Cousot, R.: Abstract interpretation: a unified lattice model for static analysis of programs by construction or approximation of fixpoints. In: Graham, R.M., Harrison, M.A., Sethi, R. (eds.) Conference Record of the Fourth ACM Symposium on Principles of Programming Languages, Los Angeles, California, USA, January 1977, pp. 238–252. ACM (1977)

11. Eén, N., Mishchenko, A., Brayton, R.K.: Efficient implementation of property directed reachability. In: Bjesse, P., Slobodová, A. (eds.) International Conference on Formal Methods in Computer-Aided Design, FMCAD '11, Austin, TX, USA, October 30 - November 02, 2011, pp. 125–134. FMCAD Inc. (2011)
12. Ernst, M.D., et al.: The daikon system for dynamic detection of likely invariants. Sci. Comput. Program. **69**(1–3), 35–45 (2007)
13. Ezudheen, P., Neider, D., D'Souza, D., Garg, P., Madhusudan, P.: Horn-ICE learning for synthesizing invariants and contracts. Proc. ACM Program. Lang. **2**(OOPSLA), 131:1–131:25 (2018)
14. Garcia-Contreras, I., K., H.G.V., Shoham, S., Gurfinkel, A.: Fast approximations of quantifier elimination. In: Enea, C., Lal, A. (eds.) Computer Aided Verification - 35th International Conference, CAV 2023, Paris, France, July 17-22, 2023, Proceedings, Part II. Lecture Notes in Computer Science, vol. 13965, pp. 64–86. Springer (2023)
15. Garg, P., Löding, C., Madhusudan, P., Neider, D.: ICE: a robust framework for learning invariants. In: Biere, A., Bloem, R. (eds.) Computer Aided Verification - 26th International Conference, CAV 2014, Held as Part of the Vienna Summer of Logic, VSL 2014, Vienna, Austria, July 18-22, 2014. Proceedings. Lecture Notes in Computer Science, vol. 8559, pp. 69–87. Springer (2014)
16. Garg, P., Neider, D., Madhusudan, P., Roth, D.: Learning invariants using decision trees and implication counterexamples. In: Bodík, R., Majumdar, R. (eds.) Proceedings of the 43rd Annual ACM SIGPLAN-SIGACT Symposium on Principles of Programming Languages, POPL 2016, St. Petersburg, FL, USA, January 20 - 22, 2016, pp. 499–512. ACM (2016)
17. Hoder, K., Bjørner, N.: Generalized property directed reachability. In: Cimatti, A., Sebastiani, R. (eds.) SAT 2012. LNCS, vol. 7317, pp. 157–171. Springer, Heidelberg (2012). https://doi.org/10.1007/978-3-642-31612-8_13
18. Jeannet, B., Miné, A.: APRON: a library of numerical abstract domains for static analysis. In: Bouajjani, A., Maler, O. (eds.) CAV 2009. LNCS, vol. 5643, pp. 661–667. Springer, Heidelberg (2009). https://doi.org/10.1007/978-3-642-02658-4_52
19. Komuravelli, A., Gurfinkel, A., Chaki, S.: SMT-based model checking for recursive programs. In: Biere, A., Bloem, R. (eds.) CAV 2014. LNCS, vol. 8559, pp. 17–34. Springer, Cham (2014). https://doi.org/10.1007/978-3-319-08867-9_2
20. McMillan, K.L.: Interpolation and SAT-based model checking. In: Hunt, W.A., Somenzi, F. (eds.) CAV 2003. LNCS, vol. 2725, pp. 1–13. Springer, Heidelberg (2003). https://doi.org/10.1007/978-3-540-45069-6_1
21. de Moura, L.M., Bjørner, N.S.: Z3: An Efficient SMT Solver. In: Ramakrishnan, C.R., Rehof, J. (eds.) Tools and Algorithms for the Construction and Analysis of Systems, 14th International Conference, TACAS 2008, Held as Part of the Joint European Conferences on Theory and Practice of Software, ETAPS 2008, Budapest, Hungary, March 29-April 6, 2008. Proceedings. Lecture Notes in Computer Science, vol. 4963, pp. 337–340. Springer (2008)
22. Padhi, S., Millstein, T., Nori, A., Sharma, R.: Overfitting in synthesis: theory and practice. In: Dillig, I., Tasiran, S. (eds.) CAV 2019. LNCS, vol. 11561, pp. 315–334. Springer, Cham (2019). https://doi.org/10.1007/978-3-030-25540-4_17
23. Padhi, S., Sharma, R., Millstein, T.D.: Data-driven precondition inference with learned features. In: Krintz, C., Berger, E.D. (eds.) Proceedings of the 37th ACM SIGPLAN Conference on Programming Language Design and Implementation, PLDI 2016, Santa Barbara, CA, USA, June 13-17, 2016, pp. 42–56. ACM (2016)

24. Reynolds, A., Barbosa, H., Nötzli, A., Barrett, C., Tinelli, C.: CVC4SY: smart and fast term enumeration for syntax-guided synthesis. In: Dillig, I., Tasiran, S. (eds.) CAV 2019. LNCS, vol. 11562, pp. 74–83. Springer, Cham (2019). https://doi.org/10.1007/978-3-030-25543-5_5
25. Ryan, G., Wong, J., Yao, J., Gu, R., Jana, S.: CLN2INV: learning loop invariants with continuous logic networks. In: 8th International Conference on Learning Representations, ICLR 2020, Addis Ababa, Ethiopia, April 26–30, 2020. OpenReview.net (2020)
26. Sharma, R., Gupta, S., Hariharan, B., Aiken, A., Nori, A.V.: Verification as learning geometric concepts. In: Logozzo, F., Fähndrich, M. (eds.) SAS 2013. LNCS, vol. 7935, pp. 388–411. Springer, Heidelberg (2013). https://doi.org/10.1007/978-3-642-38856-9_21
27. Sharma, R., Nori, A.V., Aiken, A.: Interpolants as classifiers. In: Madhusudan, P., Seshia, S.A. (eds.) CAV 2012. LNCS, vol. 7358, pp. 71–87. Springer, Heidelberg (2012). https://doi.org/10.1007/978-3-642-31424-7_11
28. Si, X., Naik, A., Dai, H., Naik, M., Song, L.: Code2Inv: a deep learning framework for program verification. In: Lahiri, S.K., Wang, C. (eds.) CAV 2020. LNCS, vol. 12225, pp. 151–164. Springer, Cham (2020). https://doi.org/10.1007/978-3-030-53291-8_9
29. Xu, R., He, F., Wang, B.: Interval counterexamples for loop invariant learning. In: Devanbu, P., Cohen, M.B., Zimmermann, T. (eds.) ESEC/FSE '20: 28th ACM Joint European Software Engineering Conference and Symposium on the Foundations of Software Engineering, Virtual Event, USA, November 8–13, 2020. pp. 111–122. ACM (2020)
30. Zhu, H., Magill, S., Jagannathan, S.: A data-driven CHC solver. In: Foster, J.S., Grossman, D. (eds.) Proceedings of the 39th ACM SIGPLAN Conference on Programming Language Design and Implementation, PLDI 2018, Philadelphia, PA, USA, June 18-22, 2018, pp. 707–721. ACM (2018)

Distributed Systems

Distributed Computation of Temporal Twins in Periodic Undirected Time-Varying Graphs

Massinissa Tighilt[1,2(✉)], Lina Azerouk[1], Camille Palisoc[2], Binh-Minh Bui-Xuan[1], and Maria Potop-Butucaru[1]

[1] LIP6, CNRS, Sorbonne Université, Paris, France
{massinissa.tighilt,lina.azerouk,buixuan,maria.potop-butucaru}@lip6.fr
[2] SITA, Geneva, Switzerland
{massinissa.tighilt,camille.palisoc}@sita.aero

Abstract. Twin nodes in a static network capture the idea of being substitutes for each other for maintaining paths of the same length anywhere in the network. In dynamic networks, we model twin nodes over a time-bounded interval, noted (Δ, d)-twins, as follows. A periodic undirected time-varying graph $\mathcal{G} = (G_t)_{t\in\mathbb{N}}$ of period p is an infinite sequence of static graphs where $G_t = G_{t+p}$ for every $t \in \mathbb{N}$. For Δ and d two integers, two distinct nodes u and v in $\mathcal{G}$ are (Δ, d)-twins if, starting at some instant, their outside neighbourhoods $N(u) \setminus \{u, v\}$ and $N(v) \setminus \{u, v\}$ have non-empty intersection and differ by at most d elements for Δ consecutive instants. In particular when $d = 0$, u and v can act during the Δ instants as substitutes for each other in order to maintain journeys of the same length in time-varying graph $\mathcal{G}$. It is known how to compute $(\Delta, 0)$-twins in polynomial time by a centralized algorithm. In this paper we propose the first distributed deterministic algorithm enabling each node to enumerate its (Δ, d)-twins in at most $2p$ rounds. We prove that the size of the messages used in our algorithm is at most $O(\delta_{\mathcal{G}} \log n + \log p)$, where n is the total number of nodes and $\delta_{\mathcal{G}}$ is the maximum degree of the graphs G_t's. Additionally, we prove that using randomized techniques borrowed from distributed hash function sampling the message size can be reduced w.h.p. down to $O(\log n + \log p)$.

Keywords: time-varying graph · twin · twin distributed computing

1 Introduction

Maintaining connectivity is an important topic for dynamic networks. For instance, in the 1-interval-connected network model, which allows for a fixed set of nodes to communicate through a temporal edge set changing at discrete

Supported by SITA – LIP6, CNRS, Sorbonne Université convention C24.0499 and ANRT grant 2024.0526.
This result has been obtained primarily by student authors.

S. Lahlou and M. Mukund (Eds.): NETYS 2025, LNCS 15736, pp. 39–56, 2026.
https://doi.org/10.1007/978-3-032-00347-8_3

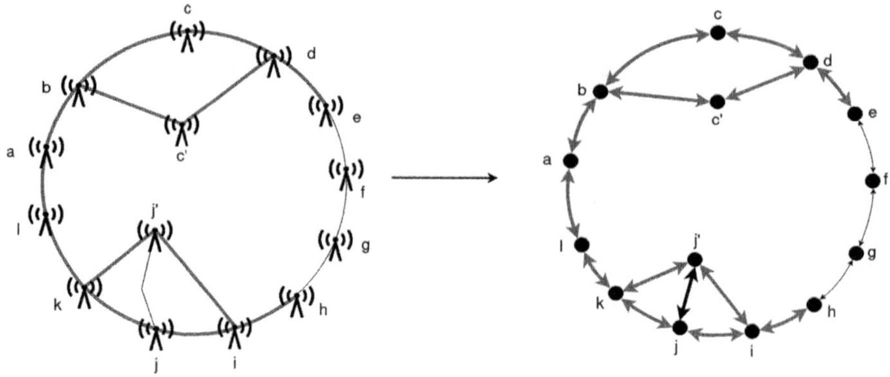

Fig. 1. Network modelled as an undirected graph. Arrows are in double direction to stress that communications are allowed both ways around. The two pairs of twins in the graph are $\{c, c'\}$ and $\{j, j'\}$. A packet traveling between node a and e can choose (a, b, c, d, e) as shortest path. If node c switches off or if it is faulty, the path of same length (a, b, c', d, e) can still be used. Between a and h, the two paths (a, l, k, j, i, h) and (a, l, k, j', i, h) are shortest, however, (a, l, k, j, j', i, h) is not a shortest path.

time units called rounds [20,22–24,29], if moreover the network structure is periodic and each node's local view can be updated entirely every round on contact of its neighbours, then a temporally optimal broadcast tree can be maintained in real time [8]. In particular, nodes do not need to process the information they receive about their neighborhood later, which is what makes this solution unique. We will refer to this kind of network structure as a time-varying graph [7,9,10,12], that is, an infinite sequence of classical graphs over the same vertex set. The first graph in the sequence is a snapshot of the network structure at the beginning of the first round of communication, and so on. Note that in the 1-interval-connected model, it is usually required for the time-varying graph to be connected at each round in order to address broadcasting concerns.

In our study, we consider all the above assumptions, including periodicity. However, we do not require the time-varying graph to be connected at every round. This is convenient to model adhoc networks with both dense and sparse areas with predictable periodicity such as LEO (Low Earth Orbital) satellite networks. We would like to capture by the notion of twin nodes the possibility of backup routes or of a resource saving strategy during the times when some satellites are called twins. This is why we aim at a formalism where the connectivity in the rest of the network are maintained by journeys of the same length even though one of the twin satellites switches off for sleeping or maintenance during some time window of a given desired length, *cf.* Fig. 1. Other applications of such a backup strategy arise in emerging datacenter networks via optical circuit switches [1,2,25], and resilient distribution in smart grids via transformers [26].

Here, IoT captors of a corrupted node need to send the list of its temporal twins to its in-neighbours for replanning backup routes.

In a static graph, such concept can be formalised using the model of ϵ-modules [17] and d-contractions [4]: given an integer d, two nodes $u \neq v$ are d-twins if their outside neighbourhoods have non-empty intersection, $N(u) \cap N(v) \setminus \{u, v\} \neq \emptyset$, while their symmetric difference has size smaller than d, that is, $|N(u) \setminus N(v) \setminus \{u, v\}| + |N(v) \setminus N(u) \setminus \{u, v\}| \leq d$. Note that in previous models [4,17], the outside neighbourhoods of d-twins are not required to have a non-empty intersection. However, in our model, we assume non-empty intersection for obtaining efficient computational results. At the same time, isolated nodes or nodes without common neighbours are bad models of backup routes as in the above example of network of satellites. Hence, we discard them from our definition of d-twins which requires nodes to have at least one common neighbour. From this point, our extension to the dynamic case will follow that of Δ-twins [6]: given two integers Δ and d, two nodes $u \neq v$ are (Δ, d)-twins in a time-varying graph $\mathcal{G} = (G_t)_{t \in \mathbb{N}}$ if there exists $t_0 \in \mathbb{N}$ such that u and v are d-twins in every graph G_t, for $t_0 \leq t < t_0 + \Delta$.

Related Work. In graph theory, modular decomposition is a recursive simplification of an input graph down to terminal cases which are edgeless graphs [15]. Formally, a module $A \subseteq V$ of a graph $G = (V, E)$ is a subset of nodes all having the same neighbourhood outside the module, that is, $N(v) \setminus A$ is the same set for every $v \in A$. Informally, a module with no internal edges could be understood as duplicates since its nodes then have exactly the same neighbourhood (both externally and internally). This very special case of module having no internal edges is called a set of (false) twins. These twin nodes would then have the same characteristics such as node degree, centrality measures, LexBFS order, and so on. Notably, a consequence for their connectivity to the rest of the network is that any path using one node can as well use the other nodes instead. These nodes can thus be seen as substitutes for each other in order to preserve paths in the graph, as exemplified in Fig. 1.

Historically, the general notion of modules has been studied mainly for their structural properties independently from network communication and connectivity. The set of overlapping modules are closed by intersection, union, difference, and symmetric difference. A family of sets satisfying such closure properties is also called *siba – semi infinite boolean algebra* – for their similar closure properties as with classical algebraic objects [13]. Using further properties developed in the context of *siba*, where [13] gives a formal overview, a series of linear time algorithms have been found to compute the modular decomposition tree of any input graph, from which all possible modules of the graph can be enumerated, see, *e.g.* [18] and the extensive references therein. However, these are centralised algorithms and to the best of our knowledge, there has not been much study focusing on designing distributed algorithms computing modules. In a sense, we propose in this paper to initiate such a study, beginning with the simpler case of modules of size 2, also called a pair of twins (either true twins or false twins).

At the same time, we relax the definition of modules, allowing for nodes in a module to have their neighbourhood differ by a fixed number of elements.

Such a relaxation of modules is not new. Habib et al. initiated the investigation of the structural properties of these, first under the terminology of an ϵ-module [17] and then (α, β)-module [16] where some set properties are still preserved, namely Moore families' closure (that is, closure under intersection) and loosely partitivity of *siba* (which is a variant of union and symmetric difference closures). However, few algorithmic results were obtained for enumerating these relaxed modules.

Letting general modules aside, Bonnet et al. focus on twins and address their relaxation down to what is called d-contractions, resulting in a long series of works on twin-width of graphs similar to what was obtained in graph minor theory [4]. The related results include a Courcelle-like meta theorem for twin-width. Here, Courcelle-like meta theorems refer to statements where every problem expressible in some logic, resp. first order logic, can be polynomially tractable on graphs where some width parameter, resp. twin-width, is bounded [4]. Loosely related to the above, twins have also been generalised to Δ-twins of temporal graphs, where a centralised computation can be performed in polynomial time for identifying behavioural similarities in a time-dependent user story of an e-commercial website [6]. In this paper, we address the intersection of these two pieces of work, at the same time considering distributed algorithms. Our main goal is thus to provide, up to our knowledge, the first investigation of twins and their relaxed variant in a dynamic distributed setting. Our work follows the broad line of research related to distributed algorithms for time varying graphs [3,5,11,21] under various contexts including graph optimization [30], structural properties of social networks [31], and machine learning [27,34].

Our Contribution. We give a distributed deterministic algorithm for every node in a periodic undirected time-varying graph of period p to compute its (Δ, d)-twins after $2p$ rounds. We give an upper bound in $O(\delta_{\mathcal{G}} \log n + \log p)$ for the size of the messages used in the algorithm, where $\delta_{\mathcal{G}}$ is the maximum degree of the graphs G_t's and n the total number of nodes. When randomized by sampling techniques from [19], their size can be reduced to $O(\log n + \log p)$ w.h.p.

The main idea in our algorithm can be divided into two steps. In the first step, we show how to solve the problem of finding d-twins in a static graph G after 2 rounds. Roughly, while in 2 rounds every node can receive messages sent by its 2-neighbourhood, the receiver node need to detect those sent by its d-twins. In particular, note that while a path over 3 vertices u–v–w admits two 0-twins which are u and w, a path over $n \geq 4$ vertices u–v–w–t has none (in particular, u has no 0-twin because t which is from its 3-neighbourhood breaks down the 0-twin definition for the pair $\{u, w\}$). However, to reduce the messages' size sent from nodes to nodes, we would like to design algorithms only using neighbourhoods or 2-neighbourhoods. Then, in order to avoid examining messages from k-neighbourhoods with $k \geq 3$, we exhibit a set property involving the number of paths of length 2 which allows to detect d-twins. The main idea is to use inclusion-exclusion properties on the neighbourhoods of nodes in order to restrict the message size to $O(\delta_G \log n)$. Furthermore, by exploiting very simple twist inspired from distributed hash function sampling [19], we reduce the message size down to $O(\log n)$ w.h.p. In a second step, we address the dynamic case. The main idea here is for the receiver nodes to store information while waiting for the time-varying graph to repeat its edges, using periodicity.

Eventually, we remark that our algorithm requires the time-varying graph to be undirected, meaning communication on an edge uv must be allowed both way around between u and v. This is because of the step in the static setting where every node attempts to count the number of paths of length 2 linking itself to every of its d-twins.

Outlines. The paper is organised as follows. The formal framework of periodic time-varying graphs and (Δ, d)-twins is defined in Sect. 2. In Sect. 3 we briefly present a property of twins in static graphs, before using it to show a distributed algorithm for every node to compute its (Δ, d)-twins and prove its correctness. We also show how to reduce the message size w.h.p. by randomizing parts of the algorithm. We conclude the paper in Sect. 4 along with some open remarks for future works.

2 Model and Problem Definition

We consider distributed systems which are fault-free, message-passing, synchronous, with a unique ID for each process. This will be formalised as a time-varying graph [9] defined by $\mathcal{G} = (V, E, T, \rho)$, where V is a finite set of nodes representing processes, $E \subseteq \binom{V}{2}$ is the underlying set of all possible edges and $\rho : E \times T \rightarrow \{0, 1\}$ is the presence function defining whether an edge exists in a given round. Temporal edges are those bound to a specific time instant: $E_t = \{e \in E : \rho(e, t) = 1\}$. Alternatively, a time-varying graph can also be seen as a sequence of static graphs $\mathcal{G} = (G_t)_{t \in T}$, where $G_t = (V, E_t)$. It is not necessary for the graphs G_t's to be connected at every time instant. The maximum degree in $(G_t)_{t \in T}$ is also called the degree of $\mathcal{G}$, it is noted $\delta_{\mathcal{G}}$.

Inspired by the models of dynamic networks in [9,20,22,28,29,32,33], we suppose furthermore that the time-varying graph is characterized by a periodicity, non-anonymity, synchronicity, and local knowledge.

- The **periodicity** means the existence of a specific value p such that, every edge present in the graph at a particular time t has its presence in the graph repeated periodically at $t + p$. Because of periodicity, we restrict our domain of study down to the cyclic group of p elements and abusively refer to it as $T = \mathbb{Z}/p\mathbb{Z} = \{0, 1, \ldots, p-1\} = [\![0, p-1]\!]$, and subsequently restrict the input time-varying graph to the first p instants, $\mathcal{G} = (G_t)_{0 \leq t < p}$.
- The **non-anonymity** of the graph means that each node v has a unique $ID \in \mathbb{N}$, we assume that each ID is represented using at most $O(\log n)$ bits, where $n = |V|$.

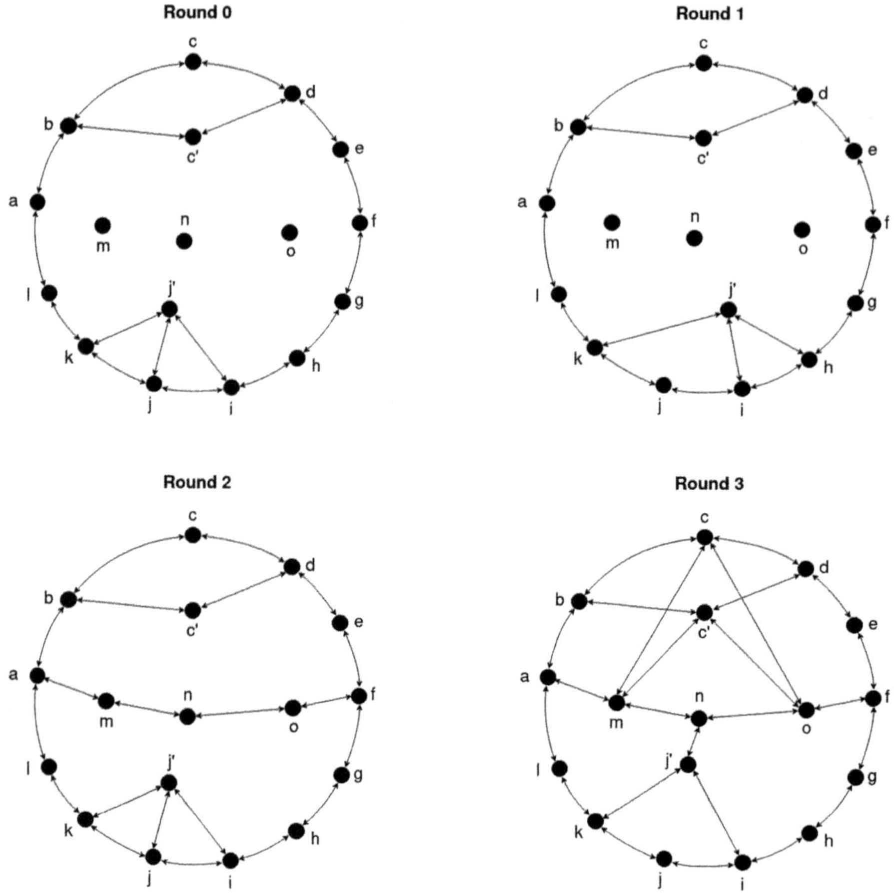

Fig. 2. A 4-periodic time-varying graph. Nodes c and c' are $(4, 0)$-twins.

- The **synchronicity** within the graph implies the presence of a global clock that ticks regularly for each $t \in T$, beginning with $t = 0$. During each tick of this clock, every node v in the graph performs three sequential actions: sending a message to each neighbouring node, receiving the message from each neighbour, and executing computational tasks. Each occurrence of the clock ticking is called *round* [20].
- By **local knowledge**, we assume that each node v in the graph has the knowledge of the number of its neighbours at any given time $t \in T$, but not their *IDs*. The set of neighbours of node v at time t is denoted as $N_t(v)$ [9].

For $u \neq v$ two nodes of $\mathcal{G}$, we say that u and v are (Δ, d)-twins if, starting from a specific time instant $t_0 \in T$, their outside neighbourhoods have a non-empty intersection while the difference between these two sets is less than or equal to a fixed value d for Δ consecutive rounds, that is, $N_t(u) \cap N_t(v) \neq \emptyset$ and $|N_t(u) \backslash N_t(v) \backslash \{u, v\}| + |N_t(v) \backslash N_t(u) \backslash \{u, v\}| \leq d$, for every $t \in [\![t_0, t_0 + \Delta - 1]\!]$

if $t_0 + \Delta \le p$ and for every $t \notin]\!]t_0 + \Delta - 1 \mod p, t_0[\![$ otherwise. The assumption of non-empty intersection is important to model the fact that isolated (Δ, d)-twins or (Δ, d)-twins of far distance from each other cannot act as backup routes. Figure 2 exemplifies (Δ, d)-twins. We address the following problem.

PERIODIC(Δ, d)-TWINS
INPUT: $\mathcal{G} = (G_t)_{t \in T}$ with $T = [\![0, p-1]\!]$ representing a time-varying graph of period p; integers $\Delta \le p$ and d.
OUTPUT: for every node u in $\mathcal{G}$, a list of all its (Δ, d)-twins, that is, a list of (v, t)'s with v being a node ID and t the starting time instant where u and v become d-twins for Δ instants.

For more clarity, we first consider the scenario where period p is given among the input of every node. In the next section, we prove for this scenario that PERIODIC(Δ, d)-TWINS can be solved after $2p$ rounds, using messages of size $O(\delta_{\mathcal{G}} \log n)$, where n is the total number of nodes and $\delta_{\mathcal{G}} \le n$ is the maximum degree of the graphs G_t's. For the scenario where nodes do not have knowledge of p, we will show how to modify the algorithm to achieve the same goal using an overhead of size $O(\log p)$ in every message.

3 Distributed Computation of (Δ, d)-Twins

The main idea of our solution is based on the following property of static graphs, which hints that every node can compare its 1-neighbourhood with the 1-neighbourhood of any other node in its 2-neighbourhood in order to determine whether that node is one of its d-twins. For $u \ne v$ two nodes of a static graph $G = (V, E)$, we say that u and v are d-twins if they have at least one common neighbour and that the difference between the sets of their outside neighbours is at most d, namely $|N(u) \setminus N(v) \setminus \{u, v\}| + |N(v) \setminus N(u) \setminus \{u, v\}| \le d$. A path of length 2 between u and v is a path having 2 edges and 3 nodes, of the form (u, w, v) with $uw \in E$ and $vw \in E$, for some $w \ne u$ and $w \ne v$.

Lemma 1. *Let $G = (V, E)$ be an undirected static graph, let $u \ne v$ be two distinct nodes in V with a common neighbour and let $k = |N(u) \cup N(v) \setminus \{u, v\}|$ be the number of distinct neighbors of u and v, excluding the nodes u and v. Then, u and v are d-twins if and only if $d \ge k$ or there are at least $k - d$ paths of length 2 between u and v.*

Proof. The case when $d \ge k$ is clear. Otherwise let $A = N(u) \setminus \{u, v\}$ and $B = N(v) \setminus \{u, v\}$. Then, $k = |A \cup B|$. The paths of length 2 between u and v are only paths passing through their common neighbours. Therefore, the number of such paths is $n_p = |A \cap B|$. We need to prove that u and v are d-twins if and only if $n_p \ge k - d$. From the definition of d-twins, we have $|A \setminus B| + |B \setminus A| \le d$. Since $|A \cup B| - |A \cap B| = |A \setminus B| + |B \setminus A|$, this is equivalent to $|A \cup B| - |A \cap B| \le d$, in other words, $k - n_p \le d$. □

The rough idea that we will use for our algorithm is as follows. Each node will identify a list of its (Δ, d)-twins in a distributed manner. Our process begins with initialization, where each node sets up local tables to record messages received from neighbors, count unique IDs, and store any potential twins identified. These tables are continuously updated throughout each round to keep track of both direct and forwarded neighborhood information, which is essential for identifying (Δ, d)-twins. During the first period, each node broadcasts its neighborhood data to direct neighbors. As neighboring nodes receive this information, they store it in their local tables. This step prepares them for the forwarding phase. In the subsequent forwarding phase, each node sends all collected neighborhood data to its 1-hop neighbors. This process allows each node to build a 2-hop view of the network, providing the necessary data to detect potential twin relationships within this extended neighborhood range. Lemma 3, which will be presented later in this section, formalizes this step. Using it, each node then verifies potential twin relationships by comparing neighborhood sizes and calculating the intersections with other nodes' neighborhoods. If the comparison meets the twin criteria, the node records this twin relationship and tracks it over multiple rounds, ensuring that the (Δ, d)-twin property is sustained over time. Through this approach, each node independently determines twin relationships without the need for global network synchronization, maintaining efficiency and accuracy in a distributed network setting.

3.1 Scenario 1: Period p is Known by Every Node

Let $\mathcal{G} = (G_t)_{t \in T}$ be a p-periodic time-varying graph with $T = [\![0, p-1]\!]$. We first describe our algorithm idea for the simpler scenario where every node has the knowledge of p in advance. For every node to compute its list of d-twins, we would need 2 rounds per static graph G_t, so that the node collects information about its 2-neighbourhood. Since the time-varying graph is periodic, we can proceed a first phase of p rounds for passing every node's 1-neighbourhood information to its neighbours. Then, in a second phase consisting of p extra rounds, every node can forward all the pieces of information it has already collected from its neighbours during the first phase. The information received in this second phase informs every node about its 2-neighbourhood. There are however two drawbacks of the above idea.

Firstly, we need to control the size of the messages sent from each node, especially in the second phase. In Lemma 3 below, we prove that the information related to the entire neighbourhood is not necessary, but only the size of it. Roughly, we plan to only send the size of the neighbourhood each time we need to forward this information, see Algorithm 2, lines 3–4. An example of messages sent by nodes during Algorithm 2 is given in Fig. 3. More specifically, following Lemma 3 each node u in $\mathcal{G}$ can determine whether a node v in $\mathcal{G}$ is such that u and v are d-twins at round t, by adding the number of u's neighbours, obtained at round t, to the number of v's neighbours, obtained at round $t' = t + p$ and subtracting the number of common neighbours between them, see Algorithm 1,

Algorithm 1. Finding the (Δ, d)-twins, all tables are dictionary data structures

```
1: procedure PERIODIC(Δ, d)-TWINS(p, Δ, d)
                                                        ▷ Initialisation
2:     Table Tab with p associating to each round the set of neighbours and the number
       of their neighbours
3:     Table Count associating to a given ID, the number of times it has been received
       in the current round
4:     nbMsg ← 0                              ▷ The number of messages received.
5:     Table Neighbors associating to a given ID its number of neighbours in the
       current round
6:     Table Twins storing the consecutive d-twins of the node, updated at each round,
       initially empty
7:     Table dTwinsRound associating to each round the found d-twins of the node
8:     Set Delta_d_Twins initially empty
9:     for each round do
10:        Call Algorithm 2                                 ▷ Sending a message
11:        Call Algorithm 3                              ▷ For received messages
12:    if round = 2p − 1 then
13:        i ← 0
14:        while i < p and Twins ≠ ∅ do
15:            for id in Twins do
16:                if id in dTwinsRound[i] then
17:                    Twins[id] ← Twins[id] + 1
18:                    if Twins[id] = Δ then
19:                        Append {id, p + i − Δ + 1} to Delta_d_Twins
20:                        Remove id from Twins
21:                else
22:                    Remove id from Twins
23:            i ← i + 1
24:        return Delta_d_Twins
```

line 14. Then, if the result is less than d, they are d-twins, according to the inequality given in Lemma 3, this is implemented in Algorithm 1, lines 15–16.

Secondly, we aim at computing (Δ, d)-twins in $\mathcal{G}$, with Δ representing a continuous window of Δ consecutive time instants starting at $t_0 \in T$. For most t_0 this can be done using in the receiver node's internal storage a counter per sender node, which increments every time the receiver node detects a sender node as its d-twin at some G_t, see Algorithm 3, line 18. The counter is reset to zero whenever that sender node is detected as a non-d-twin at some (other) G_t, see Algorithm 3, line 20. However, cases involving extremities of interval T such as when $t_0 + \Delta \geq p$ will have their time window divided into two disjoint intervals: $[\![0, t_0 + \Delta - 1 \mod p]\!]$ and $[\![t_0, p-1]\!]$. If we proceed as with all other cases, the information will be ready at some round after the $2p$-th round for this case. We can accelerate this to be as early as in the $2p$-th round using internal storage of a table in each receiver node, instead of the previously mentioned incremental counters. Another positive consequence of using a table instead of

Algorithm 2. Send messages

```
procedure SendMessage(p, Δ, d, round)
    if round < p then
        msg ←< myId, nbNeighbors >
        Send msg to all neighbours.
    else if p ≤ round < 2 * p then
        msg ← ∅
        for elem ∈ Tab[round − p] do
            Append elem to msg
        Send msg to all neighbours
```

Algorithm 3. Upon Receiving a Message **msg**

```
procedure ReceiveMessage(p, Δ, d, round)
    if round < p then
        Append msg to Tab[round]
    else if p ≤ round < 2 * p then
        nbMsg ← nbMsg + 1
        for < id, nb > in msg do
            Count[id] ← Count[id] + 1
            Neighbors[id] ← nb
        if nbMsg = nbNeighbors then
            for each id in Twins do
                if id not in Count then
                    Remove id from Twins
            for each id in Count do
                dTwin ← nbNeighbors + Neighbors[id] − 2 * Count[id]
                if dTwin ≤ d then
                    Append id to dTwinsRound[round − p]
                    if id in Twins then
                        Twins[id] ← Twins[id] + 1
                    else
                        Twins[id] ← 1
                    if Twins[id] ≥ Δ then
                        Append {id, round − Δ + 1} to Delta_d_Twins
                else
                    Remove id from Twins
```

using incremental counters is that, starting from round $p + \Delta$, every node has access in real time to its (Δ, d)-twins of previous Δ rounds. Then, at the $2p$-th round, every node has access to the full list of its (Δ, d)-twins, where the computation terminates.

Algorithm 1 implements the above ideas, calling as subroutines both Algorithms 2 and 3 at every round. All tables in Algorithm 1 are dictionary data structures. The result for every node u will be stored in table `Delta_d_Twins`. For its computation, node u maintains furthermore two tables, called `Twins` and `Count`. For a node $v \neq u$ with identifier id, a strictly positive value of `Twins[`id`]`

means that v and u have been twin vertices for the last `Twins[`id`]` number of rounds. Hence, when `Twins[`id`]` is at least Δ, we append id to the resulting list `Delta_d_Twins` along with the number of rounds where they start to be (Δ, d)-twins. This is implemented in Algorithm 3, lines 21–22.

Round 4

Sender node	Message
a	{<a, 2>, <b, 3>, <l, 2>}
b	{<b, 3>, <a, 2>, <c, 2>, <c', 2>}
c	{<c, 2>, <b, 3>, <d, 3>}
c'	{<c', 2>, <b, 3>, <d, 3>}
j	{<j, 3>, <i, 3>, <j', 3>, <k, 3>}
j'	{<j', 3>, <i, 3>, <j, 3>, <k, 3>}

Round 5

Sender node	Message
a	{<a, 2>, <b, 3>, <l, 2>}
b	{<b, 3>, <a, 2>, <c, 2>, <c', 2>}
c	{<c, 2>, <b, 3>, <d, 3>}
c'	{<c', 2>, <b, 3>, <d, 3>}
j	{<j, 2>, <i, 3>, <k, 3>}
j'	{<j', 3>, <i, 3>, <k, 3>, <h, 3>}

Round 6

Sender node	Message
a	{<a, 3>, <b, 3>, <l, 2>, <m, 2>}
b	{<b, 3>, <a, 3>, <c, 2>, <c', 2>}
c	{<c, 2>, <b, 3>, <d, 3>}
c'	{<c', 2>, <b, 3>, <d, 3>}
j	{<j, 3>, <i, 3>, <j', 3>, <k, 3>}
j'	{<j', 3>, <i, 3>, <j, 3>, <k, 3>}

Round 7

Sender node	Message
a	{<a, 3>, <b, 3>, <l, 2>, <m, 4>}
b	{<b, 3>, <a, 3>, <c, 4>, <c', 4>}
c	{<c, 4>, <b, 3>, <d, 3>, <m, 4>, <o, 4>}
c'	{<c', 4>, <b, 3>, <d, 3>, <m, 4>, <o, 4>}
j	{<j, 2>, <i, 3>, <k, 3>}
j'	{<j', 3>, <i, 3>, <k, 3>, <n, 3>}

Fig. 3. Tables describing the messages sent to the direct neighbourhood of nodes in the example presented in Fig. 2. The messages described here-above are sent through the second period of the time-varying graph, corresponding to the information collected during the first period.

In case we conclude that id is not a twin with u, such as with Algorithm 3's lines 12 and 24, a quick way to save this information is to remove key id from (dictionary) `Twins`. Table `Count` is to be used in Algorithm 3 and related to the current round. We use an alternative computation for what is stored in table `Count`: rather than using Lemma 1 which would force us to count the number of paths of length 2, we use the equivalent quantities showed in Lemma 3 below instead. These quantities are encoded precisely at line 14 of Algorithm 3. The size of the message in the second phase is composed by two additive terms. The first term is the number of neighbours, multiplied by the size of the nodes ID's. The second term is the size of the neighbourhood of every neighbour, which is upper bounded by the first term. Thus, the maximum size of messages are bounded by $O(\delta_\mathcal{G} \log n)$, where n is the total number of nodes and $\delta_\mathcal{G} \leq n$ is the maximum degree of the graphs G_t's, *cf.* Lemma 2 below. Figure 3 exemplifies the messages received in the second phase of every node in the example of Fig. 2.

We now prove the correctness of the algorithm, as well as the maximum size of the messages used in the algorithm.

Lemma 2. *Given a p-periodic time-varying graph $\mathcal{G} = (G_t)_{t \in T}$, with n nodes, if each node sends the list of IDs of its neighbours associated with the number of their neighbours collected at a round t in Algorithm 3 in line 3, then the maximum size of a message sent at round $t+p$ as stated in Algorithm 2 lines 6–9 is $O(\delta_\mathcal{G} \log(n\delta_\mathcal{G}))$.*

Proof. A node u can have at most $\delta_\mathcal{G} = n-1$ neighbours. For every neighbour w of u, u needs to store the ID of w, which requires a size of $O(\log n)$, and the number of neighbours of w, which can be at most $\delta_\mathcal{G}$, requiring a size $\log \delta_\mathcal{G}$. So for a neighbour w of u, u stores information of size $O(\log n) + \log \delta_\mathcal{G} = O(\log n\delta_\mathcal{G})$, and for all neighbours of u, it stores information of size $O(\delta_\mathcal{G} \log n\delta_\mathcal{G})$, and this information represents the size of the message that u will send in the second phase. □

Lemma 3. *Given a p-periodic time-varying graph $\mathcal{G} = (G_t)_{t \in T}$, and two distinct nodes $u \neq v$, u and v are (Δ, d)-twins if $|N_t(u) \setminus \{u,v\}| + |N_t(v) \setminus \{u,v\}| - 2 \times |((N_t(u) \setminus \{u,v\}) \cap (N_t(v) \setminus \{u,v\}))| \leq d$ for $t_0 \leq t < t_0 + \Delta$ that is, for Δ consecutive rounds.*

Proof. The proof is very similar to that of Lemma 1. Let $A = N_t(u) \setminus \{u,v\}$ and $B = N_t(v) \setminus \{u,v\}$. From the definition of d-twins, we have $|A \setminus B| + |B \setminus A| \leq d$. Since $|A| + |B| - 2 \times |A \cap B| = |A \setminus B| + |B \setminus A|$, this is equivalent to $|A| + |B| - 2 \times |A \cap B| \leq d$. □

The latter lemma allows us to store the d-twins in Algorithm 3 and check the number of consecutive round two nodes are d-twins in Algorithm 3 line 22 and Algorithm 1 line 19. We have proved the following theorem.

Theorem 1. *In a p-periodic time-varying graph $\mathcal{G} = (G_t)_{t \in T}$ where integers p, Δ, d are given as input to every node, problem* Periodic(Δ, d)-Twins *can be solved after $2p$ rounds, using messages of size $O(\delta_\mathcal{G} \log n)$, where n is the total number of nodes and $\delta_\mathcal{G} \leq n$ is the maximum degree of the graphs G_t's.*

Proof. The theorem follows from Lemma 2 and Lemma 3. The algorithm is described in details in Algorithms 1, 2 and 3. □

3.2 Scenario 2: Period p Exists, but it is Unknown

There are two solutions that we can consider. The first solution is to try to determine the period p. However, this method is complex and difficult. Several problems have solutions when the period p is known, but no solutions when p is unknown, see [14]. Understanding the limitations of an unknown period p is crucial for developing robust algorithms in dynamic graph. When p is known, synchronization and message passing become significantly easier, as nodes can coordinate actions precisely at specific intervals. However, in the absence of a known p, additional steps must be taken to ensure accurate information transfer, as explored below. The second solution, which we will explore here, is the one detailed in the following.

The main trick in using Lemma 3 for characterising d-twins is as follows. By keeping the same notations used in the lemma, let u and v be two distinct nodes having a common neighbour s. For u to conclude that v is one of its twin nodes, it is sufficient that the intermediary node s send to u the neighbourhood of v[1]. This information must have been sent to s by v. In an ideal model, v sends its neighbourhood to s at round j, and *in the same round* $i = j$, s forwards this information to u, then u can conclude immediately at round i using Lemma 3. Unfortunately, it is forbidden in our model to pass messages in the same round. This restriction against same-round messaging reflects real-world communication constraints, where direct message passing without latency or delays is often unrealistic. Network protocols generally enforce sequential messaging to account for physical or processing limitations, which adds complexity to our model.

Looking at the sending phase, described in Algorithm 2, v sent (lines 3-4 of Algorithm 2) at a past round $j < p$ its neighbourhood to s; then, at exactly round $i = j + p$, node s forwards this information received at past round $i - p$ (line 7 of Algorithm 2) to u, along with such information from v', v'', ... Note at round i that s does not forward any information of the current round i, but only information *in the past*, at round j. This means that the forwarding process relies on previously stored information. Node s essentially acts as a relay, passing data it has retained from previous interactions. This delayed forwarding ensures compliance with the round-based message restriction. Then, u can conclude using Lemma 3 during round i if v was its d-twin in the past, at round j (lines 14-15 of Algorithm 3 explicitly follow the inequality of Lemma 3: *nbNeighbours* are neighbours of u, `Neighbors`[*id*] are neighbours of v, and `Count`[*id*] is a way to count the size of their intersection).

We can extend this idea to the scenario when period p is unknown from the nodes. Here nodes do not try to compute p. They will keep in memory their previous neighborhoods. For this, we design the nodes to send three fields of information, where the third field will be used to store a pointer to some previous round j, while the second field will serve as the memory of the node's neighbourhood at that past round j. In the sequel, the rough idea is as follows. The next paragraph depicts in details the message to be sent, with three fields. The subsequent paragraph depicts how every node can use the pieces of information stored in the second and third fields of the message to "remember about its past neighbours".

---

[1] Note that if v is already a neighbour of u, it could be the case that s is not needed, but in our algorithm, we still use s as intermediary for this case, for the sake of generality.

The first field is as before, that is, as in lines 3-4 of Algorithm 2. This ensures node v sends its neighbourhood to s at round j. The second field is either empty, or it is as in line 7 of Algorithm 2. The second field is empty if and only if the third field is empty. When the second field is not empty at some instant i, the third field contains integer j, representing some past instant $j < i$; in this case, the second field contains Tab[j] instead of Tab[$round - p$] as in line 7 of Algorithm 2. This mostly ensures s forward the correct information from v to u, at the correct moment. The decision for the third field is as follows. At every round i, every node checks if its neighbourhood is the same as some neighbourhood in a past round $j < i$, using information stored in Tab[j]. If this is the case, j is the desired value.

Then, in Algorithm 3, line 3 is always performed for the first field of the received messages. Furthermore, when the second and third fields are not empty, lines 5-4 are performed with appropriate values at line 16 (j instead of $round - p$); line 22 remains the same. Note that this will trigger unnecessary work for node u, which calls Algorithm 3 in many rounds when $i \neq j + p$ but when the neighbourhood of node s repeats. This repetitive computation may seem inefficient but does not impact the final list of twin nodes. By systematically checking each round, the algorithm avoids errors that could arise from missed messages. A part from the extra computations, this will not affect the output list of twin nodes because at round i, node u will only receive information about round j (in the past), which u can check with its own information of that past round j. This allow nodes to double-check historical data, adding a layer of accuracy to the algorithm's output despite the redundant calculations. The extra size is then from the third field of messages, which is bounded by $O(\log p)$. The total message size is then $O(\delta_G \log n + \log p)$.

The bound on message size shows that the algorithm scales reasonably even with the addition of the third field. While the $\log p$ term might increase if the period is large, the impact on network resources remains within manageable limits. The overall message complexity suggests that this approach is suitable for large, distributed systems with unknown periods.

Example of Execution of the Algorithm for Scenario 2: As an example, consider nodes u and v attempting to determine if they are d-twins, with node s as their common neighbor. In round 0, nodes u and v each have s as their only neighbor, making them 0-twins at this round. In round 1, however, u and v have no neighbors in common, so they are no longer considered twins in this round. Finally, in round 3, both nodes u and v have s as a neighbor again.

The process unfolds as follows: in round 0, both u and v send their respective IDs and the number of neighbors they have to node s. Then, in round 3, node s sends a message to node u, informing it that v had one neighbor in round 0, and to node v, informing it that u had one neighbor in round 0 as well. Upon receiving this information in round 3, u know that it had exactly one neighbor in round 0 (which was s) and also receives information from s that v had one neighbor at the same round. Similarly, v receives information that u had a single neighbor in round 0. This information received by v from s allows v to confirms that u was its 0-twin in round 0. This calculation is repeated for every node and each round, allowing nodes to establish twin relationships based on historical neighborhood data, even when the period is unknown.

3.3 Twin Sampling with O(log n) Message Size

We can further reduce the message size following a randomized approach depicted in Lemma 2 in [19]. For every node v, after receiving its neighbourhood from the first round, it will not send this neighbourhood in the subsequent round. Instead, it applies a hash function on the received neighbourhood before sending. The choice of the hash function is determinant for the size of the message in this approach (the size of the hash value to be sent). For reducing the size of the message, Ref. [19] proposes to sample the hash function from a universe $\mathcal{U}$allowing for every node u to compute the approximate size of $|N_t(u) \cap N_t(v)|$ within a factor of $\epsilon \max(n_u, n_v)$ with high probability $1 - \nu$, where $n_u = |N_t(u)|$ and $n_v = |N_t(v)|$. The process uses $O(1)$ messages of size $O(\epsilon^4 \log(1/\nu) + \log\log|\mathcal{U}| + \log\max(n_u, n_v))$ bits. Thus, with high probability, the inequality in Lemma 3 can be decided using messages of $O(\log n)$ bits.

All in all, the hash function applied here is designed to capture the overlap between neighborhoods while maintaining privacy and reducing the size of the transmitted data. By hashing, each node effectively compresses its neighborhood data, allowing neighboring nodes to estimate the intersection without the need for exact transmission.

Reducing message size to $O(log\ n)$ bits is significant in large networks, where bandwidth and message congestion are limiting factors. This hashing-based approach aligns well with distributed system goals, as it limits overhead without compromising accuracy. In dynamic cases, where the time-varying nature of the graph must be considered, the extension follows a similar logic. Each node still computes the hashed value for its neighborhood but must also account for periodic changes over rounds. When the period p is unknown, nodes incorporate an additional lookup mechanism to align their current hashed neighborhood data with previously stored values, enabling them to maintain accurate estimates across the time-varying graph.

4 Conclusion and Perspectives

We introduce the problem of finding (Δ, d)-twins and propose a distributed algorithm to compute them in any p-periodic time-varying graph $\mathcal{G} = (G_t)_{t\in\mathbb{N}}$ under a distributed model similar to the 1-interval-connected network. After $2p$ rounds, every node can compute the nodes that are its (Δ, d)-twins using messages of size $O(\delta_{\mathcal{G}} \log n + \log p)$, where n is the total number of nodes and $\delta_{\mathcal{G}}$ is the maximum degree of the graphs G_t's. Moreover, using techniques borrowed from [19], we reduce the message size down to $O(\log n + \log p)$ w.h.p. If furthermore every node knows in advance the period p, the additive term $\log p$ is not necessary. Finding (Δ, d)-twins can be useful in several ways. For instance, it could be used for alternately scheduling sleeping times of the twin nodes to save resources, while maintaining connectivity for the rest of the network. Furthermore, it can be used in order to compute disjoint paths or disjoint broadcast trees. As for the next steps of research, it would be useful to extend our algorithm to compute ϵ-modules as defined in [17].

References

1. Addanki, V., Avin, C., Schmid, S.: Mars: Near-optimal throughput with shallow buffers in reconfigurable datacenter networks. Proc. ACM Meas. Anal. Comput. Syst. **7**(1), 2:1–2:43 (2023). https://doi.org/10.1145/3579312, https://doi.org/10.1145/3579312
2. Ballani, H., et al.: Sirius: a flat datacenter network with nanosecond optical switching. In: Schulzrinne, H., Misra, V. (eds.) Proceedings of the Conference of the ACM Special Interest Group on Data Communication, SIGCOMM, 2020, pp. 782–797. ACM (2020). https://doi.org/10.1145/3387514.3406221, https://doi.org/10.1145/3387514.3406221
3. Bhadra, S., Ferreira, A.: Computing multicast trees in dynamic networks and the complexity of connected components in evolving graphs. J. Internet Serv. Appl. **3**(3), 269–275 (2012). https://doi.org/10.1007/S13174-012-0073-Z
4. Bonnet, E., Kim, E., Thomassé, S., Watrigant, R.: Twin-width I: tractable FO model checking. In: 61st IEEE Annual Symposium on Foundations of Computer Science, pp. 601–612. IEEE (2020)
5. Braud-Santoni, N., Dubois, S., Kaaouachi, M., Petit, F.: The next 700 impossibility results in time-varying graphs. Int. J. Netw. Comput. **6**(1), 27–41 (2016)
6. Bui-Xuan, B., Hourcade, H., Miachon, C.: Computing temporal twins in time logarithmic in history length. In: 9th International Conference on Complex Networks and their Applications. SCI, vol. 944, pp. 651–663 (2020)
7. Casteigts, A., Chaumette, S., Ferreira, A.: Characterizing topological assumptions of distributed algorithms in dynamic networks. In: Kutten, S., Žerovnik, J. (eds.) Structural Information and Communication Complexity, pp. 126–140. Springer, Berlin Heidelberg, Berlin, Heidelberg (2010)
8. Casteigts, A., Flocchini, P., Mans, B., Santoro, N.: Measuring temporal lags in delay-tolerant networks. IEEE Trans. Computers **63**(2), 397–410 (2014)
9. Casteigts, A., Flocchini, P., Quattrociocchi, W., Santoro, N.: Time-varying graphs and dynamic networks. Int. J. Parallel Emergent Distrib. Syst. **27**(5), 387–408 (2012)
10. Casteigts, A., Dubois, S., Petit, F., Robson, J.M.: Robustness: a new form of heredity motivated by dynamic networks. Theor. Comput. Sci. **806**, 429–445 (2020)
11. Casteigts, A., Flocchini, P., Godard, E., Santoro, N., Yamashita, M.: On the expressivity of time-varying graphs. Theor. Comput. Sci. **590**, 27–37 (2015)
12. Casteigts, A., Flocchini, P., Mans, B., Santoro, N.: Shortest, fastest, and foremost broadcast in dynamic networks. Int. J. Found. Comput. Sci. **26**(4), 499–522 (2015)
13. Ehrenfeucht, A., Harju, T., Rozenberg, G.: The Theory of 2-Structures: a framework for decomposition and transformation of graphs. World Scientific (1999)
14. Flocchini, P., Mans, B., Santoro, N.: On the exploration of time-varying networks. Theoret. Comput. Sci. **469**, 53–68 (2013). https://doi.org/10.1016/J.TCS.2012.10.029

15. Gallai, T.: Transitiv orientierbare Graphen. Acta Mathematica Academiae Scientiarum Hungaricae **18**, 25–66 (1967)
16. Habib, M., Mouatadid, L., Sopena, E., Zou, M.: (α, β)-modules in graphs. CoRR **abs/2101.08881** (2021). https://arxiv.org/abs/2101.08881
17. Habib, M., Mouatadid, L., Zou, M.: Approximating Modular Decomposition Is Hard. In: Changat, M., Das, S. (eds.) CALDAM 2020. LNCS, vol. 12016, pp. 53–66. Springer, Cham (2020). https://doi.org/10.1007/978-3-030-39219-2_5
18. Habib, M., Paul, C.: A survey of the algorithmic aspects of modular decomposition. Comput. Sci. Rev. **4**(1), 41–59 (2010)
19. Halldórsson, M., Nolin, A., Tonoyan, T.: Overcoming congestion in distributed coloring. In: 2022 ACM Symposium on Principles of Distributed Computing, pp. 26–36. ACM (2022)
20. Kuhn, F., Lynch, N., Oshman, R.: Distributed computation in dynamic networks. In: 42nd ACM Symposium on Theory of Computing, pp. 513–522. ACM (2010)
21. Kumar, G., Garland, M.: Visual exploration of complex time-varying graphs. IEEE Trans. Visual Comput. Graphics **12**(5), 805–812 (2006). https://doi.org/10.1109/TVCG.2006.193
22. Luna, G.D., Viglietta, G.: Computing in anonymous dynamic networks is linear. In: 63rd Annual Symposium on Foundations of Computer Science, pp. 1122–1133. IEEE (2022)
23. Luna, G.A.D., Viglietta, G.: Efficient computation in congested anonymous dynamic networks. In: Královic, R., Kucera, A. (eds.) 49th International Symposium on Mathematical Foundations of Computer Science, MFCS 2024, August 26-30, 2024, Bratislava, Slovakia. LIPIcs, vol. 306, pp. 49:1–49:19
24. Luna, G.A.D., Viglietta, G.: Computing in anonymous dynamic networks is linear. In: 63rd IEEE Annual Symposium on Foundations of Computer Science, FOCS 2022, Denver, CO, USA, October 31 - November 3, 2022, pp. 1122–1133. IEEE (2022)
25. Mellette, W., et al.: A scalable, low-complexity, optical datacenter network. In: Proceedings of the Conference of the ACM Special Interest Group on Data Communication, SIGCOMM, 2017, pp. 267–280. ACM (2017). https://doi.org/10.1145/3098822.3098838, https://doi.org/10.1145/3098822.3098838
26. Mengxiang Liu, M., Teng, F., Zhang, Z., Ge, P., Sun, M., Deng, R., Cheng, P., Chen, J.: Enhancing cyber-resiliency of der-based smart grid: a survey. IEEE Trans. Smart Grid **15**(5), 4998–5030 (2024). https://doi.org/10.1109/TSG.2024.3373008
27. Natali, A., Isufi, E., Coutino, M., Leus, G.: Learning time-varying graphs from online data. IEEE Open J. Signal Process. **3**, 212–228 (2022). https://doi.org/10.1109/OJSP.2022.3178901
28. Nedić, A., Olshevsky, A.: Distributed optimization over time-varying directed graphs. IEEE Trans. Autom. Control **60**(3), 601–615 (2015). https://doi.org/10.1109/TAC.2014.2364096
29. O'Dell, R., Wattenhofer, R.: Information dissemination in highly dynamic graphs. In: DIALM-POMC Joint Workshop on Foundations of Mobile Computing, pp. 104–110. ACM (2005)
30. Schneider, J., Wattenhofer, R.: An optimal maximal independent set algorithm for bounded-independence graphs. Distrib. Comput. **22**, 349–361 (2010). https://doi.org/10.1007/s00446-010-0097-1
31. Tang, J., Scellato, S., Musolesi, M., Mascolo, C., Latora, V.: Small-world behavior in time-varying graphs. Phys. Rev. E **81**, 055101 (2010). https://doi.org/10.1103/PhysRevE.81.055101

32. Wehmuth, K., Ziviani, A., Fleury, E.: A unifying model for representing time-varying graphs. In: 2015 IEEE International Conference on Data Science and Advanced Analytics (DSAA), pp. 1–10 (2015). https://doi.org/10.1109/DSAA.2015.7344810
33. Whitbeck, J., Dias de Amorim, M., Conan, V., Guillaume, J.: Temporal reachability graphs. In: Akan, Ö.B., Ekici, E., Qiu, L., Snoeren, A.C. (eds.) The 18th Annual International Conference on Mobile Computing and Networking, Mobicom'12, Istanbul, Turkey, August 22-26, 2012, pp. 377–388. ACM (2012https://doi.org/10.1145/2348543.2348589
34. Zhang, T., et al.: Application of time-varying graph theory over the space information networks. IEEE Netw. **34**(2), 179–185 (2020). https://doi.org/10.1109/MNET.001.1900245

Verifying Parameterized Networks Specified by Vertex-Replacement Graph Grammars

Radu Iosif[1], Arnaud Sangnier[2], and Neven Villani[1(✉)]

[1] CNRS, Grenoble INP, VERIMAG, University of Grenoble Alpes, 38000 Grenoble, France
{Radu.Iosif,Neven.Villani}@univ-grenoble-alpes.fr
[2] DIBRIS, University of Genova, Genoa, Italy
Arnaud.Sangnier@unige.it

Abstract. We consider the parametric reachability problem (PRP) for families of networks described by vertex-replacement (VR) graph grammars, where network nodes run replicas of finite-state processes that communicate via binary handshaking. We show that the PRP problem for VR grammars can be effectively reduced to the PRP problem for hyperedge-replacement (HR) grammars, at the cost of introducing extra edges for routing messages. This transformation is motivated by the existence of several parametric verification techniques for families of networks specified by HR grammars, or similar inductive formalisms. Our reduction enables applying the verification techniques for HR systems to systems with dense architectures, such as user-specified cliques and multi-partite graphs.

1 Introduction

As pointed out in recent literature, "*network verification is a necessary part of deploying modern hyperscale datacenters*" [19]. In this context, verification considers global properties of routing control, such as access between point A and point B. Very often, the intended functionality of a network can be derived from its architecture, typically known at early stages of network design.

The huge scale of present-day datacenters, of $\sim 10^4$ routers for a regional hub and continuously growing, requires *parametric* verification techniques, that work no matter how many servers in a rack, switches in a cluster, clusters in a layer, etc. Despite decades of theoretical research and an impressive body of results (see [7] for a nice survey), these techniques consider mostly hard-coded architectures, either dense (*e.g.,* cliques [16]) or sparse (*e.g.,* rings [11]) families of graphs with a common topological pattern.

The problem of verifying networks with user-specified architecture has gained recent momentum, with the development of parametric verification techniques for systems described using logic [5] or graph grammars [20]. In principle, logic-based graph specification languages are good at describing global properties, such as planarity, k-colorability or reachability, which make them more suitable for the specification of correctness properties, than network design.

On the other hand, graph grammars are appealing for their constructive aspect, *i.e.,* defining how large graphs are built from smaller subgraphs. Moreover, this recursive way of describing sets of graphs is common among programmers and software

S. Lahlou and M. Mukund (Eds.): NETYS 2025, LNCS 15736, pp. 57–80, 2026.
https://doi.org/10.1007/978-3-032-00347-8_4

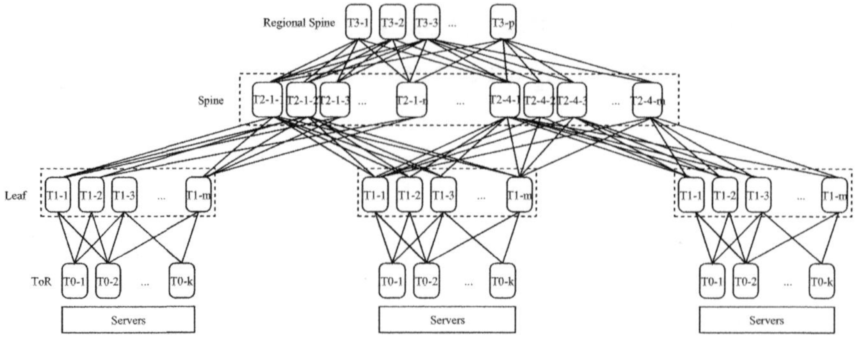

Fig. 1. Azure Datacenter Switching Topology.

engineers, who are familiar with inductively defined datastructures (lists, trees, etc.) used in both imperative and functional programming. Graph grammars are at the core of the theory of formal languages (see [13] for a comprehensive survey). Based on the underlying set of operations (*i.e.,* graph algebra), we distinguish between *vertex-replacement* (VR) and *hyperedge-replacement* (HR) grammars. In principle, HR graph grammars can specify families of graphs having bounded tree-width, such as chains, rings, stars, trees (of unbounded rank) and beyond, *e.g.,* overlaid structures such as trees or stars with certain nodes linked in a list. Since cliques and grids are families of unbounded tree-width, neither can be specified using HRgraph grammars. On the other hand, *vertex-replacement* (VR) grammars are strictly more expressive [12]. For instance, VR grammars can describe the sets $\{K_n\}_{n\geq 1}$ of cliques and $\{K_{n,m}\}_{n,m\geq 1}$ of complete bipartite graphs, among others.

A concrete motivation for using VR grammars to design datacenter networks can be found in the informal description of the Azure datacenter architecture [17,19], deployed in the Microsoft hyperscale cloud network (Fig. 1). The *top-of-rack* (ToR) switches connect servers hosted in a rack. Several ToR switches are connected together by a number of *leaf* switches. Leaf switches are in turn connected together by a set of *spine* switches, that connect the datacenter to the Azure regional network. These networks cannot be described as cliques, because of their layered structure. However, the links between each layer (*i.e.,* ToR, leaf, spine, regional spine) and its adjacent layers form a complete bipartite graph, thus lying outside the scope of HR grammars, which cannot define complete bipartite graphs of unbounded sizes[1].

The precise relation between the expressivity of VR and HR grammars has been elegantly coined in a result by Courcelle, stating that a set defined by a VR grammar can also be defined by an HR grammar if and only if it is sparse [12]. Moreover, each VR grammar can be transformed into an HR grammar producing a set of graphs with ε-edges, such that the elimination of these edges from the HR language yields the original VR language. For instance, the elimination of ε-edges from the graph from Fig. 2 (b) yields the complete bipartite graph $K_{4,3}$ from Fig. 2 (a).

[1] Each set $\{K_{n,m}\}_{n\in N,m\in M}$ for N,M infinite subsets of $\mathbb{N}$, has unbounded tree-width, whereas HR-grammars define bounded tree-width sets.

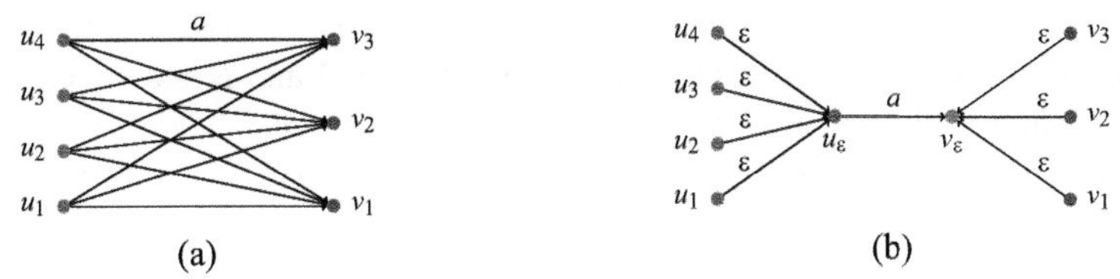

Fig. 2. The complete bipartite graph $\overrightarrow{K}_{4,3}$ (a) and one possible encoding using ε-edges (b).

Contribution. We leverage the idea of transforming VR grammars into HR grammars modulo elimination of ε-edges to define a reduction from the parametric reachability problem (PRP) for systems described by VR grammars and finite-state local behaviors, with correctness properties given by unrestricted arithmetic formulæ over a set of variables, tracking how many processes are in a given local state, to the PRP problem for systems described by HR grammars, having the same correctness property. This is motivated by several recent developments in the verification of parametric systems with HR-style architecture descriptions. In particular, [10] reports on an inference of structural invariants (*i.e.,* over-approximations of the reachable set, that can be derived from the structure of the network) for architectures described using a variant of Separation Logic with inductive definitions (same expressivity as HR grammars) Moreover, [9] gives an abstraction technique that folds similar network nodes into a finite Petri net, whose coverability problem over-approximates the original parametric coverability problem. In this paper, we give a more general reduction method, that preserves all safety properties specified by arithmetic assertions, rather than the particular case of coverability.

Related Work. The literature on parametric verification is too large to be recalled here. We point to [7] for a survey on the (un)decidability results, typically concerning clique or ring architectures. The specification of network architectures using inductive definitions can be traced back to the work on *network grammars* [18,20,22], that use inductive rules to describe systems with linear (pipeline, token-ring) architectures. These initial works target mainly safety properties, by inferring network invariants [21,23]. Pipeline and clique architectures are also considered by methods based on the theory of well-structured transition systems [1], such as monotonic abstraction [2,3].

A prominent exception, that considers the verification of clique-width bounded architectures specified using Monadic Second Order Logic (MSO) against $\mathsf{CTL}^* \setminus \bigcirc$ properties is [5]. Their result uses a reduction from the parametric model checking problem (PMCP) to the decidability of MSO over graphs of bounded clique-width [13]. Our result is orthogonal, because we consider VR grammars that strictly subsume the MSO-definable sets of bounded clique-width. It is, however, an interesting question if our reduction can be used to establish a more general decidability result. A promising lead would be to use the decidability of PMCP for HR systems with local behaviors that mimick the passing of a pebble from one node to another [9].

Notation. We denote by $\mathbb{Z}$ ($\mathbb{N}$) the set of (positive) integers. For $i, j \in \mathbb{N}$, we denote by $[i, j]$ the set $\{i, \dots, j\}$, considered empty if $i > j$. The cardinality of a finite set A is written $\|A\|$. A singleton $\{a\}$ is simply denoted a. The union of two disjoint sets A and B is denoted as $A \uplus B$. The Cartesian product of two sets A and B is denoted $A \times B$. As usual, we define A^* the set of (possibly empty) finite sequences of elements from A, and A^∞ the set of finite or infinite sequences over A. Finally $\mathcal{P}(A)$ is the powerset of A.

2 Graphs

For simplicity reasons, in this paper we consider only networks whose topologies are described by oriented binary graphs, where vertices model processes and edges model a symmetric rendezvous between two processes, *i.e.,* we do not distinguish the process initiating the communication and consider that both participants have equal roles.

Let Λ and Δ be finite disjoint alphabets of vertex and edge labels, respectively. A *graph* is a tuple $\mathsf{G} = (\mathsf{V_G}, \mathsf{E_G}, \lambda_\mathsf{G})$, where $\mathsf{V_G}$ is a finite set of vertices, $\mathsf{E_G} \subseteq \mathsf{V_G} \times \Delta \times \mathsf{V_G}$ is a set of edges, such that $(v, \delta, v') \in \mathsf{E_G}$ implies $v \neq v'$ (*i.e.,* graphs have no self-loops) and $\lambda_\mathsf{G} : \mathsf{V_G} \rightarrow \mathcal{P}(\Lambda)$ assigns a set of labels to each vertex. We do not distinguish graphs that are isomorphic. We denote by $\mathcal{G}(\Lambda, \Delta)$ the set of graphs with vertex and edge labels from Λ and Δ, or simply $\mathcal{G}$, if Δ and Λ are understood.

We shall consider parameterized networks described as infinite sets of graphs. Albeit infinite, these sets have a finite description, given by finitely many inductive rules stating how the graphs in the set are built from smaller graphs. This constructive[2] approach to the specification of infinite sets of graphs relies on graph algebras, being at the core of an impressive body of theoretical work (see [13] for a survey).

2.1 Algebras

We present two classical graph algebras, namely *vertex-replacement* (VR) and *hyperedge-replacement* (HR). Let Λ and Δ be fixed in the following. We consider a set $\Pi \subseteq \Lambda$ of distinguished vertex labels, called *ports*, such that $\|\lambda_\mathsf{G}(v) \cap \Pi\| \leq 1$, for each graph $\mathsf{G} \in \mathcal{G}(\Lambda, \Delta)$ and each vertex $v \in \mathsf{V_G}$. In other words, a vertex is labeled with at most one port. We say that a vertex $v \in \mathsf{V_G}$ is a π-port of G whenever $\pi \in \lambda_\mathsf{G}(v)$. The *sort* of a graph is the set of ports that occur in the labels of the vertices from the graph.

The labels from $\Lambda \setminus \Pi$ will be needed later to associate vertices with local behaviors, referred to as process types. For the time being, we assume the set of process types to be $\Lambda \setminus \Pi = \{\lambda_1, \ldots, \lambda_n\}$ and that the set of port labels is partitioned accordingly, *i.e.,* $\Pi = \Pi_{\lambda_1} \uplus \ldots \uplus \Pi_{\lambda_n}$. We say that the *process type* of a port $\pi \in \Pi$ is $\lambda \in \Lambda \setminus \Pi$, denoted $\mathrm{ptype}(\pi) = \lambda \stackrel{\mathsf{def}}{\iff} \pi \in \Pi_\lambda$. A partial function $\alpha : \Pi \rightharpoonup \Pi$ is *type-preserving* iff $\alpha(\pi)$, if defined, has the same process type as π, for each $\pi \in \Pi$.

The domain of the *VR-algebra* is the set $\mathcal{G}$ of graphs. The operations of VR are the following, see Fig. 3 (a) for an illustration:

- *Disjoint union*: $\mathsf{G}_1 \oplus_{\mathbf{p}_1} \mathsf{G}_2 \stackrel{\mathsf{def}}{=} H$ iff the sorts of G_1 and G_2 are $\mathbf{p}_1$ and $\mathbf{p}_2$, respectively, $\mathsf{V}_H = \mathsf{V}_{\mathsf{G}_1} \uplus \mathsf{V}_{\mathsf{G}_2}$, $\mathsf{E}_H = \mathsf{E}_{\mathsf{G}_1} \uplus \mathsf{E}_{\mathsf{G}_2}$ and $\lambda_H = \lambda_{\mathsf{G}_1} \uplus \lambda_{\mathsf{G}_2}$ where, if $\mathsf{V}_{\mathsf{G}_1} \cap \mathsf{V}_{\mathsf{G}_2} \neq \emptyset$ or $\mathsf{E}_{\mathsf{G}_1} \cap \mathsf{E}_{\mathsf{G}_2} \neq \emptyset$, we replace G_2 by an isomorphic copy disjoint from G_1. We write $\oplus$ instead of $\oplus_{\mathbf{p}_1}$ when the argument sorts are understood.

[2] As opposed to the descriptive method of defining sets of graphs by their common properties, using *e.g.,* monadic second-order logic.

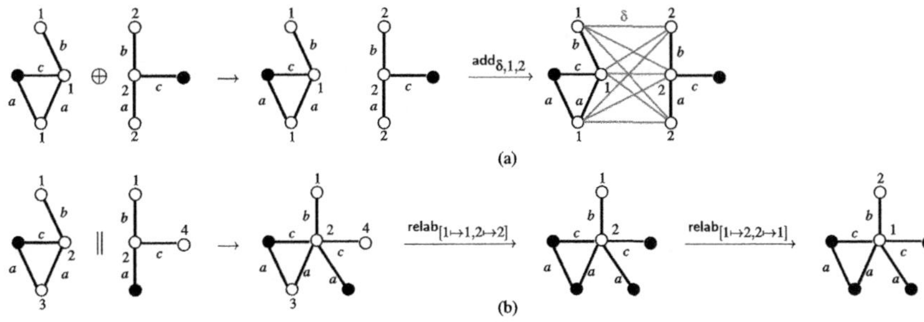

Fig. 3. VR operations (a) HR operations (b). Ports are depicted as shallow circles; port labels are natural numbers.

- *Edge creation*: for an edge label $\delta \in \Delta$ and port labels $\pi_1 \neq \pi_2 \in \Pi$, $\mathsf{add}_{\delta,\pi_1,\pi_2}(\mathsf{G}) \stackrel{\text{def}}{=} H$ iff $\mathsf{V}_H = \mathsf{V}_\mathsf{G}$, $\mathsf{E}_H = \mathsf{E}_\mathsf{G} \cup \{(v_1,\delta,v_2) \mid v_1,v_2 \in \mathsf{V}_\mathsf{G},\ \pi_i \in \lambda_\mathsf{G}(v_i),\ i = 1,2\}$ and $\lambda_H = \lambda_\mathsf{G}$; in other words, $\mathsf{add}_{\delta,\pi_1,\pi_2}$ adds a directed δ-edge from each π_1-port to each π_2-port of its argument. No edge is added if such an edge already exists. Moreover, because π_1 and π_2 are different labels and each vertex has at most one port label, no self-loops are introduced by this operation.
- *Port redefinition*: for a type-preserving partial function $\alpha : \Pi \rightharpoonup \Pi$, $\mathsf{relab}_\alpha(\mathsf{G}) \stackrel{\text{def}}{=} H$ iff $\mathsf{V}_H = \mathsf{V}_\mathsf{G}$, $\mathsf{E}_H = \mathsf{E}_\mathsf{G}$ and $\lambda_H(v) = \{\alpha(\pi) \mid \pi \in \lambda_\mathsf{G}(v) \cap \Pi\} \cup (\lambda_\mathsf{G}(v) \setminus \Pi)$, for each $v \in \mathsf{V}_H$, *i.e.,* the port labels are redefined according to α (if $\alpha(\pi)$ is undefined, the port label is erased) and the other labels are unchanged.
- *Single-vertex graphs*: for a port label $\pi \in \Pi$, $\bullet\pi \stackrel{\text{def}}{=} H$ iff $\mathsf{V}_H = \{u\}$ for some vertex u, $\mathsf{E}_H = \emptyset$ and $\lambda_H(u) = \{\pi, \mathrm{ptype}(\pi)\}$.

For simplicity, we use the same notation for a VR operation above and its corresponding function symbol. Since Δ and Π are finite sets, the above set of function symbols is finite. A VR-term $\theta[x_1,\ldots,x_n]$ consists of function symbols (*i.e.,* the binary $\oplus$ and unary $\mathsf{add}_{\delta,\pi_1,\pi_2}$ and relab_α) and the variables $x_1,\ldots,x_n$ of arity zero. A term is ground if it has no occurrences of variables. We write $\mathrm{val}^{\mathsf{VR}}(\theta)$ for the graph obtained by interpreting the function symbols in the ground term θ as the corresponding VR-operations.

Example 1. The VR-term $\theta \stackrel{\text{def}}{=} \mathsf{relab}_\emptyset(\mathsf{add}_{a,\pi,\pi'}((\bigoplus_{i\in 1,\ldots,4} \bullet\pi) \oplus (\bigoplus_{j\in 1,\ldots,3} \bullet\pi')))$ evaluates to the complete bipartite graph $\mathrm{val}^{\mathsf{VR}}(\theta) = \overrightarrow{K}_{4,3}$ with directed edges a, see Fig. 2 (a). Edge labels are $\Delta = \{a\}$, port labels are $\Pi = \{\pi,\pi'\}$, and vertex labels are $\Lambda = \Pi \cup \{\mathrm{ptype}(\pi), \mathrm{ptype}(\pi')\}$. The π-ports are $u_1,\ldots,u_4$ and the π'-ports are $v_1,\ldots,v_3$ in Fig. 2 (a). We write $\emptyset$ for the empty partial function, that removes all port labels.

The domain of the *HR-algebra* is the set $\mathcal{G}^{\mathsf{HR}}(\Lambda,\Delta) \subseteq \mathcal{G}(\Lambda,\Lambda)$ of graphs G, written $\mathcal{G}^{\mathsf{HR}}$ when Λ and Δ are understood, where $\lambda_\mathsf{G}(v_1) \cap \lambda_\mathsf{G}(v_2) \cap \Pi \neq \emptyset$ implies $v_1 = v_2$, for any two vertices $v_1, v_2 \in \mathsf{V}_\mathsf{G}$. In other words, a port labels at most one vertex. In the usual terminology, ports are called *sources*, when the HR-algebra is understood from the context. The operations of HR are the following, see Fig. 3 (b) for an illustration:

- *Composition*: $\mathsf{G}_1 \parallel_{\mathbf{p}_1} \mathsf{G}_2 \stackrel{\mathsf{def}}{=} H$ iff H is obtained from the disjoint union of $\mathsf{G}_1, \mathsf{G}_2 \in \mathcal{G}^{\mathsf{HR}}$ of sorts $\mathbf{p}_1$ and $\mathbf{p}_2$, respectively (taking an isomorphic copy of G_2 disjoint from G_1, if necessary) by joining all pairs of vertices $v_i \in \mathsf{V}_{\mathsf{G}_i}$, for $i = 1,2$ such that $\lambda_{\mathsf{G}_1}(v_1) \cap \lambda_{\mathsf{G}_2}(v_2) \cap \Pi \neq \emptyset$. The label of a vertex v obtained by joining $v_1 \in \mathsf{V}_{\mathsf{G}_1}$ with $v_2 \in \mathsf{V}_{\mathsf{G}_2}$ is $\lambda_{\mathsf{G}_1}(v_1) \cup \lambda_{\mathsf{G}_2}(v_2)$. Since the label of a vertex in a graph from $\mathcal{G}^{\mathsf{HR}}$ contains at most one source, the composition of any two graphs from $\mathcal{G}^{\mathsf{HR}}$ is contained in $\mathcal{G}^{\mathsf{HR}}$. We write $\parallel$ instead of $\parallel_{\mathbf{p}_1}$ when the argument sorts are understood.
- *Source redefinition*: relab_α is defined in the same way as for VR, with the further restriction that α is an injective partial function. This restriction is necessary to ensure that $\mathsf{relab}_\alpha(\mathsf{G}) \in \mathcal{G}^{\mathsf{HR}}$ if $\mathsf{G} \in \mathcal{G}^{\mathsf{HR}}$.
- *Single-vertex graphs*: are defined in the same way as for VR.
- *Single-edge graphs*: for an edge label $\delta \in \Delta$ and two port labels $\pi_1 \neq \pi_2 \in \Pi$, $\overrightarrow{\delta}_{\pi_1,\pi_2} \stackrel{\mathsf{def}}{=} H$ iff $\mathsf{V}_H = \{v_1, v_2\}$, $\mathsf{E}_H = \{(v_1, \delta, v_2)\}$, $\lambda_H(v_i) = \{\pi_i, \mathrm{ptype}(\pi_i)\}$, for $i = 1,2$.

HR-terms are defined just as VR-terms and $\mathsf{val}^{\mathsf{HR}}(\theta)$ denotes the graph obtained by interpreting the function symbols in the ground term θ as the corresponding HR-operations.

Example 2. We write (π) for the partial function that acts as the identity on $\{\pi\}$, erasing all source labels except π. The HR-term $\theta' \stackrel{\mathsf{def}}{=} \mathsf{relab}_\emptyset(\overrightarrow{a}_{\pi_\varepsilon,\pi'_\varepsilon}) \parallel (\parallel_{i\in 1,\ldots,4} \mathsf{relab}_{(\pi_\varepsilon)}(\overrightarrow{\varepsilon}_{\pi,\pi_\varepsilon})) \parallel (\parallel_{j\in 1,\ldots,3} \mathsf{relab}_{(\pi'_\varepsilon)}(\overrightarrow{\varepsilon}_{\pi',\pi'_\varepsilon}))$ evaluates to the graph shown in Fig. 2 (b). The edge labels are $\Delta = \{a, \varepsilon\}$, the port labels are $\Pi = \{\pi, \pi', \pi_\varepsilon, \pi'_\varepsilon\}$, the vertex labels are $\Lambda = \Pi \cup \{\mathrm{ptype}(\pi), \mathrm{ptype}(\pi'), \mathrm{ptype}(\pi_\varepsilon), \mathrm{ptype}(\pi'_\varepsilon)\}$. The π, π', π_ε and π'_ε-ports in Fig. 2 are respectively $u_{1,\ldots,4}$, $v_{1,\ldots,3}$, u_ε, v_ε.

2.2 Grammars

Graph grammars are a standard way to represent sets of graphs. Let Ω be an algebra, either VR or HR. A *Ω-grammar* is a pair $\Gamma = (\Xi, \Pi)$ consisting of a finite set Ξ of *nonterminals* and a finite set Π of *rules* of the form, either (1) $X \to t[X_1, \ldots, X_n]$, where $X, X_1, \ldots, X_n \in \Xi$ are nonterminals and t is a Ω-term whose only variables are $X_1, \ldots, X_n$, or (2) $\to X$, where $X \in \Xi$; the rules of this form are called *axioms*. Given Ω-terms θ and η, a *step* $\theta \Rightarrow_\Gamma \eta$ obtains η from θ by replacing an occurrence of a nonterminal X with the term t, for some rule $X \to t[X_1, \ldots, X_n]$ of Γ. A *X-derivation* is a sequence of steps starting with a nonterminal X. The derivation is *complete* if it ends with a ground term. Let $\mathcal{L}_X(\Gamma) \stackrel{\mathsf{def}}{=} \{\mathsf{val}^\Omega(\theta) \mid X \Rightarrow^*_\Gamma \theta \text{ is a complete derivation}\}$ and $\mathcal{L}(\Gamma) \stackrel{\mathsf{def}}{=} \bigcup_{\to X \in \Pi} \mathcal{L}_X(\Gamma)$ be the *language* of Γ, the algebra Ω being understood from the rules of Γ. A set of graphs is VR (*resp.* HR) iff it is the language of a VR (*resp.* HR) grammar.

Example 3. The VR-grammar Γ below produces the term θ from Example 1. The language of this grammar contains Fig. 2 (a). The HR-grammar Γ' produces the term θ' from Example 2. The language of this grammar contains Fig. 2 (b).

$$\Gamma : \begin{cases} \rightarrow S \\ S \rightarrow \mathsf{relab}_\emptyset(\mathsf{add}_{a,\pi,\pi'}(K)) \\ K \rightarrow \bullet\pi \\ K \rightarrow \bullet\pi' \\ K \rightarrow K \oplus K \end{cases} \qquad \Gamma' : \begin{cases} \rightarrow S \\ S \rightarrow \mathsf{relab}_\emptyset(\overrightarrow{a}_{\pi_\varepsilon,\pi'_\varepsilon} \parallel K) \\ K \rightarrow \mathsf{relab}_{(\pi_\varepsilon)}(\overrightarrow{\varepsilon}_{\pi,\pi_\varepsilon}) \\ K \rightarrow \mathsf{relab}_{(\pi'_\varepsilon)}(\overrightarrow{\varepsilon}_{\pi',\pi'_\varepsilon}) \\ K \rightarrow K \parallel K \end{cases}$$

It is known that the expressivity of VR-grammars strictly subsumes that of HR-grammars [15]. The relation between VR and HR is made precise by the following:

Definition 1. *Let $\mathcal{E}$ be a set of edge labels disjoint from Δ. An $\mathcal{E}$-graph is a graph* $\mathsf{G} \in \mathcal{G}(\Lambda, \Delta \cup \mathcal{E} \cup \overleftarrow{\mathcal{E}})$ *such that*

- $\overleftarrow{\mathcal{E}} \stackrel{\text{def}}{=} \{\overleftarrow{e} \mid e \in \mathcal{E}\}$*, and for every edge* (u,e,v)*,* $e \in \mathcal{E}$*, there exists an edge* $(v, \overleftarrow{e}, u)$*.*
- *the subgraph of* G *consisting of* $\mathcal{E}$*-labeled edges and the vertices that have incoming* $\mathcal{E}$*-labeled edges is a forest, i.e., every non-root vertex points to a single parent.*

The expansion *of an* $\mathcal{E}$*-graph* $\mathsf{G} \in \mathcal{G}(\Lambda, \Delta \cup \mathcal{E} \cup \overleftarrow{\mathcal{E}})$ *is* $\exp(\mathsf{G}) \in \mathcal{G}(\Lambda, \Delta)$*, where:*

- $\mathsf{V}_{\exp(\mathsf{G})}$ *is the set of vertices of* G *that are not the target of an* $\mathcal{E}$*-labeled edge,*
- $\mathsf{E}_{\exp(\mathsf{G})}$ *is the set of edges* (v_1, δ, v_2) *for which there exist* $\mathcal{E}$*-labeled paths from* v_i *to some vertices* $v'_i \in \mathsf{G}$*, for* $i = 1,2$*, such that* $(v'_1, \delta, v'_2) \in \mathsf{E}_\mathsf{G}$*, for some* $\delta \in \Delta$*,*
- $\lambda_{\exp(\mathsf{G})}(v) \stackrel{\text{def}}{=} \lambda_\mathsf{G}(v)$*.*

Proposition 1 (Proposition 2.4 in [12]). *For each VR-grammar* Γ*, one can build a HR-grammar* Γ' *such that* $\mathcal{L}(\Gamma) = \exp(\mathcal{L}(\Gamma'))$*.*

Example 4. The HR-grammar Γ' from Example 3 is obtained by transformation of the VR-grammar Γ from the same example, such that $\mathcal{L}(\Gamma) = \exp(\mathcal{L}(\Gamma'))$, where $\mathcal{E} = \{\varepsilon\}$. We omit $\overleftarrow{\mathcal{E}}$-edges from this figure: their placement is simply the inverse of $\mathcal{E}$-edges.

3 Parameterized Systems

We aim at describing a family of networks by a VR-grammar. To model the behavior of a network, we associate to each vertex in the graph a *process type*, which is a finite-state machine represented as a Petri net of a particular form. We denote by $\mathbb{P}$ the fixed and finite set of process types. In the rest of this paper, the alphabet of vertex labels is assumed to be $\Lambda \stackrel{\text{def}}{=} \mathbb{P} \uplus \Pi$, where $\Pi = \biguplus_{\mathsf{p} \in \mathbb{P}} \Pi_\mathsf{p}$ is a set of port labels partitioned according to the process types, *i.e.,* Π_p is the set of ports corresponding to the process type p. The intuition is that different vertices labeled with a process type run copies of that process type, called *processes*. Neighbouring processes communicate by joining their transitions in a symmetric synchronous rendezvous, represented by a pair of transitions, that labels the edge between their host vertices. Hence, the alphabet Δ of edge labels is considered to be the set of pairs of transitions from the process types $\mathbb{P}$.

3.1 Petri Nets

We make the definition of process types precise by recalling Petri nets. A *net* is a tuple $\mathsf{N} = (\mathsf{Q_N}, \mathsf{T_N}, \mathsf{W_N})$, where $\mathsf{Q_N}$ is a finite set of *places*, $\mathsf{T_N}$ is a finite set of *transitions*, disjoint from $\mathsf{Q_N}$, and $\mathsf{W_N} : (\mathsf{Q_N} \times \mathsf{T_N}) \cup (\mathsf{T_N} \times \mathsf{Q_N}) \to \mathbb{N}$ is a *weighted incidence relation* between places and transitions. For all $x, y \in \mathsf{Q_N} \cup \mathsf{T_N}$ such that $\mathsf{W_N}(x,y) > 0$, we say that there is an *edge of weight* $\mathsf{W_N}(x,y)$ between x and y. For an element $x \in \mathsf{Q_N} \cup \mathsf{T_N}$, we define the set of *predecessors* ${}^\bullet x \stackrel{\text{def}}{=} \{y \in \mathsf{Q_N} \cup \mathsf{T_N} \mid \mathsf{W_N}(y,x) > 0\}$, *successors* $x^\bullet \stackrel{\text{def}}{=} \{y \in \mathsf{Q_N} \cup \mathsf{T_N} \mid \mathsf{W_N}(x,y) > 0\}$ and predecessor-successor pair ${}^\bullet x^\bullet \stackrel{\text{def}}{=} ({}^\bullet x, x^\bullet)$. If not obvious from the context, we will specify the net in which the predecessor and successor and considered: $({}^\bullet x)_\mathsf{N}$, $(x^\bullet)_\mathsf{N}$, $({}^\bullet x^\bullet)_\mathsf{N}$.

A *marking* of N is a function $\mathsf{m} : \mathsf{Q_N} \to \mathbb{N}$. A transition t is *enabled* in the marking m if $\mathsf{m}(q) \geq \mathsf{W_N}(q,t)$, for each place $q \in \mathsf{Q}$. For all markings m, m' and transitions $t \in \mathsf{T}$, we write $\mathsf{m} \stackrel{t}{\rightsquigarrow} \mathsf{m}'$ whenever t is enabled in m and $\mathsf{m}'(q) = \mathsf{m}(q) - \mathsf{W_N}(q,t) + \mathsf{W_N}(t,q)$, for all $q \in \mathsf{Q_N}$. Given a marking m, a sequence of transitions $\rho = (t_1, t_2, \ldots) \in (\mathsf{T}_\mathcal{N})^\infty$ is a *firing sequence* iff either (i) ρ is empty, or (ii) there exist markings $\mathsf{m}_1, \mathsf{m}_2, \ldots$ such that $\mathsf{m} \stackrel{t_1}{\rightsquigarrow} \mathsf{m}_1 \stackrel{t_2}{\rightsquigarrow} \mathsf{m}_2 \stackrel{t_3}{\rightsquigarrow} \cdots$. When ρ has finite length n, we can write $\mathsf{m} \stackrel{\rho}{\rightsquigarrow} \mathsf{m}_n$, and we say that ρ is a firing sequence from m to m_n.

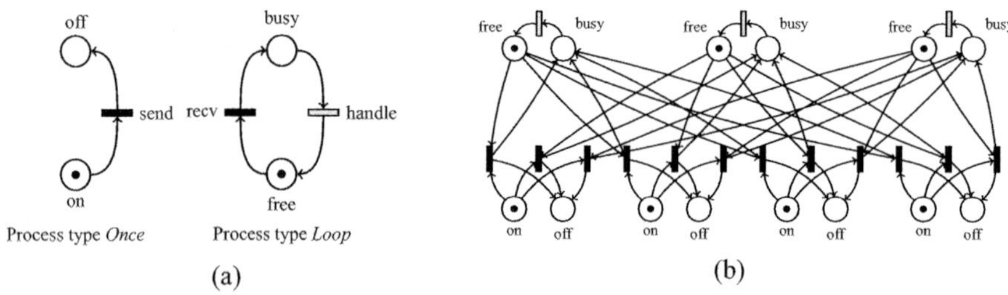

Fig. 4. Examples of process types (a). The behavior of a $\overrightarrow{K}_{4,3}(\text{send}, \text{recv})$ system (b)

A *Petri net* (PN) is a pair $\mathcal{N} = (\mathsf{N}, \mathsf{m}_0)$, where N is a net and m_0 is the *initial marking* of N. For simplicity, we write $\mathsf{Q}_\mathcal{N} \stackrel{\text{def}}{=} \mathsf{Q_N}$, $\mathsf{T}_\mathcal{N} \stackrel{\text{def}}{=} \mathsf{T_N}$, $\mathsf{W}_\mathcal{N} \stackrel{\text{def}}{=} \mathsf{W_N}$ and $\mathsf{init}_\mathcal{N} \stackrel{\text{def}}{=} \mathsf{m}_0$ for the elements of $\mathcal{N}$. A marking m is *reachable* in $\mathcal{N}$ iff there exists a finite firing sequence ρ such that $\mathsf{m}_0 \stackrel{\rho}{\rightsquigarrow} \mathsf{m}$. We denote by *Paths*$(\mathcal{N})$ the set of finite or infinite firing sequences of $\mathcal{N}$ starting from $\mathsf{init}_\mathcal{N}$.

3.2 Behaviors

We formalize the behavior of a system (*i.e.*, a graph whose vertices are labeled by process types) using PNs. To do so, we associate to each process type a PN having a special form:

Definition 2. *A* process type p *is a PN having weights at most* 1 *and exactly one marked place initially, whose transitions are partitioned into* observable $\mathsf{T}_\mathsf{p}^{obs}$ *and* internal $\mathsf{T}_\mathsf{p}^{int}$, *i.e.*, $\mathsf{T}_\mathsf{p} = \mathsf{T}_\mathsf{p}^{obs} \uplus \mathsf{T}_\mathsf{p}^{int}$, *such that each transition has exactly one predecessor and one successor. Let* $\mathbb{P} = \{\mathsf{p}_1, \ldots, \mathsf{p}_k\}$ *be a finite fixed set of process types such that* $\mathsf{Q}_{\mathsf{p}_i} \neq \emptyset$, *for all* $i \in [1,k]$ *and* $\mathsf{Q}_{\mathsf{p}_i} \cap \mathsf{Q}_{\mathsf{p}_j} = \emptyset$, *for all* $1 \leq i < j \leq k$.

Because a process type has exactly one initial token and all transitions have one predecessor and one successor, every reachable marking of a process type has exactly one token. We denote by $\mathsf{Q}_\mathbb{P} \stackrel{\text{def}}{=} \biguplus_{\mathsf{p} \in \mathbb{P}} \mathsf{Q}_\mathsf{p}$ and $\mathsf{T}_\mathbb{P}^{obs} \stackrel{\text{def}}{=} \biguplus_{\mathsf{p} \in \mathbb{P}} \mathsf{T}_\mathsf{p}^{obs}$ the sets of places and observable transitions from some $\mathsf{p} \in \mathbb{P}$, respectively.

Example 5. Figure 4 (a) shows two examples of process types, *Once* and *Loop*. Observable transitions are shown in black, and internal transitions in yellow. They have $\mathsf{Q}_{Once} = \{\text{on}, \text{off}\}$, $\mathsf{T}_{Once}^{obs} = \mathsf{T}_{Once} = \{\text{send}\}$, $\mathsf{Q}_{Loop} = \{\text{free}, \text{busy}\}$, $\mathsf{T}_{Loop}^{obs} = \{\text{recv}\}$ and $\mathsf{T}_{Loop}^{int} = \{\text{handle}\}$.

Definition 3. *A* system $\mathsf{S} = (\mathsf{V}_\mathsf{S}, \mathsf{E}_\mathsf{S}, \lambda_\mathsf{S}) \in \mathcal{G}(\mathbb{P} \uplus \Pi, \mathsf{T}_\mathbb{P}^{obs} \times \mathsf{T}_\mathbb{P}^{obs})$ *is a graph whose vertices* $v \in \mathsf{V}_\mathsf{S}$ *are labeled with exactly one process type* $\text{proc}_\mathsf{S}(v) = \mathsf{p} \stackrel{\text{def}}{\iff} \lambda_\mathsf{S}(v) \cap \mathbb{P} = \{\mathsf{p}\}$ *and at most one port* $\text{port}_\mathsf{S}(v) = \pi \stackrel{\text{def}}{\iff} \lambda_\mathsf{S}(v) \cap \Pi = \{\pi\}$. *Edges* $v_1 \xrightarrow{(t_1,t_2)} v_2 \in \mathsf{E}_\mathsf{S}$ *are labeled with pairs of observable transitions, such that* $t_i \in \mathsf{T}_{\text{proc}_\mathsf{S}(v_i)}^{obs}$, *for* $i = 1,2$. *We denote by* $\mathcal{S}(\mathbb{P}) \stackrel{\text{def}}{=} \mathcal{G}(\mathbb{P}, \mathsf{T}_\mathbb{P}^{obs} \times \mathsf{T}_\mathbb{P}^{obs})$ *the set of systems of empty sort, i.e., without ports.*

The communication (*i.e.*, synchronization between processes) in a system is formally captured by the following notion of behavior:

Definition 4. *A* behavior *is a PN* $\mathcal{N}$ *such that* $1 \leq \|{}^\bullet t\| = \|t^\bullet\| \leq 2$, *for each* $t \in \mathsf{T}_\mathcal{N}$. *The* behavior of a system S *is* $\beta(\mathsf{S}) \stackrel{\text{def}}{=} (\mathsf{N}, \mathsf{m}_0)$, *where:*

- $\mathsf{Q}_\mathsf{N} \stackrel{\text{def}}{=} \{(q,v) \mid q \in \mathsf{Q}_{\text{proc}_\mathsf{S}(v)},\ v \in \mathsf{V}_\mathsf{S}\}$, *a place* (q,v) *corresponds to the place* q *of the process type that labels the vertex* v,
- $\mathsf{T}_\mathsf{N} \stackrel{\text{def}}{=} \mathsf{E} \cup \{(t,v) \mid t \in \mathsf{T}_{\text{proc}_\mathsf{S}(v)}^{int},\ v \in \mathsf{V}_\mathsf{S}\}$, *the transitions are either edges of the system (i.e., modeling the synchronizations of two processes) or pairs* (t,v) *corresponding to an internal transition* t *of the process type that labels the vertex* v,
- *the weight function* W_N *is such that internal transitions are preserved, and observable transitions are merged according to edge labels. That is, for every* v *such that* $({}^\bullet t^\bullet)_{\text{proc}_\mathsf{S}(v)} = (\{q\},\{q'\})$ *we have* $({}^\bullet(t,v)^\bullet)_\mathsf{N} = (\{(q,v)\},\{(q',v')\})$, *and for every edge* $e = (v \xrightarrow{(t,t')} v')$ *with* $({}^\bullet t^\bullet)_{\text{proc}_\mathsf{S}(v)} = (\{q_1\},\{q_2\})$ *and* $({}^\bullet t'^\bullet)_{\text{proc}_\mathsf{S}(v')} = (\{q_1'\},\{q_2'\})$ *we have* $({}^\bullet e^\bullet)_\mathsf{N} = (\{(q_1,v),(q_1',v')\},\{(q_2,v),(q_2',v')\})$.
- $\mathsf{m}_0(q,v) \stackrel{\text{def}}{=} \text{init}_{\text{proc}_\mathsf{S}(v)}(q)$, *for all* $v \in \mathsf{V}_\mathsf{S}$ *and* $q \in \mathsf{Q}_{\text{proc}_\mathsf{S}(v)}$.

Example 6. Figure 4 (b) shows the behavior of $\overrightarrow{K}_{4,3}(\text{send},\text{recv})$, having the architecture shown in Fig. 2 (a), with the red vertices $u_{1\ldots4}$ labeled with the process type *Once* and blue vertices $v_{1\ldots3}$ labeled with the process type *Loop*, from Fig. 4. The edges are labeled by the pair (send, recv) of observable transitions from *Once* and *Loop*.

3.3 The Parametric Reachability Problem

A *parametric* VR (*resp.* HR) *system* is described by a VR (*resp.* HR) grammar Γ. We define our decision problem as a parametric reachability problem asking if there exists an instance of a parametric system, described by a grammar, whose behavior reaches an error configuration from a given set. If the answer is negative, we have a proof that the parametric system is correct.

Let $\mathbb{X}$ be a fixed countably infinite set of variables, interpreted over natural numbers. An arithmetic formula α is a (possibly quantified) first-order formula using variables in $\mathbb{X}$, constants denoting natural numbers, the binary operations of addition and multiplication and the (in)equality relation. We denote by $\mathbb{A}$ the set of such formulæ. Let $\mathcal{N}$ be a PN and $\ell : \mathsf{Q}_{\mathcal{N}} \rightharpoonup \mathbb{X}$ be a partial function that labels certain places of $\mathcal{N}$ with variables. The boolean value $[\![\alpha]\!]^{\ell}_{\mathsf{m}} \in \{\mathsf{true}, \mathsf{false}\}$ of an arithmetic formula α in a marking $\mathsf{m} : \mathsf{Q}_{\mathcal{N}} \rightarrow \mathbb{N}$ is obtained by replacing each variable x that occurs free in α by the integer value $\sum_{q \in \ell^{-1}(x)} \mathsf{m}(q)$, *i.e.*, the total number of tokens from the places associated with x in m. We further define $Atoms^{\ell}(\mathsf{m}) \stackrel{\mathsf{def}}{=} \{\alpha \in \mathbb{A} \mid [\![\alpha]\!]^{\ell}_{\mathsf{m}} = \mathsf{true}\}$, *i.e.*, the set of arithmetic formulæ satisfied by a given marking and a variable labeling. A PN $\mathcal{N}$ satisfies a reachability specification α for a place labeling ℓ, written $(\mathcal{N}, \ell) \models \alpha$, iff there exists a finite firing sequence ρ leading to a reachable marking $\mathsf{init}_{\mathcal{N}} \stackrel{\rho}{\rightsquigarrow} \mathsf{m}'$ such that $\alpha \in Atoms^{\ell}(\mathsf{m}')$.

We specialize the satisfiability of a reachability specification by an arbitrary PN to the satisfiability by the behavior of a system $\mathsf{S} \in \mathcal{S}(\mathbb{P})$ and a labeling $\mathsf{L} : \mathsf{Q}_{\mathbb{P}} \rightharpoonup \mathbb{X}$ of the places from the process types $\mathbb{P}$ with variables:

$$(\mathsf{S}, \mathsf{L}) \models \alpha \stackrel{\mathsf{def}}{\iff} (\beta(\mathsf{S}), \mathsf{L} \circ \downharpoonright_1) \models \alpha$$

where $\downharpoonright_1$ is the projection of a pair on its first component, *i.e.*, $\mathsf{L} \circ \downharpoonright_1$ labels each pair $(q, v) \in \mathsf{Q}_{\beta(\mathsf{S})}$ by the variable $\mathsf{L}(q)$, if the latter is defined. Intuitively, we require of ℓ that it assigns the same variable to all "copies" of the same place $\{(q, v) \mid v \in \mathsf{V}_{\mathsf{S}}\}$. Hence, the boolean value $[\![\alpha]\!]^{\mathsf{L} \circ \downharpoonright_1}_{\mathsf{m}}$ of an atomic proposition in a marking m of $\beta(\mathsf{S})$ is obtained by mapping each free variable x from α to the total number of tokens from a place $(q, v) \in \mathsf{Q}_{\beta(\mathsf{S})}$ such that $\mathsf{L}(q) = x$. This paper is concerned with the following problem:

Definition 5. *Let* $\mathbb{P}$ *be a set of process types. The Parametric Reachability Problem* $\mathsf{PRP}_{\mathbb{P}}(\Gamma, \alpha, \mathsf{L})$ *takes as input a grammar* Γ *such that* $\mathcal{L}(\Gamma) \subseteq \mathcal{S}(\mathbb{P})$*, a reachability formula* α *and a place labeling* $\mathsf{L} : \mathsf{Q}_{\mathbb{P}} \rightharpoonup \mathbb{X}$*, and asks if there exists some system* $\mathsf{S} \in \mathcal{L}(\Gamma)$ *for which* $(\mathsf{S}, \mathsf{L}) \models \alpha$ *holds.*

Example 7. Choosing Γ the VR-grammar (Example 3), the set of variables $\mathbb{X} \stackrel{\mathsf{def}}{=} \{x, y\}$, the place labeling $\mathsf{L} = [\mathsf{on} \mapsto x, \mathsf{off} \mapsto y]$ defined on the process types from Fig. 4 (a), and the formula $\alpha \stackrel{\mathsf{def}}{=} y \geq x + 2$, we find that $\mathsf{PRP}_{\mathbb{P}}(\Gamma, \alpha, \mathsf{L})$ has a positive answer, because the behavior Fig. 4 (b) which belongs to $\beta(\mathcal{L}(\Gamma))$ admits a reachable marking m with 3 tokens on off and 1 token on on, satisfying $[\![\alpha]\!]^{\mathsf{L} \circ \downharpoonright_1}_{\mathsf{m}} = [\![3 \geq 1 + 2]\!] = \mathsf{true}$.

In the light of inherent theoretical boundaries, related to the undecidability of the above parametric verification problem [14], several semi-algorithmic methods have been proposed, for parametric HR systems [9] and parametric systems described using similar formalisms, such as a dialect of separation logic with inductive definitions [10] and a recursive term algebra [8]. In particular, the architecture description languages used in [8,10] have similar graph composition and relabeling as the more standard HR grammars. For these methods, the verification of certain coverability properties (*e.g.,* absence of deadlocks and critical section violations) relies on the generation of structural invariants for the parametric family of behaviors, directly from the specification of the architectures and the process types. Examples include *trap invariants, i.e.,* sets of places that, once marked, remain forever marked, and *mutex invariants, i.e.,* sets of places of which at most one is marked. The generation of structural invariants can be redefined for HR grammars at little cost.

In contrast, there is virtually no verification method for parametric VR systems. Many decidability results in the literature consider parametric systems with clique architectures [16], that can be described by simple VR-grammars. A prominent result is the decidability of the more general parametric model checking problem (PMCP) for *token-passing systems* (where communication is restricted to the passing of a token between processes) with MSO-definable bounded clique-width architectures [4, Theorem 26]. It is known that each MSO-definable set of bounded clique-width is definable by a VR grammar, but not viceversa. Moreover, an orthogonal[3] decidability result for parametric HR token-passing systems is given in [9, Theorem 4]. It is an interesting open problem whether this decidability result for HR systems carries over to VR systems, but this exceeds the scope of the current paper, and will be considered in future work.

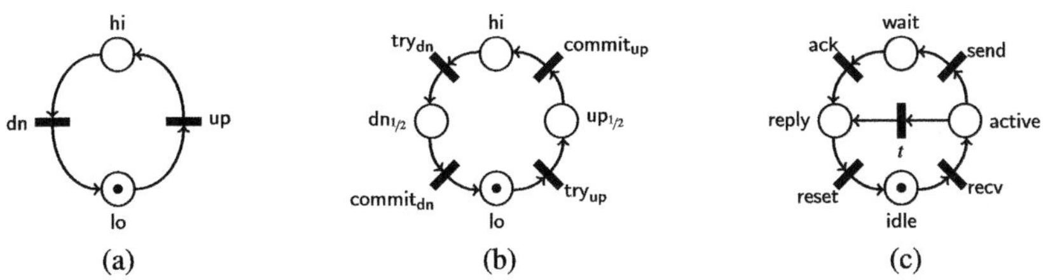

Fig. 5. A process type p (a), the corresponding process type $p_{1/2}$ (b), and ε_t (c).

4 Translating VR to HR Systems

The existence of several verification techniques for parametric systems with HR architectures and the scarsity of similar results for VR systems motivates us to define a translation from VR to HR systems, that preserves the answer of the PRP decision problem (Definition 5). This translation uses expansion to encode dense graphs as sparse graphs (see Fig. 2). Since labeled graphs are used as system models (Definition 3), the behavior

[3] This result applies to all HR sets of architectures, not just the MSO-definable ones.

of a sparse graph must be equivalent to the behavior of its expansion, on what concerns the satisfiability of reachability formulæ, thus reducing each instance of the PRP problem for a VR grammar to an instance of the same problem for an HR grammar.

Theorem 1. *There exist computable* $\mathbb{P}^{\mathcal{H}}$ *and* $\mathsf{L}^{\mathcal{H}}$, *process types and place labeling respectively, such that for any VR-grammar* Γ, *variable labeling* $\mathsf{L} : \mathsf{Q}_{\mathbb{P}} \to \mathbb{X}$ *and reachability formula* α, *one can effectively build a HR-grammar* Γ' *such that* $\mathsf{PRP}_{\mathbb{P}}(\Gamma, \alpha, \mathsf{L}) \iff \mathsf{PRP}_{\mathbb{P}^{\mathcal{H}}}(\Gamma', \alpha, \mathsf{L}^{\mathcal{H}})$

This result shows that it is possible to solve each instance of the parametric model checking problem that takes a VR grammar as input by an effective reduction to an instance of the same problem for a HR grammar, which, as previously mentioned, has received more attention lately [9].

Intuitively the translation works as follows: vertices in the HR system are either "real" vertices from the original VR system, or routing nodes. A unique vertex of the HR system will act as representative of all vertices currently π-ports in the VR system, and communication between a π-port v and a π'-port v' in the VR system will in the HR system roughly take the form of (1) a request from v to its representative v_π through a chain of routing nodes, (2) similarly a request from v' to its representative $v_{\pi'}$, (3) a direct communication between v_π and $v_{\pi'}$ (4) an acknowledgement from v_π to v following the inverse chain of routing nodes, (5) an acknowledgement from $v_{\pi'}$ to v'. This is a simplification because in reality steps (1–2) and (4–5) above may be interleaved, and rather than a single representative there is one representative per observable transition. We define below the process types that correspond to routing nodes, give an intuition of how they function, then show the actual inductive translation.

Let $\mathbb{P}$ be the set of process types used by the VR grammars, in the rest of this section. We define a new set of process types $\mathbb{P}^{\mathcal{H}}$ such that $\mathsf{Q}_{\mathbb{P}} \subseteq \mathsf{Q}_{\mathbb{P}^{\mathcal{H}}}$, see Fig. 5 (b) for an example. First, let $\mathbb{P}_{1/2} \stackrel{\text{def}}{=} \{\mathsf{p}_{1/2} \mid \mathsf{p} \in \mathbb{P}\}$ be a set of process types disjoint from $\mathbb{P}$. A generic $\mathsf{p}_{1/2}$ is defined below from $\mathsf{p} \in \mathbb{P}$. Intuitively, $\mathsf{p}_{1/2}$ simulates the behavior of p in the context of communication through routing nodes: each observable transition is split into two halves, one sending a request, then eventually receiving the acknowledgement.

- $\mathsf{Q}_{\mathsf{p}_{1/2}} \stackrel{\text{def}}{=} \mathsf{Q}_\mathsf{p} \uplus \{t_{1/2} \mid t \in \mathsf{T}_\mathsf{p}^{obs}\}$, each $t_{1/2}$ is a new place associated with the transition t,
- $\mathsf{T}_{\mathsf{p}_{1/2}} \stackrel{\text{def}}{=} \mathsf{T}_\mathsf{p}^{int} \uplus \{\mathsf{try}_t, \mathsf{commit}_t \mid t \in \mathsf{T}_\mathsf{p}^{obs}\}$, *i.e.*, each observable transition t of p is split into try_t (an attempt at firing t) and commit_t (t has been fired remotely),
- $\mathsf{W}_{\mathsf{p}_{1/2}} \stackrel{\text{def}}{=} \mathsf{W}_\mathsf{p}\downharpoonright_{\mathsf{Q}_\mathsf{p} \times \mathsf{T}_\mathsf{p}^{int} \uplus \mathsf{T}_\mathsf{p}^{int} \times \mathsf{Q}_\mathsf{p}} \uplus \{(q, \mathsf{try}_t, 1), (\mathsf{try}_t, t_{1/2}, 1) \mid q \in \mathsf{Q}_\mathsf{p}, t \in \mathsf{T}_\mathsf{p}^{obs}, \mathsf{W}_\mathsf{p}(q,t) = 1\} \uplus \{(t_{1/2}, \mathsf{commit}_t, 1), (\mathsf{commit}_t, q, 1) \mid t \in \mathsf{T}_\mathsf{p}^{obs}, \mathsf{W}_\mathsf{p}(t,q) = 1\}$, *i.e.*, whenever t is an observable transition from q to q', there are observable transitions try_t from q to $t_{1/2}$ and commit_t from $t_{1/2}$ to q' in $\mathsf{p}_{1/2}$.
- $\mathsf{init}_{\mathsf{p}_{1/2}} \stackrel{\text{def}}{=} \mathsf{init}_\mathsf{p}$.

Second, for each observable transition $t \in \mathsf{T}_{\mathbb{P}}^{obs}$, we consider a new process type ε_t, defined below. See Fig. 5 (c) for an example. This is what we call the "routing nodes".

- $\mathsf{Q}_{\varepsilon_t} \stackrel{\text{def}}{=} \{\mathsf{idle}_t, \mathsf{active}_t, \mathsf{wait}_t, \mathsf{reply}_t\}$,

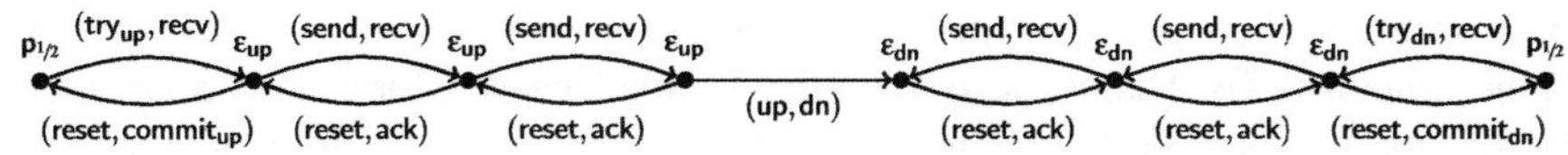

Fig. 6. An $\varepsilon_{\mathsf{up}}$-path meeting an $\varepsilon_{\mathsf{dn}}$-path to simulate the interaction $(\mathsf{up}, \mathsf{dn})$ between two vertices of type p from Fig. 5 (a).

- $\mathsf{T}_{\varepsilon_t} = \mathsf{T}^{obs}_{\varepsilon_t} \stackrel{\text{def}}{=} \{\mathsf{recv}, \mathsf{send}, \mathsf{ack}, \mathsf{reset}, t\}$,
- $\mathsf{W}_{\varepsilon_t}$ consists of the following edges, all of weight 1:

$$^\bullet\mathsf{recv}^\bullet \stackrel{\text{def}}{=} (\mathsf{idle}_t, \mathsf{active}_t) \;\; ^\bullet\mathsf{send}^\bullet \stackrel{\text{def}}{=} (\mathsf{active}_t, \mathsf{wait}_t) \;\; ^\bullet t^\bullet \stackrel{\text{def}}{=} (\mathsf{active}_t, \mathsf{reply}_t)$$
$$^\bullet\mathsf{ack}^\bullet \stackrel{\text{def}}{=} (\mathsf{wait}_t, \mathsf{reply}_t) \;\; ^\bullet\mathsf{reset}^\bullet \stackrel{\text{def}}{=} (\mathsf{reply}_t, \mathsf{idle}_t)$$

- $\mathsf{init}_{\varepsilon_t}(\mathsf{idle}_t) \stackrel{\text{def}}{=} 1$ and $\mathsf{init}_{\varepsilon_t}(\mathsf{active}_t) = \mathsf{init}_{\varepsilon_t}(\mathsf{wait}_t) = \mathsf{init}_{\varepsilon_t}(\mathsf{reply}_t) \stackrel{\text{def}}{=} 0$.

Finally, $\mathbb{P}^{\mathcal{H}} \stackrel{\text{def}}{=} \mathbb{P}_{1/2} \cup \{\varepsilon_t \mid t \in \mathsf{T}^{obs}_{\mathsf{p}}\}$, "real vertices" and "routing nodes" respectively.

Example 8. Figure 5 (a) shows examples of p, $\mathsf{p}_{1/2}$, and ε_t. Instances of ε_t exist for $t \in \mathsf{T}^{obs}_{\mathsf{p}} = \{\mathsf{up}, \mathsf{dn}\}$. Two processes of type p communicate via a $(\mathsf{up}, \mathsf{dn})$ transition, which is encoded by a sequence of transitions, see Fig. 6:

$$(\underbrace{\mathsf{try_{up}}}_{\mathsf{p}_{1/2}}, \underbrace{\mathsf{recv}), (\mathsf{send}, \mathsf{recv}), \ldots, (\mathsf{send}, \mathsf{recv}), (\mathsf{up}}_{\varepsilon_{\mathsf{up}}}, \underbrace{\mathsf{dn}}_{\varepsilon_{\mathsf{dn}}}), \underbrace{(\mathsf{reset}, \mathsf{ack}), \ldots, (\mathsf{reset}, \mathsf{ack}), (\mathsf{reset}}_{\varepsilon_{\mathsf{up}}}, \underbrace{\mathsf{commit_{up}}}_{\mathsf{p}_{1/2}})$$

This matches the earlier intuition: the leftmost process tries to execute up and sends a request through routers $\varepsilon_{\mathsf{up}}$. At the same time, the right process tries to execute dn and sends a request through routers $\varepsilon_{\mathsf{dn}}$. When both requests reach adjacent routers, the transition $(\mathsf{up}, \mathsf{dn})$ is jointly executed. Following that, an acknowledgement is sent back to the processes that initiated the communication as a sequence of $(\mathsf{reset}, \mathsf{ack})$.

The variable labeling $\mathsf{L} : \mathsf{Q}_{\mathbb{P}} \rightharpoonup \mathbb{X}$ induces the following labeling $\mathsf{L}^{\mathcal{H}} : \mathsf{Q}_{\mathbb{P}^{\mathcal{H}}} \rightharpoonup \mathbb{X}$:

$$\mathsf{L}^{\mathcal{H}}(q) \stackrel{\text{def}}{=} \mathsf{L}(q), \text{ for each } q \in \mathsf{Q}_{\mathbb{P}}$$
$$\mathsf{L}^{\mathcal{H}}(\mathsf{active}_t) \stackrel{\text{def}}{=} \mathsf{L}(^\bullet t) \qquad \mathsf{L}^{\mathcal{H}}(\mathsf{reply}_t) \stackrel{\text{def}}{=} \mathsf{L}(t^\bullet), \text{ for each } t \in \mathsf{T}^{obs}_{\mathbb{P}}$$
$$\text{undefined everywhere else}$$

The rest of the paper is the proof of Theorem 1, instanciated with these $\mathbb{P}^{\mathcal{H}}$ and $\mathsf{L}^{\mathcal{H}}$.

4.1 Proof of Theorem 1

The main idea is to use the ε_t processes to define, for a VR-term θ, a HR-term $\mathcal{H}(\theta)$ that evaluates to a sparse system, from which the system $\mathrm{val}^{\mathsf{VR}}(\theta)$ can be retrived using graph expansion, *i.e.*, $\mathrm{val}^{\mathsf{VR}}(\theta) = \exp(\mathrm{val}^{\mathsf{HR}}(\mathcal{H}(\theta)))$ (Definition 1). Using the set of port labels $\Pi^{\mathcal{H}} \stackrel{\text{def}}{=} \{\pi_{1/2}, (\pi, t), \overline{(\pi, t)} \mid \pi \in \Pi, t \in \mathsf{T}^{obs}_{\mathrm{ptype}(\pi)}\}$ where the process type of $\pi_{1/2}$ is

$(\mathsf{ptype}(\pi))_{1/2}$ and the process type of (π,t) and $\overline{(\pi,t)}$ is ε_t, we define $\mathcal{H}(\theta)$ inductively on the structure of θ. That is, in addition to a source label $\pi_{1/2}$ for each port label $\pi \in \Pi$ that occurs in θ, we add two copies of each port label for each observable transition. Intuitively, (π,t) will be the port label denoting the root of the tree of ε_t processes, and $\overline{(\pi,t)}$ will be used as backup when we need a fresh copy of (π,t). We define a renaming function $\mathsf{fresh} : \Pi^{\mathcal{H}} \rightharpoonup \Pi^{\mathcal{H}}$ by $\mathsf{fresh}(\overline{(\pi,t)}) = (\pi,t)$, and undefined everywhere else. That way fresh substitutes each source for its copy and forgets the original one. We also use the renaming function $\mathsf{obs} : \Pi^{\mathcal{H}} \rightharpoonup \Pi^{\mathcal{H}}$ which is the identity on $\Pi \times \mathsf{T}^{obs}_{\mathbb{P}}$ and undefined everywhere else, *i.e.*, obs forgets every port label except the (π,t) labels.

Concretely, creating new edges between ε_t-vertices is done by the below functions:

$$E^t_\varepsilon(\pi,\pi') \stackrel{\text{def}}{=} \overrightarrow{(\mathsf{send},\mathsf{recv})}_{(\pi,t),\overline{(\pi',t)}} \parallel \overrightarrow{(\mathsf{reset},\mathsf{ack})}_{\overline{(\pi',t)},(\pi,t)}$$

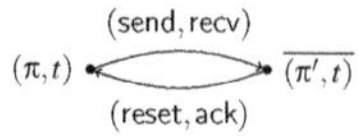

$$E^t_{1/2}(\pi) \stackrel{\text{def}}{=} \overrightarrow{(\mathsf{try}_t,\mathsf{recv})}_{\pi_{1/2},(\pi,t)} \parallel \overrightarrow{(\mathsf{reset},\mathsf{commit}_t)}_{(\pi,t),\pi_{1/2}}$$

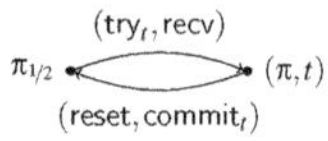

Recall that the main invariant during the translation is that whenever v in the VR system is a π-port, its corresponding vertex in the HR system is linked to the unique representative of (π,t) through a chain of routers ε_t.

An essential gadget used by the construction is the encoding of a relabeling function $\alpha : \Pi \rightharpoonup \Pi$ (which is by definition type-preserving) by a graph denoted $\mathsf{enc}(\alpha)$. We show an example of $\mathsf{enc}(\alpha)$, where α is the function $[\pi_1 \mapsto \pi_2, \pi_2 \mapsto \pi_1, \pi_3 \mapsto \pi_4]$. So as to not clutter the figure, we simply write E_ε to label the entire bundle of edges $\{E^t_\varepsilon \mid t \in \mathsf{T}^{obs}_{\mathbb{P}}\}$ and we write $(\pi,\_)$ for $\{(\pi,t) \mid t \in \mathsf{T}^{obs}_{\mathsf{ptype}(\pi)}\}$.

$$\mathsf{enc}(\alpha) \stackrel{\text{def}}{=} \mathop{\Big\|}_{\substack{\pi,\pi' \in \Pi \\ \alpha(\pi)=\pi'}} \; \mathop{\Big\|}_{t \in \mathsf{T}^{obs}_{\mathsf{ptype}(\pi)}} E^t_\varepsilon(\pi,\pi')$$

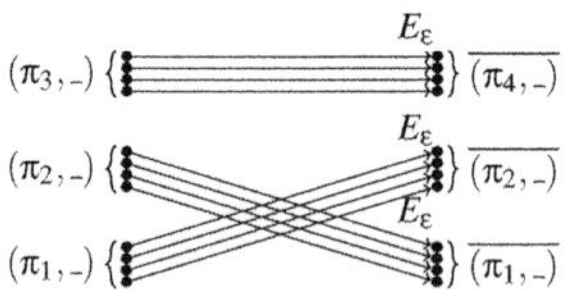

Intuitively, as the renaming α turns every π-port into an $\alpha(\pi)$-port, $\mathsf{enc}(\alpha)$ links the previous representatives of $(\pi,\_)$ to the new representatives of $(\alpha(\pi),\_)$, preserving the invariant. The translation $\mathcal{H}$ is defined inductively on the structure of the term θ:

$$\mathcal{H}(\bullet\pi) \stackrel{\text{def}}{=} \mathsf{relab}_{\mathsf{obs}}\Big(\bullet\pi_{1/2} \parallel \Big(\mathop{\|}_{t \in \mathsf{T}^{obs}_{\mathsf{ptype}(\pi)}} E^t_{1/2}(\pi)\Big)\Big) \quad \text{Figure7(a)}$$

$$\mathcal{H}(\mathsf{add}_{(t,t'),\pi,\pi'}(\theta_1)) \stackrel{\text{def}}{=} \overrightarrow{(t,t')}_{(\pi,t),(\pi',t')} \parallel \mathcal{H}(\theta_1) \quad \text{Figure 7(b)}$$

$$\mathcal{H}(\mathsf{relab}_\alpha(\theta_1)) \stackrel{\text{def}}{=} \mathsf{relab}_{\mathsf{fresh}}\Big(\mathcal{H}(\theta_1) \parallel \mathsf{enc}(\alpha)\Big) \quad \text{Figure 7(c,c',c'')}$$

$$\begin{aligned}\mathcal{H}(\theta_1 \oplus_{\mathbf{p}_1} \theta_2) \stackrel{\text{def}}{=} {} & \mathsf{relab}_{\mathsf{fresh}}\,(\mathcal{H}(\theta_1) \parallel \mathsf{enc}(\mathsf{id}_{\mathbf{p}_1 \cap \mathbf{p}_2})) \\ & \parallel \mathsf{relab}_{\mathsf{fresh}}\,(\mathcal{H}(\theta_2) \parallel \mathsf{enc}(\mathsf{id}_{\mathbf{p}_1 \cap \mathbf{p}_2})) \quad \text{Figure 7(d,d',d'')}\end{aligned}$$

These are quite straightforward once we understand the invariant: the translation of $\bullet\pi$ creates a new vertex and links it to all relevant routing nodes, the rule for $\mathsf{add}_{(t,t'),\pi,\pi'}$ establishes a communication between the representatives of (π,t) and (π',t'), the one for $\oplus$ creates a unique common representative, and the relabeling is as explained earlier.

The relation between the systems $\mathsf{val}^{\mathsf{VR}}(\theta)$ and $\mathsf{val}^{\mathsf{HR}}(\mathcal{H}(\theta))$ is captured by the below lemma. Its proof is the same as in [12, Proposition 2.4], where the new edges

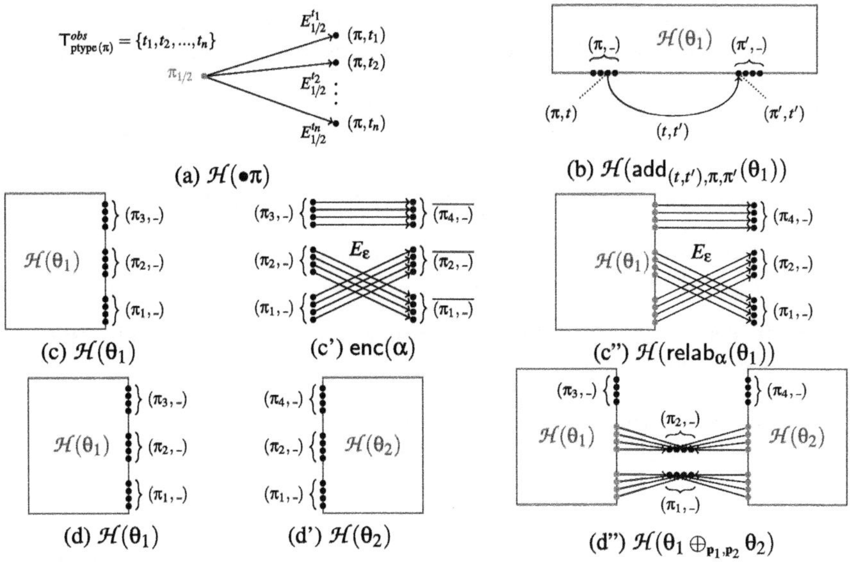

Fig. 7. Construction of $\mathcal{H}$ for each VR symbol. Relabeling uses $\alpha = [\pi_1 \mapsto \pi_2, \pi_2 \mapsto \pi_1, \pi_3 \mapsto \pi_4]$, and composition uses $\mathbf{p}_1 = \{\pi_1, \pi_2, \pi_3\}$ and $\mathbf{p}_2 = \{\pi_1, \pi_2, \pi_4\}$. Ports in gray are hidden during a relabeling.

have the same label, instead of the following sets of edge labels (Definition 1):

$$\mathcal{E} \stackrel{\text{def}}{=} \{(\mathsf{try}_t, \mathsf{recv}) \mid t \in \mathsf{T}^{obs}_{\mathbb{P}}\} \cup \{(\mathsf{send}, \mathsf{recv})\}$$
$$\overleftarrow{\mathcal{E}} \stackrel{\text{def}}{=} \{(\mathsf{reset}, \mathsf{commit}_t) \mid t \in \mathsf{T}^{obs}_{\mathbb{P}}\} \cup \{(\mathsf{reset}, \mathsf{ack})\}$$

We denote $(\mathsf{commit}_t, \mathsf{reset}) \stackrel{\text{def}}{=} \overleftarrow{(\mathsf{try}_t, \mathsf{recv})}$ and $(\mathsf{ack}, \mathsf{reset}) \stackrel{\text{def}}{=} \overleftarrow{(\mathsf{send}, \mathsf{recv})}$ (Definition 1). The meaning and orientation of these edges are shown on an example in Fig. 6.

Lemma 1. *Let* θ *be a ground VR-term,* $\mathsf{S} \stackrel{\text{def}}{=} \mathrm{val}^{\mathsf{VR}}(\theta)$ *and* $\mathsf{S}' \stackrel{\text{def}}{=} \mathrm{val}^{\mathsf{HR}}(\mathcal{H}(\theta))$*. Then,* $\mathsf{S} = \exp(\mathsf{S}')$*. For each* $v, v' \in \mathsf{V}_{\mathsf{S}'}$*, if* $E \neq \emptyset$ *is the set of edges from* v *to* v'*, then exactly one of the following holds:*

1. $(\mathrm{proc}_{\mathsf{S}'}(v), \mathrm{proc}_{\mathsf{S}'}(v')) = (\mathsf{p}_{1/2}, \varepsilon_t)$, $E = \{(\mathsf{try}_t, \mathsf{recv}), (\mathsf{commit}_t, \mathsf{reset})\}$ *and* $t \in \mathsf{T}^{obs}_{\mathsf{p}}$;
2. $(\mathrm{proc}_{\mathsf{S}'}(v), \mathrm{proc}_{\mathsf{S}'}(v')) = (\varepsilon_t, \varepsilon_{t'})$ *and* $E = \{(t, t')\}$;
3. $\mathrm{proc}_{\mathsf{S}'}(v) = \mathrm{proc}_{\mathsf{S}'}(v') = \varepsilon_t$ *and* $E = \{(\mathsf{send}, \mathsf{recv}), (\mathsf{ack}, \mathsf{reset})\}$.

Proof. The proof of $\mathsf{S} = \exp(\mathsf{S}')$ is the same as [12, Proposition 2.4]. The rest of the points follow from the definition of $\mathcal{H}$. □

The behaviors of $\mathrm{val}^{\mathsf{VR}}(\theta)$ and $\mathrm{val}^{\mathsf{HR}}(\mathcal{H}(\theta))$ are related by the following notion of path stuttering (inspired by [6, Definition 7.89]):

Definition 6. *Let* $\mathsf{S} \in \mathcal{S}(\mathbb{P})$ *and* $\mathsf{S}' \in \mathcal{S}(\mathbb{P}^{\mathcal{H}})$ *be two systems and* $\mathsf{L} : \mathsf{Q}_{\mathbb{P}} \rightharpoonup \mathbb{X}$ *be a variable labeling. Given two finite or infinite firing sequences* $\rho \in \mathit{Paths}(\beta(\mathsf{S}))$ *and*

$\rho' \in Paths(\beta(\mathsf{S}'))$, we say that ρ' is a stuttering of ρ, and write $\rho \trianglelefteq_{\mathsf{L}} \rho'$, when there exists a finite or infinite sequence $A_0, A_1, \ldots \in \mathbb{A}^\infty$ and integers $n_0, n_1, \ldots \geq 1$ such that:

$$Atoms^{\mathsf{L} \circ \downarrow_1}(\rho) = A_0, A_1, \ldots \quad \text{and} \quad Atoms^{\mathsf{L}^{\mathcal{H}} \circ \downarrow_1}(\rho') = \underbrace{A_0, \ldots, A_0}_{n_0 \text{ times}}, \underbrace{A_1, \ldots, A_1}_{n_1 \text{ times}}, \ldots$$

This relation is lifted to systems as $\mathsf{S} \trianglelefteq_{\mathsf{L}} \mathsf{S}'$, if and only if the following hold:

1. *for each $\rho \in Paths(\beta(\mathsf{S}))$ there exists $\rho' \in Paths(\beta(\mathsf{S}'))$ such that $\rho \trianglelefteq_{\mathsf{L}} \rho'$,*
2. *for each $\rho' \in Paths(\beta(\mathsf{S}'))$ there exists $\rho \in Paths(\beta(\mathsf{S}))$ such that $\rho \trianglelefteq_{\mathsf{L}} \rho'$.*

In particular $\mathsf{S} \trianglelefteq \mathsf{S}'$ implies that S and S' have sets of reachable configurations that satisfy the same atoms.

Theorem 2. *Let $\mathsf{S} \in \mathcal{S}(\mathbb{P})$ and $\mathsf{S}' \in \mathcal{S}(\mathbb{P}^{\mathcal{H}})$ be systems and $\mathsf{L} : \mathsf{Q}_{\mathbb{P}} \rightharpoonup \mathbb{X}$ be a variable labeling such that $\mathsf{S} \trianglelefteq_{\mathsf{L}} \mathsf{S}'$. Then, for any arithmetic formula α, we have*

$$(\mathsf{S}, \mathsf{L}) \models \alpha \iff (\mathsf{S}', \mathsf{L}^{\mathcal{H}}) \models \alpha$$

Finally, applying Theorem 2 to the lemma below (proof in Appendix 5) gives Theorem 1.

Lemma 2. *Let θ be a VR-term over the alphabets $\Lambda \stackrel{\text{def}}{=} \mathbb{P} \uplus \Pi$ and $\Delta \stackrel{\text{def}}{=} \mathsf{T}_{\mathbb{P}}^{obs} \times \mathsf{T}_{\mathbb{P}}^{obs}$, and $\mathsf{L} : \mathsf{Q}_{\mathbb{P}} \to \mathbb{X}$ be a variable labeling. Then $\mathrm{val}^{\mathsf{VR}}(\theta) \trianglelefteq_{\mathsf{L}} \mathrm{val}^{\mathsf{HR}}(\mathcal{H}(\theta))$.*

For the proof of Theorem 1, let Γ' be the HR grammar obtained by replacing each occurrence of a VR operation op from Γ by the HR operation $\mathcal{H}(\mathsf{op})$. "$\Rightarrow$" If $\mathsf{PRP}_{\mathbb{P}}(\Gamma, \alpha, \mathsf{L})$ has a positive answer, there exists a system $\mathsf{S} \in \mathcal{L}(\Gamma)$ such that $(\mathsf{S}, \mathsf{L}) \models \alpha$. Hence, there exists a ground VR-term θ such that $\mathrm{val}^{\mathsf{VR}}(\theta) = \mathsf{S}$ and θ is the result of a complete derivation of Γ. By the definition of Γ', $\mathcal{H}(\theta)$ is a ground HR-term resulting from a complete derivation of Γ'. By Lemma 2, $\mathrm{val}^{\mathsf{VR}}(\theta) \trianglelefteq_{\mathsf{L}} \mathrm{val}^{\mathsf{HR}}(\mathcal{H}(\theta))$, hence we obtain $(\mathrm{val}^{\mathsf{HR}}(\mathcal{H}(\theta)), \mathsf{L}^{\mathcal{H}}) \models \alpha$, by Theorem 2 and $\mathsf{PRP}_{\mathbb{P}^{\mathcal{H}}}(\Gamma', \phi, \mathsf{L}^{\mathcal{H}})$ has a positive answer. The "$\Leftarrow$" direction uses a symmetric argument. □

5 Conclusions and Future Work

We consider the parametric reachability problem for families of networks of finite-state processes specified using VR graph grammars. Our approach is to reduce the problem to HR grammars, for which several verification techniques have been developed lately. The reduction is based on a construction of an HR grammar that expands to the language of a given VR grammar, by elimination of epsilon-edges. We prove that this construction preserves any reachability property expressed using first-order arithmetic over variables that count the number of processes in each state.

Future work involves an implementation of the proposed reduction, based on existing tools for parametric verification of networks specified using HR grammars [9]. In particular, we plan to experiment with Azure-like network topologies and suitable routing (existence of an available route) properties. We also plan to extend the decidability result for pebble-passing systems with HR grammars [9] to VR grammars.

Acknowledgements. This research is supported by the French National Research Agency project"Parametric Verification of Dynamic Distributed Systems" (PaVeDyS) under grant number ANR-23-CE48-0005. We also wish to thank the anonymous reviewers for their helpful suggestions.

Disclosure of interests. The authors have no competing interests to declare that are relevant to the content of this article.

Appendix

Proof of Lemma 2

In this entire section, let θ be a fixed ground VR-term written using the set $\Lambda = \mathbb{P} \uplus \Pi$ of vertex labels. It is easy to check that $\mathcal{H}(\theta)$ is a ground HR-term written using the set $\Lambda^{\mathcal{H}} \stackrel{\text{def}}{=} \mathbb{P}^{\mathcal{H}} \uplus \Pi^{\mathcal{H}}$ of vertex labels, where the sets $\mathbb{P}^{\mathcal{H}}$ of process types and $\Pi^{\mathcal{H}}$ of ports have been defined above. We write S (*resp.* S') for $\mathrm{val}^{\mathsf{VR}}(\theta)$ (*resp.* $\mathrm{val}^{\mathsf{HR}}(\mathcal{H}(\theta))$).

Take a reachable marking m of $\beta(\mathsf{S}')$, and any transition $t \in \mathsf{T}_{\mathsf{p}}^{obs}$. We say that a vertex v of type ε_t is *idle* if $\mathsf{m}(\mathsf{idle}_t, v) = 1$. We say that v of type ε_t is *waiting on t* if $\mathsf{m}(\mathsf{wait}_t, v) = 1$. We say that v of type $\mathsf{p}_{1/2}$ is *waiting* on t if $\mathsf{m}(t_{1/2}, v) = 1$. Finally, given a label $\delta \in \mathcal{E}$ and an edge $(v', \delta, v) \in \mathsf{E}_{\mathsf{S}'}$, we say that v' is an $\mathcal{E}$-predecessor of v.

Fact 1. *For any reachable marking* m *of* $\beta(\mathsf{S}')$*, a vertex* v *of type* ε_t *is non-idle in* m *if and only if there exists a* $\mathcal{E}$*-predecessor of* v *that is waiting on* t *in* m*. Furthermore if there exists such an* $\mathcal{E}$*-predecessor, there will be exactly one.*

Proof. This proof is by induction. Since the property must hold for any reachable marking, we show that it holds for $\mathsf{init}_{\beta(\mathsf{S}')}$, then that is it preserved by every firing of a transition.

In $\mathsf{init}_{\beta(\mathsf{S}')}$ all vertices of type ε_t are in their initial state and thus have a token in idle_t. All vertices of type $\mathsf{p} \in \mathbb{P}$ have a token in a place of $\mathsf{Q}_{\mathbb{P}}$, not a place from $(\mathsf{T}_{\mathbb{P}})_{1/2}$. Therefore in the initial configuration, non-idle processes do not exist, and no process is waiting. The property is thus easy to verify.

For the inductive step, consider any transition that can occur in $\beta(\mathsf{S}')$, resulting in the firing $\mathsf{m} \overset{\delta}{\rightsquigarrow} \mathsf{m}'$. The structural properties that we established in Lemma 1 guarantee that the following case analysis is exhaustive:

- firing an internal transition t in v: no vertex of type ε_t is involved, and the vertex v in which the transition occurs is not waiting in either m or m' since ${}^\bullet t$ and $t^\bullet$ are both places of $\mathsf{Q}_{\mathbb{P}}$ not $(\mathsf{T}_{\mathbb{P}})_{1/2}$. Therefore the property holds in m'.
- firing $(v', (\mathsf{try}_t, \mathsf{recv}), v)$: for this interaction to be fireable requires that $\mathsf{m}({}^\bullet t, v') = 1$ (v' is not waiting in m) and $\mathsf{m}(\mathsf{idle}_t, v) = 1$ (v is idle in m). The inductive hypothesis applied to the latter fact yields that all $\mathcal{E}$-predecessors of v are not waiting on t in m, so when the firing makes v non-idle and v' waiting on t by $\mathsf{m}'(t_{1/2}, v') = 1$ and $\mathsf{m}'(\mathsf{active}_t, v) = 1$, it makes v' the unique $\mathcal{E}$-predecessor of v that is waiting on t in m'. Meanwhile v' is not of type ε_t so is not subject to the condition, v did not become waiting on t so the possible $\mathcal{E}$-successor of v is not affected, and all other processes retain the same state so must satisfy the same property in m' as they did in m. Therefore $\mathsf{m} \overset{(v', (\mathsf{try}_t, \mathsf{recv}), v)}{\rightsquigarrow} \mathsf{m}'$ preserves the desired property.

- firing $(v', (\mathsf{send}, \mathsf{recv}), v)$: in the same spirit as the previous case, this transition makes the token of v' move from active_t to wait_t, so v' remains non-idle and additionally becomes waiting on t in m', and at the same time the token of v moves from idle_t to active_t, so v becomes non-idle but remains non-waiting.
  Once again, v has gained exactly one waiting $\mathcal{E}$-predecessor, and all other vertices are unaffected, so m' satisfies the property.
- firing $(v', (t', t), v)$: this time we must have $\mathsf{m}(\mathsf{active}_t, v') = \mathsf{m}(\mathsf{active}_{t'}, v') = 1$, and $\mathsf{m}(\mathsf{reply}_t, v') = \mathsf{m}(\mathsf{reply}_{t'}, v') = 1$. All vertices are non-idle in m' if and only if they are non-idle in m, and they are waiting on t in m' if and only if they are waiting on t in m. The desired property is thus easily preserved.
- firing $(v', (\mathsf{commit}_t, \mathsf{reset}), v)$: this transition makes v' (waiting in m) return to non-waiting in m', and v (non-idle in m) return to idle in m'. This case is exactly symmetrical to the firing of $(v', (\mathsf{try}_t, \mathsf{recv}), v)$ and an analoguous reasoning shows that it preserves the property at hand.
- firing $(v', (\mathsf{ack}, \mathsf{reset}), v)$: similarly this case is symmetrical to $(v', (\mathsf{send}, \mathsf{recv}), v)$ and accordingly can be handled by the same reasoning.

Thus the property is preserved by all firings of transitions of $\beta(\mathsf{S}')$, and therefore holds in all reachable markings. □

We define a relation $\approx$ between markings $\mathsf{m} : \mathsf{Q}_{\beta(\mathsf{S})} \to \mathbb{N}$ and $\mathsf{m}' : \mathsf{Q}_{\beta(\mathsf{S}')} \to \mathbb{N}$, where $\mathsf{m} \approx \mathsf{m}'$ if for every place $(q, v) \in \mathsf{Q}_{\beta(\mathsf{S})}$ such that $\mathsf{m}(q, v) = 1$ we have one of the following properties:

(i) $\mathsf{m}'(q, v) = 1$, or
(ii) $\exists t \in q^\bullet.\ \exists v' \in \mathsf{V}_{\mathsf{S}'}.\ \mathsf{WaitPath}_{\mathsf{m}'}(v, v') \wedge \mathsf{m}'(t_{1/2}, v) = 1 \wedge \mathsf{m}'(\mathsf{active}_t, v') = 1$, or
(iii) $\exists t \in {}^\bullet q.\ \exists v' \in \mathsf{V}_{\mathsf{S}'}.\ \mathsf{WaitPath}_{\mathsf{m}'}(v, v') \wedge \mathsf{m}'(t_{1/2}, v) = 1 \wedge \mathsf{m}'(\mathsf{reply}_t, v') = 1$.

where we define the predicate $\mathsf{WaitPath}_{\mathsf{m}'}(v, v')$ as the existence of an $\mathcal{E}$-labeled path $v, v_1, v_2, \ldots, v_k, v'$ from v to v' such that $\mathsf{m}'(\mathsf{wait}_t, v_i) = 1$ for every $1 \le i \le k$. Furthermore we say that m' is *canonical* if only condition (i) is ever satisfied.

Intuitively m' is canonical and $\mathsf{m} \approx \mathsf{m}'$ when m' has tokens in the same places as m does. For non-canonical m', we can tolerate transitions that are partially executed and depending on whether the partial execution of t is less or more than half we count the token as being either in ${}^\bullet t$ or in $t^\bullet$ (recall: an $\mathcal{E}$-labeled path of S' simulates a transition of S, and the progress of this simulation is less than half if we have a path of wait_t until an active_t, and more than half if we have a path of wait_t until a reply_t).

Fact 2. *For any* $\mathsf{m} \approx \mathsf{m}'$*, we have* $\mathit{Atoms}^{\ell}(\mathsf{m}) = \mathit{Atoms}^{\ell^{\mathcal{H}}}(\mathsf{m}')$

Proof. Due to Lemma 1 and Fact 1, we know that when in the definition of $\approx$ above we talk about an $\mathcal{E}$-labeled path $\mathsf{WaitPath}_{\mathsf{m}'}(v, v')$ in the form of $v, v_1, \ldots, v_k, v'$, it necessarily means that all $v_1, \ldots, v_k$ are vertices of type ε_t, and that they are disjoint from any other instanciation of $\mathsf{WaitPath}_{\mathsf{m}'}$ for a different place. In particular this implies that the conditions (i), (ii), (iii) are mutually exclusive, and any token in a place active_t or reply_t can be injectively mapped to some vertex v with a token in $t_{1/2}$ from which there is a $\mathsf{WaitPath}_{\mathsf{m}'}$ as described.

This induces a bijection between $\{v \in \mathsf{V_S} \mid \mathsf{m}(q,v) = 1\}$, and $\{v \in \mathsf{V_{S'}} \mid \mathsf{m}'(q,v) = 1\} \uplus \{v \in \mathsf{V_{S'}} \mid \mathsf{m}'(\mathsf{active}_t, v) = 1 \text{ for } t \in q^\bullet\} \uplus \{v \in \mathsf{V_{S'}} \mid \mathsf{m}'(\mathsf{reply}_t, v) = 1 \text{ for } t \in {}^\bullet q\}$, implying that they have the same cardinal. It happens that $\sum_{q \in \ell^{-1}(x)} \mathsf{m}(q)$ is exactly the cardinal of the first set, and $\sum_{q \in (\ell^{\mathcal{H}})^{-1}(x)} \mathsf{m}'(q)$ is the cardinal of the second. We conclude that ℓ and $\ell^{\mathcal{H}}$ have the same interpretation of x, and since this applies to every $x \in \mathbb{X}$ we conclude that the same atoms are satisfied in m and in m'. □

Fact 3. *If* $\mathsf{m}'_0 \overset{\delta}{\rightsquigarrow} \mathsf{m}'_1$ *in* $\beta(\mathsf{S}')$ *and* $\delta \in \mathcal{E} \cup \overleftarrow{\mathcal{E}}$*, then for all* m *marking of* $\beta(\mathsf{S})$ *we have* $\mathsf{m} \approx \mathsf{m}'_0$ *if and only if* $\mathsf{m} \approx \mathsf{m}'_1$.

Proof. Once again we rely on Lemma 1 and Fact 1. Consider an interaction that can be fired between some v and v', and assume that it results in the transition from m'_0 to m'_1. Since $\approx$ is defined pointwise on each place of $\beta(\mathsf{S})$ that holds a token, and since m is unchanged, it suffices to look at exactly the places of $\beta(\mathsf{S}')$ that are changed by $\mathsf{m}'_0 \overset{\delta}{\rightsquigarrow} \mathsf{m}'_1$. In all configurations we will show that the equivalence is preserved simply by changing which of the conditions (i), (ii), (iii) hold on each place. In all that follows we will write t the transition that we consider (fully determined by the type ε_t of v'), and $v_0 \in \mathsf{V_S}$ the vertex that is currently being considered for the equivalence. The cases are as follows:

- $(v, (\mathsf{try}_t, \mathsf{recv}), v')$: m is linked to m'_0 on $({}^\bullet t, v)$ by condition (i). Furthermore $v_0 = v$. We show that after firing $\delta = (\mathsf{try}_t, \mathsf{recv})$ the markings are now linked by condition (ii) on the path v, v'.
  In m'_0, the vertex v which is of type $\mathsf{p}_{1/2}$ has a token in place ${}^\bullet t$. We know this because it is the only way that its transition try_t is fireable, and this is why condition (i) is satisfied. Similarly there must be a token in (idle_t, v') so that recv is fireable.
  After firing δ we now have $\mathsf{m}'_1(t_{1/2}, v) = 1$ and $\mathsf{m}'_1(\mathsf{active}_t, v') = 1$. This satisfies the condition for (ii) with $\mathsf{WaitPath}_{\mathsf{m}'_1}(v, v')$ instanciated by the trivial path v, v'. Every step of this reasoning is in fact an equivalence, so we also get the other direction of the statement.
- $(v, (\mathsf{send}, \mathsf{recv}), v')$: m and m'_0 are linked on $({}^\bullet t, v_0)$ by condition (ii), in the form of $\mathsf{WaitPath}_{\mathsf{m}'_0}(v_0, v)$ instanciated by some $v_0, v_1, \ldots, v_k, v$. We show that m and m'_1 are still linked by condition (ii), but on v' instead of v.
  The interaction $(\mathsf{send}, \mathsf{recv})$ belongs to $\mathcal{E}$, so $v_0, v_1, \ldots, v_k, v, v'$ is still an $\mathcal{E}$-labeled path. In fact after we fire δ, we get $\mathsf{m}'_1(\mathsf{wait}_t, v) = 1$ which means that $v_0, v_1, \ldots, v_k, v, v'$ instanciates $\mathsf{WaitPath}_{\mathsf{m}'}(v_0, v')$. Lastly we have $\mathsf{m}'_1(\mathsf{active}_t, v') = 1$, thus satisfying condition (ii).
- $(v, (\mathsf{commit}_t, \mathsf{reset}), v')$: m is linked to m'_0 on $(t^\bullet, v_0)$ by condition (iii). With a reasoning analoguous to the first case, including the fact that $v_0 = v$, we can prove that m and m'_1 are instead linked by condition (i).
- $(v, (\mathsf{ack}, \mathsf{reset}), v')$: m is linked to m'_0 on $(t^\bullet, v_0)$ by condition (iii). With a reasoning analoguous to the second case, we can prove that m and m'_1 are still linked by condition (iii), but using a shorter $\mathsf{WaitPath}(v_0, v)$ instead of $\mathsf{WaitPath}(v_0, v')$.

□

Fact 4. *For any markings* $\mathsf{m}_1, \mathsf{m}_2 : Q_{\beta(\mathsf{S})} \rightarrow \mathbb{N}$, *transition* $\delta \in T_{\beta(\mathsf{S})}$ *such that* $\mathsf{m}_1 \overset{\delta}{\rightsquigarrow} \mathsf{m}_2$ *in* $\beta(\mathsf{S})$, *and any* $\mathsf{m}'_1 : Q_{\beta(\mathsf{S}')} \rightarrow \mathbb{N}$, *if* $\mathsf{m}_1 \approx \mathsf{m}'_1$ *and* m'_1 *is canonical then there exist a marking* $\mathsf{m}'_2 : Q_{\beta(\mathsf{S}')} \rightarrow \mathbb{N}$, *an* $\mathcal{E}$*-sequence* $\mathbf{p}$, *and an* $\overleftarrow{\mathcal{E}}$*-sequence* $\mathbf{q}$, *such that* $\mathsf{m}'_1 \overset{\mathbf{p}\cdot\delta\cdot\mathbf{q}}{\rightsquigarrow} \mathsf{m}'_2$ *in* $\beta(\mathsf{S}')$ *and* $\mathsf{m}_2 \approx \mathsf{m}'_2$ *with* m'_2 *canonical.*

Proof. Firstly if δ is an internal transition, then the canonicity of $\mathsf{m}_1 \approx \mathsf{m}_2$ and the fact that process types in $\mathbb{P}_{1/2}$ have the same internal transitions as those of $\mathbb{P}$, give that δ must also be fireable in m_2. We thus choose both $\mathbf{p}$ and $\mathbf{q}$ to be the empty sequence.

Otherwise, we assume that from m_1 to m_2, the interaction $\delta = (t, t')$ occurs between vertices v and v'. As we hinted at in Example 8, we choose $\mathbf{p}$ to be $(\mathsf{try}_t, \mathsf{recv}), (\mathsf{send}, \mathsf{recv}), ..., (\mathsf{send}, \mathsf{recv})$ on an ε_t-path starting from v, followed by $(\mathsf{try}_{t'}, \mathsf{recv}), (\mathsf{send}, \mathsf{recv}), ..., (\mathsf{send}, \mathsf{recv})$, on an $\varepsilon_{t'}$-path starting from v'. After that we execute

(t, t'), then propagate backwards for $\mathbf{q}$ as $(\mathsf{reset}, \mathsf{ack}), ..., (\mathsf{reset}, \mathsf{ack}), (\mathsf{reset}, \mathsf{commit}_t)$ and $(\mathsf{reset}, \mathsf{ack}), ..., (\mathsf{reset}, \mathsf{ack}), (\mathsf{reset}, \mathsf{commit}_{t'})$ along the same two paths in reverse.

Since m'_1 is canonical, all vertices of type ε_t and $\varepsilon_{t'}$ in S' have a token in idle_t in m'_1. Since $\mathsf{S} = \exp(\mathsf{S}')$, the existence of an interaction (t, t') between v and v' implies that there are some u, u' in S' and there exist an ε_t-path from v to u and an $\varepsilon_{t'}$-path from v' to u'. Along such paths, the sequence of transitions described above is a firing sequence if initially all vertices of type ε_t and $\varepsilon_{t'}$ are in state idle_t and $\mathsf{idle}_{t'}$ respectively, and they will return to state idle_t or $\mathsf{idle}_{t'}$ once the entire sequence is fired.

Thus $\mathsf{m}'_1 \overset{\mathbf{p}\cdot\delta\cdot\mathbf{q}}{\rightsquigarrow} \mathsf{m}'_2$, m'_2 is canonical, and $\mathsf{m}_2 \approx \mathsf{m}'_2$. □

Fact 5. *Every (finite or infinite) firing sequence in Paths*$(\beta(\mathsf{S}))$ *admits a stuttering firing sequence in Paths*$(\beta(\mathsf{S}'))$.

Proof. Let $\mathsf{init}_{\beta(\mathsf{S})} = \mathsf{m}_0 \overset{\delta_0}{\rightsquigarrow} \mathsf{m}_1 \overset{\delta_1}{\rightsquigarrow} \mathsf{m}_2 \overset{\delta_2}{\rightsquigarrow} \cdots$ be a (finite or infinite) firing sequence $\rho \in$ *Paths*$(\beta(\mathsf{S}))$. Using the initialization that $\mathsf{init}_{\beta(\mathsf{S})} \approx \mathsf{init}_{\beta(\mathsf{S}')}$, and the latter is canonical (since the initial token of ε_t is in idle_t for all t), we can inductively apply Fact 4 at every step to construct a firing sequence $\mathsf{init}_{\beta(\mathsf{S}')} = \mathsf{m}'_0 \overset{\mathbf{p}_0\cdot\delta_0\mathbf{q}_0}{\rightsquigarrow} \mathsf{m}'_1 \overset{\mathbf{p}_1\cdot\delta_1\cdot\mathbf{q}_1}{\rightsquigarrow} \mathsf{m}'_2 \overset{\mathbf{p}_2\cdot\delta_2\cdot\mathbf{q}_2}{\rightsquigarrow} \cdots$ which is a path $\rho' \in$ *Paths*$(\beta(\mathsf{S}'))$. In this construction all $\mathbf{p}_i$ and $\mathbf{q}_i$ are $\mathcal{E}$-sequences and $\overleftarrow{\mathcal{E}}$-sequences respectively, thus invariant for $\approx$ (Fact 3). This in turn implies that they do not change the set of atomic propositions that hold (Fact 2).

A path $Atoms^{\ell}(\rho) = A_0 A_1 A_2 \cdots$, where $\rho \in$ *Paths*$(\beta(\mathsf{S}))$ is thus transformed by this construction into a path $Atoms^{\ell^{\mathcal{H}}}(\rho') = A_0^{1+|\mathbf{p}_0|} A_1^{1+|\mathbf{q}_0|+|\mathbf{p}_1|} A_2^{1+|\mathbf{q}_1|+|\mathbf{p}_2|} \cdots$ which gives $\rho \trianglelefteq_{\mathsf{L}} \rho'$, for some $\rho' \in$ *Paths*$(\beta(\mathsf{S}'))$. □

Fact 6. *Any firing sequence of* $\mathcal{E} \cup \overleftarrow{\mathcal{E}}$*-transitions must be finite.*

Proof. In principle, the proof is straightforward: we define a cost function on places and show that every $\mathcal{E}$-labeled transition moves a token to a place that has a strictly smaller cost. Let $c : \mathsf{Q}_{\beta(\mathsf{S}')} \to \mathbb{N}$ be defined as follows:

$$\begin{aligned}
c(\mathsf{wait}_t, v) = c(\mathsf{idle}_t, v) = c(t_{1/2}, v) &= 0 && \text{for any } t, v \\
c(\mathsf{active}_t, v) &= 1 + c(\mathsf{active}_t, v') && \text{if } \exists v'.\ v \xrightarrow{\mathcal{E}} v' \\
c(\mathsf{active}_t, v) &= 0 && \text{otherwise} \\
c(q, v) &= 1 + \max_{t \in q^\bullet} \max_{v' : v \xrightarrow{\mathcal{E}} v'} c(\mathsf{active}_t, v') && \text{for any } q, v \\
c(\mathsf{reply}_t, v) &= 1 + \max_{v' : v' \xrightarrow{\mathcal{E}} v} c(t^\bullet, v) + \max_{v' : v' \xrightarrow{\mathcal{E}} v} c(\mathsf{reply}_t, v') && \text{for any } t, v
\end{aligned}$$

This function, apart from being obviously nonnegative, is well-defined everywhere: the acyclicity of the subgraph of S' composed only of $\mathcal{E}$-edges guarantees that the system of equations above has a solution. More precisely:

- c is obviously well-defined for places of the form (wait_t, v), (idle_t, v), or $(t_{1/2}, v)$;
- when a token is in a place (active_t, v) it can only be involved in transitions in the direction of $\mathcal{E}$ which is acyclic. Furthermore vertices ε_t form a forest so if v' such that $v \xrightarrow{\mathcal{E}} v'$ exists then it is unique, thus c is also well-defined for places of the form (active_t, v);
- finally c over (q, v) and (reply_t, v) is defined in terms of $\mathcal{E}$-predecessors, which are not unique (thus why we need a max), but still form an acyclic graph.

Given a marking m, we define

$$\mathsf{fuel}(\mathsf{m}) \stackrel{\mathsf{def}}{=} \sum_{q \in \mathsf{Q}_{\mathsf{S}'}} \mathsf{m}(q) c(q)$$

Observe that since $\mathsf{m}(q)$ can only take the value 0 or 1, the fuel of a marking is the sum of the cost of overy place with a token. Our objective is now to show that whenever $\mathsf{m} \overset{t_0}{\rightsquigarrow} \mathsf{m}'$ for $t_0 \in \mathsf{T}_{\beta(\mathsf{S}')}$ labeled by $\delta \in \mathcal{E} \cup \overleftarrow{\mathcal{E}}$, we have $\mathsf{fuel}(\mathsf{m}) > \mathsf{fuel}(\mathsf{m}')$. We do this by showing the equivalent fact that $\mathsf{fuel}(\mathsf{m}) - \mathsf{fuel}(\mathsf{m}') > 0$ because most of it cancels out: partition the set of vertices into ${}^\bullet t_0$ (loses a token when we fire t_0), $t_0^\bullet$ (receives a token when we fire t_0), and the rest (unchanged), and we are left with simply

$$\mathsf{fuel}(\mathsf{m}) - \mathsf{fuel}(\mathsf{m}') = \sum_{q \in {}^\bullet t} c(q) - \sum_{q \in t^\bullet} c(q)$$

Now for the case analysis on δ:

- $(v, (\mathsf{try}_t, \mathsf{recv}), v')$: $\mathsf{fuel}(\mathsf{m}) - \mathsf{fuel}(\mathsf{m}') = c({}^\bullet t, v) + c(\mathsf{idle}_t, v') - c(t_{1/2}, v) - c(\mathsf{active}_t, v') = c({}^\bullet t, v) - c(\mathsf{active}_t, v')$. Since $v \xrightarrow{\mathcal{E}} v'$, (active_t, v') is already accounted for in $c({}^\bullet t, v) = 1 + \max_{t \in ({}^\bullet t)^\bullet} \max_{v' : v \xrightarrow{\mathcal{E}} v'} c(\mathsf{active}_t, v')$, and thus $c({}^\bullet t, v) > c(\mathsf{active}_t, v')$. We easily conclude that $\mathsf{fuel}(\mathsf{m}) - \mathsf{fuel}(\mathsf{m}') > 0$.
- $(v, (\mathsf{send}, \mathsf{recv}), v')$: $\mathsf{fuel}(\mathsf{m}) - \mathsf{fuel}(\mathsf{m}') = c(\mathsf{active}_t, v) + c(\mathsf{idle}_t, v') - c(\mathsf{idle}_t, v) - c(\mathsf{active}_t, v') = c(\mathsf{active}_t, v) - c(\mathsf{active}_t, v') = (1 + c(\mathsf{active}_t, v')) - c(\mathsf{active}_t, v') = 1$ strictly positive as expected.

- $(v,(\mathsf{commit}_t,\mathsf{reset}),v')$: $\mathsf{fuel}(\mathsf{m}) - \mathsf{fuel}(\mathsf{m}') = c(t_{1/2},v) + c(\mathsf{reply}_t,v') - c(t^\bullet,v) - c(\mathsf{idle}_t,v') = c(\mathsf{reply}_t,v') - c(t^\bullet,v)$. Since the quantity $c(\mathsf{reply}_t,v)$ occurs in $\max_{v:v \xrightarrow{\mathcal{E}} v'} c(\mathsf{reply}_t,v)$ which is part of the sum that constructs $c(\mathsf{reply}_t,v')$, the inequality is obvious.
- $(v,(\mathsf{ack},\mathsf{reset}),v')$: The same reasoning as the previous case applies, since this time $\mathsf{fuel}(\mathsf{m}) - \mathsf{fuel}(\mathsf{m}') = c(\mathsf{reply}_t,v) - c(\mathsf{reply}_t,v')$ and once again $c(\mathsf{reply}_t,v')$ occurs in $\max_{v:v \xrightarrow{\mathcal{E}} v'} c(\mathsf{reply}_t,v)$ leading to $c(\mathsf{reply}_t,v) - c(\mathsf{reply}_t,v') > 0$.

In all cases we obtain $\mathsf{fuel}(\mathsf{m}) > \mathsf{fuel}(\mathsf{m}')$. The function fuel, as we have already justified, is a well-defined finite nonnegative quantity. It follows that an infinite firing sequence of $\mathcal{E} \cup \overleftarrow{\mathcal{E}}$-labeled edges cannot exist. □

Fact 7. *For any markings* $\mathsf{m}'_1, \mathsf{m}'_2 : \mathsf{Q}_{\beta(\mathsf{S}')} \to \mathbb{N}$, *transition* $\delta \in \mathsf{T}_{\beta(\mathsf{S}')}$ *such that* $\mathsf{m}'_1 \overset{\delta}{\rightsquigarrow} \mathsf{m}'_2$ *in* $\beta(\mathsf{S})$, *and any* $\mathsf{m}_1 : \mathsf{Q}_{\beta(\mathsf{S})} \to \mathbb{N}$, *if* $\mathsf{m}_1 \approx \mathsf{m}'_1$ *and* $\delta \notin \mathcal{E} \cup \overleftarrow{\mathcal{E}}$ *then there exists a marking* $\mathsf{m}_2 : \mathsf{Q}_{\beta(\mathsf{S})} \to \mathbb{N}$ *such that* $\mathsf{m}_1 \overset{\delta}{\rightsquigarrow} \mathsf{m}_2$ *in* $\beta(\mathsf{S})$ *and* $\mathsf{m}_2 \approx \mathsf{m}'_2$.

Proof. If $\delta = t$ is an internal transition, it means that for some $(q,v) = {}^\bullet t$ we have $\mathsf{m}'_1(q,v) = 1$. Thee definition of $\approx$ this implies $\mathsf{m}_1(q,v) = 1$ and thus δ is also fireable in $\beta(\mathsf{S})$ and obviously leads to $\mathsf{m}_2 \approx \mathsf{m}'_2$.

Otherwise $\delta = (t,t')$ is an observable transition. It must occur between some e and e' of respective types ε_t and $\varepsilon_{t'}$, and in m_2 they must have a token in active_t and $\mathsf{active}_{t'}$ respectively. By the characterization from Fact 1, there must furthermore exist some vertices v, v' such that there is an ε_t-path from v to e and an $\varepsilon_{t'}$-path from v' to e', and all vertices along those paths have a token in wait_t or $\mathsf{wait}_{t'}$ respectively. Finally, still from Fact 1, we obtain that in m'_1, v and v' have a token in $t_{1/2}$ and $t'_{1/2}$ respectively.

Knowing that $\mathsf{m}_1 \approx \mathsf{m}'_1$, this means that $\mathsf{m}_1({}^\bullet t, v) = 1$ and $\mathsf{m}_1({}^\bullet t', v) = 1$, and thus (t,t') is fireable in m'_1. Firing it yields m'_2 with $\mathsf{m}_2(t^\bullet, v) = 1$ and $\mathsf{m}_2(t'^\bullet, v) = 1$. On the other hand m'_2 only differs from m'_1 in that instead of having $\mathsf{m}'_1(\mathsf{active}_t, e) = 1$ and $\mathsf{m}'_1(\mathsf{active}_{t'}, e') = 1$ we now have $\mathsf{m}'_2(\mathsf{reply}_t, e) = 1$ and $\mathsf{m}'_2(\mathsf{reply}_{t'}, e') = 1$. In the definition of $\approx$, we thus easily check that $\mathsf{m}_2 \approx \mathsf{m}'_2$. □

Fact 8. *Every (finite or infinite) firing sequence in* $\mathit{Paths}(\beta(\mathsf{S}'))$ *is a stuttering of a firing sequence in* $\mathit{Paths}(\beta(\mathsf{S}))$.

Proof. Let $\mathsf{init}_{\beta(\mathsf{S}')} = \mathsf{m}'_0 \overset{t_1}{\rightsquigarrow} \mathsf{m}'_1 \overset{t_2}{\rightsquigarrow} \cdots$ be a firing sequence $\rho' \in \mathit{Paths}(\beta(\mathsf{S}'))$. Let $i_0 = 0$ then $i_1, i_2, \ldots$ be an enumeration of all the indices i for which $t_i \notin \mathcal{E} \cup \overleftarrow{\mathcal{E}}$. Starting from $\mathsf{init}_{\beta(\mathsf{S}')} = \mathsf{m}_0$, we apply Fact 7 for every i_j in increasing order, to get a firing sequence ρ defined by $\mathsf{m}_0 \overset{t_{i_1}}{\rightsquigarrow} \mathsf{m}_1 \overset{t_{i_2}}{\rightsquigarrow} \cdots$ and such that $\mathsf{m}_j \approx \mathsf{m}'_{i_j}$ for every $j \geq 0$. Applying Fact 3 in-between gives that $\mathsf{m}_j \approx \mathsf{m}'_k$ for every $i_j \leq k < i_{j+1}$, and Fact 6 guarantees that there are finitely many stuttering steps. We can finally conclude $\mathit{Atoms}^{\ell}(\rho) \trianglelefteq \mathit{Atoms}^{\ell^{\mathcal{H}}}(\rho')$. □

Finally we conclude from Fact 5 and Fact 8 that $\beta(\mathsf{S}) \trianglelefteq_{\mathsf{L}} \beta(\mathsf{S}')$: $\beta(\mathsf{S})$ and $\beta(\mathsf{S}')$ have the same set of paths, up to finite stuttering on the side of S'.

References

1. Abdulla, P.A., Cerans, K., Jonsson, B., Tsay, Y.: General decidability theorems for infinite-state systems. In: Proceedings, 11th Annual IEEE Symposium on Logic in Computer Science, New Brunswick, New Jersey, USA, July 27-30, 1996, pp. 313–321. IEEE Computer Society (1996)
2. Abdulla, P.A., Delzanno, G., Henda, N.B., Rezine, A.: Monotonic abstraction: on efficient verification of parameterized systems. Int. J. Found. Comput. Sci. **20**(5), 779–801 (2009)
3. Abdulla, P.A., Delzanno, G., Rezine, A.: Approximated parameterized verification of infinite-state processes with global conditions. Formal Methods Syst. Des. **34**(2), 126–156 (2009)
4. Aminof, B., Kotek, T., Rubin, S., Spegni, F., Veith, H.: Parameterized Model Checking of Rendezvous Systems. In: Baldan, P., Gorla, D. (eds.) CONCUR 2014. LNCS, vol. 8704, pp. 109–124. Springer, Heidelberg (2014). https://doi.org/10.1007/978-3-662-44584-6_9
5. Aminof, B., Kotek, T., Rubin, S., Spegni, F., Veith, H.: Parameterized model checking of rendezvous systems. Distributed Comput. **31**(3), 187–222 (2018)
6. Baier, C., Katoen, J.: Principles of model checking. MIT Press (2008)
7. Bloem, R., et al.: Decidability of Parameterized Verification. Synthesis Lectures on Distributed Computing Theory. Morgan and Claypool Publishers (2015)
8. Bozga, M., Iosif, R.: Specification and safety verification of parametric hierarchical distributed systems. In G. Salaün and A. Wijs, (eds) Formal Aspects of Component Software - 17th International Conference, FACS 2021, Virtual Event, October 28-29, 2021, Proceedings, vol. 13077 of Lecture Notes in Computer Science, pp. 95–114. Springer (2021)
9. Bozga, M., Iosif, R., Sangnier, A., Villani, N.: Counting abstraction for the verification of structured parameterized networks. *CoRR*, abs/2502.15391 (2025)
10. Bozga, M., Iosif, R., Sifakis, J.: Verification of component-based systems with recursive architectures. Theor. Comput. Sci. **940**(Part), 146–175 (2023)
11. Browne, M., Clarke, E., Grumberg, O.: Reasoning about networks with many identical finite state processes. Inf. Comput. **81**(1), 13–31 (1989)
12. Courcelle, B.: Structural properties of context-free sets of graphs generated by vertex replacement. Inf. Comput. **116**(2), 275–293 (1995)
13. Courcelle, B., Engelfriet, J.: Graph structure and monadic second-order logic: a language-theoretic approach. Cambridge University Press, Encyclopedia of Mathematics and its Applications (2012)
14. Emerson, E.A., Namjoshi, K.S.: Reasoning about rings. In: POPL, pp. 85–94 (1995)
15. Engelfiet, J., Rozenberg, G.: A comparison of boundary graph grammars and context-free hypergraph grammars. Inf. Comput. **84**(2), 163–206 (1990)
16. German, S.M., Sistla, A.P.: Reasoning about systems with many processes. J. ACM **39**(3), 675–735 (1992)
17. Greenberg, A., et al.: Vl2: a scalable and flexible data center network. SIGCOMM Comput. Commun. Rev. **39**(4), 51–62 (2009)
18. Hirsch, D., Inverardi, P., Montanari, U.: Graph grammars and constraint solving for software architecture styles. In: Proceedings of the Third International Workshop on Software Architecture, ISAW '98, pp. 69–72, New York, NY, USA, 1998. Association for Computing Machinery
19. Jayaraman, K., et al.: Validating datacenters at scale. In Wu, J., Hall, W., (eds) Proceedings of the ACM Special Interest Group on Data Communication, SIGCOMM 2019, Beijing, China, August 19-23, 2019, pp. 200–213. ACM (2019)
20. Metayer, D.: Describing software architecture styles using graph grammars. IEEE Trans. Softw. Eng. **24**(7), 521–533 (1998)

21. Lesens, D., Halbwachs, N., Raymond, P.: Automatic verification of parameterized linear networks of processes. In: The 24th ACM SIGPLAN-SIGACT Symposium on Principles of Programming Languages, pp. 346–357. ACM Press (1997)
22. Shtadler, Z., Grumberg, O.: Network grammars, communication behaviors and automatic verification. In Sifakis, J., (ed) Automatic Verification Methods for Finite State Systems, International Workshop, vol. 407 of LNCS, pp. 151–165. Springer (1989)
23. Wolper, P., Lovinfosse, V.: Verifying properties of large sets of processes with network invariants. In: Automatic Verification Methods for Finite State Systems, International Workshop, vol. 407 of LNCS, pp. 68–80. Springer (1989)

Secure Lineage Storage on Public and Private Blockchains

Bilel Zaghdoudi(✉) and Maria Potop-Butucaru

LIP6, CNRS, Sorbonne Université, Paris, France
{Bilel.Zaghdoudi,maria.potop-butucaru}@lip6.fr

Abstract. This paper reports the experimental results related to Lineage Event storage via smart-contracts deployed on private and public Blockchains. In our experiments we measure three key metrics: the cost to deploy the storage Smart Contract on the Blockchain. This metric captures the initial expenditure, typically in gas units, required to deploy the Smart Contract that facilitates Lineage Event storage, then the time and gas costs needed to store a Lineage Event. We investigated both single and multi-clients scenarios. We considered the following public Blockchains (largely used by industry): Hedera, Fantom, Harmony Shard0, Polygon Amoy, Ethereum Sepolia, Optimism Sepolia, Klaytn Baobab and Arbitrum Sepolia. Furthermore, we investigate the performances of Hyperledger Besu with different consensus algorithms as private Blockchains. Additionally, we explore an alternative case study involving hash-based batch Lineage Event storage using the QBFT consensus algorithm on a private Blockchain, and analyze the impact of client scaling on transaction times.

Keywords: secure lineage storage · public Blockchains · private Blockchains · gas and time cost

1 Introduction

The rapid expansion of data across various domains, fueled by the rise of the Internet of Things (IoT) and its evolution into the Artificial Intelligence of Things (AIoT), has led to increasingly complex data ecosystems. These ecosystems, characterized by diverse data sources, intricate data transformations, and multifaceted consumption patterns, present significant challenges in ensuring data quality, traceability, and security. The AIoT, with its connected devices ranging from simple sensors to autonomous vehicles and drones, produces vast amounts of data that require careful management to ensure their integrity and compliance with regulatory requirements. This complexity is compounded by the decentralized and distributed nature of modern data architectures, which often involve multiple static and mobile domains, leading to vulnerabilities in data transmission and transformation processes.

The interest in securing data lineage has grown significantly across various domains due to the increasing reliance on data-driven systems and the need

S. Lahlou and M. Mukund (Eds.): NETYS 2025, LNCS 15736, pp. 81–96, 2026.
https://doi.org/10.1007/978-3-032-00347-8_5

for traceability and compliance. In the healthcare sector, managing sensitive information with secure data lineage is crucial for ensuring patient privacy and complying with regulations like HIPAA [15,18]. Similarly, in the financial industry, data lineage is essential for maintaining the integrity of transactional data and adhering to regulatory requirements such as Basel II [3,25]. Cloud computing environments also face challenges in securing data lineage, particularly in the context of detecting anomalous behavior and ensuring end-to-end data security [14,24]. In big data ecosystems like Hadoop, ensuring secure provenance and preventing data spillage are critical for maintaining trust in large-scale distributed systems [12,19].

Traditional data lineage platforms, including OpenLineage [20], Apache Atlas [4], and DataHub [10], have emerged to address these challenges by providing solutions for metadata management, data governance, and lineage visualization. These tools enable organizations to track and visualize data flows across systems, ensuring data quality and compliance. However, these platforms are centralized, which introduces single points of failure and security risks, and they lack robust mechanisms for protecting against unauthorized access, data breaches, and malicious alterations. This has been highlighted in recent academic research, which emphasizes the importance of secure and decentralized solutions for managing data lineage and governance.

In addition to these challenges, the decentralized architecture of AIoT applications and the integration of third-party services into cloud-based infrastructures amplify the risk of security incidents. As data flows through various systems, it becomes vulnerable to breaches, unauthorized access, and tampering. These vulnerabilities can lead to substantial financial losses, reputational damage, and legal repercussions for organizations. Furthermore, the lack of comprehensive visibility and control over data movement complicates the enforcement of security policies and compliance with data protection regulations.

Related Work. The state of the art focused so far on designing new Blockchain architectures tailored to specific use cases rather than using existing public Blockchains like Ethereum. LineageChain [22] and ForensiBlock [2] for example propose custom solutions to improve efficiency, security, and scalability, addressing the shortcomings of generalized public chains that may lack the precision, privacy, and performance necessary for tasks like data provenance in Smart Contracts or digital forensics.

In [22], authors present a Blockchain-based solution designed to address the inefficiencies in querying data provenance in traditional Blockchain systems. LineageChain integrates a skip-list index, allowing fine-grained, tamper-evident provenance queries without the need for replaying all past transactions. Built on Hyperledger Fabric and ForkBase, LineageChain enhances the capture and retrieval of historical data, making it ideal for applications requiring precise provenance, such as Smart Contracts. Its utility lies in enabling real-time provenance tracking with minimal storage overhead, making it far more efficient than traditional systems.

ForensiBlock [2], introduces a specialized private Blockchain for digital forensics. ForensiBlock addresses gaps in existing systems, such as access control and efficient provenance extraction, by integrating a Role-Based Access Control with Staged Authorization (RBAC-SA) and a distributed Merkle root for tamper-evident case tracking. Designed specifically for forensic investigations, it provides secure data access and rapid retrieval of provenance records, ensuring both auditability and privacy.

In [21] the authors explore the challenges of managing data provenance in Blockchain environments. This paper focuses on capturing fine-grained provenance securely and efficiently using a Merkle DAG structure integrated with a Deterministic Append-only Skip List (DASL) to improve query performance and integrity in Blockchain systems. Implemented on Hyperledger Fabric, the proposed system supports runtime provenance access, making it particularly useful for applications requiring real-time data lineage queries, such as Smart Contracts.

In [23] the authors present a Blockchain-based solution for ensuring tamper-proof data provenance in IoT applications, using a layered architecture with Ethereum Smart Contracts. It supports diverse IoT use cases such as vaccine supply chains and health monitoring while addressing key challenges like privacy and scalability. The performance evaluation shows linear increases in gas consumption with context size and input records, with transaction latencies ranging from 14 to 36 s. These results highlight public Blockchain's limitations in handling high-throughput IoT scenarios. None of the previous works compare the performances of the existing Blockchains (public and private) in the context of distributed secure lineage.

Our Contribution. This paper reports the experimental results related to Lineage Event storage on various existing Blockchain architectures and in particular those frequently used by the industry. We challenge these Blockchains targeting the following metrics: the cost of deploying a smart-contract, time and gas consumption for registering a Lineage Event. We investigated both single and multi-client scenarios. We considered the following public Blockchains: Hedera, Fantom, Harmony Shard0, Polygon Amoy, Ethereum Sepolia, Optimism Sepolia, Klaytn Baobab, and Arbitrum Sepolia. Furthermore, we explore the performances of Hyperledger Besu with different consensus algorithms for private Blockchains. Additionally, we present a case study using a hash-based Lineage Event storage approach on a private Blockchain utilizing QBFT focusing on the impact of increasing the number of clients on transaction times.

Our study can be of interest for practitioners willing to use existing public or private Blockchains as a secure distributed storage environment but also for academics willing to design Blockchain-based dedicated architectures for lineage in order to compare the performances of their system on a common ground.

Paper Roadmap. The paper is organized as follows. Section 2 presents the use case and the architecture of a system generating secure Lineage Events. Section 3 presents the extensive experiments we performed on various public and private Blockchains.

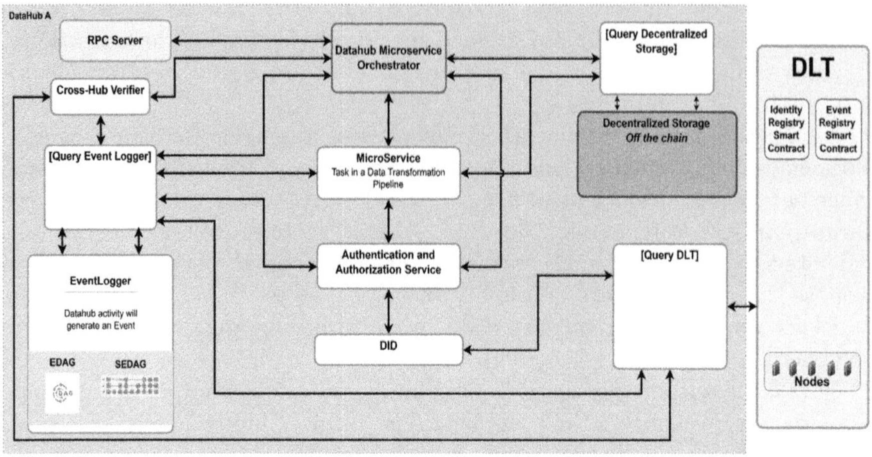

Fig. 1. Secure lineage one hub architecture.

2 Blockchain-Secured Data Lineage Architecture

In the following we propose a secure lineage architecture that ensures traceable, tamper-proof, and verifiable data transformations across all stages of data processing. By integrating Blockchain technology, the system creates an immutable, auditable record of data activities, meeting the demands of sensitive or regulated industries.

2.1 Secure Data Lineage Scenario

The system securely manages data processing from ingestion to transformation. Each stage is logged to produce a tamper-resistant, auditable history. This is particularly important in sectors handling high-stakes data where trust and accountability are critical. Our architecture matches several use cases. For example, in healthcare, maintaining the integrity of patient records is critical. A second case study concerns sensitive data collected by multiple data collectors (planes, cars etc.) and stored and modified by a data hub. A data hub can log every update, ensuring information remains consistent and unaltered while allowing real-time access for authorized staff. Blockchain complements this by generating cryptographic proofs, enabling secure and verifiable data transformations.

This approach builds trust by ensuring real-time proof of data integrity and reliability, enabling secure collaboration and efficient compliance with regulatory requirements.

2.2 Architecture Services and Workflow

The architecture presented in Fig. 1 incorporates the following components to support secure workflows:

- **RPC Server**: Acts as an entry point for external systems to interact with the DataHub. It routes incoming requests to appropriate internal services.
- **Cross-Hub Verifier**: Ensures data integrity and consistency between multiple DataHubs. It validates inter-hub transactions and provides APIs to update received data and to generate an integrity proof for audit purposes.
- **Event Logger**: Tracks all activity within the DataHub, generating events that can be queried or stored on-chain. The EventLogger plays a key role in maintaining data lineage, stores events and to update the Events trust DAG.
- **DataHub Microservice Orchestrator**: Manages workflows and assigns tasks among microservices. It helps generate event metadata and manage the transformation pipeline.
- **Authentication and Authorization Service**: Uses decentralized identifiers to ensure secure access control and authenticate interactions with the DataHub components.
- **Decentralized Storage**: Manages off-chain storage of large data that is not suitable for direct on-chain recording.
- **Distributed Ledger Technology**: Responsible for managing identity and event registries through Smart Contracts. It provides immutable and verifiable records of events.

2.3 Workflow Overview

Data is processed by authenticated microservices, with each transformation generating metadata logged by the Event Logger. Lineage Events are stored off-chain for scalability and on-chain for verification, ensuring a tamper-proof history of data transformations.

3 Experimental Results

In our experiments we measure three key metrics: the cost to deploy the storage Smart Contract on the Blockchain. This metric captures the initial expenditure, typically in gas units, required to deploy the Smart Contract that facilitates Lineage Event storage, then the time and gas costs needed to store a Lineage Event.

For the following experimentation scenarios, the deployed Smart Contract had a size of 6,032 bytes. Additionally, the average size of each storage event recorded was approximately 2,200 bytes.

We complete our experiments in Sect. 4 by studying the impact of the storage of the hash of events instead of full events. The Blockchain platforms evaluated include Hedera Testnet [6], Fantom Testnet [9], Harmony Shard0 Testnet [17],

Polygon Amoy Testnet [7], Ethereum Sepolia Testnet [8], Optimism Sepolia Testnet [5], Klaytn Baobab Testnet [13] and Arbitrum Sepolia Testnet [16] for public Blockchains and Hyperledger Besu [11] with different consensus algorithms for private networks. Our choice of Hyperledger Besu instead of Hyperledger Fabric is motivated by the analysis of [1].

The hardware environment for the private networks consists of 3 virtual machines with 4vCPUs and 8 GB RAM each, running Ubuntu 22.04. Performance metrics are collected using custom monitoring scripts and analyzed using statistical methods to determine significance.

3.1 Single-Batch Execution Scenario

In this scenario, we execute 100 transactions sequentially on each Blockchain system. Smart Contract deployment costs further underscore the cost efficiency of private Blockchains. Hyperledger Besu configurations (IBFT2.0 and QBFT) maintain deployment costs at approximately 1,304,759 gas units, while the Hedera Testnet shows an exceptionally low cost of 144,959 gas units. In stark contrast, public Blockchains like Arbitrum Sepolia Testnet and Ethereum Sepolia Testnet incur much higher costs, with Arbitrum Sepolia reaching 5,951,321 gas units. This significant variation underscores the economic considerations that organizations must evaluate when selecting a Blockchain platform for deploying Smart Contracts. The Lineage Event storage time comparison shows a similar trend, with private Blockchains outperforming public ones. Arbitrum Sepolia Testnet stands out with the lowest storage time of approximately 814.65 ms. Hyperledger Besu configurations also demonstrate low storage times, with IBFT2.0 BP 1 achieving around 1,081.75 ms. Conversely, public Blockchains like Ethereum Testnet Sepolia and Hedera Testnet exhibit higher storage times, around 13,761.73 ms and 7,240.37 ms, respectively. These results suggest that

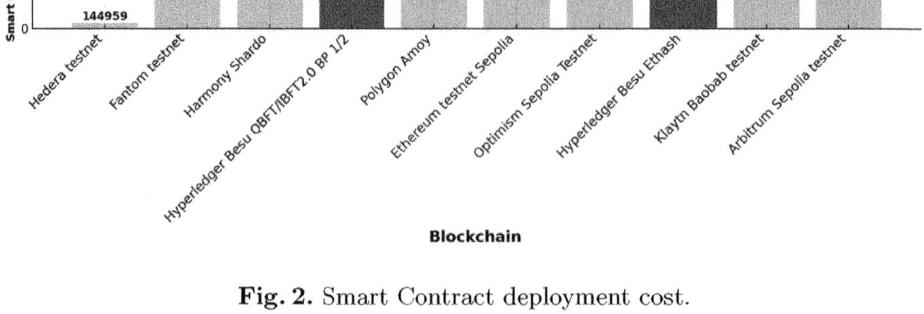

Fig. 2. Smart Contract deployment cost.

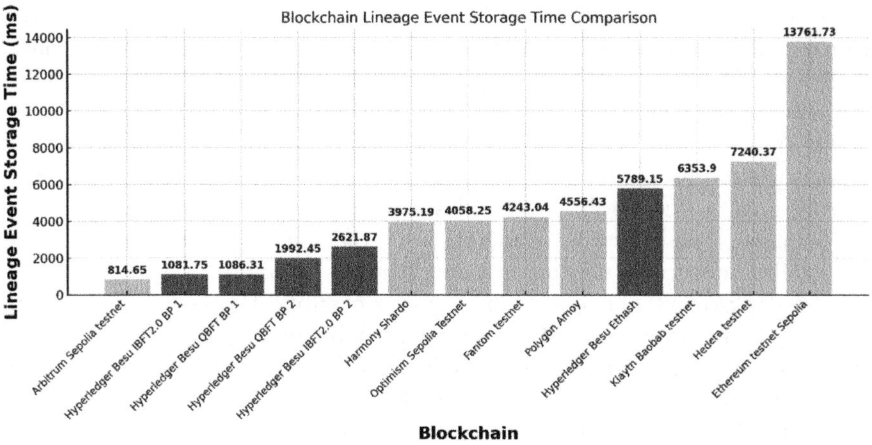

Fig. 3. Lineage Event Storage Time.

while public Blockchains offer broader accessibility, they may face latency issues, impacting their suitability for applications requiring rapid data storage.The chart in 4 illustrating the Lineage Event storage cost across different Blockchains reveals significant disparities. The private Blockchains (Hyperledger Besu) demonstrate remarkably low storage costs, around 39,444 gas units across various configurations. This indicates efficient performance and cost-effectiveness in a controlled environment. On the other hand, public Blockchains, such as Arbitrum Sepolia, incur significantly higher costs, peaking at 2,623,302 gas units. Notably, Ethereum testnet Sepolia and Optimism Sepolia Testnet also exhibit high costs, around 1,035,042 gas units. This discrepancy highlights the cost

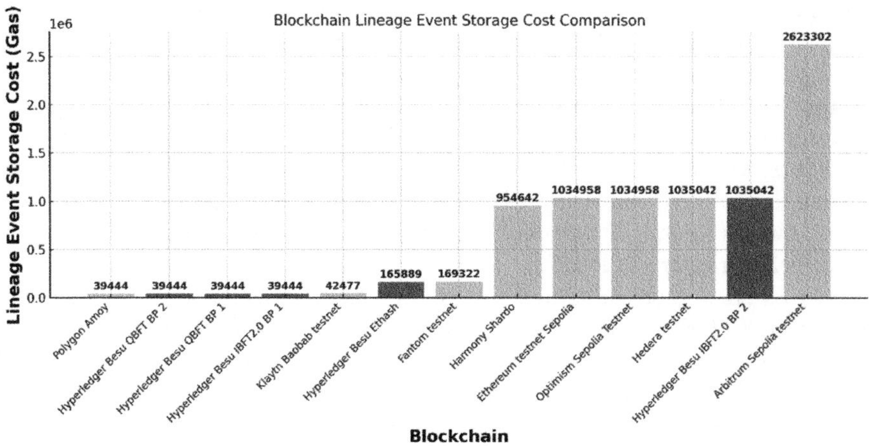

Fig. 4. Lineage Event Storage Cost.

implications of leveraging public Blockchains for storage-intensive operations, primarily due to their broader network and higher operational complexities.

Private Blockchains (Hyperledger Besu configurations) consistently demonstrate lower costs and faster storage times, highlighting their efficiency in controlled environments. This efficiency makes them preferable for enterprise applications where cost and performance are critical. Public Blockchains, despite offering greater decentralization and security, exhibit higher costs and slower performance. These attributes might be a trade-off for their broader network accessibility and robustness against single points of failure.

The deployment and operational costs on public Blockchains can be prohibitively high. For instance, the cost on the Arbitrum Sepolia Testnet is significantly higher than on private Blockchains, which may deter cost-sensitive applications. Organizations need to balance the benefits of decentralization offered by public Blockchains against the economic efficiencies of private Blockchains. The performance metrics indicate that for applications requiring high throughput and low latency, private Blockchains provide a more suitable infrastructure. The higher storage times on public Blockchains suggest potential latency issues, which can impact real-time applications and services.

3.2 Multi-worker scenario

In this scenario, we studied Lineage Event storage using Hyperledger Besu private Blockchain under three consensus algorithms: Ethash, QBFT, and IBFT2.0.

The experiment was conducted with a block period of 1 and 2 s, while multiple workers executed 100 transactions each simultaneously. Configurations ranged from 4 to 16 workers to assess the scalability and performance of each consensus algorithm under increased loads.

Ethash exhibited the highest variability in storage times across all worker configurations. For 4 workers (Fig. 5), the median storage time was approximately 5000 ms, but significant fluctuations were observed, with some transactions taking much longer due to occasional network congestion. This pattern became more pronounced with 8 workers, as shown in Fig. 6, where outliers increased, leading to higher transaction times.As the number of workers increased to 16 (Fig. 8), the variance in transaction times further escalated. This indicates that the Ethash consensus algorithm struggles to efficiently handle high concurrency, leading to more frequent delays. The increasing outliers suggest that the network is reaching its limits, with transactions being delayed by temporary bottlenecks or inefficient resource allocation.

Across all worker configurations, the median storage time remained consistent around 5000 ms, but the presence of frequent outliers demonstrates the limitations of Ethash when scaling for larger transaction volumes. This variability reflects Ethash's underlying reliance on Proof-of-Work (PoW), which is less suited to high-throughput environments requiring low-latency operations.

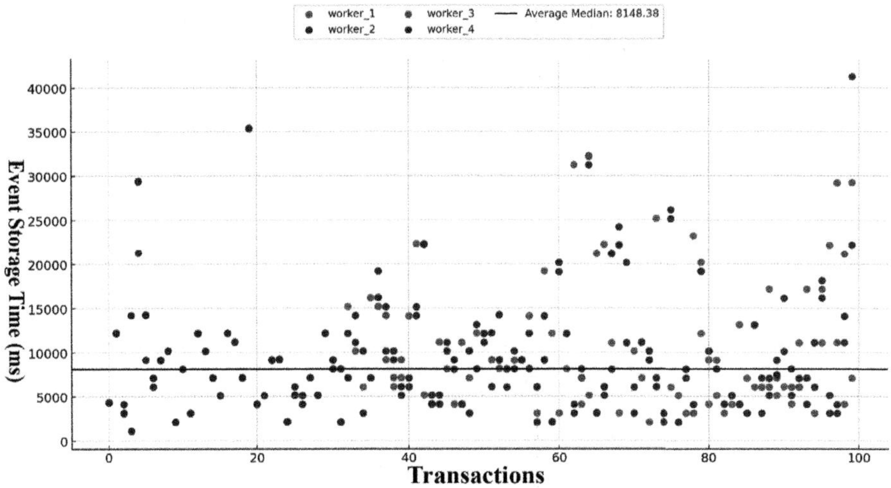

Fig. 5. Ethash Lineage Storage Time with 4 Workers.

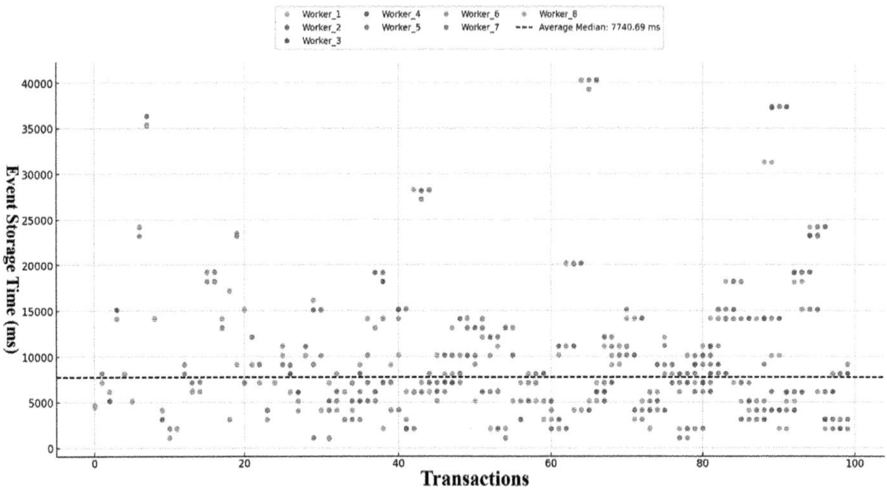

Fig. 6. Ethash Lineage Storage Time with 8 Workers.

IBFT 2.0 displayed more stable performance across all worker configurations compared to Ethash. With 4 workers (Fig. 9), the median storage time was approximately 1200 ms, with few outliers. This stability persisted even as the number of workers increased. The performance for 8 and 12 workers (Figs. 10 and 11) remained largely consistent, although slight increases in transaction times were observed, particularly with higher concurrency levels.

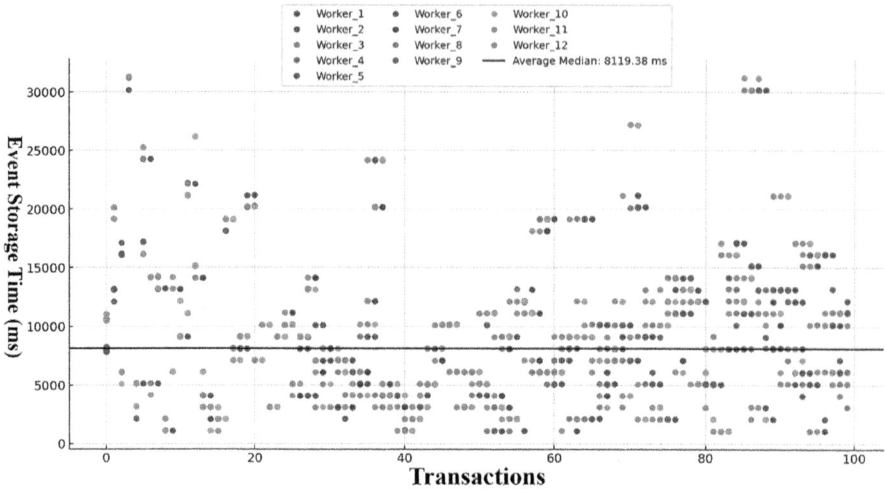

Fig. 7. Ethash Lineage Storage Time with 12 Workers.

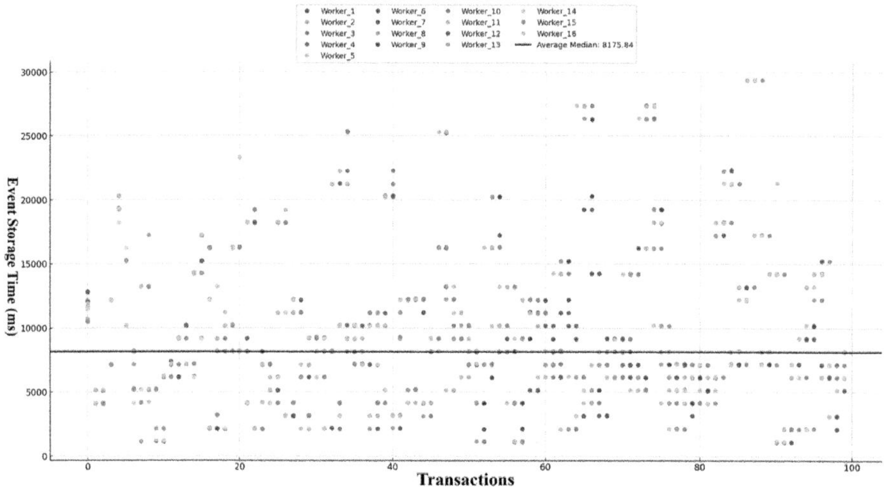

Fig. 8. Ethash Lineage Storage Time with 16 Workers.

However, as the worker count increased to 16 (Fig. 12), more outliers began to appear. This reflects a mild scalability issue, as IBFT 2.0 still managed to handle most transactions within reasonable times, but occasional latency spikes occurred due to network or resource contention.

Despite this, IBFT 2.0 proved to be significantly more reliable than Ethash, with fewer outliers and lower median storage times, making it better suited for environments that require more predictable performance under moderate to high concurrency loads.

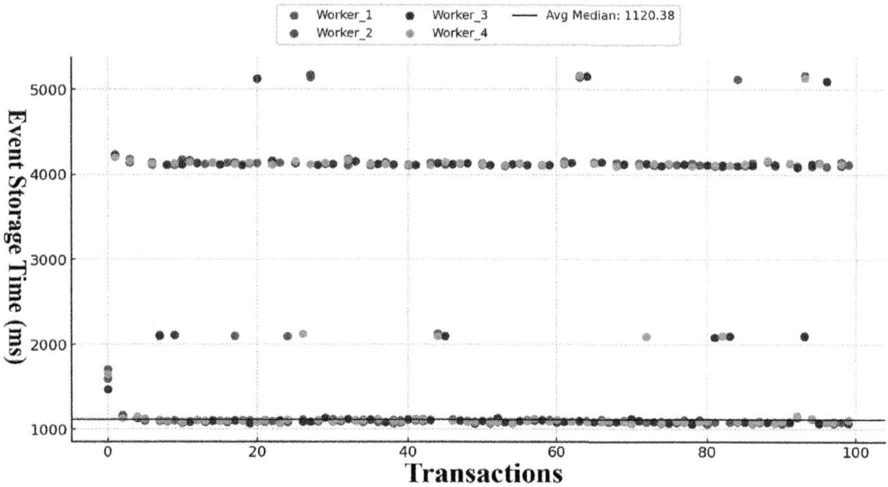

Fig. 9. IBFT 2.0 Lineage Storage Time with 4 Workers/1 s Block Period.

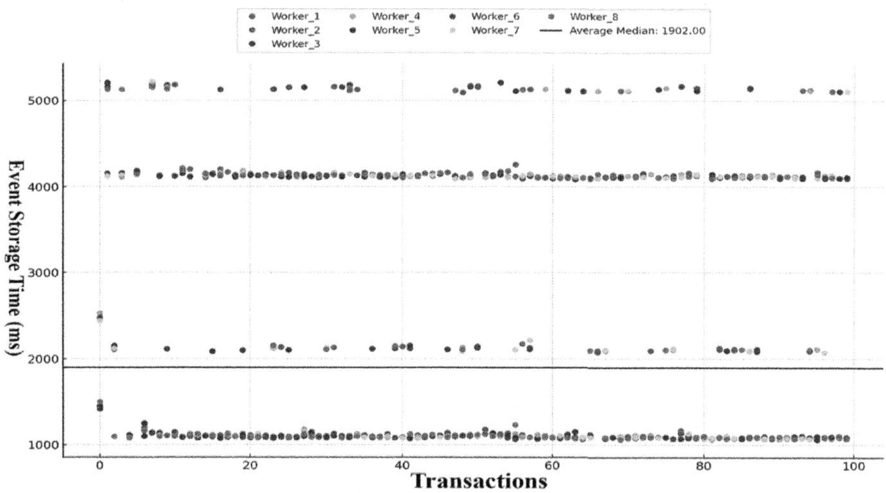

Fig. 10. IBFT 2.0 Lineage Storage Time with 8 Workers/1 s Block Period.

QBFT consistently provided the best performance across all worker configurations, with minimal variability in transaction times. The median storage time for 4 workers was around 1100 ms, and even as the number of workers increased to 16 (Fig. 13), the storage times remained highly consistent, with only a slight increase in variability.

The QBFT consensus mechanism maintained lower latency and fewer outliers across all configurations, demonstrating superior scalability and stability. The minimal increase in outliers as the worker count rose indicates that QBFT

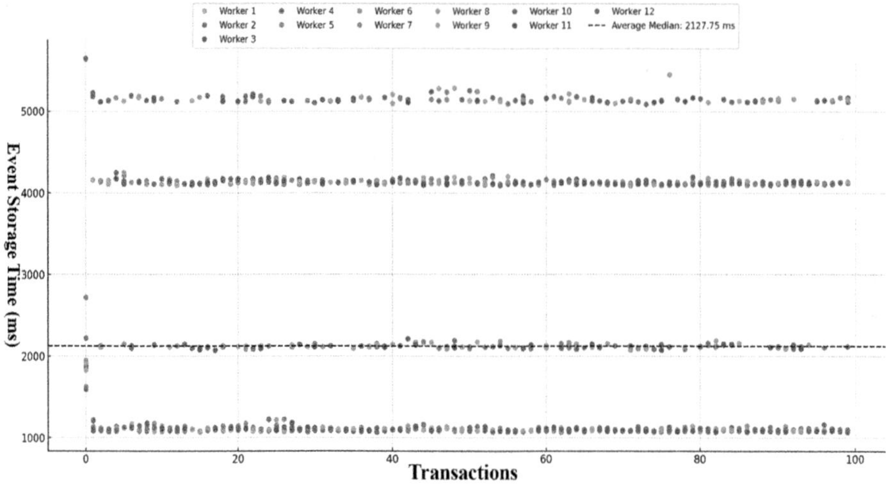

Fig. 11. IBFT 2.0 Lineage Storage Time with 12 Workers/1 s Block Period.

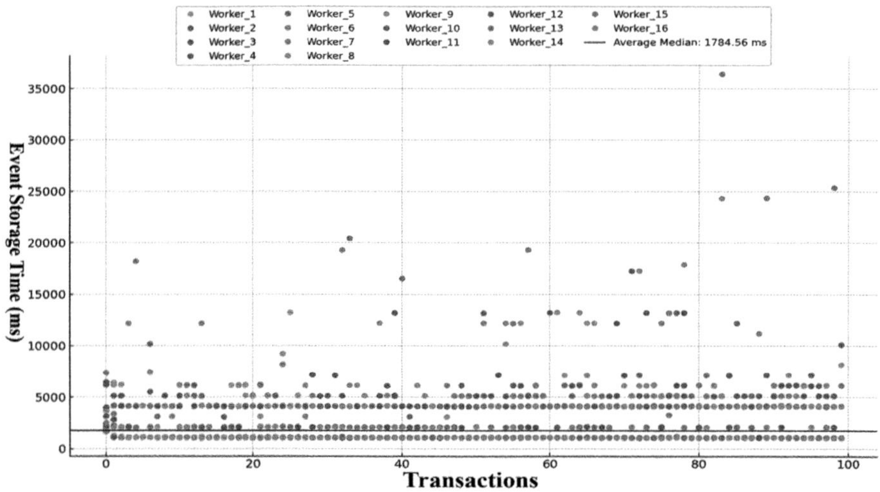

Fig. 12. IBFT 2.0 Lineage Storage Time with 16 Workers/1 s Block Period.

handles concurrent transactions efficiently without sacrificing performance. This makes QBFT the best-suited consensus algorithm for high-throughput environments, where consistent transaction times are crucial.

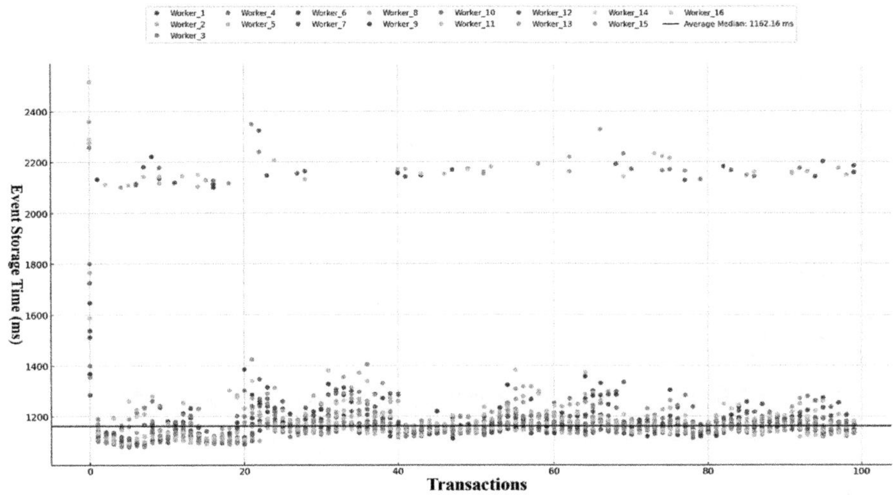

Fig. 13. QBFT Lineage Storage Time with 16 Workers/1 s Block Period.

4 Hash-Based Batch Lineage Event Storage Scenario (QBFT Blockchain, 1s Block Period)

In this experimental scenario, we used a QBFT Blockchain configuration with a 1-second block period to evaluate hash-based Lineage Event storage. Instead of storing full event data, only the hash of each Lineage Event was stored. The Smart Contract defined a mapping from a Lineage Event ID to the corresponding

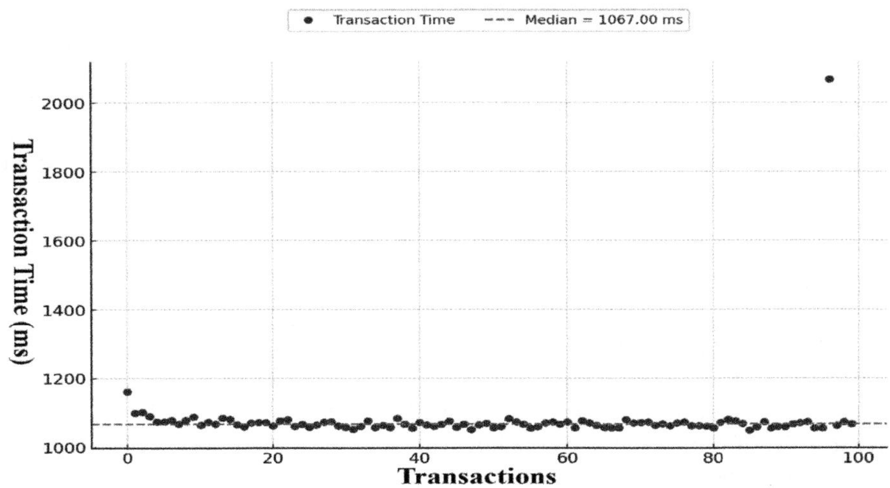

Fig. 14. Transaction Time for 1 Client.

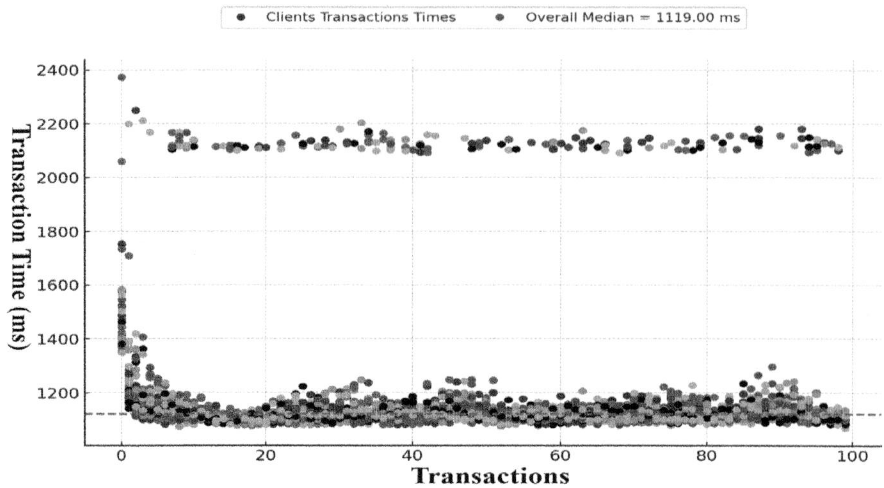

Fig. 15. Transaction Time for 32 Clients.

event hash. Each client executed 100 transactions, storing 50 events per transaction.

We tested client configurations ranging from 1 to 32 clients. At lower concurrency levels (1 to 8 clients), the median transaction times remained stable around 1100 ms, with minimal variation, as seen in Fig. 14. However, as the number of clients increased, variability grew. At 32 clients (Fig. 15), outliers became more frequent, with transaction times ranging between 1100 ms and 2400 ms. This suggests that while QBFT remains efficient even at higher client loads, resource contention starts to impact performance under extreme concurrency conditions.

Across all client configurations, QBFT maintained low median transaction times, indicating its robustness for hash-based event storage. The system displayed resilience to increasing client loads, though variability increased with higher concurrency, particularly beyond 16 clients. Despite this, QBFT demonstrated superior performance for applications requiring efficient storage and retrieval of hashed events, making it a strong candidate for scalable environments.

5 Conclusions

In conclusion, our analysis indicates that while public Blockchains offer the advantages of decentralization and security, they come with higher costs and slower performance compared to private Blockchains. Private Blockchains like Hyperledger Besu present a compelling case for applications where cost efficiency and performance are paramount.

Moreover, for applications prioritizing low latency and efficient storage times, QBFT is the preferred consensus algorithm, offering the best performance in the tested configurations. ETHASH, despite its widespread industrial use, is not optimal for storage-intensive operations due to its high latency. IBFT2.0, while better than ETHASH, still lags behind QBFT in both efficiency and scalability. Our study motivated by the storage of Lineage Events is agnostic to the technology that generates Lineage Events. Therefore, this study can be of interest for practitioners willing to use Blockchains as a secure distributed storage environment.

The hash-based Lineage Event storage scenario utilizing the QBFT Blockchain configuration demonstrates that while the median transaction times remain stable across increasing client loads, the variability in execution times grows with higher concurrency.

The system shows resilience in maintaining low median transaction times, but resource contention becomes a limiting factor in high-client scenarios, as evidenced by the increasing number of outliers. This analysis shows that the QBFT consensus algorithm provides robust performance under moderate concurrency but may face challenges under extreme loads.

References

1. Ethereum vs fabric vs corda: blockchain protocols compared. https://www.kaleido.io (2023)
2. Akbarfam, A.J., Heidaripour, M., Maleki, H., Dorai, G., Agrawal, G.: Forensiblock: a provenance-driven blockchain framework for data forensics and auditability. arXiv preprint arXiv:2308.03927 (2023)
3. Alabi, O., Beckman, J., Dark, M., Springer, J.: Towards a data spillage prevention process in hadoop using data provenance. In: Workshop on Changing Landscapes in HPC Security, pp. 9–13. ACM (2015). https://doi.org/10.1145/2874676.2874681
4. Apache atlas community: apache atlas documentation. Apache Software Foundation (2024), https://atlas.apache.org/. Accessed 17 Sep 2024
5. Armstrong, M.: Ethereum, smart contracts and the optimistic roll-up (2021)
6. Baird, L., Harmon, M., Madsen, P.: Hedera: a public hashgraph network and governing council. White Paper **1**(1), 9–10 (2019)
7. Bjelic, M., Nailwal, S., Chaudhary, A., Deng, W.: Pol: one token for all polygon chains (2017)
8. Buterin, V., et al.: A next-generation smart contract and decentralized application platform. white paper **3**(37), 2–1 (2014)
9. Choi, S.M., Park, J., Nguyen, Q., Cronje, A.: Fantom: a scalable framework for asynchronous distributed systems. arXiv preprint arXiv:1810.10360 (2018)
10. DataHub Community: DataHub Documentation. LinkedIn (2024). https://datahubproject.io/docs/. Accessed 17 Sep 2024
11. Fan, C., Lin, C., Khazaei, H., Musilek, P.: Performance analysis of hyperledger besu in private blockchain. In: 2022 IEEE international conference on decentralized applications and infrastructures (DAPPS), pp. 64–73. IEEE (2022)
12. Groves, W., et al.: Data lineage in big data systems: provenance management in apache hadoop. In: Proceedings of the Workshop on Secure Data Management, pp. 17–32. Springer (2015). https://doi.org/10.1007/978-3-319-12727-9_2
13. Guidi, B.: An overview of blockchain online social media from the technical point of view. Appl. Sci. **11**(21), 9880 (2021)

14. Haider, W., Hu, J., Xie, Y., Yu, X., Wu, Q.: Detecting anomalous behavior in cloud servers by nested-arc hidden semi-markov model with state summarization. IEEE Trans. Big Data **5**(3), 305–316 (2017). https://doi.org/10.1109/TBDATA.2017.2701362
15. Hammad, R., Barhoush, M., Abed-alguni, B.: A semantic-based approach for managing healthcare big data: a survey. J. Healthcare Eng. (2020). https://doi.org/10.1155/2020/8865808
16. Kalodner, H., Goldfeder, S., Chen, X., Weinberg, S.M., Felten, E.W.: Arbitrum: scalable, private smart contracts. In: 27th USENIX Security Symposium (USENIX Security 18). pp. 1353–1370 (2018)
17. Kaur, G., Gandhi, C.: Scalability in blockchain: challenges and solutions. In: Handbook of Research on Blockchain Technology, pp. 373–406. Elsevier (2020)
18. Khan, F., Soiland-Reyes, S., Goble, C.: Sharing interoperable workflow provenance: a review of best practices and their practical application in cwlprov. GigaScience **8**(11) (2019). https://doi.org/10.1093/gigascience/giz095
19. Maccioni, A., Torlone, R.: Kayak: a framework for just-in-time data preparation in a data lake. In: Krogstie, J., Reijers, H.A. (eds.) CAiSE 2018. LNCS, vol. 10816, pp. 474–489. Springer, Cham (2018). https://doi.org/10.1007/978-3-319-91563-0_29
20. OpenLineage community: openlineage documentation. The Linux Foundation (2024). https://openlineage.io/docs/. Accessed 17 Sep 2024
21. Ruan, P., Dinh, T.T.A., Lin, Q., Zhang, M., Chen, G., Ooi, B.C.: Revealing every story of data in blockchain systems. In: Proceedings of the 2019 ACM SIGMOD International Conference on Management of Data, pp. 123–140 (2019).https://doi.org/10.1145/3422648.3422665
22. Ruan, P., Dinh, T.T.A., Lin, Q., Zhang, M., Chen, G., Ooi, B.C.: Lineagechain: a fine-grained, secure and efficient data provenance system for blockchains. VLDB J. **30**(3), 3–24 (2020)
23. Sigwart, M., Borkowski, M., Peise, M., Schulte, S., Tai, S.: A secure and extensible blockchain-based data provenance framework for the internet of things. Pers. Ubiquit. Comput. **28**(1), 309–323 (2020)
24. Suen, C., Ko, R., Tan, Y., Jagadpramana, P., Lee, B.: S2logger: end-to-end data tracking mechanism for cloud data provenance. In: 12th IEEE International Conference on Trust, Security and Privacy in Computing and Communications, pp. 594–602. IEEE (2013). https://doi.org/10.1109/TrustCom.2013.70
25. Zhang, O., Ko, R., Kirchberg, M., Suen, C., Jagadpramana, P., Lee, B.: How to track your data: rule-based data provenance tracing algorithms. In: IEEE 11th International Conference on Trust, Security and Privacy in Computing and Communications, pp. 1429–1437. IEEE (2012). https://doi.org/10.1109/TrustCom.2012.404

Byzantine Fault-Tolerant Distributed Set Intersection with Redundancy and Its Relationship with Byzantine Optimization

Shuo Liu(✉) and Nitin H. Vaidya

Georgetown University, Washington DC 20057, USA
{sl1539,nitin.vaidya}@georgetown.edu

Abstract. In this paper, we study the problem of Byzantine fault-tolerant distributed set intersection and the importance of redundancy in solving this problem. Specifically, consider a distributed system with n agents, each of which has a local set. There are up to f agents that are Byzantine faulty. The goal is to find the intersection of the sets of the non-faulty agents. We are the first to consider the Byzantine set intersection problem with redundancy, and our problem formulation differs from prior works on related problems in different ways.

We derive the Byzantine set intersection problem from the Byzantine optimization problem. We present the definition of $2f$-set-redundancy for Byzantine set intersection, derived from $2f$-redundancy in Byzantine optimization – a necessary condition for Byzantine optimization to be solvable in server-based systems [11]. We study Byzantine set intersection in decentralized (server-less) systems, presenting the necessary and sufficient condition on the communication graph for the Byzantine set intersection problem to be solvable with $2f$-set-redundancy. Finally, we present solvability results for Byzantine optimization in decentralized systems, derived from our findings on Byzantine set intersection. Aside from the theoretical results, we also present two practical algorithms for Byzantine set intersection and optimization.

Keywords: Byzantine fault tolerance · Distributed algorithm

1 Introduction

Consider a distributed system of n agents, where each agent i has a local input set X_i. The goal of the Byzantine set intersection problem for the non-faulty agents is to collectively compute the intersection of the X_i's for all non-faulty agents i's despite the presence of up to f faulty agents, i.e., to find

$$\bigcap_{i\in\mathcal{V}\setminus F} X_i \tag{1}$$

where $\mathcal{V}$ is the set of all agents, and F is the set of Byzantine faulty agents with $|F| \leq f$. The identity of the Byzantine agents is unknown to other participants

S. Lahlou and M. Mukund (Eds.): NETYS 2025, LNCS 15736, pp. 97–113, 2026.
https://doi.org/10.1007/978-3-032-00347-8_6

in the system, the only assumption of the algorithms is the upper bound on the number of Byzantine agents f.

We call an algorithm that achieves this goal (1) f-set-resilient, or formally:

Definition 1 (f-set-resilience). *We say that an algorithm for Byzantine set intersection is* f-set-resilient *if it outputs the intersection of the sets of all non-faulty agents, defined in* (1), *in the presence of up to f Byzantine agents.*

It can be shown that the f-resilience for set intersection is generally not achievable when $f \geq 1$. Instead, in this paper, we consider the necessary and sufficient conditions such that an f-set-resilient algorithm exists.

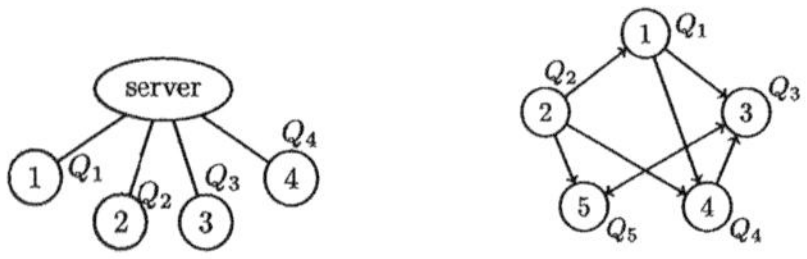

Fig. 1. Distributed system architectures. Server-based (left) and decentralized (right). The decentralized communication graph is directed and does not need to be fully connected.

There are two major architectures of a distributed system, shown in Fig. 1: (i) A *server-based* system consists of a (trusted) server and n agents, and communications happen only between the server and each agent, but not between pairs of agents. In this case, the server produces the final output. (ii) A *decentralized* system consists of only n agents, and communications happen between pairs of agents directly. In this case, all non-faulty agents should reach a consensus on the output. In a decentralized system, a directed graph $G(\mathcal{V}, \mathcal{E})$ can be used to describe the communication graph, where $\mathcal{V}$ is the set of agents, and $\mathcal{E}$ is the set of directed edges where $(i, j) \in \mathcal{E}$ if agent i can send messages to agent j. Unless otherwise stated, this paper assumes a *synchronous* and *decentralized* system.

Motivation. As we will show in Sect. 3, the Byzantine set intersection problem is related to the Byzantine optimization problem. Specifically, prior work has shown for a class of optimization algorithms that it is necessary for the cost functions to satisfy a redundancy property called $2f$*-redundancy* to solve the synchronous server-based Byzantine optimization problem exactly [11]. The $2f$-redundancy property indicates that the sets of minimum points of all non-faulty agents *intersect*, and the set of minimum points of the aggregate cost functions of non-faulty agents is the same as the *intersection* of the set of minimum points of each non-faulty agent. Inspired by this result, we find that the Byzantine set intersection problem is worth studying.

Also inspired by [11], we study the importance of *redundancy in the input* to the solvability of the Byzantine set intersection problem under various settings. In this paper, we pay special attention to the solvability of Byzantine set intersection when *$2f$-set-redundancy is satisfied*, due to the importance of $2f$-redundancy in Byzantine optimization. We will also discuss other fault models and other similar redundancy properties.

The Byzantine set intersection problem itself is significant to investigate, as the intersection is a fundamental mathematical operation with various applications, for example in wireless sensor networks or information retrieval [29].

We will also show in Sect. 5 that the solvability for Byzantine set intersection can in reverse also derive solvability of Byzantine optimization. Prior work focuses more on server-based [11] or fully connected communication graphs [10], while in this paper we study the problem in decentralized systems with communication graphs that are not necessarily fully connected. Byzantine optimization finds its various applications in swarm robotics [19], distributed sensing [18], and distributed machine learning [4], which also motivates this paper.

Our Contribution. In this paper, the main question we consider is the solvability of the Byzantine set intersection problem: given redundancy in the input sets, what conditions on the communication graphs are necessary and sufficient.

We first discuss the relationship between Byzantine set intersection and Byzantine optimization in Sect. 3. In Sect. 4, we propose a *$2f$-set-redundancy* property for Byzantine set intersection and present the conditions on the communication graph under which an f-set-resilient algorithm exists when $2f$-set-redundancy is satisfied. We will discuss two types of algorithms. We also extend these results to an asynchronous system, a generalized redundancy, and a link-failure model. Lastly, we present some necessity and sufficiency results on *decentralized Byzantine optimization* in Sect. 5 that are related to the results we obtain for Byzantine set intersection.

We present an efficient Byzantine set intersection algorithm for special cases in Sect. 4.2, demonstrating that some constraints on the input sets can help improve the efficiency of the algorithm. For Byzantine optimization, we also present a practical approximate Byzantine optimization algorithm inspired by our studies in Byzantine set intersection in Sect. 5.2.

Most of the *proofs* of results in this paper are omitted, but will be included in a full version made available on arXiv [14].

2 Related Work

To the best of our knowledge, we are the first to consider the Byzantine set intersection problem with redundancy in the input. However, there are previous studies on problems related to the Byzantine distributed set intersection problems. *Certified propagation algorithms* (CPA) [12,17,24,25] are proposed for a problem in the presence of Byzantine faults, where there is a source agent in a distributed network with an initial input, and that value needs to be transmitted to all other agents. Prior work on this problem typically assumes a *f-local* model where for every non-faulty agent, up to f incoming neighbors are Byzantine faulty. The set intersection problem can be adapted to a propagation problem:

imagine there is a "virtual" source agent in a distributed network for a set intersection problem, where for each value $y \notin \bigcap_{i \in \mathcal{V}} X_i$, it needs to propagate a value 0 to all other agents, in other words, all agents should end up with knowing that y is not in $\bigcap_{i \in \mathcal{V}} X_i$. It is worth noting that we can derive the *necessary* conditions for Byzantine set intersection from certified propagation in the above way. But we cannot directly apply CPAs to actually solve Byzantine set intersection. Instead, we present our own algorithms to show sufficiency. Also, in the certified propagation problem, the algorithm is assumed [24]; while our proof of necessary conditions for Byzantine set intersection does not assume a specific algorithm.

Another line of work studies the *lattice agreement* problem [1,31]: On a complete graph connecting n agents, each agent proposes a local value in a *finite join semi-lattice.* The goal is for each agent to decide on a value in the lattice such that the values of every pair of agents are comparable. The sets in a set intersection problem can be defined as a lattice with subset relation being the partial order and the union operation of sets being the join operation of the lattice. Then, the problems of lattice agreement and set intersection are similar. However, lattice agreement only requires each agent to decide on *comparable* values, while the set intersection problem requires agreement on the *same* intersection. Furthermore, in general, the Byzantine set intersection problem in this paper does not require a complete communication graph. Also, we explore a special case where the input sets have a certain form of redundancy, introduced later.

We borrow the notions of *reduced graph* and *source component* from prior works [20–22,26,27], introduced later in Sect. 4.1. However, some of them study other problems like distributed state estimation [21], hypothesis testing with crash failures [22], and iterative Byzantine consensus [26]. In these three works, a reduced graph is allowed to remove up to f incoming links, but only one source component is allowed in the reduced graph while we allow multiple. Byzantine consensus and non-Bayesian learning with a reduced graph are studied in [20], allowing removing up to df incoming links where d is the dimension of the target vector, while we only allow removing f. Non-Bayesian learning is studied in [27], where it allows multiple source clusters like in our results, but also allows the removal of up to mf incoming links. Apart from studying different problems, our condition is more relaxed than the above ones in one aspect or another.

Decentralized Byzantine hypothesis testing and non-Bayesian learning are studied in [15], providing necessary and sufficient conditions. However, the conditions are defined for a certain joint observation profile, while our results are for all possible input sets, resulting in a simpler algorithm. Also, the f-local model is considered in [15], while we study the f-global and link failure models.

It is pointed out in [7] that, in a synchronous undirected graph, for every node to broadcast its value to every other non-Byzantine faulty node in the graph, we need to have $(2f + 1)$-connectivity. Such a condition is both necessary and sufficient, for both *routed networks*, where every agent is aware beforehand of the routes through which other agents will send messages, and *unknown networks*, where every agent only knows its direct neighbor, but not the topology of the network or routes which it will receive messages. Also, it is shown via Menger's

Theorem [3], that if $(2f+1)$-connectivity is satisfied, for every pair of nodes in the graph, there are $2f+1$ disjoint paths. Similar results regarding the necessity of $(2f+1)$-connectivity in reliable communication are also presented in [8,9].

The solvability of Byzantine optimization in server-based systems is relatively well-studied [11,13]. Our work is inspired by [11], including the redundancy properties, discussed more in Sect. 3. However, this paper focuses on Byzantine set intersection and optimization in decentralized systems. The solvability of Byzantine optimization in a decentralized system with $2f$-redundancy is studied in [10], but the authors only examines a fully connected communication graph while our results in Sect. 5 apply to generalized communication graphs.

3 From Optimization to Set Intersection

The Byzantine set intersection problem is related to the Byzantine optimization problem. Recall that we defined $\mathcal{V}$ to be the set of all agents, and F to be the set of Byzantine agents in a given execution with $|F| \leq f$. In Byzantine optimization [2,6,11,30], each agent i has a local input cost function $Q_i(x)$, and the problem asks the non-faulty agents to collaboratively compute $\widehat{x}$, such that

$$\widehat{x} \in \arg\min_x \textstyle\sum_{i \in \mathcal{V} \setminus F} Q_i(x), \tag{2}$$

in the presence of up to f Byzantine faulty agents. Algorithms that achieve this goal are called f-resilient [11], or formally

Definition 2 (f-resilience[11]). *A distributed optimization algorithm is f-resilient, if it outputs a minimum point of the aggregate cost function of all non-faulty agents, despite the presence of up to f Byzantine faulty agents.*

Assuming cost functions are convex and differentiable and a minimum point $\arg\min_x \sum_{i \in \mathcal{V} \setminus F} Q_i(x)$ exists, for a class of algorithms it is necessary to have $2f$-redundancy for an f-resilient algorithm to exist in server-based system [11]:

Definition 3 ($2f$-redundancy, cf. [11]). *For a set $\mathcal{V}$ of n agents, the local input cost functions $Q_i(x)$'s of the n agents are said to satisfy the $2f$-redundancy if* (i) $\bigcap_{i \in \mathcal{V}} \arg\min_x Q_i(x) \neq \varnothing$, *and* (ii) *for every subset $S \subseteq \mathcal{V}$ with $|S| \geq n-2f$,*

$$\arg\min_x \textstyle\sum_{i \in S} Q_i(x) = \arg\min_x \sum_{i \in \mathcal{V}} Q_i(x). \tag{3}$$

Let us denote, for any agent i and any set of agents S, $X_i \triangleq \arg\min_x Q_i(x)$ and $X_S \triangleq \arg\min_x \sum_{i \in S} Q_i(x)$. It can be shown that the above property is equivalent to the following property over the minimum sets of $Q_i(x)$'s.

Definition 4. *The cost functions $Q_i(x)$'s of a set $\mathcal{V}$ of n agents are said to satisfy $2f$-redundancy, if $\bigcap_{i \in \mathcal{V}} X_i \neq \varnothing$, and for any point $y \notin \bigcap_{i \in \mathcal{V}} X_i$, there exist at least $2f+1$ agents i, such that $y \notin X_i$.*

Remark. Both Definitions 3 and 4 define their properties over the input functions of all n agents. However, even in executions where up to f agents are Byzantine faulty, the property still provides useful constraints on the input cost functions of non-faulty agents. Consider the following examples:

- Definition 3 states that for every $S \subseteq \mathcal{V}$ with $|S| \geq n-2f$, (3) holds. Suppose in an execution, the set $F \subset \mathcal{V}$ contains all Byzantine agents, $|F| \leq f$. Therefore, $|\mathcal{V} \backslash F| \geq n-f \geq n-2f$. Because of $2f$-redundancy, we can still derive from (3) that $\arg\min_x \sum_{i \in S} Q_i(x) = \arg\min_x \sum_{i \in \mathcal{V} \backslash F} Q_i(x)$ for all $S \subseteq \mathcal{V} \backslash F$ with $|S| \geq n-2f$, which is a useful property since the right side of the above equation is in the goal of Byzantine optimization (2).
- Similarly, suppose in an execution, the set F contains all Byzantine agents with $|F| \triangleq \phi \leq f$. Then for any point $y \notin \bigcap_{i \in \mathcal{V}} X_i$, it follows from the property in Definition 4 that $y \notin \bigcap_{i \in \mathcal{V} \backslash F} X_i$ as well, since there should be at least $2f - \phi + 1$ non-faulty agents i such that $y \notin X_i$.

Intuitively, we can imagine that each agent i has an input cost function $Q_i(x)$ (even for Byzantine agents), and these n functions satisfy the $2f$-redundancy property together. However, in any execution, up to f agents may become Byzantine: they may behave arbitrarily, and their real functions may remain unknown to the non-faulty agents. Yet the cost functions of non-faulty agents remain the same and still observe the redundancy provided by $2f$-redundancy.

Note that Definition 4 is a property on the *intersection* of minimum sets, motivating this paper to study the *Byzantine set intersection* problem. Particularly, In Sect. 4, we consider Byzantine set intersection when redundancy is provided. We present the necessary and sufficient conditions on the communication graph for the problem to be solvable.

4 Byzantine Set Intersection with 2*f*-Set-Redundancy

In this section, we study the Byzantine set intersection problem directly. Specifically, we explore the necessary and sufficient conditions for an f-set-resilient algorithm to exist if some set redundancy is satisfied.

Recall the definition of Byzantine set intersection in Sect. 1, where there are n agents in the distributed system, and each agent i has a local input set X_i. The goal is to find the intersection of all non-faulty agents $X_{\mathcal{V} \backslash F} = \bigcap_{i \in \mathcal{V} \backslash F} X_i$ in the presence of up to f Byzantine agents, where $\mathcal{V}$ is the set of all agents and F is the set of all Byzantine faulty agents in any execution.

Note that in the remainder of this paper, we concentrate on the situation where the goal (1) is not empty. However, we would like to note that all conditions are still correct if the intersection is empty.

To begin with, we formally define $2f$*-set-redundancy* from a distributed set intersection perspective, instead of a property of cost functions. Note again that the $2f$-set-redundancy property is defined with respect to the input sets of all n agents, and the behavior of Byzantine agents may not necessarily be consistent with their input sets. However, even in executions where up to f agents are faulty, the property provides useful constraints on input sets of non-faulty agents.

Definition 5 (2f-set-redundancy). *The input sets X_i's of a set $\mathcal{V}$ of n agents are said to satisfy 2f-set-redundancy, if $\bigcap_{i\in\mathcal{V}} X_i \neq \varnothing$, and for any point $y \notin \bigcap_{i\in\mathcal{V}} X_i$, there exist at least $2f+1$ agents i, such that $y \notin X_i$.*

Remark. Note that following our discussion in the previous section, 2f-redundancy for n cost functions (Definition 3) is equivalent to 2f-set-redundancy for the minimum sets of these n cost functions. We will use this property again in Sect. 5.

4.1 Constrained Algorithms in a Decentralized Architecture

Recall that in a decentralized architecture, there is no server and the n agents communicate directly to each other. The *communication graph* $G(\mathcal{V},\mathcal{E})$ can be used to describe the connections of the agents, where $\mathcal{V}$ is the set of n agents, and $\mathcal{E}$ is a set of directed edges. An edge $(i,j)\in\mathcal{E}$ represents that agent i can send information to agent j. Let us also define $N_i^- = \{j|(j,i)\in\mathcal{E}\}$ for any agent i to be the set of *incoming neighbors* of i. Note that throughout the remainder of this paper, we define $i \notin N_i^-$ for all $i\in\mathcal{V}$ (or equivalently $(i,i)\notin\mathcal{E}$), but agent i knows its local set nonetheless.

In an iterative algorithm starting with iteration 0, let us denote X_i^t to be the local set of agent i at the beginning of iteration t with $X_i^0 \triangleq X_i$. Also, recall that we denote by F the set of faulty agents in any execution.

Now, we consider a class of *constrained algorithms* that can maintain only a local set X_i^t for each agent i in each iteration t and no additional state. A *correct* f-set-resilient iterative set intersection algorithm must satisfy these criteria:

- **Validity**: $\forall t>0$, $X_i^t \subseteq X_i^{t-1}$; and
- **Convergence**: There exists a finite τ such that after τ iterations, $X_i^\tau = X_{\mathcal{V}\setminus F}$, for all $i\in\mathcal{V}\setminus F$.

In each iteration, each agent may only send their own set to their outgoing neighbors, receive the sets of incoming neighbors, and update the local set according to the received information. This class of algorithms is worth studying due to simplicity. Similar algorithms maintaining only a small amount of states are commonly studied in distributed optimization [16] and consensus [23,26].

Note that the problem becomes trivial when $n \le 2f+1$ due to 2f-set-redundancy: it is necessary to have $X_i = X_j$ for all $i,j\in\mathcal{V}$ for an f-set-resilient algorithm to exist. This condition is also sufficient: an f-set-resilient algorithm only needs each non-faulty agent to output its input set directly. For the remainder of this section, we assume $n \ge 2f+2$.

It can be shown that with 2f-set-redundancy, the condition on the communication graph in the following theorem is both necessary and sufficient for a constrained f-resilient Byzantine set intersection algorithm to exist.

Theorem 1. *Assume that the number of agents $n \ge 2f+2$. Suppose 2f-set-redundancy is satisfied. A constrained f-set-resilient algorithm exists, if and only if the communication graph satisfies the following:*

For any partition of G into L, R, F, $|F| \le f$, the following conditions hold:

a) If $|R| \geq f+1$*, there exists an agent* $i \in L$*,* $|N_i^- \cap R| \geq f+1$*, and*
b) If $|L| \geq f+1$*, there exists an agent* $i \in R$*,* $|N_i^- \cap L| \geq f+1$.

Note that, as alluded to in Sect. 2, the necessity of the above condition can also be obtained by reducing set intersection to a set of *certified propagation* problems, and then applying the results in [24]. Suppose $2f$-set-redundancy is satisfied. For every subset of agents $F \subset \mathcal{V}$ with $|F| \leq f$, for every value $y \notin \bigcap_{i \in \mathcal{V} \setminus F} X_i$, we add a virtual source node $v_{F,y}$ to the graph G that has out-going links to all nodes i such that $y \notin X_i$. Denote by $E_{v_{F,y}}$ the out-going links of $v_{F,y}$. The necessary condition for certified propagation [24] should be satisfied on the *augmented graph* $G_{v_{F,y}}(\mathcal{V} \cup \{v_{F,y}\}, \mathcal{E} \cup E_{v_{F,y}})$, such that the information of "not having y" can be propagated from $v_{F,y}$ to all other nodes in $G_{v_{F,y}}$. Therefore, the necessary graph condition for an f-set-resilient algorithm to exist given $2f$-set-redundancy is a graph G such that the necessary condition for certified propagation should be satisfied for the augmented graphs $G_{v_{F,y}}$ created by all possible F and y.

The following algorithm can be used to show the sufficiency part of the above theorem: Each agent i sets its set X_i^0 to be its input set. In each iteration t,

Step 1 Each agent i sends the set X_i^t to all agents j with $(i,j) \in \mathcal{E}$. Byzantine faulty agent may send arbitrary set.
Step 2 Each agent j receives sets from all agents in N_j^-. For each agent $k \in N_j^-$, denote the set j receives by Z_k^t. For a non-faulty agent k, $Z_k^t = X_k^t$. For a Byzantine agent l, Z_l^t can be an arbitrary set.
Step 3 Each agent i updates its set: Initiate the set Y_i^t to be empty. For any point $y \in X_i^t$, if there are more than f agents $j \in N_i^-$ such that $y \notin Z_j^t$, add y to the set Y_i^t. Then, the local set of i is updated as $X_i^{t+1} \leftarrow X_i^t \setminus Y_i^t$.

It is worth noting that this algorithm is similar to the protocols in [12,25]. However, our algorithm is for a different problem in a different system setting.

Note that the above algorithm we use to show sufficiency is only practical when the input sets have finite elements. We present an efficient algorithm for some special cases of continuous input sets in Sect. 4.2.

An Equivalent Necessary Condition. Now, we present a condition equivalent to the condition in Theorem 1. This equivalent condition provides additional insights into the structure of the communication graphs where the Byzantine set intersection problem is solvable with $2f$-set-redundancy.

Note that the terms *agent* and *node* are used interchangeably, both referring to an element in $\mathcal{V}$ in the communication graph. We first introduce some definitions based on prior work [26] on iterative consensus:

Definition 6 ([26]). *a) Let* H *be a directed graph. A strongly connected component* H_k *of* H *is said to be a* source component *if it is maximal and there is no incoming link from any other node in* H*. b) For a given graph* $G(\mathcal{V}, \mathcal{E})$ *and* $F \subset \mathcal{V}$*, a graph* $G_F(\mathcal{V}_F, \mathcal{E}_F)$ *is a* reduced graph *of* G*, if* (i) $\mathcal{V}_F = \mathcal{V} - F$*, and*

(ii) $\mathcal{E}_F$ *is obtained by first removing all links incident on the nodes in* F, *and then removing up to* f *other incoming links at each node in* $\mathcal{V}_F$.

Note that for a given graph G and set F, multiple reduced graphs G_F may exist. With the above definitions, it can be shown that the following condition is equivalent to the condition in Theorem 1.

Definition 7. *A graph is said to satisfy the* reduced graph condition, *if for any* $F \subset \mathcal{V}$ *such that* $|F| \leq f$, *in every reduced graph* G_F *obtained as per Definition 6, size of any source component is at least* $n - 2f$.

Remark 1. We have the following observations following the equivalent reduced graph condition.

- *If* $n > 3f$, *the condition in Theorem* 1 *(or equivalently, the reduced graph condition) implies that there is only one source component in any reduced graph* G_F *of graph* G. This result gives us some more insight into the communication graph structure when our problem is solvable with $2f$-set-redundancy.
- *Suppose that the condition in Theorem* 1 *holds for graph* $G(\mathcal{V}, \mathcal{E})$, *and* $n \geq 2f + 2$. *For any* $F \subset \mathcal{V}$ *such that* $|F| = \phi \leq f$, *in every reduced graph* G_F *obtained as per Definition* 6, *the size of any source component* $\geq n - \phi - f$.

4.2 An Efficient Algorithm for Special Cases

The algorithm we used to show sufficiency in Theorem 1 is impractical when the input sets are continuous. We now show that some constraints imposed on input sets can be exploited to improve the efficiency of the algorithm. The following algorithm can solve Byzantine set intersection when the input sets are hyperrectangles. For convenience, we discuss this algorithm for the cases where the input sets are in the 1-dimensional space, i.e., they are line segments, but the algorithm can be easily extended to higher dimensions.

We use the following notations: denote a line segment on $\mathbb{R}^1$ with endpoints A and B by $[A, B]$ if the set is closed at both endpoints, by $[A, B)$ if it is closed at A but open at B, and by (A, B) if it is open at both endpoints. The *size* of a line segment $[A, B]$ is defined as its length $B - A$.

We make the following assumptions: (i) the intersection of all non-faulty agents is non-empty, (ii) the input sets satisfy $2f$-set-redundancy, and (iii) the communication graph satisfies the condition in Theorem 1. Note that any point t on $\mathbb{R}^1$ is equivalent to a closed segment $[t, t]$ too, with its two endpoints identical.

With the above assumptions, we now present an algorithm for set intersection in the case when the input set of each agent i is a closed line segment $X_i = [L_i, R_i]$, where $L_i \leq R_i$ are the two endpoints of the line segment. The algorithm below ensures that the set at each agent i at the start of each round $t > 0$ is also a closed line segment, which will be denoted as $X_i^t = [L_i^t, R_i^t]$. Since the problem is defined on $\mathbb{R}^1$, we use the terms "point" and "value" interchangeably.

It can be shown that the following iterative algorithm solves the above special case of Byzantine set intersection problem: In each iteration $t = 0, 1, 2, ...,$

Step 1 Each agent i sends the two endpoints L_i^t and R_i^t of its local line segment X_i^t to all agents j with $(i, j) \in \mathcal{E}$. Byzantine agent may send arbitrary values.

Step 2 Each agent j receives two endpoints from all agents in N_j^-. For each agent $k \in N_j^-$, denote the two endpoints j receives from k by LI_k^t and RI_k^t. For a non-faulty agent k, $LI_k^t = L_k^t$ and $RI_k^t = R_k^t$. For a Byzantine agent l, LI_l^t and RI_l^t can be two arbitrary values. If an agent l does not send two points LI_l^t and RI_l^t with $LI_l^t \leq RI_l^t$, then agent l must be Byzantine, and j assumes $LI_l^t = L_j^t$ and $RI_l^t = R_j^t$ as placeholders.

Step 3 Each agent i updates its set by the following rule: Denote by $Z_j^t \triangleq [LI_j^t, RI_j^t]$. Initialize Y_i^t as an empty set. For any point $y \in X_i^t$, if there are more than f agents $j \in N_j^-$ such that $y \notin Z_j^t$, add y to the set Y_i^t.
Recall that the size of $[A, B]$ is $B - A$. X_i^{t+1} is chosen as the subset of X_i^t with the smallest size such that X_i^{t+1} is a closed segment and $X_i^t - X_i^{t+1} \subseteq Y_i^t$.

Compared to the algorithm in the sufficiency proof of Theorem 1, this section's algorithm requires each agent's input set to be convex and closed. However, instead of sending the whole local set, this algorithm only requires sending two points per communication. Also, in Step 3, each agent i does not need to iterate through every point $y \in X_i^t$, but only to iterate through the endpoints that agent i receives to determine if each segment between neighboring endpoints is in Y_i^t. In each iteration, an agent can receive at most $2n$ endpoints.

The algorithm can be extended to a 2-dimensional, and further to a d-dimensional case, where integer $d \geq 1$ and the local set of each non-faulty agent is a closed d-dimensional hyperrectangle with edges in parallel with coordinate lines in d-dimensional Euclidean space. Such a hyperrectangle is diametrically representable: it can be specified using two diametrically opposite corner points.

With the algorithms in this section, we have shown that some additional knowledge on the input sets can be exploited to reduce communication overhead.

4.3 Unconstrained Algorithms in a Decentralized Architecture

In this section, we remove the constraints over the algorithms in the previous section, that is, the algorithm can maintain more information than a local set. As such, the requirement of Validity and Convergence are also removed. Instead, suppose $F \subset \mathcal{V}$ is the set of Byzantine agents with $|F| \leq f$, an unconstrained f-set-resilient set intersection algorithm must satisfy the following criteria:

- **Correctness**: Each agent $i \in \mathcal{V} \backslash F$ will decide on $X_{\mathcal{V} \backslash F}$ as its output in finite time.

Let us denote by $G - S$ with $S \subseteq \mathcal{V}$ the graph obtained by removing all nodes in S and all edges incident on the nodes in S. Recall the following definitions of k-connectivity in graph theory [28]: A *separating set* or a *vertex cut* of a directed graph G is a set $S \subseteq \mathcal{V}$ such that the graph $G - S$ is not strongly connected. A directed graph G is *k-connected* if every separating set has at least k vertices.

The result below can be derived using similar techniques and arguments for previous results in unanimity and reliable communication [7,9], where it states that for every node to broadcast its value to every correct node we need $(2f+1)$-connectivity. Similar findings are also presented in [8].

Theorem 2. *Suppose $2f$-set-redundancy is satisfied, and $n \geq 2f+2$. An f-set-resilient Byzantine set intersection algorithm exists, if and only if the communication graph G is $(2f+1)$-connected.*

This result indicates that $(2f+1)$-connectivity is still necessary even when $2f$-set-redundancy is satisfied. This result is included for completeness.

4.4 Extensions of the Constrained Case

The results for constrained algorithms can be easily extended to the following three cases, each has a necessary and sufficient condition similar to Theorem 1 when a variation of the redundancy condition is provided:

- Constrained algorithms in *asynchronous* systems, where any message sent will be delivered *eventually*, but with unbounded delay, with $3f$-set-redundancy provided and $n \geq 3f+2$.
- *Link failure model*, where there are no Byzantine agents in the system, but in each iteration up to f links are Byzantine faulty and may relay arbitrary messages, with f-set-redundancy provided and $n \geq f+2$.
- When provided with a more generalized $(2f+k)$-set-redundancy ($k \geq 0$), the Byzantine set intersection problem is solvable with a generalization of the condition in Theorem 1. This result suggests that when more redundancy is provided, the condition on the communication graph for Byzantine set intersection becomes weaker.

The $3f$-, f-, and $(2f+k)$-set-redundancy are defined similar to $2f$-set-redundancy, by replacing $2f+1$ in Definition 5 with $3f+1$, $f+1$, and $2f+k+1$, respectively.

5 From Set Intersection to Optimization

Recall from Sect. 2 that, although the Byzantine optimization problem in a server-based architecture is well studied in its solvability [11,13], it is not so for the problem in a decentralized architecture.

Inspired by the relationship between the Byzantine set intersection and optimization problems, discussed in Sect. 3, we now derive some solvability results of Byzantine distributed optimization in a decentralized system using the results in the previous two sections.

Let us first recall that we defined constrained and unconstrained set intersection algorithms in Sects. 4.1 and 4.3, respectively. In this section, we also consider constrained and unconstrained optimization algorithms.

5.1 Theoretical Results

Let us start by revisiting some related results bridging optimization and set intersection from the previous sections: Theorem 1 shows a necessary and sufficient condition for an f-set-resilient algorithm to exist if $2f$-set-redundancy is satisfied. Also, in Sect. 3 we discussed that $2f$-redundancy on n cost functions derives $2f$-set-redundancy on the minimum sets of these cost functions.

Now, we consider a specific type of constrained optimization algorithms, similar to the constrained set intersection algorithms defined in Sect. 4.1. Specifically, the algorithm is iterative, and in each iteration t, each agent i of a constrained Byzantine optimization algorithm in a decentralized system is constrained to maintain only a local estimate x_i^t and no additional state. Each agent arbitrarily chooses the initial local estimate at the beginning of the algorithm. In each iteration, each non-faulty agent can only send its local estimate to its outgoing neighbors, receive its local estimate from its incoming neighbors, and update its local estimate.

Suppose the optimization problem is defined on an arbitrary region $\mathcal{W} \subseteq \mathbb{R}^d$. Consider the following assumptions:

Assumption 1. *The cost functions of non-faulty agents are convex and differentiable.*

Assumption 2. *The minimum set of the aggregate of all cost functions* $\arg\min_{x\in\mathcal{W}} \sum_{i\in\mathcal{V}} Q_i(x)$ *only has 1 point.*

Note that Assumption 2 is rather strong, but to utilize our set intersection results from previous sections to derive results in this section, we need this assumption.

Suppose Assumption 2 is satisfied, F is the set of all Byzantine faulty agents with $|F| \leq f$, and $x_{\mathcal{V}\backslash F} = \arg\min_{x\in\mathcal{W}} \sum_{i\in\mathcal{V}\backslash F} Q_i(x)$ is the unique minimum of the aggregate cost function of all non-faulty agents. A *correct* f-resilient constrained Byzantine optimization algorithm should satisfy the following criteria:

- **Convergence**: When the number of iterations $t \to \infty$, $x_i^t \to x_{\mathcal{V}\backslash F}$ for all $i \in \mathcal{V}\backslash F$; and
- **Stability**: Once the local estimate x_i^t of a non-faulty agent i is updated to $x_{\mathcal{V}\backslash F}$, it will no longer change in any of the following iterations.

It can be shown that with $2f$-redundancy, the condition in Theorem 1 is also necessary for a constrained Byzantine optimization algorithm to exist, using techniques similar to the necessity proof of Theorem 1.

Theorem 3. *Suppose* $2f$*-redundancy is satisfied, and* $n \geq 2f + 2$. *If Assumptions 1 and 2 hold, a deterministic constrained* f*-resilient Byzantine optimization algorithm exists only if the graph condition in Theorem 1 is satisfied.*

For *sufficiency*, it is possible to solve the Byzantine optimization problem in decentralized systems by utilizing constrained Byzantine set intersection algorithms discussed in the previous sections, with the conditions in Theorem 3 satisfied. The algorithm showing sufficiency is as follows: Each agent computes the minimum set of their local cost function, runs a constrained Byzantine set intersection algorithm to find the intersection of those sets, and outputs an identical point in the output of the Byzantine set intersection algorithm.

Note that this Byzantine optimization algorithm is not the constrained algorithm defined in this section. However, it is still worth pointing out that this algorithm is f-resilient and can solve the Byzantine optimization problem if the conditions in Theorem 3 are satisfied.

For unconstrained algorithms, there is no restriction on what state each agent can maintain. Suppose $F \subset \mathcal{V}$ is the set of Byzantine agents with $|F| \leq f$, an unconstrained f-resilient optimization algorithm must satisfy this criteria:

- **Correctness**: Each agent $i \in \mathcal{V} \backslash F$ will decide on the same minimum point of the aggregate cost function of all non-faulty agents $x^* \in \arg\min_{x \in \mathcal{W}} \sum_{i \in \mathcal{V} \backslash F} Q_i(x)$ as its output in finite time.

For the Byzantine optimization problem on a decentralized distributed system with $2f$-redundancy, we have the following necessity and sufficiency results on the communication graph:

Theorem 4. *Suppose $2f$-redundancy is satisfied, and $n \geq 2f+2$. (i) If Assumptions 1 and 2 hold, a deterministic unconstrained f-resilient Byzantine optimization algorithm exists only if the graph condition in Theorem 2 is satisfied. (ii) If Assumption 1 holds, a deterministic unconstrained f-resilient Byzantine optimization algorithm exists if the graph condition in Theorem 2 is satisfied.*

5.2 Practical Approximate Byzantine Optimization Algorithm with Byzantine Set Intersection Algorithms

The algorithms in the previous part of this section only show the sufficiency of Byzantine optimization. We now present a framework of a more practical approach that applies a Byzantine set intersection algorithm to solve a decentralized Byzantine optimization problem assuming $2f$-redundancy in cost functions.

Consider a decentralized Byzantine optimization problem on a convex and compact region $\mathcal{W} \subseteq \mathbb{R}^d$. We make Assumption 1 and the following assumptions on the cost functions of agents. Note that these assumptions are also common in analysis of the practical algorithms in prior work on server-based Byzantine optimization [11,13].

Assumption 3 (Lipschitz smoothness). *For each non-faulty cost function $Q_i(x)$ of agent i, we assume that the gradient of its cost function $\nabla Q_i(x)$ is Lipschitz continuous, i.e., there exists a finite real value $\mu > 0$ such that*

$$\left\| \nabla Q_i(x) - \nabla Q_i(x') \right\| \leq \mu \left\| x - x' \right\|, \quad \forall x, x' \in \mathcal{W}. \tag{4}$$

Assumption 4 (Relaxed strong convexity). *For a non-empty set of non-faulty agents S, let $Q_S(x)$ denote the average cost function of the agents in S, i.e.,*

$$Q_S(x) = \frac{1}{|S|} \sum_{i \in S} Q_i(x).$$

Denote by $X_S \triangleq \arg\min_{x\in\mathcal{W}} \sum_{i\in S} Q_i(x)$*, and* $[x]_{X_S}$ *the Euclidean projection of any point* $x \in \mathcal{W}$ *on the set* X_S*. For each such set* S *with* $|S| = n - 2f$*, we assume that there exists a finite real value* $\gamma > 0$ *such that, for all* $x \in \mathcal{W}$*,*

$$\langle \nabla Q_S(x), x - [x]_{X_S} \rangle \geq \gamma \left\| x - [x]_{X_S} \right\|^2, \quad \forall x \in \mathcal{W}.$$

Assumption 5 (Existence of solution). *For every non-empty set of non-faulty agents* S*, we assume that the set* $\arg\min_{x\in\mathcal{W}} \sum_{i\in S} Q_i(x)$ *is non-empty and closed, and that* $\arg\min_{x\in W} \sum_{i\in S} Q_i(x) = \arg\min_{x\in\mathbb{R}^d} \sum_{i\in S} Q_i(x)$*, i.e., the minimum set of the aggregate cost function of agents in* S *in* $\mathcal{W}$ *is the same as that in* $\mathbb{R}^d$*.*

Note that following Assumptions 1 and 5, the minimum set of each non-faulty cost function Q_i, $X_i = \arg\min_{x\in\mathcal{W}} Q_i(x)$, is also convex, and therefore, the Euclidean projection of every point x on X_S exists and is unique [5].

For convenience, for a parameter $\epsilon > 0$, let us call the points that can be parameterized by the format of $(a_1\epsilon, ..., a_d\epsilon)$, where $a_1, ..., a_d$ are d integers, ϵ-*parameterizable* in $\mathbb{R}^d$. Furthermore, let us call the set of all points in $\mathcal{W}$ that are ϵ-parameterizable an ϵ-*grid* in $\mathcal{W}$. Two points x and y on an ϵ-grid are *neighbors*, if $x = (a_1\epsilon, ..., a_d\epsilon)$ and $y = (b_1\epsilon, ..., b_d\epsilon)$ for integers a_i's and b_i's and $\sum_{i=1}^d |a_i - b_i| = 1$.

Suppose the cost functions of non-faulty agents satisfy the $2f$-redundancy property, and the graph condition in Theorem 1 is satisfied. We also assume that $\mathcal{W}$ is large enough to contain at least one ϵ-parameterizable point. Consider the following algorithm with a predetermined hyperparameter ϵ:

Step 1 Search all points on the ϵ-grid in $\mathcal{W}$, and let the set $\widehat{X}_i$ be the set of all points $\widehat{x}_i$'s on the discrete grid with $\|\nabla Q_i(\widehat{x}_i)\| \leq \frac{\sqrt{d}}{2}\mu\epsilon$.

Step 2 Each agents run the Byzantine set intersection algorithm in the proof of Theorem 1 on the sets $\widehat{X}_i$'s for $n - f$ iterations.

Step 3 Each agent outputs one point in the output set obtained after completing the Byzantine set intersection algorithm.

Suppose $F \subseteq \mathcal{V}$ is the set of all Byzantine agents in a given execution with $|F| \leq f$. It can be shown that the above algorithm has the following property:

Theorem 5. *Suppose Assumptions 1, 3, 4, and 5 hold. The input cost functions satisfy* $2f$*-redundancy, and the graph condition in Theorem 1 is satisfied. In the presence of up to* f *Byzantine agents in a decentralized system, suppose the output of the above algorithm by each non-faulty agent* i *is* x_i*. We have:*

i) The outputs of all non-faulty agents are not guaranteed to reach consensus, i.e., it is possible to have non-faulty agents i, j*,* $x_i \neq x_j$*.*

ii) For any non-faulty agent i*, there exists a true minimum point of the Byzantine optimization problem* x_i^**, such that* $\|x_i, x_i^*\| \leq \sqrt{d}\mu\epsilon/2\gamma$*, where* d *is the dimension of the space where the functions* Q_i*'s are defined.*

iii) For any two non-faulty agents i, j,

$$\|x_i - x_j\| \leq \sqrt{d}\mu\epsilon/\gamma + d_{X_{\mathcal{V}\setminus F}},$$

where $X_{\mathcal{V}\setminus F}$ is the true minimum set of the aggregate of all non-faulty agents, and $d_{X_{\mathcal{V}\setminus F}} \triangleq \max_{p,q\in X_{\mathcal{V}\setminus F}} \|p - q\|$ is its diameter.

Intuitively, although the outputs of each agent are not guaranteed to be the same, the output of each non-faulty agent is close to at least one true solution of the Byzantine optimization problem, and the outputs of non-faulty agents are also close to each other.

It is worth noting that, the accuracy of the output is determined by the sample distance parameter ϵ. Smaller ϵ gives us a better bound, which in turn also increases the number of points in X_i's and hence the communication and computation complexity.

It is also worth noting that the generation of the set $\widehat{X}_i$ described in Step 1 of the algorithm above is computationally expensive. Alternatively, an agent i can construct the set $\widehat{X}_i$ in the following manner: locally perform any gradient-based optimization algorithm, e.g., gradient descent, on its cost function Q_i until the norm of the gradient of the estimate $\widehat{x}_i$ satisfies $\|\nabla Q_i(\widehat{x}_i)\| \leq \frac{\sqrt{d}}{2}\mu\epsilon$. The agent i can then start a heuristic search from $\widehat{x}_i$, exploring points in the ϵ-grid at progressively larger distances from $\widehat{x}_i$.

6 Summary

In this paper, we proposed and discussed a Byzantine distributed set intersection problem. We first demonstrated the relationship between this problem and the Byzantine distributed optimization problem, and propose a $2f$-set-redundancy property in parallel to $2f$-redundancy in Byzantine optimization. We then studied the solvability of Byzantine set intersection: We provided the necessary and sufficient condition on the communication graph of a distributed system when $2f$-set-redundancy is satisfied. Lastly, we discussed the necessary and sufficient conditions for the Byzantine optimization problem in a decentralized architecture. The results we provide are for synchronous systems.

We also discussed two practical algorithms in decentralized systems. For the Byzantine set intersection problem with $2f$-set-redundancy, we present an efficient algorithm for the special cases where the input sets are d-dimensional closed hyperrectangles, showing that these constraints on the input sets can be exploited to improve the efficiency of the algorithm. For the Byzantine optimization problem, we present a sampling-based approximate algorithm that utilizes a Byzantine set intersection algorithm on finite sets as a subroutine. This algorithm allows each agent to produce an output that is within a bounded distance from an actual minimum point.

Future works may include more practical and communication-efficient approximate algorithms for Byzantine set intersection problems under different system settings. For example, a continuous set in Euclidean space can be approximated by a set of discrete sample points, reducing communication and computation overhead, but with further details to be considered. Another possible future work is the solvability of Byzantine optimization problems in decentralized systems with fewer assumptions than those of the results we have presented.

References

1. Attiya, H., Herlihy, M., Rachman, O.: Atomic snapshots using lattice agreement. Distrib. Comput. **8**, 121–132 (1995). https://doi.org/10.1007/BF02242714
2. Blanchard, P., El Mhamdi, E.M., Guerraoui, R., Stainer, J.: Machine learning with adversaries: byzantine tolerant gradient descent. In: Proceedings of the 31st International Conference on Neural Information Processing Systems, pp. 118–128 (2017), https://proceedings.neurips.cc/paper_files/paper/2017/file/f4b9ec30ad9f68f89b29639786cb62ef-Paper.pdf
3. Bondy, J.A., Murty, U.S.R., et al.: Graph theory with applications, vol. 290. Macmillan London (1976)
4. Boyd, S., Parikh, N., Chu, E.: Distributed optimization and statistical learning via the alternating direction method of multipliers, vol. 3. Now Publishers Inc, Hanover, MA, USA (Jan 2011). https://doi.org/10.1561/2200000016
5. Boyd, S., Vandenberghe, L.: Convex optimization. Cambridge University Press (2004). https://doi.org/10.1017/CBO9780511804441
6. Chen, Y., Su, L., Xu, J.: Distributed statistical machine learning in adversarial settings: Byzantine gradient descent. Proc. ACM Measure. Anal. Comput. Syst. **1**(2), 1–25 (2017). https://doi.org/10.1145/3154503
7. Dolev, D.: Unanimity in an unknown and unreliable environment. In: 22nd Annual Symposium on Foundations of Computer Science (sfcs 1981), pp. 159–168. IEEE (1981https://doi.org/10.1109/SFCS.1981.53
8. Dolev, D.: The byzantine generals strike again. J. Algorithms **3**(1), 14–30 (1982). https://doi.org/10.1016/0196-6774(82)90004-9
9. Dolev, D., Dwork, C., Waarts, O., Yung, M.: Perfectly secure message transmission. J. ACM (JACM) **40**(1), 17–47 (1993). https://doi.org/10.1145/138027.138036
10. Gupta, N., Doan, T.T., Vaidya, N.H.: Byzantine fault-tolerance in decentralized optimization under 2f-redundancy. In: 2021 American Control Conference (ACC), pp. 3632–3637. IEEE (2021https://doi.org/10.23919/ACC50511.2021.9483067
11. Gupta, N., Vaidya, N.H.: Fault-tolerance in distributed optimization: the case of redundancy. In: Proceedings of the 39th Symposium on Principles of Distributed Computing, pp. 365–374 (2020https://doi.org/10.1145/3382734.3405748
12. Koo, C.Y.: Broadcast in radio networks tolerating byzantine adversarial behavior. In: Proceedings of the Twenty-third Annual ACM Symposium on Principles of Distributed Computing, pp. 275–282 (2004). https://doi.org/10.1145/1011767.1011807
13. Liu, S., Gupta, N., Vaidya, N.H.: Approximate byzantine fault-tolerance in distributed optimization. In: Proceedings of the 2021 ACM Symposium on Principles of Distributed Computing, PODC 2021, pp. 379–389. Association for Computing Machinery, New York (2021). https://doi.org/10.1145/3465084.3467902
14. Liu, S., Vaidya, N.H.: Byzantine fault-tolerant distributed set intersection with redundancy. arXiv preprint arXiv:2402.08809 (2024)

15. Mitra, A., Richards, J.A., Sundaram, S.: A new approach to distributed hypothesis testing and non-bayesian learning: improved learning rate and byzantine resilience. IEEE Trans. Autom. Control **66**(9), 4084–4100 (2020). https://doi.org/10.1109/TAC.2020.3033126
16. Nedic, A., Ozdaglar, A.: Distributed subgradient methods for multi-agent optimization. IEEE Trans. Autom. Control **54**(1), 48–61 (2009). https://doi.org/10.1109/TAC.2008.2009515
17. Pelc, A., Peleg, D.: Broadcasting with locally bounded byzantine faults. Inf. Process. Lett. **93**(3), 109–115 (2005). https://doi.org/10.1016/j.ipl.2004.10.007
18. Rabbat, M., Nowak, R.: Distributed optimization in sensor networks. In: Proceedings of the 3rd International Symposium on Information Processing in Sensor Networks, pp. 20–27. IEEE (2004https://doi.org/10.1145/984622.984626
19. Raffard, R.L., Tomlin, C.J., Boyd, S.P.: Distributed optimization for cooperative agents: application to formation flight. In: 2004 43rd IEEE Conference on Decision and Control (CDC)(IEEE Cat. No. 04CH37601), vol. 3, pp. 2453–2459. IEEE (2004). https://doi.org/10.1109/CDC.2004.1428778
20. Su, L.: Defending distributed systems against adversarial attacks: consensus, consensus-based learning, and statistical learning. ACM SIGMETRICS Perform. Evaluat. Rev. **47**(3), 24–27 (2020). https://doi.org/10.1145/3380908.3380916
21. Su, L., Shahrampour, S.: Finite-time guarantees for byzantine-resilient distributed state estimation with noisy measurements. IEEE Trans. Autom. Control **65**(9), 3758–3771 (2020). https://doi.org/10.1109/TAC.2019.2951686
22. Su, L., Vaidya, N.H.: Asynchronous distributed hypothesis testing in the presence of crash failures. arXiv preprint arXiv:1606.03418 (2016)
23. Tseng, L., Liang, G., Vaidya, N.H.: Iterative approximate byzantine consensus in arbitrary directed graphs. Distributed Comput., 1–22 (2024). https://doi.org/10.1007/s00446-024-00468-2
24. Tseng, L., Vaidya, N., Bhandari, V.: Broadcast using certified propagation algorithm in presence of byzantine faults. Inf. Process. Lett. **115**(4), 512–514 (2015). https://doi.org/10.1016/j.ipl.2014.11.010
25. Tseng, L., Wu, Y., Pan, H., Aloqaily, M., Boukerche, A.: Reliable broadcast in networks with trusted nodes. In: 2019 IEEE Global Communications Conference (GLOBECOM), pp. 1–6. IEEE (2019). https://doi.org/10.1109/GLOBECOM38437.2019.9013797
26. Vaidya, N.H., Tseng, L., Liang, G.: Iterative approximate byzantine consensus in arbitrary directed graphs. In: Proceedings of the 2012 ACM Symposium on Principles of Distributed Computing, pp. 365–374 (2012). https://doi.org/10.1145/2332432.2332505
27. Vyavahare, P., Su, L., Vaidya, N.H.: Distributed learning with adversarial agents under relaxed network condition. arXiv preprint arXiv:1901.01943 (2019)
28. West, D.B., et al.: Introduction to graph theory, vol. 2. Prentice hall Upper Saddle River (2001)
29. Xue, Q., Zhu, Y., Wang, J., Li, X.: Distributed set intersection and union with local differential privacy. In: 2017 IEEE 23rd International Conference on Parallel and Distributed Systems (ICPADS), pp. 198–205. IEEE (2017). https://doi.org/10.1109/ICPADS.2017.00036
30. Yin, D., Chen, Y., Kannan, R., Bartlett, P.: Byzantine-robust distributed learning: towards optimal statistical rates. In: International Conference on Machine Learning, pp. 5650–5659. PMLR (2018). https://proceedings.mlr.press/v80/yin18a.html
31. Zheng, X., Hu, C., Garg, V.K.: Lattice agreement in message passing systems. arXiv preprint arXiv:1807.11557 (2018)

Pattern Formation of Mobile Agents in Dynamic Grids

Masahiro Shibata[1(✉)], Sayaka Kamei[2], Fukuhito Ooshita[3], and Hirotsugu Kakugawa[4]

[1] Kyushu Institute of Technology, Iizuka, Japan
shibata@csn.kyutech.ac.jp
[2] Hiroshima University, Higashihiroshima, Japan
s10kamei@hiroshima-u.ac.jp
[3] Fukui University of Technology, Fukui, Japan
f-oosita@fukui-ut.ac.jp
[4] Ryukoku University Shiga, Shiga, Japan
kakugawa@rins.ryukoku.ac.jp

Abstract. In this paper, we consider the pattern formation problem of mobile agents in $n \times m$ dynamic grids, requiring k agents in the grid to stay at x designated (target) nodes to form some shape (pattern). We assume that at most one link is missing at each round. In this case, some agent's movement may be always blocked and the agent cannot reach any target node. In addition, if the number k of agents is smaller than the number x of target nodes, several target nodes cannot be occupied. For this reason, focusing on the relationship between the values of k and x, we consider variants of the pattern formation problem in dynamic grids and examine how differences in these requirements and the number of agents influence the design and performance of algorithms. First, we consider the case of $k \leq x$. In this case, we consider the *approximate pattern formation problem*, requiring at least $k - 1$ ($< x$) target nodes to be occupied. For this problem, we propose an algorithm to achieve approximate pattern formation in $O(kn+km)$ rounds. Next, we consider the case of $k > x$. In this case, we consider the *exact pattern formation problem*, requiring each of the x target nodes to be occupied. For this problem, we propose an algorithm to achieve exact pattern formation in $O(kn+km+mn)$ rounds. In particular, when $k-x$ is sufficiently large, we show that exact pattern formation can be achieved in $\Theta(n + m)$ rounds.

Keywords: mobile agent · pattern formation · dynamic grid

1 Introduction

1.1 Background and Related Work

A *distributed system* comprises a set of computing entities (*nodes*) connected by communication links. As a promising design paradigm for distributed systems,

S. Lahlou and M. Mukund (Eds.): NETYS 2025, LNCS 15736, pp. 114–128, 2026.
https://doi.org/10.1007/978-3-032-00347-8_7

(mobile) agents have attracted much attention [1]. Agents can traverse the system, carrying information collected at visited nodes, and execute an action at each node using the collected information to achieve a task. In other words, agents can encapsulate the process code and data, which simplifies the design of distributed systems [2].

In this paper, we consider the *pattern formation problem* as a fundamental problem for agents' coordination. This problem requires agents to stay at designated (target) nodes to form some shape (pattern). Pattern formation is useful for satisfying application users' demands. For example, considering an agent as a resource, it is useful to place many agents at some area likely having a lot of network loads. As another example, when agents are required to spread uniformly in the network and they achieve it, uniformly deployed agents can periodically patrol the system and visit each node at short intervals to check nodes' statuses [3].

The pattern formation problem has been extensively studied for the model such that agents have no or only constant memory space but can observe multiple nodes within its visibility range [4–6]. On the other hand, another agent model, that have memory but cannot observe nodes except for their currently visiting nodes, has also been considered for several problems [7–11]. In this paper, we consider this (the latter) agent model.

While all the above work on pattern formation assumed *static graphs* where a network topology does not change during an execution, recently the importance of algorithm designs for *dynamic graphs*, where a topology changes during an execution, has been increasing, since many recent networks such as IoT change their structures frequently. Hence, several problems involving agents have been studied in dynamic graphs, such as, the gathering problem [12], the exploration problem [13–15], and the uniform deployment problem [16]. However, to the best of our knowledge, pattern formation for dynamic graphs has never been considered.

1.2 Our Contribution

In this paper, we consider the pattern formation problem in $n \times m$ dynamic grids. This problem requires k agents in the grid to stay at x designated (target) nodes to form some shape (pattern). Positions of the designated nodes are represented as a multiset, and hence it is possible that several agents should stay at the same node (we give a formal explanation later). In this paper, as a first step for considering pattern formation in dynamic grids, we assume that all agents start the algorithm execution from the same node (such an assumption is called *rooted*), and at most one link is missing at each round. The position of the missing link is determined by an adversary. Agent problems in such an assumption of missing links have been broadly studied recently [12,15–20]. An example requiring agents to spread uniformly in a 5×7 dynamic grid is given in Fig. 1. In such an assumption of missing links, it is possible that, when some agent tries to move to visit some neighboring node, the corresponding link is missing and the agent fails to move. Since the agent may fail to move at every round by such missing

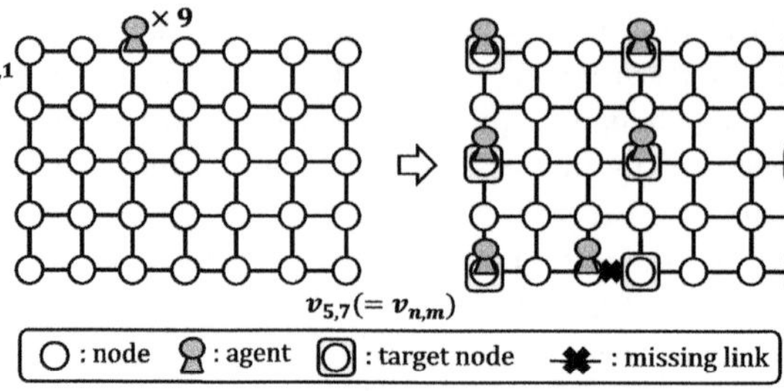

Fig. 1. Example of pattern formation in a 5×7 dynamic grid.

links, it is possible that some agent cannot reach any target node. In addition, if the number k of agents is smaller than the number x of target nodes, several target nodes cannot be occupied. For this reason, focusing on the relationship between the values of k and x, we consider variants of the pattern formation problem in dynamic grids and examine how differences in these requirements and the number of agents influence the design and performance of algorithms.

First, we consider the case of $k \leq x$. In this case, we consider the *approximate pattern formation problem*, which requires at least $k - 1$ $(< x)$ target nodes (including overlapping, if any) to be occupied. For this problem, we propose an algorithm to achieve approximate pattern formation in $O(kn + km)$ rounds. Next, we consider the case of $k > x$. In this case, we consider the *exact pattern formation problem*, which requires each of the x target nodes to be occupied. For this problem, we propose an algorithm to achieve exact pattern formation in $O(kn + km + mn)$ rounds. In particular, when $k - x$ is sufficiently large, we show that the exact pattern formation problem can be solved in $\Theta(n + m)$ rounds. These results demonstrate that, in dynamic grids, approximate pattern formation can be achieved with $k \leq x$ agents, and exact pattern formation can be achieved with $k \geq x + 1$ agents and can be achieved in asymptotically optimal rounds when using sufficiently many agents. Due to limitation of the space, we omit describing pseudocodes and proofs.

2 Preliminaries

2.1 System Model

A *dynamic* $n \times m$ *grid* $(n, m \geq 2)$ is defined as a 2-tuple $G = (V, E)$, where V is a set of nodes $\{v_{i,j} \mid 1 \leq i \leq n, 1 \leq j \leq m\}$ and E is a set of undirected links $(\{(v_{i,j}, v_{i+1,j}) \mid 1 \leq i \leq n-1\}) \vee (\{(v_{i,j}, v_{i,j+1}) \mid 1 \leq j \leq m-1)\})$. We call nodes $v_{1,1}, v_{1,m}, v_{n,1}$ and $v_{n,m}$ *corner nodes*, and the node set $\{v_{i,j} \mid (i \in \{1, n\} \oplus j \in \{1, m\})\}$ *border nodes*. Nodes are anonymous, i.e., they do not have distinct IDs (and thus the indices of nodes are employed just for the notation purpose). We call the direction from $v_{i,j}$ to $v_{i,j+1}$ for $1 \leq j \leq m-1$ (resp., $v_{i,j}$ to $v_{i+1,j}$ for $1 \leq i \leq n-1$, $v_{i,j}$ to $v_{i,j-1}$ for $2 \leq j \leq m$, and $v_{i,j}$ to $v_{i-1,j}$ for $2 \leq i \leq n$) *right* (resp., *down, left* and *up*). The *distance* between nodes $v_{i,j}$

and $v_{p,q}$ is represented as $|i-p|+|j-q|$. In addition, at each time step called a *round*, at most one link may be missing, and the position of the missing link is determined by the *adversarial scheduler*. We assume that the adversary knows the algorithm tactics in advance and determines the position of the missing link at each round so that achieving pattern formation becomes hard.

There exist several (at least 4) agents in the grid. Notice that there may exist more than mn agents because several agents may be required to stay at the same node. An agent is a state machine having two special states $s_{initial}$ and s_{final}. We assume that agents have enough memory space for executing the proposed algorithm, and we plan to analyze the space complexity in the future work. Agents can move through links, that is, from $v_{i,j}$ to $v_{i,j+1}$ (right), from $v_{i,j}$ to $v_{i+1,j}$ (down), from $v_{i,j}$ to $v_{i,j-1}$ (left), or from $v_{i,j}$ to $v_{i-1,j}$ (up). Agents can detect whether they are at a corner, a border, or another node. Agents do not have knowledge of n or m but have distinct IDs. Agents have a common sense of directions, that is, they agree on the right, down, left, and up directions in the grid. We assume that agents can communicate with other agents staying at the same node and hence can obtain information (e.g., states and IDs) of agents at the same node. When each agent changes its state to s_{final}, it never changes its state nor leaves the current node thereafter.

During an execution of the algorithm, we assume that agents move instantaneously, that is, they always exist at nodes (not on links). Each agent a_h executes the following four operations in an atomic action: 1) Agent a_h obtains information of agents at the same node $v_{i,j}$, 2) a_h executes local computation, 3) a_h changes its state (if necessary), and 4) a_h leaves $v_{i,j}$ (if it decides to move). When a_h tries to move to its neighboring node but the corresponding link is missing, we say that a_h is *blocked*, and it still exists at $v_{i,j}$ at the beginning of the next action. We assume that a_h can detect whether it is blocked or not for the current movement.

In an agent system, a (global) *configuration* is defined as the states of all agents and the locations of all agents. We define C as a set of all configurations. We assume that the initial configuration c_0 is *rooted*, that is, all the agents exist at the same node, but the location is determined by the adversary. Notice that the assumption of this rooted configuration is not unnatural by considering an agent as an object with some software package, but we will relax this rooted assumption in future work. In c_0, all agents are in the same state $s_{initial}$.

We consider a *synchronous execution*, that is, at each round, all agents perform atomic actions synchronously and simultaneously. An *execution* from c_0 is defined as $Ex = c_0, c_1, \ldots$ where each c_i $(i \geq 1)$ is the configuration reached from c_{i-1} by atomic actions of all agents. An execution is infinite, or ends in a configuration where the state of every agent is s_{final}.

2.2 The Problems to Be Solved

The pattern formation problem requires agents to stay at x designated nodes to form some shape (pattern). We call the set of designated nodes the *target nodes*. We define $T(n,m)$ as the function returning a multiset representing target nodes, from the values of n and m[1]. For example, in Fig. 1, $T(n,m) = \{v_{1,1}, v_{1,4}, v_{1,7}, v_{3,1}, v_{3,4}, v_{3,7}, v_{5,1}, v_{5,4}, v_{5,7}\}$ holds. Note that the number x of target nodes described above is equal to $|T(n,m)|$, and $T(n,m)$ may include the same node v several times since it returns a multiset (i.e., when v appears c times, c agents should stay at v). However, under the assumption that at most one link is missing at each round, it is possible that, when some agent tries to move to visit some neighboring node, the corresponding link is missing and the agent fails to move. In this case, since the agent may fail to move at every round by such link missings, it is possible that some agent cannot reach any target node. In addition, if the number k of agents is smaller than the number $|T(n,m)|$ of target nodes, several target nodes cannot be occupied. For this reason, focusing on the relationship between the values of k and $|T(n,m)|$, we consider variants of the pattern formation problem in dynamic grids.

First, we consider the case of $k \leq |T(n,m)|$. In this case, we consider the *approximate pattern formation problem*, which requires at least $k-1$ ($< |T(n,m)|$) target nodes to be occupied. Concretely, letting $posA$ be the locations of all agents, it should contain at least $k-1$ elements of $T(n,m)$, that is, $|T(n,m) \backslash posA| \leq |T(n,m)| - (k-1)$ holds. In this case, at most one agent is allowed to stay at an arbitrary node. In Fig. 1 where $k = |T(n,m)| = 9$, $posA = \{v_{1,1}, v_{1,4}, v_{1,7}, v_{3,1}, v_{3,4}, v_{3,7}, v_{5,1}, v_{5,3}, v_{5,7}\}$ and hence $|T(n,m) \backslash posA| = 1$ ($= |T(n,m)| - (k-1)$) holds. Thus, it satisfies the condition of approximate formation. Next, we consider the case of $k > |T(n,m)|$. In this case, we consider the *exact pattern formation problem*, which requires each of the $|T(n,m)|$ target nodes to be occupied. That is, $|T(n,m) \backslash posA| = 0$ should hold. In this case, at most $k - |T(n,m)|$ agents are allowed to stay at arbitrary nodes but all the $|T(n,m)|$ elements should be included in $posA$ by relaxing the number of agents.

Formally, we define the problems as follows.

Definition 1. *Given a function $T(a,b)$ returning a multiset of target nodes of an $a \times b$ grid, an algorithm solves the* approximate *pattern formation problem for k agents in $n \times m$ dynamic grids if, when $k \leq |T(n,m)|$, any execution Ex satisfies the following conditions:*

- *Execution Ex is finite (i.e., all agents terminate in state s_{final}).*
- *When Ex terminates, letting $posA$ be the multiset representing locations of all agents, $|T(n,m) \backslash posA| \leq |T(n,m)| - (k-1)$ holds.*

Definition 2. *Given a function $T(a,b)$ returning a multiset of target nodes of an $a \times b$ grid, an algorithm solves the* exact *pattern formation problem for k agents in $n \times m$ dynamic grids if, when $k > |T(n,m)|$, any execution Ex satisfies the following conditions:*

- *Execution Ex is finite (i.e., all agents terminate in state s_{final}).*

[1] Agents do not know the output of $T(n,m)$ beforehand because they do not have knowledge n or m, and hence they need to firstly know n and m during the execution.

- *When Ex terminates, letting posA be the multiset representing locations of all agents,* $|T(n,m)\backslash posA| = 0$ *holds.*

In this paper, we evaluate the algorithms by the total number of required rounds to solve the problem. Then, for some target node $v_{i,j}$, let $v_{i',j'}$ be the farthest corner node from $v_{i,j}$ (the distance between them is $\Omega(n+m)$). In this case, considering an initial configuration where the starting node of the agents is $v_{i',j'}$ and two agents are required to stay at $v_{i,j}$, obviously at least one agent requires $\Omega(n+m)$ rounds to reach $v_{i,j}$. Hence, we have the following lower bound.

Theorem 1. *A lower bound on the required number of rounds to solve the pattern formation problem (either of approximate or exact) in* $n \times m$ *dynamic grids is* $\Omega(n+m)$.

3 The Proposed Algorithm

The outline is a naive one (either of approximate or exact pattern formation): since all agents initially stay at the same node and they have distinct IDs, using the IDs, each agent calculates the position of its own target node and tries to move there. However, since they do not know n or m beforehand, they cannot recognize the positions of target nodes. Hence, agents first get the value of n and m, and calculate the locations of target nodes $T(n,m)$. Thereafter, depending on the relationship between the values of k and $|T(n,m)|$, agents determine whether they execute algorithms for approximate pattern formation or exact pattern formation.

To accomplish the above, the algorithm comprises two phases: the *size-obtaining phase* and the *formation phase*. In the size-obtaining phase, several agents move in the grid to know n and m. In the formation phase, agents determine which algorithm for formation they execute and try to move to and stay at their target nodes. In the following subsections, we explain the details of each phase.

3.1 Size-Obtaining Phase

To get the values of n and m, four agents use edge-distinct paths and try to measure the length l_{right} from the current (starting) node $v_{i,j}$ to the right border or corner node $v_{i,m}$, length l_{down} from $v_{i,j}$ to the down border or corner node $v_{n,j}$, length l_{left} from $v_{i,j}$ to the left border or corner node $v_{i,1}$, and length l_{up} from $v_{i,j}$ to the up border or corner node $v_{1,j}$, respectively. Concretely, let $a^1_{min}, a^2_{min}, a^3_{min}$, and a^4_{min} be the agents with the smallest, the second smallest, the third smallest, and the fourth smallest ID among all agents, respectively. Then, $a^1_{min}, a^2_{min}, a^3_{min}$, and a^4_{min} try to get the length of $l_{right}, l_{down}, l_{left}$, and l_{up} by moving through the paths like $p_{right}, p_{down}, p_{left}$, and p_{up} in Fig. 2(a),

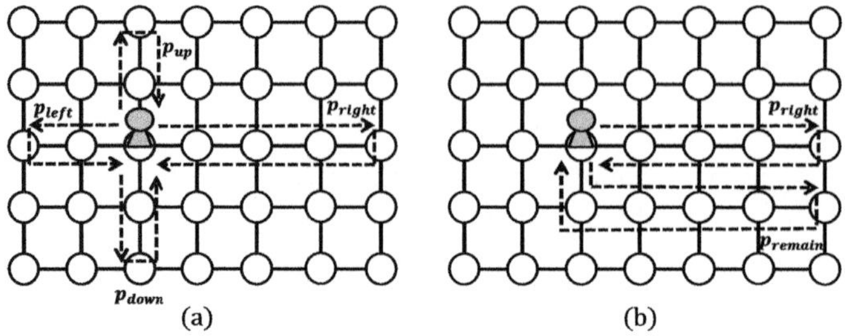

Fig. 2. (a) Four paths $p_{right}, p_{down}, p_{left}$, and p_{up} used by $a^1_{min}, a^2_{min}, a^3_{min}$, and a^4_{min}, respectively, (b) path p_{remain} used by a_{remain}.

respectively[2]. In this case, since the four paths are edge-distinct and at most one link is missing at each round, at least three of them can go through the path and eventually return to their initial node $v_{i,j}$. Without loss of generality, we assume that a^2_{min}, a^3_{min}, and a^4_{min} returned to $v_{i,j}$. In this case, a^1_{min} is still measuring the length l_{right} and it cannot return to $v_{i,j}$ due to missing links. To treat this, letting a_{remain} be the agent with the smallest ID among agents that returned to $v_{i,j}$ (a_{remain} is actually a^1_{min} or a^2_{min}), it tries to get the length of l_{right} by using the path p_{remain} that first goes vertically and then goes to a right border or corner node like Fig. 2(b)[3]. In this case, since p_{right} and p_{remain} are edge-distinct, either of them can finish the movement and return to its starting node. Without loss of generality, we assume that a_{remain} could return to $v_{i,j}$ and a^1_{min} is still moving. Hence, all the agents other than a^1_{min} can get the values of n and m by combining the obtained information of $l_{right}, l_{down}, l_{left}$, and l_{up}. In the following, we explain the way the agent a_{still} that is still exploring the grid (a^1_{min} in this case) gets the values of n and m.

Letting a^1_{share} (resp., a^2_{share}) be the agent with the smallest (resp., the second smallest) ID among agents that got the values of n and m (i.e., all agents other than a_{still}), they calculate a common ring including all the nodes used in a_{still}'s path (p_{right} in this case), by combining p_{right}, p_{remain}, and adding an edge. Then, a^1_{share} tries to move through the ring in some (forward) direction and a^2_{share} tries to move in the opposite (i.e., backward) direction (see Fig. 3(a)). In this case, since at most one link is missing at each round, a^1_{share} or a^2_{share} can move to the next node in each movement. However, only with this movement, it is possible that, when a_{still} and a^1_{share} or a^2_{share} stay at neighboring nodes, they cross at the next round without meeting if the corresponding link is present (see Fig. 3(b)). In this case, a_{still} cannot get the values of n and m. To treat this, agents $a^1_{min}, a^2_{min}, a^3_{min}, a^4_{min}$, and a_{remain} (either of them is a_{still}) in the previous paragraph move only in odd rounds, and a^1_{share} and a^2_{share} move only in even

[2] In order to use this technique, in this paper we assume $k \geq 4$. Note that three agents are actually sufficient if they conduct the movement sequentially, but we assume $k \geq 4$ to simplify the behavior (or pseudocode).

[3] The cases where a^2_{min}, a^3_{min} or a^4_{min} cannot return to $v_{i,j}$ can be treated similarly.

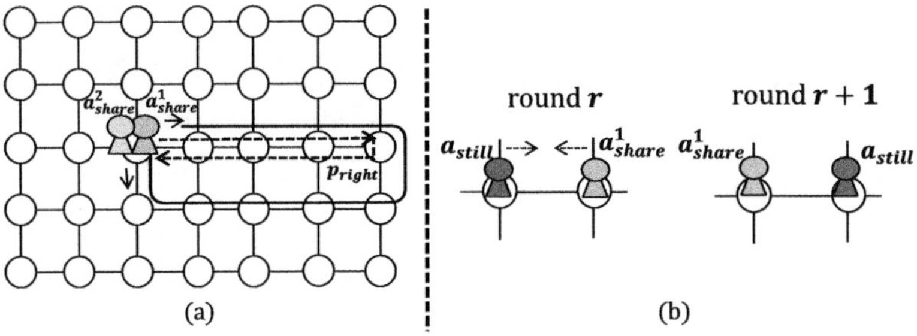

Fig. 3. (a) A ring that a^1_{share} and a^2_{share} move through, (b) an example that a_{still} and a^1_{share} or a^2_{share} cross without meeting.

rounds. By doing this, when a^1_{share} or a^2_{share} moves to the next node at some round, a_{still} stays at the current node for the round, and thus it eventually meets a^1_{share} or a^2_{share} and gets the values of n and m.

Concerning the size-obtaining phase, we have the following lemma.

Lemma 1. *The size-obtaining phase terminates in $O(n+m)$ rounds. After the termination, all the k agents get the values of n and m.*

3.2 Formation Phase

After getting n, m, and $T(n,m)$ (see Sect. 2.2), depending on the relationship between the values of k and $|T(n,m)|$, agents determine which algorithm they use to achieve (approximate of exact) pattern formation.

3.2.1 The Case of $k \leq |T(n,m)|$: Approximate Pattern Formation. In this subsection, when $k \leq |T(n,m)|$, agents achieve approximate pattern formation in $O(kn+km)$ rounds. By Lemma 1, since all the k agents got the values of n and m, using $T(n,m)$ and its ID, each agent a_h can calculate the position of its own target node v_t^h in a way that, if a_h has the ℓ-th smallest ID, it determines v_t^h as the ℓ-th target node. Note that, by the information obtained in Sect. 3.1, e.g., the distance l_{right} from the starting node to the right border or corner node, each agent a_h can know the coordinate information of i and j for the current node $v_{i,j}$ and which directions and how far it is apart from v_t^h. Then, basically, a_h tries to stay at v_t^h via a shortest path. However, since at most one link is missing, if all the agents staying at the same node try to move in the same direction to visit a common neighboring node, it is possible that the corresponding link is missing and they all are blocked. To avoid this, using IDs, at most half of the agents try to move in some common direction and the other agents choose other direction(s). Concretely, a_h calculates two paths p_h^{c1} and p_h^{c2} from the current node v_c^h to v_t^h such that (i) p_h^{c1} (resp., p_h^{c2}) prioritizes the horizontal (resp., vertical) direction first and then the vertical

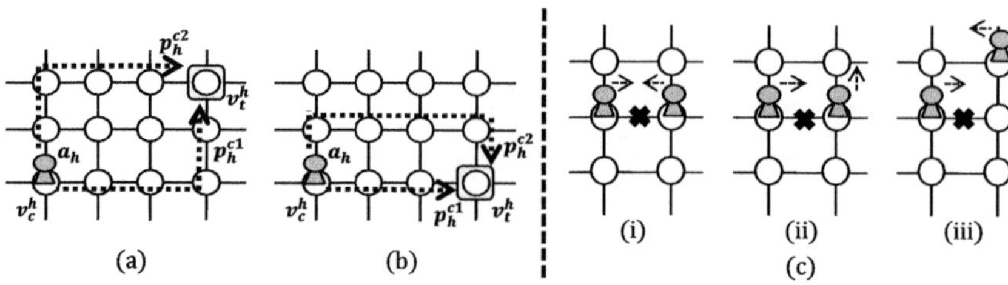

Fig. 4. (a): Two paths p_h^{c1} and p_h^{c2} (dir_h^{c1} is "right" and dir_h^{c2} is "up" in this case), (b): paths p_h^{c1} and p_h^{c2} for the case when v_c^h is distant only in one direction from v_t^h, (c): moving example of two agents after all agents other than them reached their targets.

(resp., horizontal) direction (see Fig. 4(a)), and (ii) the first direction dir_h^{c1} on p_h^{c1} and the first direction dir_h^{c2} on p_h^{c2} are different. When v_t^h is at least one node distant vertically and at least one node distant horizontally from v_c^h, both p_h^{c1} and p_h^{c2} are the shortest. On the other hand, when v_t^h is distant only in one direction, a_h calculates p_h^{c1} as the shortest but p_h^{c2} not as the shortest, that is, dir_h^{c1} is the direction closer to v_t^h but dir_h^{c2} is the direction moving away from v_t^h like Fig. 4(b) (but we show in Lemma 2 that this does not matter). In addition, let k_h be the number of agents staying at the same node as a_h's currently staying node (including a_h), and let $a'_1, a'_2, \ldots a'_{k_h}$ be the agents. We assume that the ID value of a'_p is smaller than that of a'_q for any p and q ($1 \leq p < q \leq k_h$). Then, agent a'_q first calculates the next directions of agents $a'_1, a'_2, \ldots a'_{q-1}$ in this order and then calculates its next direction as follows. First, a'_q calculates dir_p^{c1} and dir_p^{c2} for each agent a'_p ($1 \leq p < q$). Next, a'_q recognizes that agent a'_1 chose dir_1^{c1} as its next direction. Thereafter, in general, on the next direction of agent a'_p, among $p-1$ agents, if at least (resp., at most) $\lceil k_h/2 \rceil$ agents chose dir_p^{c1} as their direction, a'_q recognizes that a'_p chose dir_p^{c2} (resp., dir_p^{c1}) as its next direction. After calculating the next directions of the $q-1$ agents, a'_q similarly calculates its next direction. After deciding its direction (path), a_h tries to move through the path for the current round and the next round (a_h tries to use the same path for two rounds). Thereafter, a_h recalculates its paths p_h^{c1} and p_h^{c2} (and directions dir_h^{c1} and dir_h^{c2}) from the current node and determines which path (and direction) it uses for the next two rounds. By repeating such behaviors, we can show in Lemma 2 that, until the number of agents not reaching their target nodes becomes at most two, the sum of distances to destinations decreases every four rounds, indicating that at least $k-2$ agents reach their target nodes in $O(kn + km)$ rounds.

However, after the above movements, it is possible that some two agents a and b continue to be blocked and do not reach their target nodes yet, when a tries to move in some direction (e.g., right) from some node $v_{i,j}$ and b tries to move in the opposite direction (e.g., left) from a neighboring node (e.g., $v_{i,j+1}$) but the corresponding link continues to be missing. To treat this, as an additional behavior, depending on the direction in which agents failed to move, they determine whether they change their directions or not for the following three rounds. In the first round, agents use the directions that have been used. In the second round, when agent a_h was blocked in trying to move right or up in the first round, it uses the direction also in the second round. Conversely, when a_h was blocked in trying to move left or down, between dir_h^{c1} and dir_h^{c2}, it uses the direction not used in the previous (first) round (see (i) and (ii) of Fig. 4(c)). Finally, if a_h was blocked in trying to move right or up in both the first and second rounds, it continues to use the direction. If a_h was blocked in trying to move left or down in the first round, it tries to move in the direction of the first round in the third round (see (iii) of Fig. 4(c)). By this behavior, either agent a or b can move to another node and it does not happen that both of them continue to be blocked for the following rounds. As a result, either a or b can reach its target node and thus agents eventually achieve approximate pattern formation.

Concerning the formation phase of this subsection, we have the following lemmas.

Lemma 2. *After executing the formation phase of this subsection for* $12k(m+n)$ *rounds,* $|T(n,m)\backslash posA| \leq |T(n,m)| - (k-2)$ *holds.*

Lemma 3. *After finishing the formation phase of this subsection,* $|T(n,m)\backslash posA| \leq |T(n,m)| - (k-1)$ *holds.*

We have the following theorem for the approximate pattern formation problem.

Theorem 2. *When* $k \leq |T(n,m)|$*, the proposed algorithm solves the approximate pattern formation problem with* $O(kn + km)$ *rounds in* $n \times m$ *dynamic grids.*

3.2.2 The Case of $k = |T(n,m)| + 1$: Exact Pattern Formation with One Redundant Agent. In this subsection, when $k = |T(n,m)| + 1$, agents achieve exact pattern formation in $O(kn + km + mn)$ rounds. The basic idea is the same as that for approximate pattern formation in Sect. 3.2.1. However, without any modification, at least one target node may not be occupied, although exact pattern formation requires all the $|T(n,m)|$ target nodes to be occupied. To treat this, in the formation phase, the agent a_{still} that could not reach its target node (if any) and the agent a_{max} with the largest ID among all agents move through some embedded ring that passes all (or almost all) the target nodes, after some rounds such that at least $|T(n,m)| - 1$ target nodes are occupied in spite of missing links. In a way that a_{still} moves through the ring in some direction and a_{max} moves in the opposite direction, either a_{still} or a_{max} can reach a_{still}'s target node and stay there. Then, all the $|T(n,m)|$ target nodes are occupied and agents achieve exact pattern formation.

Concretely, agents other than a_{max} first execute the formation phase in the previous subsection. In this case, at least $|T(n,m)| - 1$ target nodes are occupied, in other words, at most one agent a_{still} does not reach its target node. Thereafter,

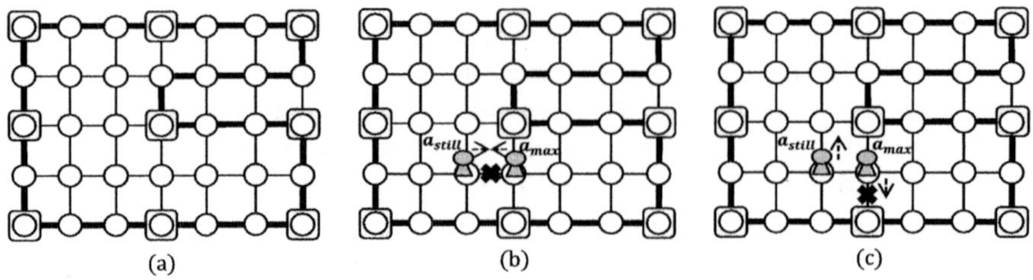

Fig. 5. (a): Embedded ring R_{dep} (represented by bold lines), (b): movements of a_{still} and a_{max} for the first m rounds, (c): movements for the next n rounds.

a_{still} and a_{max} calculate a common ring R_{dep} with the minimum length that (i) includes at least $|T(n,m)|-1$ target nodes and all border and corner nodes and (ii) does not pass any node more than once (see Fig. 5(a) for the case where all the $|T(n,m)|$ target nodes are included). Note that, in any $n \times m$ grid, there exists an embedded ring that includes at least $|T(n,m)|-1$ target nodes because (a) when n or m is even, there is a Hamiltonian cycle in the grid (Fig. 6(a)), and (b) when both n and m are odd, there is an embedded ring including all the nodes other than node $v_{n-1,m-1}$ (Fig. 6(b)). After the calculation, a_{still} and a_{max} determine the forward and backward directions of the ring. Thereafter, if it is not on a node of R_{dep}, a_{still} (resp., a_{max}) tries to move right (resp., left) for m rounds (Fig. 5(b)) and then tries to move up (resp., down) for the next n rounds (Fig. 5(c)). By this behavior, either a_{still} or a_{max} can reach a node of R_{dep} (actually some border or corner node). Thereafter, if it is on a node of R_{dep}, a_{still} (resp., a_{max}) tries to move forward (resp., backward) through R_{dep} for $2|R_{dep}|$ rounds and then tries to move backward (resp., forward) for the next $|R_{dep}|$ rounds. If a_{still} or a_{max} is not on a node of R_{dep} yet, the agent tries to move right until it is on a node of R_{dep} for the $3|R_{dep}|$ rounds. By this behavior, even if both a_{still} and a_{max} cannot visit a new node in R_{dep}, it occurs at most m rounds (when an agent on R_{dep} is blocked, the other agent not on R_{dep} moves closer to a node in R_{dep} and reaches the node within the m rounds). Hence, if a_{still}'s target node is on R_{dep}, either a_{still} or a_{max} can visit the node within these $3|R_{dep}|$ rounds and agents can achieve exact pattern formation. If a_{still}'s target node is $v_{n-1,m-1}$, a_{still} and a_{max} further move to visit $v_{n-1,m-1}$ by executing the first $12k(m+n)$ rounds of the formation phase in the previous subsection. Then, a_{still} or a_{max} can reach $v_{n-1,m-1}$ and agents can achieve exact pattern formation.

Concerning the formation phase of this subsection, we have the following lemma.

Lemma 4. *After finishing the formation phase of this subsection,* $|T(n,m) \setminus posA| = 0$ *holds.*

We have the following theorem for the exact pattern formation problem with $|T(n,m)|+1$ agents.

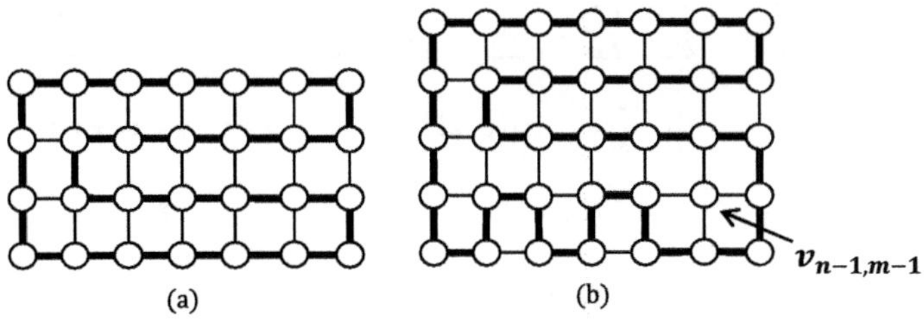

Fig. 6. (a): Embedded ring in the $n \times m$ grid where either n or m is even, (b) embedded ring in the $n \times m$ grid where both n and m are odd.

Theorem 3. *When $k = |T(n,m)| + 1$, the proposed algorithm solves the exact pattern formation problem with $O(kn + km + |R_{dep}|)$ rounds in $n \times m$ dynamic grids.*

Remark: By Theorem 3, the time complexity depends on the value of k and the length of R_{dep} (in other words, the locations of target nodes). For example, if $k = O(1)$ and the formation requires all the agents to stay at some common node, agents can achieve exact pattern formation in $O(n+m)$ rounds using R_{dep} with length $O(n+m)$ with the shape like Fig. 5(a) (assume that $v_{3,4}$ is the target node). If the formation requires agents to spread uniformly in the $n \times m$ grid with $n = m$, since the distance between nearest two target nodes is around $n/\sqrt{k}$ and there exist k target nodes, the length of R_{dep} is around $k \times n/\sqrt{k} = O(n\sqrt{k})$ and hence the total time complexity is $O(kn)$.

3.2.3 The Case of $k > |T(n,m)| + 1$: Exact Pattern Formation with More Than One Redundant Agents. In the previous subsection, we considered exact pattern formation when $k = |T(n,m)| + 1$. In this subsection, we assume $|T(n,m)| + 2 \leq k \leq 2 \times |T(n,m)|$ and consider how fast agents can achieve exact pattern formation. Let $c = k - |T(n,m)|$. In this case, there are two kinds of approaches each of whose time complexity depends on the value of c and agents select the appropriate approach that can achieve exact pattern formation faster.

In the first approach, the basic idea is to partition agents into c groups and partition the whole grid into c sub-areas, and apply the method in Sect. 3.2.2 separately. Concretely, letting $rank^h_{all}$ be the variable representing how small its ID is among all agents in the grid, when $1 \leq rank^h_{all} \leq |T(n,m)|$, a_h calculates $\lceil rank^h_{all}/\lfloor |T(n,m)|/c \rfloor \rceil$ for its group number. If the value i is less than c, a_h belongs to the i-th group. If the value is at least c, it belongs to the c-th group. On the other hand, when $|T(n,m)|+1 \leq rank^h_{all} \leq |T(n,m)|+c$, a_h belongs to the $(rank^h_{all} - |T(n,m)|)$-th group. A grouping example when $c = 3$ is given in Fig. 7. In this case, we can recognize that one redundant agent (a_{max} in Sect. 3.2.2) is assigned to each group, that is, when group g_i has num_i target nodes, $num_i + 1$ agents are assigned to g_i. Thus, agents can achieve exact pattern formation in a way such that each group executes the algorithm in Sect. 3.2.2 independently. In

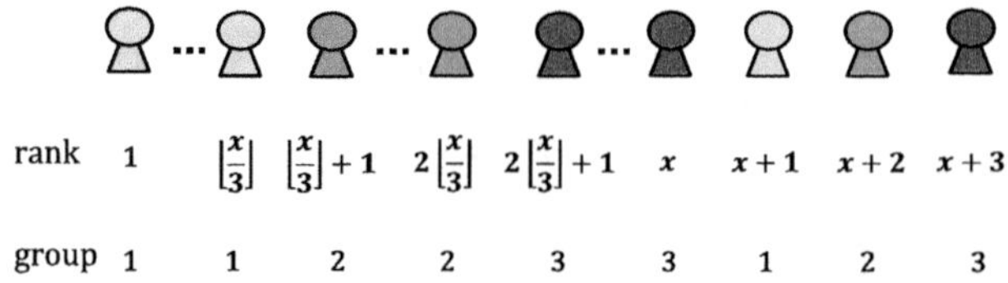

Fig. 7. Partition of agents into groups for the case of $c = 3$ (assume $x = |T(n,m)|$).

addition, similar to R_{dep} in Sect. 3.2.2, letting R^i_{dep} be an embedded ring with the minimum length that (i) includes at least $num_i - 1$ target nodes and four nodes forming a rectangle that includes all the $num_i - 1$ target nodes, and (ii) does not pass any node more than once, it is obviously expected that $|R^i_{dep}|$ is smaller than $|R_{dep}|$ including at least $|T(n,m)|-1$ target nodes used in Sect. 3.2.2. Thus, in accordance with the values of c and $\max_{1 \le i \le c} |R^i_{dep}|$, agents in this section can achieve exact pattern formation faster than those in Sect. 3.2.2.

We have the following theorem on this approach.

Theorem 4. *Assume $|T(n,m)| + 2 \le k \le 2 \times |T(n,m)|$. In this case, letting $c = k - |T(n,m)|$, the proposed method solves the exact pattern formation problem with $O(kn + km + \max_{1 \le i \le c} |R^i_{dep}|)$ rounds in $n \times m$ dynamic grids.*

The second approach is useful particularly when $c = k - |T(n,m)|$ is near or equal to $|T(n,m)|$. The basic approach is the same as that in the previous first approach, that is, to partition agents into c groups so that $num_i + 1$ agents in group g_i respectively try to occupy num_i target nodes. However, in this approach, each group g_i repeats behaviors such that two agents try to stay at a target node in g_i one by one. Concretely, the algorithm comprises several loops. In the 1-st loop, in each group g_i, agents with the smallest and the second smallest ID in g_i try to reach the 1-st target node v_t^{i1} of the group, using the moving tactics of Sect. 3.2.1. In this case, since the two agents use different directions when they are at the same node, eventually one of them reaches v_t^{i1}. Next, in the 2-nd loop, two agents try to reach the 2-nd target node v_t^{i2}. In this loop, among agents with the first or second smallest ID, the agent that (i) did not reach v_t^{i1} when one of them cannot reach there, or (ii) the agent with the second smallest ID when both of them reach there, continues to move. In addition to the agent, the agent with the third smallest ID moves to reach v_t^{i2}. The movement in the ℓ-th loop is explained similarly. Agents repeat such behavior for each target node one by one. In this case, since the above movement for reaching one target node takes $O(n + m)$ rounds, the time complexity depends on the maximum number of agents in all groups. That is, when $c = k - |T(n,m)|$ is large, since the number of groups also becomes large and hence the number of agents in each group becomes small, agents can achieve exact pattern formation faster. In particular, when $k - |T(n,m)| = \Theta(|(T(n,m)|)$, they can solve the problem in $O(n+m)$ (i.e., asymptotically optimal) rounds.

We have the following theorem and corollary on the second approach.

Theorem 5. *Assume* $|T(n,m)| + 2 \leq k \leq 2 \times |T(n,m)|$. *In this case, letting* $c = k - |T(n,m)|$, *the proposed method solves the exact pattern formation problem with* $O(\frac{k}{c}(n+m))$ *rounds in* $n \times m$ *dynamic grids.*

Corollary 1. *When* $c = \Theta(|T(n,m)|)$, *the proposed method achieves the exact pattern formation with* $O(n+m)$ *rounds in* $n \times m$ *dynamic grids.*

4 Conclusion

In this paper, we considered the pattern formation problems in $n \times m$ dynamic grids. We proposed several algorithms focusing on the relationship between the values of k and $|T(n,m)|$. When $k \leq |T(n,m)|$, we proposed the algorithm to achieve *approximate* pattern formation in $O(kn + km)$ rounds. When $k \geq |T(n,m)| + 1$, we proposed several methods to achieve *exact* pattern formation, whose time complexity depends on the number of agents (when the number is more, agents can achieve exact pattern formation faster). Future works are as follows. First, we plan to analyze the space complexity and the move complexity of the proposed algorithm, and consider whether the time complexity of the current methods is actually smaller by analyzing deeply. Second, we plan to consider situations such that more than one link may be missing at each round, and for initial configurations where agents are placed at distinct nodes. Third, we plan to consider the agent model such that they can communicate when they are within several constant hops.

Acknowledgments. This work was partially supported by JSPS KAKENHI Grant Number JP20KK0232, JP23K11059, JP23K28037, JP25K14995, and JP25K03101.

References

1. Gray, R.S., Cybenko, G., Kotz, D., Peterson, R.A., Rus, D.: D'agents: applications performance of a mobile-agent system. Softw.: Pract. Exper. **32**(6), 543–573 (2002)
2. Lange, D.B., Oshima, M.: Seven good reasons for mobile agents. CACM **42**(3), 88–89 (1999)
3. Bieszczad, B., Pagurek, A., White, T.: Mobile agents for network management. IEEE Commun. Surv. **1**(1), 2–9 (1998)
4. Bose, K., Adhikary, R., Kundu, M.K., Sau, B.: Arbitrary pattern formation on infinite grid by asynchronous oblivious robots. Theoret. Comput. Sci. **815**, 213–227 (2020)
5. Dieudonné, Y., Petit, F., Villain, V.: Leader election problem versus pattern formation problem. In: Proceedings of the 24th International Symposium on Distributed Computing, pp. 267–281 (2010)
6. Kundu, M.K., Goswami, P., Ghosh, S., Sau, B.: Arbitrary pattern formation by opaque fat robots on infinite grid. Int. J. Parallel Emergent Distrib. Syst. **37**(5), 542–570 (2022)
7. Shibata, M., Kakugawa, H., Masuzawa, T.: Space-efficient uniform deployment of mobile agents in asynchronous unidirectional rings. Theoret. Comput. Sci. **809**, 357–371 (2020)

8. Shibata, M., Mega, T., Ooshita, F., Kakugawa, H., Masuzawa, T.: Uniform deployment of mobile agents in asynchronous rings. J. Parall. Distrib. Comput. **119**, 92–106 (2018)
9. Pattanayak, D., Bhagat, S., Gan Chaudhuri, S., Molla, A.R.: Maximal independent set via mobile agents. In: Proceedings of the 25th International Conference on Distributed Computing and Networking, pp. 74–83, (2024)
10. Gorain, B., Kaur, T., Mondal, K.: Distance-2-dispersion with termination by a strong team. In: Proceedings of Conference on Algorithms and Discrete Applied Mathematics, pp. 44–58 (2024)
11. Chand, P.K., Molla, A.R., Sivasubramaniam, S. Run for cover: dominating set via mobile agents. In: Proceedings of International Symposium on Algorithmics of Wireless Networks, pp. 133–150 (2023)
12. Di Luna, G.A., Flocchini, P., Pagli, L., Prencipe, G., Santoro, N., Viglietta, G.: Gathering in dynamic rings. Theor. Comput. Sci. **811**, 79–98 (2020)
13. Gotoh, T., Flocchini, P., Masuzawa, T., Santoro, N.: Exploration of dynamic networks: tight bounds on the number of agents. J. Comput. Syst. Sci. **122**, 1–18 (2021)
14. Gotoh, T., Sudo, Y., Ooshita, F., Kakugawa, H., Masuzawa, T.: Exploration of dynamic tori by multiple agents. Theoret. Comput. Sci. **850**, 202–220 (2021)
15. Di Luna, G., Dobrev, S., Flocchini, P., Santoro, N.: Distributed exploration of dynamic rings. Distrib. Comput. **33**(1), 41–67 (2018). https://doi.org/10.1007/s00446-018-0339-1
16. Agarwalla, A., Augustine, J., Moses Jr, W.K., Madhav, S.K., Sridhar, A.K.: Deterministic dispersion of mobile robots in dynamic rings. In: Proceedings of the 19th International Conference on Distributed Computing and Networking, pp. 1–4 (2018)
17. Das, S., Di Luna, G.A., Gasieniec, L.A.: Patrolling on dynamic ring networks. In: International Conference on Current Trends in Theory and Practice of Informatics, pp. 150–163 (2019)
18. Shibata, M., Sudo, Y., Nakamura, J., Kim, Y.: Almost uniform deployment of mobile agents in dynamic rings. Inf. Comput. **289**, 104949 (2022)
19. Shibata, M., Sudo, Y., Nakamura, J., Kim, Y.: Partial gathering of mobile agents in dynamic rings. In: Proceedings of International Symposium on Stabilizing, Safety, and Security of Distributed Systems, pp. 440–455 (2021)
20. Saxena, A., Kaur, T., Mondal, K.: Dispersion on time varying graphs. In: Proceedings of International Conference on Distributed Computing and Networking, pp. 269–273 (2025)

An Automaton Model to Succinctly Represent Suffix-Based Specifications of a Concurrent System

R Keerthan[1,2], B Srivathsan[2,3(✉)], and R Venkatesh[1]

[1] Tata Consultancy Services - Innovation Labs, Pune, India
{keerthanr,r.venky}@tcs.com
[2] Chennai Mathematical Institute, Chennai, India
sri@cmi.ac.in
[3] CNRS, ReLaX, IRL 2000, Siruseri, India

Abstract. Deterministic Suffix-reading Automata (DSA) were introduced recently as a concise model for regular languages. DSAs can succinctly capture formal specifications that are based on *sequences* of input actions (and not just single actions). For a concurrent system, specifications may further depend on combinations of input sequences seen across multiple components (ports). For such systems, DSAs consider all possible interleavings, resulting in large and unreadable automata.

In this work, we enrich DSAs to include a $\|$ operator in its transitions. The resulting *multi-port DSAs (mDSAs)* can succinctly represent concurrent suffix-based specifications. Subsequently, we extend mDSAs to produce outputs on transitions, and show that state reachability becomes PSPACE-complete in the presence of outputs. Finally, we apply our results to the formal analysis of Expressive Decision Tables (EDT) – an industry notation for specifying requirements of reactive systems.

Keywords: Formal verification · automata theory · concurrency

1 Introduction

Finite state automata are all-pervasive, adopting different roles in different contexts. We focus on the role of automata as *formal models of system requirements* and their subsequent application in Model Based Testing (MBT). MBT is a paradigm in formal methods where the requirements of a system under test (SUT) are first converted to a formal model. This formal model is then used to automatically generate test cases for the SUT. There are many MBT tools (see [4,13] for a survey) and in several of them, the formal model is given by some extension of finite automata.

Converting requirements to a Deterministic Finite Automaton (DFA) or a Non-deterministic Finite Automaton (NFA) is often cumbersome. This is because DFAs and NFAs describe low level computations which reason about

S. Lahlou and M. Mukund (Eds.): NETYS 2025, LNCS 15736, pp. 129–145, 2026.
https://doi.org/10.1007/978-3-032-00347-8_8

individual actions. There are various ways in which automata can be made consise. In Generalized Automata [5,6], transitions contain words instead of single actions. A transition $q \xrightarrow{abb} q'$ is fired from q if the word abb is seen after the automaton reaches q. Therefore, requirements which depend on an exact sequence of actions can be represented using generalized automata more concisely. A natural extension is to allow for regular expressions in transitions, resulting in the model of Expression Automata [8] and its deterministic variant. Deterministic Expression Automata (DEA) impose restrictions on the regular expressions that can be used: they should result in a prefix-free language, and moreover, every pair of regular expressions out of state is language disjoint. This results in DEA recognizing a subset of regular languages. On the other hand, in (non-deterministic) Expression Automata, the transitions are so powerful that the states have almost no meaning: the entire automaton can be reduced to a single state and a single transition labeled by the regular expression representing the language. For languages leading to big automata, the corresponding regular expression can be complicated and incomprehensible. The goal is to hit a sweet spot where the transition labels are not too complicated, and at the same time there are fewer states than a DFA.

Deterministic suffix-reading automata (DSAs) [10] are a recently introduced automaton model for regular languages. Transitions are labeled with words (as in a generalized automaton), however, the semantics is different. A transition (q, abb, q') is fired from q if a word *ending* with the suffix abb is seen. When there are multiple transitions out of a state, the first transition that matches is fired. Figure 1 gives some examples of DSAs.

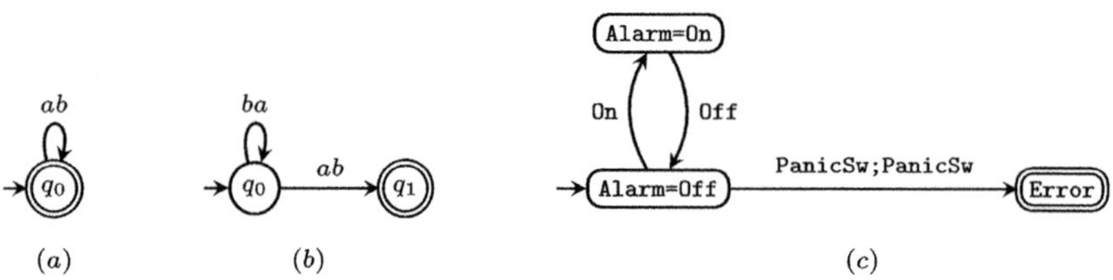

Fig. 1. Examples of Deterministic Suffix-reading Automata (DSA)

In Fig. 1(a), the DSA accepts all words that end with ab, for instance $bab, bbab, babaab$, etc. The transition $q_0 \xrightarrow{ab} q_0$ is fired as soon as a word ending with ab is seen after reaching q_0. For instance, on the word $babaab$, the transition is first triggered on the prefix bab since this is the first time ab appears as suffix; once the transition is triggered, the prefix bab has been consumed, and now we are left with aab; on reading aab fully, the transition $q_0 \xrightarrow{ab} q_0$ is triggered again. In Fig. 1(b), we can view the state q_0 as tracking two suffixes ba and ab. When ba is seen before ab, the self-loop is triggered; otherwise when ab is seen first, the transition to q_1 is taken. For example, on word $bbab$, the automaton starts at q_0, and on *bba* it fires $q_0 \xrightarrow{ba} q_0$ (since *ba* is a suffix of *bba*), then reads *b* and remains there. However, on *bbaab*, the run loops on *bba* back to q_0, and then reads the next *ab* to reach q_1, and accept. The final example Fig. 1(c) is a *suffix-based specification* of a part of an automotive software: when the alarm is off, and the panic switch is pressed twice within one second, flag an error. Here, we assume there is a symbol `tick` to denote the elapse of 1 unit of time. So, on a word `tick`; `On`; `tick`; `Off`; `PanicSw`; `PanicSw`, an error should be flagged (we have added a separator symbol ; just for clarity). This specification is succinctly represented by the DSA in Fig. 1(c).

Since transitions in a DSA wait for specific patterns to appear, DSAs are able to represent suffix-based specifications succinctly. When we consider systems with multiple components (which we call ports), the requirements can talk about different combinations of inputs. Here are two examples.

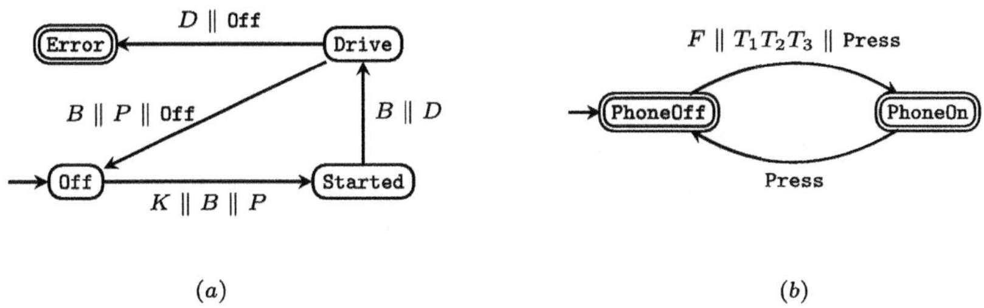

Fig. 2. Concurrent suffix-based specifications as multi-port DSAs.

Car Security System. For a car to start, you need: key in ignition (K), brake pedal pressed (B), and transmission in park (P). The actions K, P and B can occur in any order. A DSA would need to represent this requirement using all 6 permutations. Instead, we assume an alphabet that is distributed across different *ports* – ignition, brake pedal, transmission, and denote the concurrent actions as $K \parallel B \parallel P$. Here are some requirements of a car security system. Figure 2(a) illustrates the enriched DSA.

- When the brake pedal is pressed (B), transmission is in park (P) and key is in ignition (K), the car can be started.
- If the brake pedal is pressed (B) and the transmission is moved to drive (D), the car goes to the drive mode.
- When the brake pedal is pressed (B), transmission is in park (P), and the ignition becomes off (`Off`), the car is switched off. If ignition is switched off when brake is not pressed or when transmission is in drive/reverse, signal an error.

Smartphone Lock Pattern. Figure 2(b) represents the enriched DSA modeling the requirements below for a smartphone lock.

- When the button is pressed (`Press`), fingerprint verified (F) and a correct pattern is received ($T_1T_2T_3$), then the phone is switched on.
- If the phone is on, and the button is pressed, the phone is switched off.

To the best of our knowledge, no automaton model can succinctly represent the combination of suffix-based patterns across a concurrent system. Incorporating concurrency into the specification is paramount when requirements talk about different components of a concurrent system.

Contributions. The goal of this paper is to investigate the addition of a parallel operator $\|$, into the transition syntax of DSAs. We call the resulting model as *multi-port DSAs*, where the alphabet is distributed (partitioned) across multiple ports. The challenge lies in describing an operational semantics that matches with our intentions. As our first technical contribution, we provide a formal operational semantics for multi-port DSAs, or mDSAs.

Next, we include the feature to produce outputs on transitions, giving us mDSA-with-outputs. When the produced outputs also influence suffix-based input conditions, the behaviours become more complex. In fact, we then show that state reachability for mDSA-with-outputs is PSPACE-complete. When there are no outputs, reachability is simply linear in the input size.

As our next contribution, we apply the mDSA framework to provide a formal semantics for Expressive Decision Tables (EDTs), a notation introduced by [14] to incorporate both state-based and stream-based requirements in one convenient tabular form. The EDT notation has been successfully deployed in many industrial projects. In [14] it has also been observed that the time and effort involved in writing EDT specifications was considerably low compared to other formalisms like Statecharts. Many test generation tools for EDT specifications have been developed: given an EDT, and a row, the tool can generate a sequence of input actions that can trigger the input-side conditions of the particular row [2,15]. Although EDTs have been used extensively for test generation, the notation does not yet have a formal operational semantics because of a complex interplay between concurrency and suffix-based rules. We close these gaps using the mDSA technology: we consider a fragment of the EDT notation, and map each EDT to an mDSA-with-outputs. This in turn gives an operational semantics for the EDT. Moreover, test generation for EDTs reduces to state reachability in mDSA-with-outputs. We also develop a prototype implementation for state reachability in mDSA-with-outputs, using which we generate test cases for an intricate EDT example.

Related Work. Use of automata to model concurrent systems has been explored widely. Esterel [3] is a synchronous programming language that provides a parallel composition operator. Harel's Statecharts [9] also support parallel composition of state transition systems. In both these languages the reaction of a system in response to inputs on each port can be specified separately and the different specifications can be composed using the parallel operator. A system model can then refer to the states of each port's specification to model the system behaviour. In mDSAs, we do not compose automata. Instead there is a single automaton, but the transitions include a parallel composition operator. More importantly, mDSA allows for suffix-based event triggers. Petri nets [12] have been studied extensively to model concurrent systems. In Petri nets each letter of each port's alphabet will have to be represented using a place and the places combined to model the system. There is no mechanism to include suffix-based triggers. The work that is closest to ours is Input/Output Partial Order Automata (IOPOA) [7]. In their work, transitions execute non-atomically reacting to asynchronous inputs on several ports. The main differences between IOPOA and mDSA: in mDSA transitions react atomically, transition labels can be strings representing a suffix for each port and not just letters, and different transitions may trigger on the same string at a port. For example consider the mDSA in Fig. 2(a), the transition from `Off` to `Started` and `Started` to `Drive` can be taken on the same input B. In an IOPOA this will require two occurences of B. IOPOA was primarily designed to enable test generation whereas the aim of mDSAs is succinct specification of requirements.

Structure of the Paper. Section 2 briefly recalls the syntax and semantics of Deterministic Suffix-reading Automata (DSA). In Sect. 3, we extend DSA with the parallel operator, and in Sect. 4, we add the feature to produce outputs. Finally in Sect. 5, we describe the EDT notation and the translation from EDT to multi-port DSA with outputs.

2 Deterministic Suffix-Reading Automata (DSA)

In this section, we recall the formal syntax and semantics of deterministic suffix-reading automata (DSA) [10]. For a finite alphabet Σ, we write Σ^+ for $\Sigma^* \setminus \{\epsilon\}$.

Definition 1 (Deterministic Suffix-reading Automata (DSA)). *Let Σ be a finite alphabet. A DSA $\mathcal{A}$ is given by a tuple $(Q, \Sigma, q_0, \delta, F)$ where Q is a finite set of states, q_0 is the initial state and $F \subseteq Q$ is a set of final states, and $\delta \subseteq Q \times \Sigma^+ \times \Sigma$, is a finite transition relation. Each transition therefore is of the form (q, u, q') where $q, q' \in Q$ and $u \in \Sigma^+$. We write* $\text{Out}(q) := \{w \in \Sigma^+ \mid (q, u, q') \in \delta\}$.

A *configuration* of a DSA is given by (q, w) where q is the current state, and w is the word seen *after reaching* q. The initial configuration is (q_0, ϵ). Transitions are as follows:

- $(q, w) \xrightarrow{a} (q, wa)$ if no string in $\text{Out}(q)$ is a suffix of wa,
- $(q, w) \xrightarrow[u]{a} (q', \epsilon)$ if u is the longest string of $\text{Out}(q)$ which is a suffix of wa, and (q, u, q') is the corresponding transition.

A configuration (q, w) is accepting if $q \in F$ and $w = \epsilon$, signifying that the accepting state was reached on the last input.

We illustrate the semantics on an example. Consider the DSA in Fig. 1 (b). Here is the sequence of configurations obtained on the word *bbaab*:

$$(q_0, \epsilon) \xrightarrow{b} (q_0, b) \xrightarrow{b} (q_0, b) \xrightarrow[ba]{a} (q_0, \epsilon) \xrightarrow{a} (q_0, a) \xrightarrow[ab]{b} (q_1, \epsilon)$$

3 Extending DSA to Accommodate Multiple Ports

Consider a special kind of alphabet $\Sigma = \langle \Sigma_1, \Sigma_2, \ldots, \Sigma_k \rangle$ such that $\Sigma_i \cap \Sigma_j = \emptyset$ for all $i, j \in \{1, \ldots, k\}$. We will call Σ_i as the alphabet of *port* i, and Σ as a *multi-port* alphabet. For instance, in the *Car Security System specification* of Sect. 1, there are three ports: brake, transmission and ignition, with $\Sigma_{\mathsf{brake}} = \{B\}$, $\Sigma_{\mathtt{trm}} = \{P, D\}$ and $\Sigma_{\mathtt{ig}} = \{K, \mathtt{Off}\}$ respectively.

We look at DFAs over such multi-port alphabets. Such DFAs model properties of systems that listen to inputs from different components and perform actions based on them. Sometimes the order in which the system receives its inputs from different ports is not relevant. For example, at a state s, if the system receives a from port 1 and b from port 2, in any order, then it has to go to state t. A DFA would model this with transitions: $s \xrightarrow{a} s_a \xrightarrow{b} t$ and $s \xrightarrow{b} s_b \xrightarrow{a} t$. A DSA would contain two transitions $s \xrightarrow{ab,ba} t$ (and some other transitions, if needed, to take care of aa, bb). To get a more succinct notation we will use a $\|$ operator. We will write $s \xrightarrow{a\|b} t$ to mean that at state s, when both a and b are received, the automaton moves to t. When there are several components, this notation leads to significant succinctness, for instance $a_1 \parallel a_2 \cdots \parallel a_n$ stands for all the $n!$ permutations of a_1 to a_n. We will also allow expressions of the form $a_1a_2 \parallel b$, which stands for the set of words $\{a_1a_2b, a_1ba_2, ba_1a_2\}$ which shuffles a_1a_2 and b. Section 1 illustrates further examples of the use of $\|$ operator in Fig. 2. We will now formalize this idea. We begin with some notation.

Notation. For a word $w \in \Sigma^*$, we write $\mathsf{P}_i(w)$ for the projection of w onto the set Σ_i. For instance, if $\Sigma_1 = \{a_1, a_2\}, \Sigma_2 = \{b_1, b_2\}$ and $w = a_1b_1a_2a_1b_2b_2$, we have $\mathsf{P}_1(w) = a_1a_2a_1$ and $\mathsf{P}_2(w) = b_1b_2b_2$. Notice that if for two words w_1, w_2 suppose $\mathsf{P}_i(w_1) = \mathsf{P}_i(w_2)$ for all ports i, then w_1 and w_2 have the same order of events within each port, but could have a different ordering between letters from different ports.

3.1 Some Challenges in Extending to Multiport

For a DSA, a configuration was given by (q, w) where q is the current state and w is the word seen after reaching q. Moreover, if a transition matches, the DSA moves to a configuration (q', ϵ) by fully consuming the word seen so far. Now consider the car security system example (Fig. 2 (a)) . On receiving inputs $P; B; K$, the automaton moves to $\mathtt{Started}$ state. If the brake remains pressed and the transmission is moved to park, we would like the car to go into the drive mode. Therefore, on the word $P; B; K; D$, the automaton should go to the `Drive` state. This intention is summarized below as what we require as the run of the automaton:

$$\texttt{Off} \xrightarrow{P;B;K} \texttt{Started} \xrightarrow{D} \texttt{Drive}$$

If we had consumed the prefix $P; B; K$ while moving to the `Started` state, then the transition $B \parallel D$ would not match anymore, since there is no B after reaching `Started`. What we really need is that: the last seen input in the brake port is B and the last seen input in the transmission port is D. Therefore, one option is to simply not consume any letters and say that a transition $u_1 \parallel u_2 \parallel \cdots \parallel u_k$ matches a word w if u_i is a suffix of projection $\mathsf{P}_i(w)$. However, this creates other problems as we will now illustrate.

Consider the smartphone lock pattern specification (Fig. 2 (b)). On a word $F; T_1; T_2; T_3;$`Press`, the phone is unlocked and the automaton goes to the `PhoneOn` state. At this state, there is an outgoing transition that listens to `Press`. If we do not consume the word seen so far, the last seen input in the button port is still `Press`, and hence the automaton would go back to the `PhoneOn` state without seeing additional inputs. In fact, this looping behaviour would continue forever, with no inputs seen. Therefore, for the outgoing transition `Press` in the `PhoneOn` state, the intention is that we need to receive a fresh signal `Press`.

To summarize: on a transition match, we do not want to consume the word seen so far (car security specification example); but simply not consuming the word leads to problems (smartphone lock pattern example). In the following, we adopt an intermediate approach, where we mark the position θ in the word where the last transition matched. For a new transition $u_1 \parallel u_2 \parallel \cdots \parallel u_k$ to match, in addition to having each u_i as a suffix of $\mathsf{P}_i(w)$, we require at least one u_i to appear entirely after the marked position θ. We include an additional condition that every u_i appears either entirely to the left of θ or to the right of θ to account for such examples:

$$s_0 \xrightarrow{c \| a} s_1 \xrightarrow{cc \| b} s_2$$

Action c can denote a `click`. So, the pattern cc denotes a double click. On seeing $a; c$ the automaton moves to s_1. Now if the inputs received are $b; c$, we do not want the transition $cc \parallel b$ to match. Instead, we want two clicks and a b after the last match. The condition that every pattern appears entirely after this match, or entirely before this match takes care of this situation.

3.2 Multi-port DSAs: Formal Syntax and Semantics

We first describe the formal syntax and then proceed to an operational semantics given by a labeled transition system.

Definition 2 (Multi-port DSA). *Let* $\Sigma = \langle \Sigma_1, \Sigma_2, \ldots, \Sigma_k \rangle$ *be a multi-port alphabet.* A multi-port (deterministic) suffix-reading automaton *(written mDSA* *in short)* $\mathcal{A}$ *is a tuple* $(Q, \Sigma, q_0, \delta, F)$ *where* Q, q_0 *and* F *are a finite set of states, the initial state and a set of accept states, respectively. The transition relation* $\delta \subseteq Q \times \Sigma_1^* \times \Sigma_2^* \times \cdots \times \Sigma_k^* \times Q$*: each transition is of the form* $(q, (u_1 \parallel u_2 \parallel \cdots \parallel u_k), q')$ *where* $u_i \in \Sigma_i^*$ *(not all of them can be* ϵ*). We assume there are only finitely many transitions.*

Figure 2 gives two mDSAs adhering to this syntax.

For the semantics, it is convenient to assume that there is a *tape* on which the automaton writes all its inputs. Initially, the tape is ϵ. Each time an input letter $a \in \Sigma$ is received, the automaton appends it to the right of the tape.

Notation. For a word $w = a_1 \ldots a_n$, with $a_i \in \Sigma$, we write $w(i)$ to denote the letter a_i. We remark our convention that the indices of w start from 1 (and not 0). The length of w, denoted as $|w|$, equals n (the number of letters). For $j \in \{1, \ldots, n\}$ we write $w[i, j]$ to denote the substring $a_i a_{i+1} \cdots a_j$.

mDSA semantics. A *configuration* of an mDSA is given by (q, w, θ) where

- q is the current state,
- w is the word read so far, from the beginning
- $\theta \in \mathbb{N}$ marks a position in the word where the last match of a transition appeared.

We refer to the pair (w, θ) as the *tape configuration.*

The formal semantics of an mDSA $\mathcal{A}$ is given by a transition system $\mathbb{TS}^{\mathcal{A}} = (S, S_0, \rightarrow, S_F)$ over the configurations: the set of nodes S is the set of all configurations (q, w, θ) (notice that this set is infinite); the initial node s_0 is $(q_0, \epsilon, 0)$, also called *the initial configuration*; S_F is the set of *accepting configurations* which are configurations (q, w, θ) where $q \in F$ and $\theta = |w|$ (signaling reaching an accepting state immediately after a match); to describe the transition relation $\rightarrow$, we first explain when a transition label matches with a tape configuration.

Definition 3. *We say that a transition label* $(u_1 \parallel u_2 \parallel \cdots \parallel u_k)$ *matches a tape configuration* (w, θ) *if:*

- u_i *is a suffix of* $\mathsf{P}_i(w)$ *for all ports* i,
- *each* u_i *appears entirely before or entirely after* θ*: that is,* u_i *is a subword of* $w[1, \theta]$ *or* $w[\theta + 1, |w|]$,
- *at least one* u_i *appears entirely after* θ.

Let $\rho : (q, (u_1 \parallel u_2 \parallel \cdots \parallel u_k), q')$ be an outgoing transition from q.

- In $\mathbb{TS}^{\mathcal{A}}$, there is a following transition:

$$(q, w, \theta) \xrightarrow[u_1 \| u_2 \| \cdots \| u_k]{a} (q', wa, \theta') \qquad \text{if}$$

$(u_1 \parallel u_2 \parallel \cdots \parallel u_k)$ matches the tape configuration (wa, θ), and $\theta' = |wa|$ (tape head moves to the end of the tape).

- There is a transition of the form:

$$(q, w, \theta) \xrightarrow{a} (q, wa, \theta)$$

  if no transition out of q matches the tape configuration (wa, θ). In this case, the tape head remains at its position.

The transition relation $\rightarrow$ of $\mathbb{TS}^{\mathcal{A}}$ is a union over all $\xrightarrow[u_1\|u_2\|\cdots\|u_k]{a}$ and $\xrightarrow{a}$.

For all examples described in Sect. 3.1, the above semantics of transitions adheres to the required intention.

Remark 1. We remark that the labeled transition system $\mathbb{TS}^{\mathcal{A}}$ defined as above is non-deterministic, since multiple transitions can, in principle, be enabled at (q, w, θ) on seeing an a. In order to make the automaton deterministic, a specific priority function can be added to resolve the non-determinism. If multiple transitions match at a configuration, the priority function is used to resolve the non-determinism. We did not explicitly add it to the syntax for technical simplicity.

Remark 2. A DSA is an mDSA with a single port. To resolve non-determinism, DSAs employ the longest match criterion: among all strings that are a suffix, pick the one with the maximum length.

4 Multiport DSAs with Outputs

In Sect. 3, we have seen multi-port DSAs which process inputs across several ports and match transitions. In many situations, requirements also talk about outputting values to certain ports when transitions match. Here is an example of some requirements of a *Car Alarm module*, adapted from [15].

1. If the most recent values on *Ignition* (I) and *Alarm* (A) are `Off`, and the last two values on the Panic Switch (P) are `Press;Press`, then the value `On` is output on the port *Alarm*.
2. If the last three values on the Panic Switch are `Release;Release;Release`, and the Alarm is `On`, then output `False` on *Flash* (F) and *Alarm*.
3. If last value on *Ignition* is `On`, then `False` is output on *Flash* and `Off` is output on *Alarm*.

The first requirement checks for I : `Off` $\|$ A : `Off` $\|$ P : `Press;Press` and immediately writes A : `On`. The check-and-update is a fully atomic operation. One way to model this requirement as an mDSA would be to absorb port A as part of the state: that is the state of the mDSA is defined using values of such ports that are used both for inputs and outputs. However, this would lead to an exponential blowup in the number of states when there are multiple such ports that are both read and written on transitions. To succinctly capture requirements with outputs, we allow both reads and writes on all ports and define *mDSAs with outputs*. Later, in Sect. 5 we will use these mDSAs-with-outputs to give a semantics for the industry notation Expressive Decision Tables (EDTs).

4.1 mDSA-with-Outputs: Formal Syntax and Semantics

The syntax of mDSA-with-outputs is almost the same as that of mDSAs. The only difference is in the syntax of transitions. As before, there is a multiport alphabet $\Sigma = \langle \Sigma_1, \ldots, \Sigma_k \rangle$. An mDSA-with-outputs $\mathcal{B}$ is a tuple (Q, Σ, q_0, δ) where Q is a finite set of states, q_0 is the initial state and δ is a finite set of transitions. We do not view these automata as language acceptors, and so we do not specifically define accept states. We will instead discuss state reachability.

Transitions. A transition now looks like:

$$q \xrightarrow[O_1:b_1 \;\|\; O_2:b_2 \;\|\; \cdots \;\|\; O_m:b_m]{I_1:u_1 \;\|\; I_2:u_2 \;\|\; \cdots \;\|\; I_\ell:u_\ell} q'$$

where q, q' are states; each u_j is a word in the port alphabet of I_j; and each b_j is a letter in the port alphabet of O_j. We remark that $\{I_1, \ldots, I_k\} \cap \{O_1, \ldots, O_m\}$ may be non-empty. In other words, some of the ports may appear both as input and output in a transition.

Semantics. Configurations of $\mathcal{B}$ are the same as before, given by (q, w, θ) with q a state, w the word seen so far and θ a position of the tape head. The semantics is a transition system $\mathbb{TS}^{\mathcal{B}} = (S, s_0, \rightarrow)$ where S is the set of configurations, with s_0 being the initial configuration $(q_0, \epsilon, 0)$. Let $\rho = (q, (I_1 : u_1 \| \cdots I_\ell : u_\ell), (O_1 : b_1 \| \cdots \| O_m : b_m), q')$. There are three kinds of transitions in $\mathbb{TS}^{\mathcal{B}}$:

- *ϵ-transitions.* $(q, w, \theta) \xrightarrow[\rho]{\epsilon} (q', wb_1b_2 \ldots b_m, |w|)$ if the input condition $(I_1 : u_1 \| \cdots \| I_\ell : u_\ell)$ matches the tape configuration (w, θ); in that case move the tape head to the end of w and write all the outputs to the right of w (order of writing does not matter).
- *transitions on input letters.* if no outgoing transition from q has a label that matches the current tape configuration (w, θ), then there is no ϵ transition out of (q, w, θ) and the mDSA-with-outputs listens to further input letters:
  - $(q, w, \theta) \xrightarrow[\rho]{a} (q', wab_1b_2 \ldots b_m, |wa|)$ if $I_1 : u_1 \| \cdots \| I_\ell : u_\ell$ matches (wa, θ); then, move the tape head to the end of wa and write the outputs after that,
  - $(q, w, \theta) \xrightarrow{a} (q, wa, \theta)$ if no transition out of q matches (wa, θ).

Notice that the transitions on input letters have the same matching semantics as in an mDSA, except now they also write all the outputs to the end of the word. The main change is the presence of ϵ-transitions. Since we write outputs after matching a transition, on reaching a new state q' there could already be transitions out of q' that match the current tape. Previously, in mDSA, this would not happen, since the tape head would be at the end of the word, and at least one port should see a fully fresh match.

Surprisingly, this ability to produce outputs which can in turn be consumed by input conditions, creates complex behaviours. We illustrate this additional difficulty by presenting an mDSA-with-outputs that can succinctly encode an N-bit counter.

N-bit counter. We wish to implement addition of an N-bit counter using an mDSA-with-outputs that has 3 states $\{q^{init}, q_0, f\}$, $N+1$ ports and $\mathcal{O}(N)$ transitions. Suppose $b_{N-1}b_{N-2}\dots b_1b_0$ are the N bits, with b_{N-1} the most significant bit and b_0 the least significant bit. Addition can be implemented using N rules: for $j \in \{0, \dots, N-1\}$

- if $b_j = 0$ and $b_{j-1} = b_{j-2} = \dots = b_0 = 1$, then change $b_j := 1$ and $b_{j-1} = b_{j-2} = \dots = b_0 := 0$

Starting from 0 for all bits, there will be exactly one rule that will be applicable each time. Applying the relevant rule each time will lead to $b_{N-1} = b_{N-2} = \dots = b_0 = 1$ in $2^N - 1$ steps.

To model this counter using an mDSA-with-outputs, we can use N ports $b_{N-1}, b_{N-2}, \dots, b_0$ each having two values $\{0, 1\}$. From the initial state q^{init}, we can first read a dummy letter (in a fresh port), write 0 to all ports $b_{N-1}, \dots, b_0$, and move to state q_0. From q_0 to q_0, there is a transition for each $j \in \{0, \dots, N-1\}$ in the following form:

$$q_0 \xrightarrow[b_j{:}1 \ \| \ b_{j-1}{:}0 \ \| \ \cdots \ \| \ b_0{:}0]{b_j{:}0 \ \| \ b_{j-1}{:}1 \ \| \ \cdots \ \| \ b_0{:}1} q_0$$

These transitions start a sequence of $2^N - 1$ ϵ transitions which finally result in all ports b_{N-1} to b_0 being 1. To mark the end of the computation, we add an extra transition from q_0 that checks if $b_{N-1} : 1 \ \| \ b_{N-1} : 1 \ \| \ \cdots \ \| \ b_0 : 1$ and moves to f. Notice that the length of the tape when the automaton reaches f is exponential in the size of the input automaton. Therefore, the witness for reachability is exponential. We have crucially used the ability to have ports that can be used both as inputs and outputs. We will now pin down the complexity of the reachability problem in mDSA-with-outputs.

4.2 Complexity of State Reachability

We now look at the state reachability problem: given an mDSA-with-outputs $\mathcal{B}$ and a state q, does there exist a word that reaches q? Without outputs, this problem is simply a graph reachability problem, like in a DFA or a DSA. The presence of outputs makes this problem harder, as seen in the N-bit counter.

Theorem 1. *Emptiness for mDSA with outputs is PSPACE-complete.*

Proof. PSPACE *upper bound.* Let $\mathcal{B}$ be an mDSA-with-outputs. Consider the transition system $\mathbb{TS}^{\mathcal{B}}$ describing the semantics of $\mathcal{B}$. Each node in the transition system is of the form (q, w, θ) where w can become arbitrarily long. Therefore, the transition system, viewed as it is, is infinite. Suppose M is the maximum length among all words used in the transition labels of $\mathcal{A}$. This is the maximum length of a suffix that will be checked for in a transition. To detect whether

$u_1 \parallel u_2 \parallel \cdots \parallel u_k$ matches a configuration (q, w, θ), it is sufficient to maintain the last M letters seen in each port. We now explain how this can be implemented.

Assume that in configuration (q, w, θ), every projection $\mathsf{P}_i(w)$ of the word w has at most M letters. We apply the criteria for verifying if $(u_1 \parallel u_2 \parallel \cdots \parallel u_k)$ matches the tape configuration (w, θ) as in Definition 3. Now, when we append $a \in \Sigma_i$ to the end of w: if wa contains $M+1$ letters in port i, that is $|\mathsf{P}_i(wa)| = M+1$, then let w' be the word obtained by deleting from wa the first occurrence of a letter in Σ_i. Let b be this letter. If b appeared at a position strictly greater than θ in wa, then we do not need to change the tape head ($\theta' = \theta$); otherwise, b appears on or before θ, and we reduce tape position by 1 ($\theta' = \theta - 1$). This gives a new tape configuration (w', θ'). Transitions point to the new truncated configuration. Call the new truncated transition system as $\mathbb{TS}^{\mathcal{B}}_{\mathsf{finite}}$.

This bounds the tape length to $M \times k$, where k is the total number of ports. So, the total size of the truncated transition system is exponential in the size of the input. To verify emptiness, it is sufficient to guess a path in this transition system. Since each node requires polynomial space, and the length of the witness is bounded by an exponential in the size of the input, we deduce a PSPACE upper bound for the emptiness problem, following standard complexity theoretic arguments.

PSPACE-*hardness.* For the hardness, we give a reduction from this problem: given DFAs $D_1, D_2, \ldots, D_n$ over a common alphabet Σ, the DFA-intersection-emptiness asks if there exists a word in the language of all the n DFAs. This is known to be PSPACE-complete [11]. Let $D_j = (Q_j, q_j^{init}, \delta_j, F_j)$ be the description of DFA D_j. The mDSA-with-outputs $\mathcal{B}^D$ that we will construct makes use of n ports to store the state reached by each of the DFAs.

We will have one input port I with Σ as alphabet, and n ports S_j (for $j \in \{1, \ldots, n\}$), with $\Sigma_j = Q_j$ being the states of DFA D_j. We add a special port L with alphabet \$ that will be used for book-keeping. Let s^{init} be the initial state of $\mathcal{B}^D$. There is an initial transition that reads the special character \$ and writes the initial state of each DFA to the respective ports, and moves to s_0:

$$s^{init} \xrightarrow[S_1:q_1^{init} \,\parallel\, S_2:q_2^{init} \,\parallel\, \cdots \,\parallel\, S_n:q_n^{init}]{L:\$} s_0$$

From s_0 we have a gadget that reads the next input and then sequentially updates the states of each DFA by writing the new states in the respective ports.

- the process starts with a transition $s_0 \xrightarrow[L:\$]{I:a} s_1^a$;
- there are states s_j^a for all $j \in \{1, \ldots, n\}$, and for all $a \in \Sigma$;
- for every transition (q_j, a, q_j') in D_j we have: $s_j^a \xrightarrow[L:\$ \,\parallel\, S_j:q_j']{L:\$ \,\parallel\, S_j:q_j} s_{j+1}^a$, with $s_{n+1}^a := s_0$.

When an a is read at s_0, the automaton moves to s_1^a and the tape head moves to the position of a. Since the same transition also writes a \$ to L, there will be an outgoing transition from s_1^a that matches: this transition would be the one corresponding to the current state of D_1. Then, the automaton goes to s_2^a, and the process continues until the automaton comes back to s_0, giving rise to a sequence of n ϵ-transitions from s_1^a back to s_0.

This is the basic construction that simulates the n DFAs using an mDSA-with-outputs. To detect acceptance, we can add special ports $B_1, B_2, \ldots, B_n$. Whenever we reach an accepting state in Q_j we write 1 to this port, and when we reach a non-accepting state, we write 0. Add a transition $B_1 = 1 \parallel B_2 = 1 \parallel \cdots \parallel B_n = 1$ from s_0 to a special state f. The intersection of $D_1, \ldots, D_n$ is empty iff f is reachable.

For every letter a and every port j there is a state s_j^a. There are transitions s_j^a to s_{j+1}^a for each every transition in D_j. Total number of states is $(|\Sigma| \cdot n) + 2$, and the total number of transitions is proportional to $\sum_j \delta_j$. Therefore, the overall construction is polynomial-time.

5 Expressive Decision Tables

Expressive Decision Tables (EDTs) [14] are a tabular notation for specifying software requirements and have been used in various industrial settings [2,15]. An EDT specification consists of tables where columns specify input, output and input/output (I/O) ports, and rows specify the relationship between input and output values on these ports. Each port is associated with an alphabet and each cell in the table consists of a string of letters from this alphabet. The original work on EDTs contained timing constraints in the cells and interpreted the EDT over a notion of discrete-time. In this paper we consider EDT without time. A cell in an EDT table is said to match when the string given in that cell is a suffix of the values seen for the input port corresponding to that cell's column. A row of an EDT matches when all the cells corresponding to that row match and one cell matches on the last input. Table 1 gives the EDT specification of the Car Alarm module described in the beginning of Sect. 4. We write F for `Off` and `False`, N for `On`, P for `Press` and R for `Release`.

Table 1. EDT for an Alarm module

s.no	in I	in P	in A	out A	out F
1	F	P;P	F	N	
2		R;R;R	N	F	F
3	N			F	F

In the example EDT the input ports are prefixed with *in* and output ports are prefixed with *out*. Input/Output ports are prefixed with both *in* and *out*. These are the ports that appear on both sides of the EDT, as inputs as well as outputs.

A *test case* for a requirement is a sequence of values that match the EDT row corresponding to that requirement. The use of EDTs and test case generation algorithms from EDT specifications have been widely studied. [2,15]. However, the notation lacks a rigorous formal semantics, except for a brief description of key elements of formal semantics in [14]. Hence, none of the test case algorithms use formal techniques like model checking and instead rely on random generation using heuristics. These algorithms, therefore, cannot prove that an EDT row cannot be matched and also find it hard to match certain rows. We overcome both these limitations by providing a formal semantics for EDTs (without timing) through a translation to mDSA-with-outputs.

5.1 Translating EDT to mDSA-with-Outputs

An EDT with C columns and R rows is translated to an mDSA, with one state q_0 and an alphabet $\Sigma = \langle \Sigma_1 \cdots \Sigma_{|C|} \rangle$. Each Σ_i corresponds to the port of column i and the letters of the alphabet correspond to the values that the signal can take, prefixed by $\langle Portname :\rangle$. Thus if the Port name of the first column is A and its alphabet is $a_1, a_2, \cdots, a_k$ then the corresponding alphabet $\Sigma_1 = A : a_1, A : a_2 \cdots A : a_k$. Each EDT row is translated to an mDSA as follows:

- The mDSA has exactly one state q_0
- There is a transition corresponding to each row with q_0 as both the source and target state.
- The label of each transition consists of all the strings in the cells of the input columns of the row combined using the $||$ operator.
- The output of the transitions are the strings in the cell corresponding to the output columns, combined using the $||$ operator.

The mDSA in Fig. 3 is an mDSA specification corresponding the EDT given in Table 1

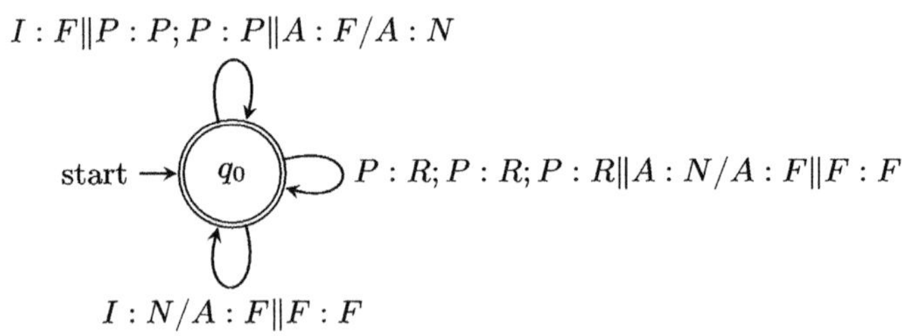

Fig. 3. mDSA of the Alarm EDT.

To generate a test for a certain row r, we can first add a special state q_r, and make the transition corresponding to this row point to q_r instead of q_0. A test for r then reduces to a witness for the reachability of q_r.

5.2 Experiments

We have implemented a prototype test generator for EDTs using the translation of EDTs to mDSA-with-outputs [1]. In our implementation, we translate the given EDT $\mathcal{T}$ into an mDSA-with-outputs $\mathcal{B}^{\mathcal{T}}$ and simulate the semantics of $\mathcal{B}^{\mathcal{T}}$ using the finite transition system $\mathbb{TS}^{\mathcal{B}^{\mathcal{T}}}_{\mathsf{finite}}$ described in the proof of Theorem 1.

First we look at a couple of small EDTs. Suppose we want a testcase for Row 1 in Table 1. Encoding this in our tool gives a testcase $(P; P)$ for Row 1, when default values for I and A are set to F. Next we look at Table 2, a partial representation of a wiper module in a car. The tool finds a testcase (park;notpark) for Row 2.

Table 2. EDT for a Wiper module

sno	in ignition	in wiperswitch	in parksensor	in error	out wipercmd	out error
1	on	on		false	wipe	
2			(park;notpark)		dontwipe	true

We now present an EDT for which our tool can solve the test generation problem, whereas randomized techniques will have low success probability. The EDT is a slight variation of the N bit counter presented in Sect. 4.1. We depict a part of the EDT for three bits in Table 3. In addition we add a row to check for all $t_i = 1$, and also have an extra letter in the port T. Therefore there is exactly one sequence that makes all the t_i equal to 1. Randomized techniques have a low probability of generating such a test case. Our prototype implementation generates a test case for $N = 5$.

Table 3. Implementing a binary counter for 3 bits

T	t_2	t_1	t_0	S_T	t_2	t_1	t_0	S_T
✓								+
			0	+			1	−
		0	1	+		1	0	−
	0	1	1	+	1	0	0	−

Our goal with the experiments was not to present a scalable tool for EDT test generation. We aimed to create an open source simulator for mDSA-with-outputs, which we have applied on EDT test case generation. As future work, we plan to investigate scalable algorithms for reachability in mDSA-with-outputs.

6 Conclusion

We have presented mDSA-with-outputs, an extension of DSA with concurrency and outputs. The resulting model captures suffix-based specifications of concurrent systems more succinctly compared to a DSA or a DFA. We have illustrated this idea over several examples. The main challenge was to provide a clean operational semantics that can account for suffixes, multiple ports and outputs. We have applied our study to the formal analysis of a fragment of Expressive Decision Tables (EDT), an industry notation for formal specifications. Although there are several automaton based models known in the literature, we believe mDSA-with-outputs gives a fresh perspective on *suffix-based* specifications in the presence of concurrency and outputs. Extending this work to the real-time setting is an interesting direction for future work.

Acknowledgement. We thank Arjun Arul for his help with the implementation of the test generator explained in Sect. 5.2. We thank Sagar Verma for helpful discussions.

References

1. https://github.com/KeerthanR/mDSA/tree/main/code
2. Agrawal, S., Venkatesh, R., Shrotri, U., Zare, A., Verma, S.: Scaling test case generation for expressive decision tables. In: 13th IEEE International Conference on Software Testing, Validation and Verification, ICST 2020, Porto, Portugal, October 24-28, 2020, pp. 364–374. IEEE (2020)
3. Berry, G., Gonthier, G.: The Esterel synchronous programming language: Design, semantics, implementation. Sci. Comput. Program. **19**(2), 87–152 (1992)
4. Dias Neto, A.C., Subramanyan, R., Vieira, M., Travassos, G.H.: A survey on model-based testing approaches: a systematic review. In: Proceedings of the 1st ACM International Workshop on Empirical Assessment of Software Engineering Languages and Technologies: Held in Conjunction with the 22nd IEEE/ACM International Conference on Automated Software Engineering (ASE) 2007, WEASELTech '07, pp. 31–36, New York, NY, USA, 2007. Association for Computing Machinery
5. Samuel Eilenberg. Automata, languages, and machines., B. Pure and applied mathematics. Academic Press (1976)
6. Giammarresi, D., Montalbano, R.: Deterministic generalized automata. Theoret. Comput. Sci. **215**(1), 191–208 (1999)
7. Haar, S., Jard, C., Jourdan, G.V.: Testing input/output partial order automata. In: Proceedings of the 19th IFIP TC6/WG6.1 International Conference, and 7th International Conference on Testing of Software and Communicating Systems, TestCom'07/FATES'07, page 171–185, Berlin, Heidelberg, 2007. Springer-Verlag (2007)
8. Han, Y.S., Wood, D.: The generalization of generalized automata: Expression automata. In: Domaratzki, M., Okhotin, A., Salomaa, K., Yu, S., eds., In: Implementation and Application of Automata, pp. 156–166, Berlin, Heidelberg, 2005. Springer Berlin Heidelberg (2005)
9. Harel, D.: Statecharts: a visual formalism for complex systems. Sci. Comput. Program. **8**(3), 231–274 (1987)

10. Keerthan, R., Srivathsan, B., Venkatesh, R., Verma, S.: Deterministic suffix-reading automata. In: Achilleos, A., Francalanza, A., eds., In: Proceedings Fifteenth International Symposium on Games, Automata, Logics, and Formal Verification, GandALF 2024, Reykjavik, Iceland, 19-21 June (2024)
11. Kozen, D.: Lower bounds for natural proof systems. In: Proceedings of the 18th Annual Symposium on Foundations of Computer Science, SFCS '77, pp. 254–266, USA, 1977. IEEE Computer Society (1977)
12. Petri, C.A.: Communication with automata. DTIC Research Report AD0630125 (1966)
13. Utting, M., Pretschner, A., Legeard, B.: A taxonomy of model-based testing approaches. Softw. Test. Verif. Reliab. **22**(5), 297–312 (2012)
14. Venkatesh, R., Shrotri, U., Krishna, G.M., Agrawal, S.: EDT: A specification notation for reactive systems. In: Fettweis, G.P., Nebel, W., editors, Design, Automation & Test in Europe Conference & Exhibition, DATE 2014, Dresden, Germany, March 24-28, 2014, pp. 1–6. European Design and Automation Association (2014)
15. Venkatesh, R., Shrotri, U., Zare, A., Agrawal, S.: On generating test cases from EDT specifications. In: Maciaszek, L.A., Filipe, J., eds., Evaluation of Novel Approaches to Software Engineering - 10th International Conference, ENASE 2015, Barcelona, Spain, April 29-30, 2015, Revised Selected Papers, volume 599 of Communications in Computer and Information Science, pp. 1–20. Springer (2015)

SmartShards: Churn-Tolerant Continuously Available Distributed Ledger

Joseph Oglio, Mikhail Nesterenko(✉), and Gokarna Sharma

Department of Computer Science, Kent State University, Kent, OH 44242, USA
joglio@kent.edu, {mikhail,sharma}@cs.kent.edu

Abstract. We present *SmartShards*: a new sharding algorithm for improving Byzantine tolerance and churn resistance in blockchains. Our algorithm places a peer in multiple shards to create an overlap. This simplifies cross-shard communication and shard membership management. We describe *SmartShards*, prove it correct and evaluate its performance.

We propose several *SmartShards* extensions: defense against a slowly adaptive adversary, combining transactions into blocks, fortification against the join/leave attack.

1 Introduction

Blockchain is a distributed digital ledger maintained by a network of independent peers. The technology provides transparency and immutability of records while promises decentralized control over the ledger. This facilitates cooperation among non-trusting entities: the peers agree on the records of the ledger. The peers usually do not belong to the same organization and may join and leave the network during its operation generating continuous churn. The peers themselves may not necessarily operate correctly. Instead, they may fail or even attack the network. Such behavior is modeled as Byzantine fault [20] where the faulty peer is allowed to behave arbitrarily.

Besides cryptocurrency [24,30], which generates a lot of recent public discourse, blockchain is used in a variety of applications: online auctions [19], marketplaces [29], supply chain [11], health care [3], Internet-of-Things [26], intellectual property rights [16], electric power industry [4] among many others.

Popular blockchains use proof-of-work based consensus algorithms [24] in which peers compete for the right to publish records on the blockchain by searching for solutions to cryptographic challenges. Such algorithms tend to be conceptually simple and robust. However, they are resource intensive and environmentally harmful [28]. Therefore, modern blockchain designs often focus on cooperative consensus algorithms. In these cooperative consensus algorithms, rather than compete, peers exchange messages to arrive at a joint decision.

Within many blockchain application domains, the size of the blockchain network needs to reach thousands and possibly hundreds of thousands of peers. This

S. Lahlou and M. Mukund (Eds.): NETYS 2025, LNCS 15736, pp. 146–162, 2026.
https://doi.org/10.1007/978-3-032-00347-8_9

necessitates systems which are highly scalable and resilient. However, traditional blockchain systems face significant scalability issues: to agree on a ledger record all peers have to communicate with each other. Hence, the communication cost grows with the network size.

Sharding is a technique that may potentially enhance blockchain scalability. In a sharded network, the peers are divided into groups called shards. Each shard processes transactions in parallel, improving overall system throughput. A number of sharded blockchain designs are presented in the literature. Refer to recent surveys [15,21,31] for an extensive review. Although promising, the scalability of shading blockchain design is hampered by the inherent features of a decentralized peer-to-peer systems. In particular, cross-shard transactions and churn.

In this paper we propose an approach of shard construction we call *SmartShards* that addresses both of these problems. *SmartShards* overlaps shards to improve shard communication coordination and membership.

Cross-Shard Transactions and Faults. A shard acts as a unit of either coordination or data ownership. For example, in Elastico [22], the shards concurrently verify different transactions. In *Rapidchain* [32], each shard stores data about a collection of wallets. A cross-shard transaction requires the coordination of multiple shards. For example, in *Rapidchain*, a transaction may be moving funds between wallets in two different shards. There are multiple ways to coordinate such transactions. Some blockchains use locking [17]. Other designs break the single transaction into sub-transactions to be executed separately. Alternatively, the system may have a dedicated reference committee that approves cross-shard transactions [22]. Regardless of the technique, the source and target shards have to communicate either directly or though intermediate coordinators.

Individual peers may be faulty. One approach to Byzantine fault-tolerance is to use cryptographic signatures. However, this may be computationally expensive or difficult to implement in a peer-to-peer system. Instead, we consider a classic approach where the correctness depends on sufficiently large majority of correct peers. To ensure information propagation correctness, multiple source shard peers have to broadcast the transaction data to multiple target shard peers. This limits the efficiency of cross-shard transaction processing. In *SmartShards* that we propose, each peer participates in multiple shards. The shard overlap is used to make inter-shard communication more efficient and robust.

Churn. Churn, continuous joining and leaving of peers, may disrupt the operation of a blockchain. In case of sharding, the problem is exacerbated since it may potentially lead to shard failure and structural network compromise. However, the problem of handling continuous churn within sharded blockchains remains underexplored.

In most systems [17,22,32], the churn is handled through periodic system re-configuration events. An epoch is the time of continuous system operation between such reconfiguration events. For such epoch-based systems, the rate of churn is considered low enough to ensure adequate system availability. If the churn is substantial, to ensure correct blockchain operation, the system has to spend significant time re-configuring itself. This downtime increases with both the rate of churn and the scale of the system.

In a sharded blockchain, peers have to maintain both their shard membership and the links to the other shards for cross-shard transactions. In traditional systems, this information has to be maintained separately. In *SmartShards*, the peers are used for internal shard recording and for inter-shard communication. Therefore, the overlapping shards integrally maintain both membership and links. This simplifies churn handling in *SmartShards*.

Related Work. There are several blockchain designs that overlap coordination between consensus groups. *Monoxide* [27] is a competitive Proof-of-Work blockchain. To improve scalability, it uses multiple asynchronous consensus zones that maintain separate blockchains. These blockchains periodically synchronize by linking blocks across zones. A peer may work on any of these local blockchains. Thus, *Monoxide* has fixed zones with floating peer membership. *Hyperledger Fabric* [5] uses cooperative consensus. It also maintains multiple blockchains. It has a centralized ordering service for transaction synchronization. Peers may join and leave the network only when the system is off-line, i.e. outside an epoch.

Churn management in distributed systems has been extensively studied. Kuhn *et al.* [18] propose simulating a robust node by a collection of peers connected to peers of other simulated nodes. These simulated nodes retain there data despite individual peer churn. In this sense, these simulated nodes are similar to shards in blockchain networks. Foreback *et al.* [12,13] explore the theoretical limits of infinite churn, proposing techniques to maintain network connectivity despite continuous churn in general peer-to-peer networks.

Malkhi and Reiter [23] study Byzatine-robust quorum systems for distributed storage. A quorum is a collection of subsets of peers where each pair of subsets intersects. This arrangement is similar to *SmartShards*. However, in their approach, quorums are used to build a robust register and to synchronize the entire network and ensure consistent reading and writing of the shared data. In *SmartShards*, the quorums are used to maintain separate data in separate shards and only synchronize if the data is affected by smart-shard transactions.

SMARTCHAIN [8] is a blockchain algorithm that uses quorums to improve performance. However, *SMARTCHAIN* uses cryptographic signatures to verify cross-shard transactions. In contrast, *SmartShards* does not need the cryptographic signatures.

Baldoni *et al.* [7] use quorums for churn resistance in Byzantine fault-tolerant distributed storage. Their approach requires bounded churn and eventual system synchrony. *SmartShards* do not need such assumptions.

García-Pérez *et al.* [14] use overlapping quorums to achieve consensus despite Byzantine faults. Similar to *SmartShards*, the quorum intersections are used for data update synchronization. However, a "trust relationship" is required for quorum formation and maintenance. *SmartShards* do not need such trust relationship.

Our Contribution. *SmartShards* presented in this paper is a novel sharded approach to Byzantine tolerance and churn resistance in blockchain systems.

Given a basic Byzantine consensus algorithm that tolerates up to f faults, and with overlap between shards x, *SmartShards* operates correctly with at most f faults in each shard, and at most $\lfloor x/2 - 1 \rfloor$ faults in the overlap.

2 Notation and Problem Definition

System Model. We assume a peer-to-peer network. Each peer has a unique identifier. A peer may send a message to any other peer so long as it has the receiver's identifier. Communication is reliable. Peers communicate through authenticated channels: the receiver of the message may always identify the sender. Identity forging, such as Sybil attacks [10], is not considered.

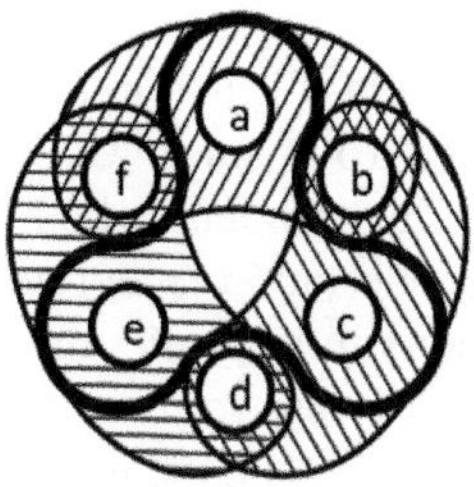

Fig. 1. *SmartShards* peer to shard allocation example. The shards are: $\{f, a, b\}$, $\{b, c, d\}$, $\{d, e, f\}$, $\{a, c, e\}$.

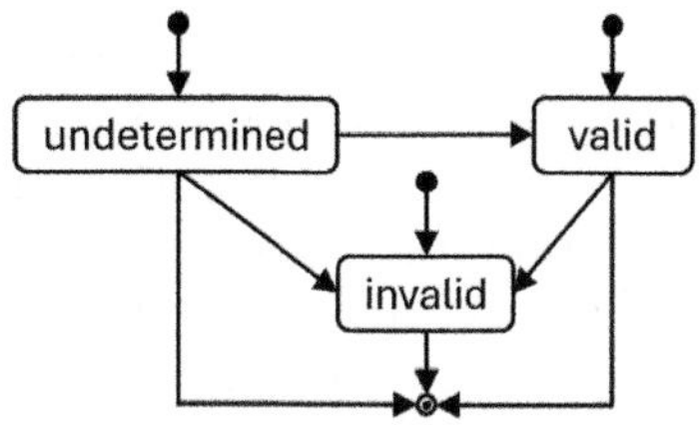

Fig. 2. Transaction validity transitions.

Shards, Transactions, Faults. A *shard* is a fully connected set of peers maintaining a blockchain. Shards A and B are considered *overlapping* if there exists at least one peer $p \in A \cap B$. For simplicity, we initially assume that a peer may belong to at most two shards. See example peer-to-shard allocation in Fig. 1.

The overlaps are used for communication between shards. We assume that the overlap size, x, is the same for all shards. Note that $x = 1$ in Fig. 4 and is not sufficient for fault tolerance. Two peers p and q that belong to the same shard are *shard mates*, or just *mates*. If q is a mate of p in some shard, then the *countershard* of p for q is the other shard to which q belongs.

A *wallet* is a means of storing funds. Each wallet has a unique identifier. A *client* is an entity that *owns* wallets. This ownership can be authenticated by the peers of the network. There may be multiple clients. A client submits transactions. A *transaction* is a transfer of funds from a *source* to a *target* wallet. For simplicity, we assume that each transaction has a single source and a single target wallet. A shard records transactions for a set of wallets. A *source shard* records the transaction if the source wallet is in this shard's set. Similarly, a *target shard* records a transaction if it maintains the target wallet. A client may have wallets in more than one shard.

There are two types of transactions. A *cross-shard transaction* moves funds between wallets of different shards. An *internal transaction* moves funds between two wallets of the same shard. Note that for an internal transaction, the single shard is both the source and the target.

The funds are transferred in the form of *UTXOs* (unspent transaction outputs). A transaction is applied to an *input* UTXO and produces an *output* UTXO.

A ledger is a sequence of transactions recorded by a shard. Each peer in the shard maintains its own copy of this ledger. The peers are initialized with the same genesis ledger.

A transaction is *confirmed* by a peer if it is recorded in this peer's ledger. An output UTXO of a confirmed transaction is either spent or unspent. A UTXO is *unspent* if it is an output of a confirmed transaction and there is no other confirmed transaction that uses it as an input. It is *spent* if used as an input to a confirmed transaction. If a transaction is unconfirmed, its output UTXO is neither spent nor unspent.

A transaction, whether confirmed or not, is *valid* if it is applied to an unspent UTXO. A transaction is *invalid* if it is applied to a spent UTXO. Note that if the input of a transaction is neither spent nor unspent, then its validity is undetermined. The validity transitions of a transaction are, therefore, as follows, see Fig. 2. A submitted transaction may be either valid, invalid, or undetermined. An undetermined transaction may eventually become either valid or invalid. A transaction of determined validity may never become undetermined again. A valid transaction may become invalid if another transaction that spends its input UTXO is confirmed. A valid confirmed transaction is never invalidated. An invalid transaction, either confirmed or unconfirmed, never becomes valid.

A *Byzantine* peer is faulty. A faulty peer behaves arbitrarily. A *correct* peer is not faulty.

Consensus and Distributed Ledger Problems.

Definition 1. *In* the Consensus Problem, *every correct process is input a value v and must output an irrevocable decision subject to the following properties:*

- **CValidity:** *if all correct peers are input the same value v, then every correct peer decides v;*
- **CAgreement:** *no two correct peers decide differently;*
- **COrder:** *any pair of decisions are ordered the same of every pair of peers;*
- **CLiveness:** *every correct peer eventually decides.*

Tolerance threshold f is the maximum number of faulty processes. An algorithm solves the Consensus Problem if it satisfies the three properties above provided that the number of faults does not exceed f.

Definition 2. *In* the Distributed Ledger Problem, *peers confirm a particular transaction with the following three properties:*

- **LValidity:** *every confirmed transaction is valid;*
- **LAgreement:** *if a transaction is confirmed by one correct peer in a shard, it is confirmed by every correct peer in the shard; and*

LLiveness: *if a client submits a valid transaction, it is eventually either confirmed or invalidated.*

Algorithm 1: *SmartShards*, Variables

Constants
p ▷ peer id
$Shards$ ▷ set of all shard ids
$shard_1, shard_2 \in Shards$ ▷ ids of the shards this peer is in
$Peers_1$, $Peers_2$ ▷ sets of peer ids for $shard_1$ and $shard_2$
$CounterShards_1 \equiv \{\langle q, s\rangle \mid q \in Peers_1, s \in Shards\}$ ▷ countershards for $Peers_1$
$CounterShards_2 \equiv \{\langle q, s\rangle \mid q \in Peers_2, s \in Shards\}$ ▷ countershards for $Peers_1$

Transaction variables
$client$ ▷ client initiating the transaction
$sWallet$ ▷ source wallet
$tWallet$ ▷ target wallet
$UTXO$ ▷ source unspent transaction output
$sShard$ ▷ shard containing the source wallet
$tShard$ ▷ shard containing the target wallet

Process variables
$Ledger_1$, $Ledger_2$ ▷ sequence of committed transactions in $shard_1$, $shard_2$
▷ record format: $\langle UTXO,\ sShard, tShard, sWallet, tWallet\rangle$
$Transfers_1$, $Transfers_2$ ▷ set of cross-shard transaction receipts for $shard_1$, $shard_2$
▷ record format: $\langle UTXO,\ sShard, tShard, sWallet, tWallet, q\rangle$

3 *SmartShards* Description and Correctness Proof

Algorithm Outline. *SmartShards* uses a consensus algorithm *Consensus* to confirm transactions. The peers of the source shard execute *Consensus* to agree on the transaction. This is sufficient for an internal transaction where the source and target shards are the same. For a cross-shard transaction, the peers that overlap the source and target shard, inform the target shard of the transaction via a Transfer message. Once a peer of the target shard receives sufficient number of Transfer messages, it initiates consensus on the cross-shard transaction.

Constants and Variables Description. The constants and variables are listed in Algorithm 1. Let us start with constants. Each peer has a unique identifier p. The peer stores a set of all shard ids in $Shards$. Out of this set, p belongs to two shards: $shard_1$ and $shard_2$. The set $Peers_1$ contains the ids of the mates of p in $shard_1$. Similarly, $Peers_2$ are mates of p in $shard_2$. For each mate q of p, $CounterShards_1$ lists a set of countershards for all mates of p in $shard_1$. $Countershards_2$ is defined similarly for $shard_2$.

The variables maintained by p are of two kinds: transaction and process variables. Transaction variables pertain to a particular transaction: client id, source and target wallet, source UTXO, and source and target shard. Note that if the transaction is internal, then the source and target shards are the same.

Algorithm 2: *SmartShards*, Actions

```
18 function VALID(client, UTXO, sShard)
19     ▷ returns true if UTXO is owned by client and is unspent

20 ▷ actions for shard_1
21 upon receive TRANSACTION (client, UTXO, sShard, tShard, sWallet, tWallet)
22     if VALID(client, UTXO, sShard) and sShard = shard_1 then
23         STARTCONSENSUSTX(UTXO, sShard, tShard, sWallet, tWallet)

24 upon ENDCONSENSUSTX(UTXO, sShard, tShard, sWallet, tWallet)
25     if VALID(client, UTXO, sShard) then
26         append (UTXO, sShard, tShard, sWallet, tWallet) to Ledger_1
27         if sShard ≠ tShard and tShard = shard_2 then
28             send TRANSFER (UTXO, sShard, tShard, sWallet, tWallet) to tShard
29         else
30             send TXCONFIRMATION (p, UTXO) to client

31 upon ENDCONSENSUSTR(UTXO, sShard, tShard, sWallet, tWallet, result)
32     if result then
33         append (UTXO, sShard, tShard, sWallet, tWallet) to Ledger_1
34         send TXCONFIRMATION (p, UTXO) to client

35 upon receive TRANSFER(UTXO, fromShard, toShard, sWallet, tWallet) from q
36     if q ∈ Peers_1 and CounterShards_1.q = fromShard and
37       (UTXO, fromShard, toShard, sWallet, tWallet, q) ∉ Transfers_1 and
38       toShard = shard_1 then
39         add (UTXO, fromShard, toShard, sWallet, tWallet, q) to Transfers_1
40         if #{(UTXO, fromShard, toShard, sWallet, tWallet, *) ∈
             Transfers_1} ≥ ⌈#{(q, s) ∈ CounterShards_1 : s = sShard}/2⌉ and
             (UTXO, fromShard, toShard, sWallet, tWallet) ∉ Ledger_1 then
41             STARTCONSENSUSTR(UTXO, fromShard, toShard, sWallet, tWallet, true)

42 ▷ actions for shard_2 similar
```

In addition to transaction variables, p maintains process variables in all transactions. Specifically, $Ledger_1$ contains records of confirmed transactions for $shard_1$. Variable $Ledger_2$ keeps the records for $shard_2$. Variable $Transfers_1$ collects notifications of confirmed transactions from the source shard peers.

Actions Description. *SmartShard* actions are listed in Algorithm 2. The function VALID is used in the actions of *SmartShards.* It examines the shard ledger of p to check if the specific $UTXO$ is in the client wallet and is unspent. That is, this $UTXO$ is not an input to another transaction in this ledger.

There are four actions in the algorithm: TRANSACTION, ENDCONSENSUSTX, ENDCONSENSUSTR, and TRANSFER. The TRANSACTION action, see Line 21, processes client transaction receipts in the source shard. If a transaction is valid, the peer starts the consensus algorithm for this transaction.

Once this consensus is done, the ENDCONSENSUSTX action, see Line 24, at the source shard checks if the transaction is still valid and confirms the transaction by recording it in the local ledger and sends a confirmation message to the client. If the transaction is cross-shard, and the peer is in both source and target shards, then the peer sends a TRANSFER message to the target shard notifying it of the successful confirmation.

Algorithm 3: *SmartShards*, Client Actions and Variables

```
43 Constants
44 client                                                        ▷ client id
45 UTXO
46 f                                          ▷ consensus tolerance threshold
47 Variables
48 confirmed                             ▷ status of the pending transaction
49 SMSmembers          ▷ set of sets of peers, history of shard membership
50 Confirmations              ▷ set of peers that confirmed the transaction
51 Actions
52 upon SubmitTx⟨UTXO⟩
53     confirmed = false
54     while ¬confirmed do             ▷ periodically resend transaction request
55         send Transaction⟨client, UTXO⟩ to SMS
56 upon receive Membership ⟨Members⟩ from SMS
57     SMSmembers := {Members} ∪ SMSmembers
58 upon receive TxConfirmation ⟨peer, UTXO⟩ from peer
59     Confirmations := Confirmations ∪ peer
60     if ∃ Members ∈ SMSmembers : #{Members ∩ Confirmations} > f then
61         confirmed := true
62 ▷ join and leave actions similar
```

The TRANSFER action handles the TRANSFER message receipt, see Line 35. A recipient peer p in $shard_1$ collects such receipts in $Transfers_1$. If p receives TRANSFER messages from greater than half of the peers in the overlap between the source and target shards, it considers the transaction to be valid and then p initiates consensus in the target shard on the cross-shard transaction. Every peer in the target shard participates in this consensus. Each peer uses the number of received TRANSFER messages to set its initial value for consensus. If the number of received TRANSFER messages is greater than half the number of peers in the overlap then the value is set to **true** otherwise **false**.

Once consensus on a transfer is reached, the ENDCONSENSUSTR action, see Line 31, at the target shard checks whether the peers agree on the validity of the transaction. If agreement is reached, and *result*, the consensus value, is **true**, the transaction is recorded in the ledger and sends a confirmation message to the client.

Correctness Proof.

Lemma 1. SmartShards *satisfies the LValidity property of the Distributed Ledger Problem.*

Proof. To satisfy LValidity, we need to show that only valid transactions are confirmed. Let us consider internal transactions first. In this case, the source and target shards are the same. Therefore, *SmartShards* executes only the TRANSACTION and ENDCONSENSUSTX actions without transmitting any TRANSFER messages. The peers of the shard execute the *Consensus* algorithm for the transaction within a single shard. An internal transaction is only confirmed by the

EndConsensusTx action. Before confirming, the action checks the transaction validity. That is, only valid transactions are confirmed. Valid confirmed transactions may not be invalidated.

Let us now deal with cross-shard transactions. Such transactions are confirmed in the source and target shards separately. By an argument similar to the above, we can show that a cross-shard transaction is confirmed in the source shard only if it is valid. If such a transaction is confirmed in the source shard, the source shard peers send a Transfer message. This initiates consensus in the target shard. A correct peer starts such consensus only after it receives a Transfer message from more than half of the peers in the overlap between the source and target shards. This means that at least one correct peer in the source shard sends such message. That is, this transaction is valid.

Note that a cross-shard transaction is confirmed by the EndConsensusTr action in the target shard. If this consensus is started by a correct peer, the transaction is valid. Alternatively, a Byzantine peer may start *Consensus* on a potentially invalid transaction. For such a transaction, correct peers do not have a sufficient number of Transfer messages. Therefore, all correct peers are input an initial value of **false**. By the CValidity property of consensus, if all correct peers are input **false**, they must decide **false**. In which case, the transaction is not confirmed. Thus, *SmartShards* satisfies LValidity for both internal and cross-shard transactions. □

Lemma 2. SmartShards *satisfies the LAgreement property of the Distributed Ledger Problem.*

Proof. We prove this property by induction. Each peer starts with the same genesis ledger which is assumed to contain valid transactions. Let the ledger at each peer contain i valid transactions. Any transaction is confirmed by either the execution of the EndConsensusTx or EndConsensusTr action. Let us consider the action for transaction $i + 1$. By COrder property, the order of EndConsensusTx and EndConsensusTr actions are the same for every peer. By CAgreement, this is the same transaction at every peer. Since the ledger up to the i-th transaction is the same for each peer, the validity of this transaction is also going to be the same. That is, this transaction is going to be either confirmed or rejected by all correct peers. Thus, the ledger remains consistent after processing $i + 1$ transactions. □

Lemma 3. SmartShards *satisfies the LLiveness property of the Distributed Ledger Problem.*

Proof. For internal transactions, the peers are running *Consensus*. Therefore, LLiveness is satisfied because the CLivenss property of *Consensus* ensures that every transaction is eventually either confirmed or invalidated.

Let us discuss cross-shard transactions. Similarly to internal transactions, the peers of the source shard are running *Consensus*. Therefore, they eventually either confirm or invalidate any cross-shard transaction. If the transaction is confirmed by the source shard, the source shard peers that overlap the target shard send TRANSFER messages. Greater than half of such peers are assumed to be correct. Therefore, each target peer eventually gets more than half such TRANSFER messages.

If a target peer gets more than half TRANSFER messages, it will start *Consensus.* If all correct peers received TRANSFER messages from more than half of the overlap, then they all use *true* as the input for *Consensus.* By CValidity, this consensus must succeed. Therefore, LLiveness holds for cross-shard transactions as well. Hence the lemma. □

The below theorem follows from Lemmas 1, 2, and 3. Recall that x is the shard overlap size.

Theorem 1. *Algorithm* SmartShards *solves the Distributed Ledger Problem with at most f Byzantine faults in each shard and at most $\lfloor x/2 - 1 \rfloor$ faults in the overlap between shards.*

Fault tolerance threshold estimation. Let us address the relation between x and f. From the above theorem it follows that $f < x/2$. However, we may be able to get a more optimistic bound. In classic sharding algorithms, it is assumed that faults are distributed across shards somewhat evenly. To put another way, the number of faults in a shard is proportional to shard size. We apply this reasoning to the shard overlap size.

Let s be the number of shards in the network and z be the shard size. Assume the shard fault tolerance threshold is $f < z/3$. Since every pair of shards overlap over x peers, the shard size is $z = x(s-1)$. If the number of faults is proportional to overlap size then the tolerance threshold can be estimated as follows:

$$f < \frac{z}{3} = \frac{x(s-1)}{3}.$$

Churn Tolerance. SmartShards may be modified to tolerate churn: peer joining and leaving. We consider only cooperative churn where joining and leaving processes are correct [13]. Faulty churning peers are assumed to be within the general tolerance thresholds f and x. There are two aspects: (i) the client needs to ascertain that the appropriate member peers confirm the transaction and (ii) the peers themselves need to agree on the current shard membership.

We assume the existence of the Shard Membership Service (SMS) – a trusted service providing membership information to the clients. A client submits its transaction to the SMS. The SMS forwards this transaction to the peers in the source shard and replies to the client with the current set of peer identifiers in this shard. Once the peers receive the transaction from the SMS, they run the consensus algorithm and send the confirmation to the client.

A client may re-send the transaction. In this case, the SMS behaves similarly: it forwards the transaction to the peers and sends the membership set to the client. Due to peer churn, the membership set may differ every time. If the peers receive a request for a transaction that is already confirmed, they re-send the confirmation to the client.

Potentially, the SMS may return the exact set of peers that handle the transaction. However, such service may be difficult to implement as it needs to synchronize its operation with peers joining and leaving. Instead, we consider a weaker SMS assumption. If the client submits infinitely many requests for a specific valid transaction, then the SMS provides infinitely many sets containing at least $f + 1$ peers that reply to the transaction request. *Weak SMS* is the SMS that satisfies this assumption. Henceforth, we refer to weak SMS as just SMS.

The client actions are shown in Algorithm 3. We show the code for a single transaction confirmation. Until confirmed, the client periodically sends the transaction requests to the SMS. The client collects membership sets sent back by the SMS in $SMSmembers$. The client also collects peer confirmations in $Confirmations$. The client considers the transaction confirmed if it gets at least $f+1$ confirmations for this transaction from one of the membership sets received from the SMS.

Let us now discuss churn. A peer wishing to join or leave *SmartShards* submits a transaction with this request. A joining peer utilizes the SMS. The process is similar to a client submitting a regular UTXO-related transaction. With their confirmation, the peers in the shard send their complete ledger to the joining peer. Once this peer receives $f + 1$ confirmations from one of the shard membership sets supplied by the SMS, the peer is ready to participate in *SmartShards*. The algorithm for a leaving peer is simpler since it knows the shard membership. The leaving peer just submits a leave request to the members of its shard. It may leave the shard once it receives $f + 1$ confirmations. After the peer leaves, it may not receive or send any messages. We summarize this discussion in the below theorem.

Theorem 2. *Algorithm* SmartShards *with weak SMS solves the Distributed Ledger Problem with at most f Byzantine faults in each shard and at most $\lfloor x/2 - 1 \rfloor$ faults in the overlap between shards despite peer churn.*

4 Performance Evaluation

Simulation Setup. We evaluate the performance of *SmartShards* in the abstract algorithm simulator QUANTAS [25]. The QUANTAS code for the *SmartShards* simulation as well as our performance evaluation data is available online [1,2].

The simulated network consists of individual peers. Each pair of peers communicate via a message-passing channel. The channels are FIFO and reliable. A single computation is modeled as a sequence of rounds. In each round, a peer receives messages that were sent to it in the previous rounds, performs local computation, and sends messages to the other peers.

The receipt of each message may be delayed up to some maximum amount which various by experiment. The network is modeled with n peers divided into s shards.

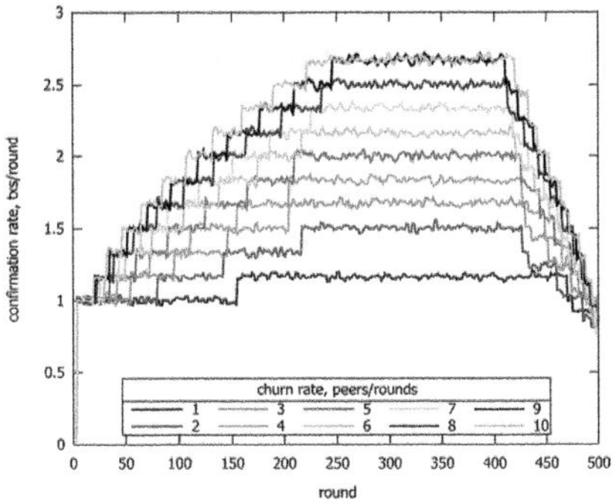

Fig. 3. Transaction confirmation rate timing diagram. Peers request to join the network every round from 1 to 250. They request to leave the network every round from 251 to 500.

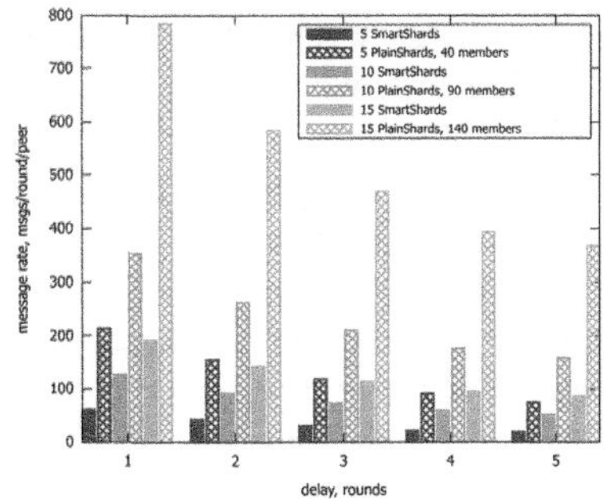

Fig. 4. Message rates for varied shard sizes and max message delay for the *SmartShards* algorithm vs. *PlainShards*.

We do not explicitly simulate clients or faults. Each shard processes transactions independently. We evaluate *SmartShards* where peers participate in multiple overlapping shards against *PlainShards* where each peer is in at most one shard. In *SmartShards* each peer is in at most two shards. If two shards overlap, x is the number of peers in this overlap. Therefore, total number of peers in the network is subject to this formula:

$$n = \frac{s(s-1)x}{2}$$

In *SmartShards*, each shard is running *PBFT*. *PBFT* [9] is a common leader-based consensus algorithm. Transactions are proposed by the *PBFT* leader of each shard. All transactions are valid and have a chance of being cross-shard that is governed by the number of shards in the network.

Peers in the network may join and leave shards. Unless otherwise stated, in each round, a single peer requests to join and a single peer requests to leave the network.

SmartShards and *PlainShards* differ in their implementation of cross-shard transactions and transaction membership. Since there is no shard overlap, in case of a cross-shard transaction, each source shard peer informs every target peer of source shard consensus decision. Also, each peer has to maintain memberships of all network shards. Therefore, once a peer joins or leaves the network, it has to inform all network peers.

We simulate computations of 500 rounds. Unless otherwise stated, each data point is an average of 10 tests.

Experiment Description. In the first experiment we observed the dynamics of *SmartShards* churn handling. The results of a representative computations are shown in Fig. 3. In every round from 1 to 250, new peers request to join the network. Then, in rounds 251 though 500, randomly selected peers request to leave the network. *PBFT* leaders and peers that have not joined yet, are not selected to leave. If there are least 25 peers in the shard overlap between each shard on average, a new shard is created, random peers from donor shards join a new shard. If there are less than 9 peers in the shard overlap between each shard on average, a shard is destroyed and its peers are randomly distributed to other shards. We plot a rolling average of transaction confirmation rate over 100 tests with a window of 3 rounds. We vary the churn rate: the number of peers requesting to join or leave the network every round.

Initially, the network contains 100 peers divided into 5 shards with an overlap of 10. The confirmation rate reflects the number of available shards: the greater the number of shards the higher the confirmation rate. The experiments show the robustness of *SmartShards* with the respect to churn.

Figure 4 compares *SmartShards* with *PlainShards*, the non-overlapping sharded implementation. We compare the message exchange rate for *SmartShards* and *PlainShards* networks of comparable sizes. The message rate is the total number of messages exchanged divided by the number of rounds in the computation and the number of peers in the network. The figure indicates that *SmartShards* outperforms *PlainShards* due to more efficient implementation of cross-shard transaction and churn handling. Each *SmartShards* experiment uses an overlap of 10.

For the next set of experiments, we vary message delay and observe its influence on network performance. In Figs. 5, 7, and 9, we change the number of shards in *SmartShards* and observe the dynamics of throughput, latency and message rate respectively. Throughput is computed as the total number of transactions confirmed during the computation. Latency is the number of rounds that elapse from when a transaction is submitted until it is confirmed by *PBFT*. The figures indicate that with the increase of the number of shards the performance of *SmartShards* improves with a relatively modest increase in message expense.

In Figs. 6, 8, and 10 we change the intersection size and observe its influence on throughput, latency and message rate. Figures 6 and 8 demonstrate that as the number of intersections between shards in the network increases, the throughput and latency remain unaffected. However, Fig. 10 shows that the increase in the number of intersections increases the message rate as expected due to the increase in shard sizes. This cost is relatively low due to the benefit of increasing the Byzantine tolerance threshold of the algorithm.

5 Extensions and Implementation Considerations

Multiple Sources and Targets Transactions. *SmartShards* can be adapted to handle a *multi-transaction* that transfers funds from multiple source wallets or to multiple target wallets atomically. If the wallets belong to the same shard, the modification is simple since the peers of the same shard confirm the transaction. However, it becomes complicated if the wallets are located in different shards.

In this case, the multi-transaction is preceded by the Consolidation Phase and followed by the Distribution Phase. The actual transaction is carried out in a *consolidation shard*. This shard may be one of the source or target shards or an unrelated shard. The *Consolidation Phase* consists of moving the source UTXOs into the consolidation shard. Each source UTXO is transferred to the consolidation shard without changing ownership of the UTXO. That is, the same client owns the wallet which contained the UTXO in the source as in the consolidation shard. After the Consolidation Phase is complete, *SmartShards* confirms the multi-transaction in a single consolidation shard. After this execution, the target UTXOs are transferred to the target shards during the *Distribution Phase*. Again, there is no ownership change during such a transfer.

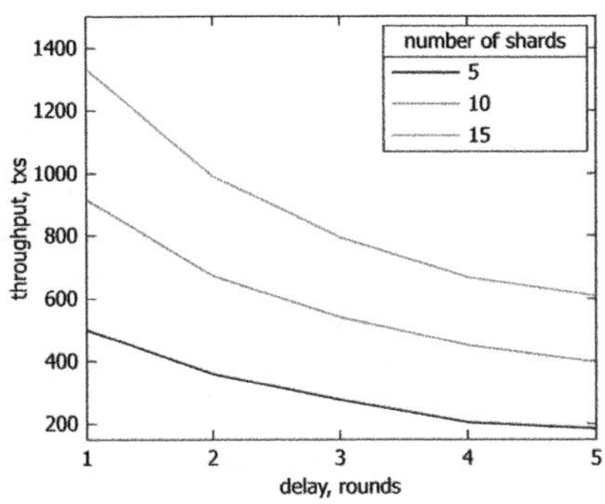

Fig. 5. Number of approved transactions depending on the message delay for various number of shards.

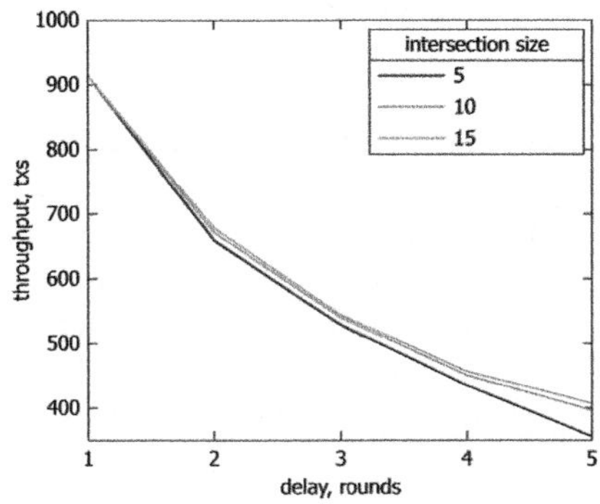

Fig. 6. Number of approved transactions depending on the message delay for various intersection sizes.

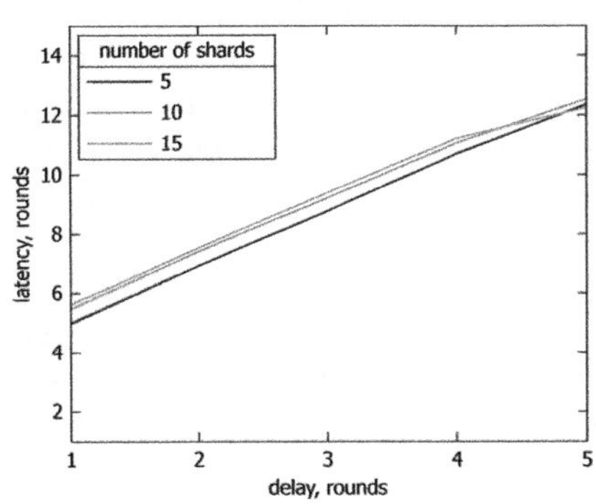

Fig. 7. Latency of approving a transaction depending on the message delay for various number of shards.

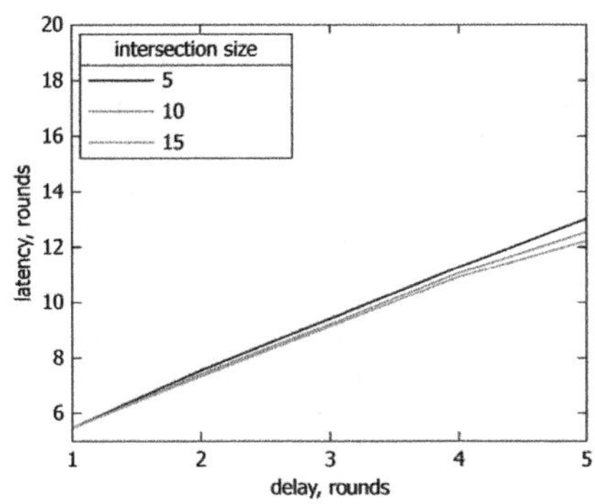

Fig. 8. Latency of approving a transaction depending on the message delay for various intersection sizes.

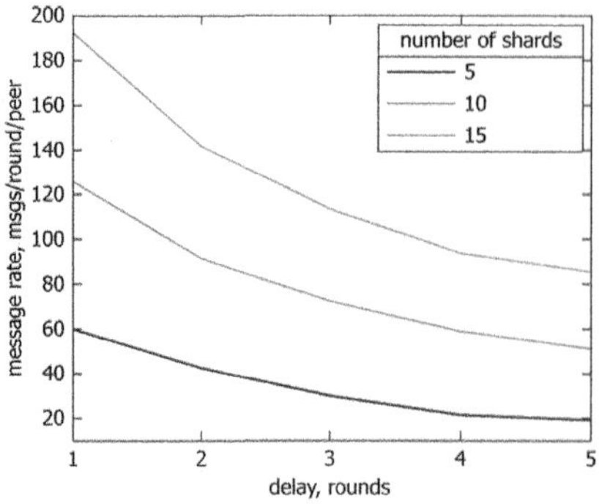

Fig. 9. Message exchange rate depending on message delay.

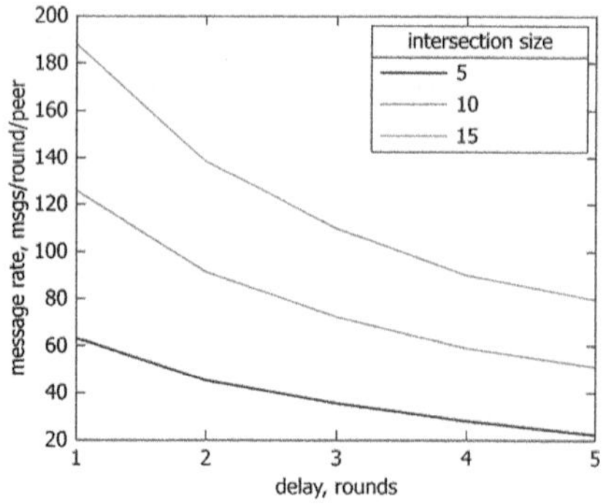

Fig. 10. Average message rate for varied intersection sizes and max message delay.

Defense Against Membership Attacks. *SmartShards* may be fortified against a *slowly adaptive adversary* [32] that requires a certain time period to corrupt new peers. Such an adversary may focus on compromising a single shard or a single shard intersection. If the corruption period is known, peers are ejected from their shards before a timer expires to prevent a Byzantine majority from compromising the system. Such peers then join a different shard shuffling the peers and distributing the faults.

Similarly, defense against a leave/join attack may be incorporated into *SmartShards*. In such an attack, the faulty nodes repeatedly join and leave the network hoping to get into the same shard in an attempt to exceed its tolerance threshold. To counteract it, a Cuckoo rule may be applied [6]. If a node joins a shard, another arbitrary node has to leave this shard and join another shard. Thus, the adversary loses control over fault node shard selection.

Implementation Considerations. As with any blockchain, to improve performance, multiple transactions may be confirmed in a block in *SmartShards*. Thus, a single round of agreement is required for confirmation of all transactions in the block. In this case, the peers of the shard confirm several transactions as a block and then carry out the transfer part of each transaction individually. The block may contain regular UTXO transactions as well as peer join and leave transactions.

Let us comment on the implementation of the Shard Membership Service (SMS) component of *SmartShards*, which clients use to keep track of membership changes. Effectively, the SMS is a trusted source of membership information. As such, it may be implemented as a side-chain of membership records, a bootstrap service, or a Byzantine-robust host that reliably answers client membership queries.

6 Concluding Remarks

In this paper we explored the idea of overlapping shards. We showed how it can be used to improve efficiency and robustness of a sharded blockchain. In the future, it would be interesting to implement *SmartShards* in a real pear-to-peer system and compare it against traditional non-overlapping sharding blockchains. Alternatively, *SmartShards* may be used directly in existing blockchains to overlap shards and enhance their fault-tolerance and functional performance.

References

1. Smartshards implementation. https://github.com/QuantasSupport/Quantas/tree/SmartShards
2. Smartshards perfromance evaluation data. http://www.cs.kent.edu/mikhail/Research/trail.output.tar.gz Feb 2025
3. Agbo, C.C., Mahmoud, Q.H., Eklund, J.M.: Blockchain technology in healthcare: a systematic review. In: Healthcare, vol. 7, p. 56. MDPI (2019)
4. Andoni, M., et al.: Blockchain technology in the energy sector: a systematic review of challenges and opportunities. Renew. Sustain. Energy Rev. **100**, 143–174 (2019)
5. Androulaki, E., et al.: Hyperledger fabric: a distributed operating system for permissioned blockchains. In: Proceedings of the Thirteenth EuroSys Conference, pp. 1–15 (2018)
6. Awerbuch, B., Scheideler, C.: Towards a scalable and robust DHT. In: Proceedings of the Eighteenth Annual ACM Symposium on Parallelism in Algorithms and Architectures, pp. 318–327 (2006)
7. Baldoni, R., Bonomi, S., Nezhad, A.S.: A protocol for implementing byzantine storage in churn-prone distributed systems. Theor. Comput. Sci. **512**, 28–40 (2013)
8. Bessani, A., Alchieri, E., Sousa, J., Oliveira, A., Pedone, F.: From byzantine replication to blockchain: Consensus is only the beginning. In: 2020 50th Annual IEEE/IFIP International Conference on Dependable Systems and Networks (DSN), pp. 424–436. IEEE (2020)
9. Castro, M., Liskov, B.: Practical byzantine fault tolerance and proactive recovery. ACM Trans. Comput. Syst. **20**(4), 398–461 (2002)
10. Douceur, J.R.: The sybil attack. In: International workshop on peer-to-peer systems, pp. 251–260. Springer (2002)
11. Dujak, D., Sajter, D.: Blockchain applications in supply chain. SMART supply network, pp. 21–46 (2019)
12. Foreback, D., Nesterenko, M., Tixeuil, S.: Infinite unlimited churn. arXiv preprint arXiv:1608.00726 (2016)
13. Foreback, D., Nesterenko, M., Tixeuil, S.: Churn possibilities and impossibilities. In: Networked Systems: 6th International Conference, NETYS 2018, Essaouira, Morocco, May 9–11, 2018, Revised Selected Papers 6, pp. 303–317. Springer (2019)
14. García-Pérez, A., Gotsman, A.: Federated byzantine quorum systems. In: 22nd International Conference on Principles of Distributed Systems (OPODIS 2018). Schloss-Dagstuhl-Leibniz Zentrum für Informatik, (2019)
15. Hafid, A., Hafid, A.S., Samih, M.: Scaling blockchains: a comprehensive survey. In: IEEE Access **8**, 125244–125262 (2020)

16. Ito, K., O'Dair, M.: A critical examination of the application of blockchain technology to intellectual property management. Business Transform. Blockchain **II**, 317–335 (2019)
17. Kokoris-Kogias, E., Jovanovic, P., Gasser, L., Gailly, N., Syta, E.,Ford, B.: Omniledger: aA secure, scale-out, decentralized ledger via sharding. In: 2018 IEEE Symposium on Security and Privacy (SP), pp. 583–598. IEEE (2018)
18. Kuhn, F., Schmid, S., Wattenhofer, R.: Towards worst-case churn resistant peer-to-peer systems. Distrib. Comput. **22**, 249–267 (2010)
19. Lafourcade, P., Nopere, M., Picot, J., Pizzuti, D., Roudeix, E.: Security analysis of auctionity: a blockchain based e-auction. In: Foundations and Practice of Security: 12th International Symposium, FPS 2019, Toulouse, France, November 5–7, 2019, Revised Selected Papers 12, pp. 290–307. Springer, 2020 ¡error l="308" c="Invalid command: paragraph not started." /¿
20. Lamport, L., Shostak, R., Pease, M.: The byzantine generals problem. ACM Trans. Program. Lang. Syst. **4**(3), 382–401 (1982)
21. Liu, X., Xie, H., Yan, Z., Liang, X.: A survey on blockchain sharding. ISA Trans. **141**, 30–43 (2023)
22. Luu, L., Narayanan, V., Zheng, C., Baweja, K., Gilbert, S., Saxena, P.: A secure sharding protocol for open blockchains. In: Proceedings of the 2016 ACM SIGSAC Conference on Computer and Communications Security, pp. 17–30 (2016)
23. Malkhi, D., Reiter, M.: Byzantine quorum systems. Distributed Comput. **11**(4), 203–213 (1998)
24. Nakamoto, S.: Bitcoin: a peer-to-peer electronic cash system (2008)
25. Oglio, J., Hood, K., Nesterenko, M., Tixeuil, S.: Quantas: quantitative user-friendly adaptable networked things abstract simulator. In: Proceedings of the 2022 Workshop on Advanced tools, programming languages, and PLatforms for Implementing and Evaluating algorithms for Distributed systems, pp. 40–46 (2022)
26. Samaniego, M., Jamsrandorj, U., Deters, R.: Blockchain as a service for Iot. In: 2016 IEEE International Conference on Internet of Things (iThings) and IEEE green computing and communications (GreenCom) and IEEE cyber, physical and social computing (CPSCom) and IEEE smart data (SmartData), pp. 433–436. IEEE (2016)
27. Wang, J., Wang, H.: Monoxide: scale out blockchains with asynchronous consensus zones. In: 16th USENIX Symposium on Networked Systems Design and Implementation (NSDI 19), pp. 95–112 (2019)
28. Wendl, M., Doan, M.H., Sassen, R.: The environmental impact of cryptocurrencies using proof of work and proof of stake consensus algorithms: a systematic review. J. Environ. Manage. **326**, 116530 (2023)
29. White, B., Mahanti, A., Passi, K.: Characterizing the OpenSea NFT marketplace. In: Companion Proceedings of the Web Conference 2022, pp. 488–496 (2022)
30. Wood, G.: Ethereum: a secure decentralized generalized transaction ledger. Ethereum Project Yellow Paper **151**, 1–32 (2014)
31. Yu, G., Wang, X., Yu, K., Ni, W., Zhang, J.A., Liu, R.P.: Sharding in blockchains: Survey. IEEE Access **8**, 14155–14181 (2020)
32. Zamani, M., Movahedi, M., Raykova, M: Rapidchain: scaling blockchain via full sharding. In: Proceedings of the 2018 ACM SIGSAC Conference on Computer and Communications Security, pp. 931–948 (2018)

On Restricting Separator Problems in the OBLOT Computational Landscape

Quentin Bramas[1,2(✉)] and Sébastien Tixeuil[2]

[1] University of Strasbourg, ICUBE, CNRS, Strasbourg, France
bramas@unistra.fr
[2] Sorbonne Université, CNRS, LIP6, IUF, Paris, France

Abstract. We study the impact of restricting the class of separator problems on the look-compute-move mobile robot model hierarchy. In particular, we show that reachability specifications are sufficient to separate the semi-synchronous and the asynchronous model variants when robots agree on the unit-distance, but the two model variants are equivalent when considering terminating problems and no coordinate system agreement.

Keywords: Mobile robots · Computational hierarchy

Motivation. Since the introduction of the now called *OBLOT* model by Suzuki and Yamashita [5], a number of problems have been tackled (see the reference book by Flocchini et al. [1] and references therein), aiming to characterize the minimal hypotheses (constituting the execution model) that enable problem solvability. A recent line of work explores the partial order hierarchy between the various models explored so far [3], making use of *separator problems*, that is, problems that are solvable in one model but unsolvable in another model (that differs from the first one on a single hypothesis or dimension).

A key separator problem between the semi-synchronous and the asynchronous model variants is the Monotone Line Convergence (MLCv) problem [4], that requires two robots to monotonically approach each other using the line joining them as a trajectory. As a result, specifying this problem requires one to define a predicate on the whole infinite execution of the system (a valid configuration at time t depends on every previous configuration). By contrast, most problems studied so far [1], *e.g.* pattern formation, gathering, scattering, mutual visibility, etc., can be defined by a single predicate on configurations, an execution satisfying such a specification when it is suffix-closed by configurations that satisfy the predicate. Obviously, suffix-closed specifications have weaker expressive power than full execution specifications.

Surprisingly, some well-known equivalences, such as the equivalence between semi-synchronous and asynchronous robots endowed with lights (robots have a light, visible to other robots, with a finite number of colors they can update) [2], does not hold when considering problems defined by a predicate on the entire

S. Lahlou and M. Mukund (Eds.): NETYS 2025, LNCS 15736, pp. 163–168, 2026.
https://doi.org/10.1007/978-3-032-00347-8_10

execution, but only holds on a class of problems where a subset of the execution satisfies a predicate (but in this class of problems, the MLCv does not separate semi-synchronous from asynchronous models anymore).

This dichotomy motivates the question raised in this short paper: do weaker specifications for separator problems change the computational landscape of mobile robot computing?

Model. We consider the OBLOT model [1] where a set of n robots is moving on an Euclidean plane. Each robot has its own coordinate system that does not change throughout execution. The coordinate system of a robot r is associated with a *similarity* function ϕ_r (a bijection of the plane preserving angles). For a given time t, $C(t)$ denotes the positions of the robots at time t in a global fixed coordinate system (unknown to the robots).

The robots are anonymous and execute the same algorithm through Look-Compute-Move cycles. In a cycle, a robot r *Looks* *i.e.*, retrieve the set $\phi_r(C(t))$ of position of the other robots in its own coordinate system at time t. Then, r *Computes* a destination based on $\phi_r(C(t))$. Finally, r *Moves* towards its destination. The movements are said to be *rigid* the destination is always reached. We consider three types of schedulers: **Fully-Synchronous** ($FSYNC$) where all robots execute their cycle synchronously, **Semi-Synchronous** ($SSYNC$), where a non-empty subset of robots execute their cycle synchronously, and **Asynchronous** ($ASYNC$) where the robots execute the phases of their cycle independently. In $ASYNC$, the look phase is atomic, but the compute and move phases can take an arbitrarily long (but finite) time. This implies that a robot may look while another robot moves (or computes), hence basing its computation on a possibly outdated configuration (a robot cannot distinguish moving robots from still ones). An *execution* is an infinite sequence of configurations. We assume only *fair* executions where every robot is activated infinitely often.

We define the following set of problems encountered in the literature.

- **General problems.** The most general type of problems where the entire execution (a sequence of configurations) must satisfy a given predicate. The set of those problems is denoted $\mathcal{G}$.
- **Terminating problems.** General problems where, eventually, the configuration remains the same forever. The set of terminating problems is denoted $\mathcal{T}$.
- **Reachability problems.** Problems where the goal is to reach configurations that all satisfy a given (unique) configuration predicate. The set of reachability problems is denoted $\mathcal{R}$.
- **Similarity-invariant problems.** Reachability problems where the configuration predicate is invariant by similarity. So the predicate does not depend on a particular coordinate system, as it is the case for the pattern formation problem for instance. The set of similarity-invariant problems is denoted $\mathcal{I} \subset \mathcal{R}$.

Model Hierarchy. We are interested in comparing different models. A model defines the core hypotheses that drive robots execution in a particular context.

We denote by $\mathbb{M}(X_1, X_2, ...)$ the model satisfying hypotheses $X_1, X_2, \ldots$, where X_i describes an hypothesis such as a scheduler, a space where the robots evolve, a number of robots, or any other assumption.

In this short paper, we focus on models that follow the description of the $OBLOT$ model described above with only two robots and rigid movements, denoted $\mathbb{M}(2, OBLOT, rigid)$. Then, we consider two schedulers, $SSYNC$ and $ASYNC$. We may add the hypothesis, denoted $same\text{-}unit$, that the coordinate systems of the robots share the same unit-distance.

We say a model X is as powerful as a model Y, denoted $X \succcurlyeq Y$, if every problem that is solvable by an algorithm in model Y can also be solved by an algorithm in model X. This transitive relation defines a partial order called the **model hierarchy**. We say a model X is *more powerful* than a model Y, denoted $X \succ Y$, if it is as powerful and there exists a problem solvable in model X that is not solvable in model Y. This kind of problem is called a **separator problem**. $X \approx Y$ means $X \succcurlyeq Y \wedge Y \succcurlyeq X$.

We usually compare two models that differ only on few assumptions. For readability, if two models differ only on one hypothesis we write $\mathbb{M}(X_1, \ldots, X_k) : Y \succ Z$ instead of $\mathbb{M}(X_1, \ldots, X_k, Y) \succ \mathbb{M}(X_1, \ldots, X_k, Z)$.

In previous work, most separator problems were in class $\mathcal{G}$. The main question we want to ask is how does the problem hierarchy change when we restrict the class of allowed separator problems to (strict) subsets of $\mathcal{G}$? We define the operator $\overset{Cl}{\succ}$, resp. $\overset{Cl}{\succcurlyeq}$, as the restriction of the operator $\succ$, resp. $\succcurlyeq$, to the class of problems Cl. So, $\succ$, resp. $\succcurlyeq$ is equivalent to $\overset{\mathcal{G}}{\succ}$, resp. $\overset{\mathcal{G}}{\succcurlyeq}$.

Summary of Our Results. We prove the following relations:

$$\mathbb{M}(2, OBLOT, rigid, same\text{-}unit): \quad SSYNC \overset{\mathcal{R}\cap\mathcal{T}}{\succ} ASYNC \tag{1}$$

$$\mathbb{M}(2, OBLOT, rigid): \quad SSYNC \overset{\mathcal{R}}{\succ} ASYNC \tag{2}$$

$$\mathbb{M}(2, OBLOT, rigid): \quad SSYNC \overset{\mathcal{T}\cup\mathcal{I}}{\approx} ASYNC \tag{3}$$

The separator results naturally extend to more general problem specifications. For instance, Relation (1) implies that the same relation is true considering a larger class of problems (such as $\mathcal{R}$, $\mathcal{T}$, or $\mathcal{G}$), because $SSYNC \succcurlyeq ASYNC$ is true by construction on any class, and a separator in $\mathcal{R} \cap \mathcal{T}$ is a separator in any super-set. Conversely, Relation (3) implies the same relation in more restricted classes of problems, because the existence of a separator in a subset would imply a separator in $\mathcal{T} \cup \mathcal{I}$.

Proof of (1). We consider the model $\mathbb{M}(2, OBLOT, rigid, same\text{-}unit)$, and we define a problem that is solvable in $SSYNC$, but not solvable in $ASYNC$.

Let $D(k, i)$ be the set of 2-robot configurations such that the two robots are at a distance $k/2^i$ for an odd integer k and an integer i. Let P be a 2-robot configuration predicate such that $P(C)$ is true if and only if the two robots are in $C \in D(k, i)$, where i is not divisible by 3. Given a team of two robots initially in a configuration in $D(k, i)$ (for any odd k and any i), the ND3 (for Non-Divisible by 3) problem consists in reaching a configuration satisfying predicate P and remaining in this configuration forever. This problem belongs to the $\mathcal{R} \cap \mathcal{T}$ class.

Let $\mathcal{A}$ be the following algorithm: Let d be the distance to the other robot, we have $d = k/2^i$ for some odd k and positive i (this is true initially and is preserved throughout the execution). If i is not divisible by three, then the activated robot remains idle. Otherwise, the activated robot moves a distance $k/2^{i+2}$ towards the other robot.

Theorem 1. *Algorithm $\mathcal{A}$ solves the ND3 problem in* $\mathbb{M}(2, \mathit{OBLOT}, \mathit{rigid}, \mathit{same-unit}, \mathit{SSYNC})$

Proof. If both robots are activated, then they end up at distance $k/2^{i+1}$ (which is $d - 2 \times k/2^{i+2}$), and the obtained configuration satisfies P (because $i+1$ is not divisible by 3). If only one robot is activated, then they end up at distance $(3k)/2^{i+2}$ (which is $d - k/2^{i+2}$), and the obtained configuration satisfies P (because $i+2$ is not divisible by 3).

Theorem 2. *ND3 is not solvable in* $\mathbb{M}(2, \mathit{OBLOT}, \mathit{rigid}, \mathit{same-unit}, \mathit{ASYNC})$

Proof. Consider for the sake of contradiction that the problem can be solved with the ASYNC hypothesis by an algorithm A. Consider the configuration where the two robots are at distance $d_0 = k/2^i$ with k an odd integer, and i is divisible by 3. Consider the execution where a robot is first activated alone and let p_1 be its target at distance d_1, from the other robot. Now consider that after the activation, the robot remains in the "move" phase and is located on the path towards its destination at distance $d_1 \in (d_0, d_1)$ (or (d_1, d_0) depending on the ordering) such that $d'_1 = k'/2^{3h}$ for some integer $h \geq 1$ and odd integer k'. Then we consider that the other robot is activated. This robot sees distance d'_1 so it has to move towards a point p_2 at distance d_2. Again, we consider the execution where this robot partially performs its movement, towards a point at distance d'_2 from the target p_1 such that d'_2 is $d'_2 = k''/2^{3h'}$. When the first robot reach its destination p_1 and is activated, it sees distance d'_2 and has to move towards a point p_3 at distance d_3. We can continue this process and show that the robots are always moving and the configuration falsifies P infinitely often.

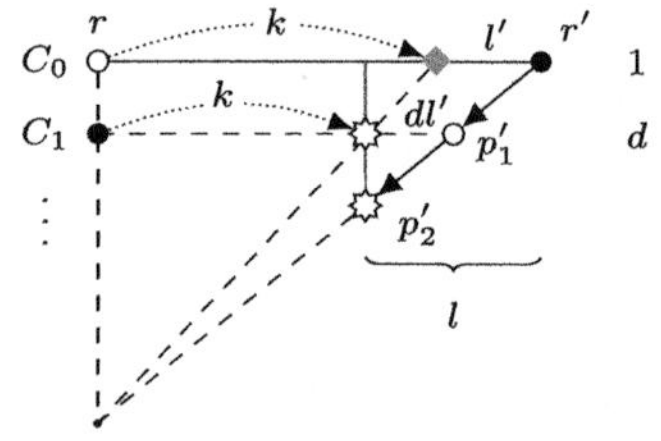

Fig. 1. Illustration accompanying the proof of Theorem 3.

Proof of (2). Now we consider the model $\mathbb{M}(2, \mathit{OBLOT}, \mathit{rigid})$, so robots may not agree on the distance unit. Starting from a configuration where the two robots are at distinct positions, we consider the reachability problem CD (Converge Distinct) defined by a configuration predicate P that is true if and only if the two robots are at distance less than 1 (in a global coordinate system, unknown to the robots) but not at the same point. The problem is not in $\mathcal{T}$, so it can be solved even if the robots move forever. Let $\mathcal{A}$ be the algorithm where the activated robot moves towards the other robot one third of the distance between them. Clearly, the problem is solved in SSYNC by $\mathcal{A}$ because the robots keep getting closer and closer, while never reaching the same point.

Theorem 3. *CD is not solvable in* $\mathbb{M}(2, OBLOT, rigid, ASYNC)$

Proof. Consider for the sake of contradiction that the problem can be solved with the ASYNC hypothesis by an algorithm A. Consider the configuration where the two robots see themselves at distance 1. The idea of the proof, illustrated by Fig. 1, is to activate one robot (r'), then, after partially moving it (to the white circle), to activate the other robot (r) k times (for some k) to reach a configuration where the two robots are gathered. To do so, we have to carefully decide the distance d between the robot when r is activated so that its destination (the star node) is exactly the destination of r'.

First, observe that there is at least a view for which an agent moves towards the other agent. Without loss of generality, let's say that this view is when the distance between the agents is 1. So we consider that agent r, initially in C_0 has this view, is activated, and is dictated to move at distance $0 < l < 1$ to a point p'_2. Second, one can show that, if a single robot is activated infinitely often, it converges towards the other robot (otherwise we can find a round-robin execution where the distance between the robots does not tend to zero).

So, for any distance $l < 1$, after a finite number of activations, say k, robot r seeing distance 1 would end up at distance $l' < l$ (in the diamond node). Hence, if the global distance is d (in C_1), we can choose a coordinate systems for r so that it sees distance 1 and after k activations, r ends up at distance dl' from p'_1. In particular, one can show that, if we activate r when the distance between r and r' is $d = \frac{1-l}{1-l'}$, then after k activations of r (and without moving r'), r ends up at the exact destination p'_2 of r'. After finishing the movement of r', both robots occupy the same position p'_2 and cannot solve the problem anymore, a contradiction. The value of d has been found so that the top star is indeed the intersection of the lines passing through it. □

Proof of (3)**.** Consider a problem in $\mathcal{I}$, *i.e.*, a reachability problem defined by a predicate P that is invariant by similarity. In the case of two robots, there are only four predicates that are invariant by similarity: two trivial predicates $\perp$ and $\top$, the Gathered predicate $G : \{p_1, p_2\} \mapsto p_1 = p_2$, and its negation $\bar{G} : \{p_1, p_2\} \mapsto p_1 \neq p_2$. The gathering problem and the $\perp$ are not solvable in SSYNC and the two other predicates are trivially solvable in ASYNC (just by staying idle).

Now consider a problem in $\mathcal{T}$. To prove the relation, we simply show that, either the problem is not solvable in *SSYNC*, or the problem is solvable in *ASYNC* by the idle algorithm. Assume for the sake of contradiction that the problem is solvable in *SSYNC* by a non-idle algorithm *i.e.*, an algorithm that orders at least one robot to move in at least one configuration. Then, this algorithm must order to move in all possible (non-gathered) views, otherwise, for any initial configuration we can choose the coordinate systems of the robots so that they never move, and since they must solve the problem also in this case, the idle algorithm as well, a contradiction. Since the robots are ordered to move in any non-gathered configuration, and we can make sure that the gathered configuration is never reached (by scheduling both robots if they move to

the other's position, and by selecting a single robot otherwise), then the robots never terminates, a contradiction.
Open Question. For each pair of model variants for which there exists a separator problem, what is the weakest possible class of the separator?

References

1. Moving and computing models: robots. In: Flocchini, P., Prencipe, G., Santoro, N. (eds.) Distributed Computing by Mobile Entities, Current Research in Moving and Computing, LNCS, vol. 11340, pp. 3–14. Springer (2019). https://doi.org/10.1007/978-3-030-11072-7_1
2. Das, S., et al.: The power of lights: synchronizing asynchronous robots using visible bits. null (2012). https://doi.org/10.1109/icdcs.2012.71
3. Flocchini, P., Santoro, N., Sudo, Y., Wada, K.: On asynchrony, memory, and communication: separations and landscapes. In: OPODIS 2023. https://doi.org/10.4230/LIPIcs.OPODIS.2023.28
4. Flocchini, P., Santoro, N., Sudo, Y., Wada, K.: On asynchrony, memory, and communication: separations and landscapes. In: Bessani, A., Défago, X., Nakamura, J., Wada, K., Yamauchi, Y. (eds.) 27th International Conference on Principles of Distributed Systems (OPODIS 2023). Leibniz International Proceedings in Informatics (LIPIcs), vol. 286, pp. 28:1–28:23. Schloss Dagstuhl – Leibniz-Zentrum für Informatik, Dagstuhl, Germany (2024). https://doi.org/10.4230/LIPIcs.OPODIS.2023.28, https://drops.dagstuhl.de/entities/document/10.4230/LIPIcs.OPODIS.2023.28
5. Suzuki, I., Yamashita, M.: Distributed anonymous mobile robots: formation of geometric patterns. SIAM J. Comput. **28**(4), 1347–1363 (1999)

Machine Learning

Going Forward-Forward in Distributed Deep Learning

Ege Aktemur[1,2(✉)], Ege Zorlutuna[1,3], Kaan Bilgili[1,4], Tacettin Emre Bök[1,4], Berrin Yanikoglu[1], and Süha Orhun Mutluergil[1]

[1] Sabanci University, Istanbul, Turkey
{berrin,suha.mutluergil}@sabanciuniv.edu
[2] TU Darmstadt, Darmstadt, Germany
ege.aktemur@stud.tu-darmstadt.de
[3] ETH Zurich, Zurich, Switzerland
ezorlutuna@ethz.ch
[4] TU Berlin, Berlin, Germany
{bilgili,boek}@tu-berlin.de

Abstract. We introduce a new approach in distributed learning, building on Hinton's Forward-Forward (FF) algorithm to speed up the training of neural networks in distributed environments without losing accuracy. Unlike traditional methods that rely on forward and backward passes, the FF algorithm employs a dual forward pass strategy, eliminating the dependency among layers required during the backpropagation period, which prevents efficient parallelization of the training process. Although the original FF algorithm focused on its ability to match the performance of the backpropagation algorithm, this work aims to reduce the training time with pipeline parallelism. We propose three novel pipelined FF algorithms that speed up training 3.75 times on the MNIST dataset while maintaining accuracy when training a four-layer network with four compute nodes. These results show that FF is highly parallelizable and its potential in large-scale distributed/federated systems to enable faster training for larger and more complex models.

Keywords: Forward-Forward Algorithm · Distributed Learning · Pipeline Parallelism

1 Introduction

Training deep neural networks, often consisting of hundreds of layers, is a very time-consuming process that can take several weeks, using the well-known backpropagation [18] as the learning algorithm. However, parallelization of this algorithm presents significant challenges due to the sequential nature of the backpropagation learning algorithm, as illustrated in Fig. 1.

During the backward pass in backpropagation-based training methods, the gradient is calculated for all layers, and they depend on the gradient calculated at the next layer. If layers are distributed to different nodes, this dependency

S. Lahlou and M. Mukund (Eds.): NETYS 2025, LNCS 15736, pp. 171–186, 2026.
https://doi.org/10.1007/978-3-032-00347-8_11

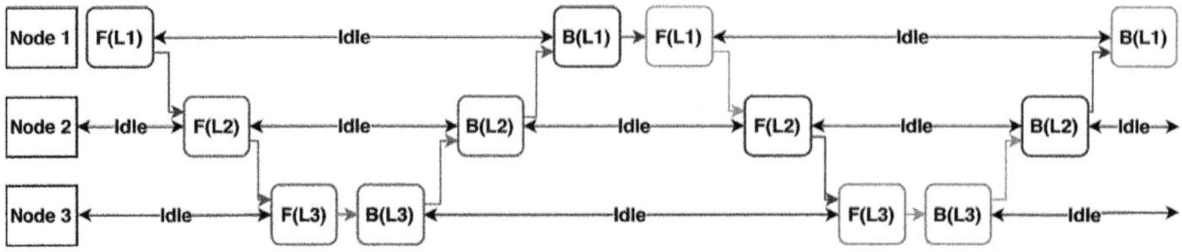

Fig. 1. Challenges in parallelizing traditional backpropagation involve managing the forward (F) and backward (B) passes, both applied to the layer specified by their first parameter.

necessitates the sequentialization of the computing nodes, as each node must wait for the gradient information to backpropagate from its successor before it can proceed with its calculations. Moreover, the need for constant communication between nodes to transfer gradient and weight information can lead to significant communication overhead. This is particularly problematic in large-scale neural networks, where the volume of data to be transferred can be substantial.

Distributed deep learning has witnessed significant advancements in recent years, driven by the ever-increasing complexity and size of neural networks. Distributed training frameworks such as PyTorch Distributed Data Parallel (DDP) [10], GPipe [6], PipeDream [13] and Flower [2] have emerged as pivotal solutions, enabling the training of massive models by optimizing for scale, speed, cost, and usability. These systems utilize sophisticated methodologies such as data, pipeline, and model parallelism to manage and process large-scale neural network training efficiently across multiple computing nodes.

In addition to the above research geared towards distributed implementations of backpropagation, the Forward-Forward Algorithm (FFA) proposed by Hinton [5] proposes a novel approach to train neural networks. Unlike traditional deep learning algorithms that rely on global forward and backward passes, the FFA only uses local (layer-wise) forward and backward passes. Although the FFA is designed to address the limitations associated with backpropagation without focusing on distribution, the layer-wise training feature of the FFA results in a less dependent architecture in a distributed environment that reduces idle time, communication and synchronization, as demonstrated in Fig. 2.

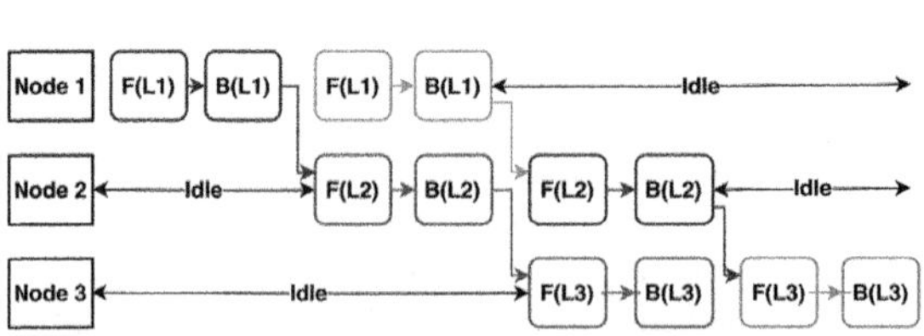

Fig. 2. Distributed training of a FFA network. F and B blocks are representing the layer local forward and backward passes. B blocks compute the gradient by considering the goodness that will be defined later and then update the weights of the corresponding layer.

This paper explores the integration of the FFA into distributed deep learning systems, particularly focusing on its potential to improve the efficiency and performance of training large-scale neural networks. We demonstrate the effectiveness of the Pipeline Forward-Forward (PFF) algorithm, which reduces the training duration by almost 5-fold for a 5-layer network while preserving the accuracy of the original algorithm.

2 Related Work

Distributed and parallel neural networks have attracted widespread interest and investigation from researchers, driven by the promise of improved computational efficiency and scalability in handling large-scale data and complex models. Comprehensive surveys from 2019 [1] and 2022 [12] provide extensive information about the recent developments on the parallelism methods including data, model and pipeline that we employ in our methods.

PipeDream [13] is a deep neural network training system that uses backpropagation that efficiently combines data, pipeline, and model parallelism by dividing the model layers into multiple stages containing consecutive layers. Unlike our method, PipeDream inherits the limitations of the classic backpropagation algorithm. Similarly, GPipe [6] is a distributed deep learning library that updates weights synchronously during the backward pass, which differentiates it from PipeDream; however, it also suffers from additional dependencies introduced by the classic backpropagation algorithm. In contrast, PyTorch Distributed Data Parallel [10] achieves near-linear scalability in distributed training by leveraging data parallelism and synchronizing gradients during the backward pass, trying to alleviate the inherent limitations of classic backpropagation.

In addition to the above methods, there are several proposed methods for efficient deep learning training that attempt to overcome the limitations of backpropagation by proposing alternatives to backpropagation. One of them is called *local parallelism* [9]. This method divides the layers into a number of blocks and uses this block's local loss to adjust the parameters of the layers that are within that block. Although this method achieves a significant speedup compared to backpropagation, its effectiveness is limited because the local loss of the blocks is not comparable to the global loss.

Forward-Forward Algorithm (FFA) [5] is a learning method for multilayer networks, proposed by Hinton. This algorithm introduces a novel way of training, which eliminates the backpropagation and the backward pass. Unlike the method proposed in this paper, the original FFA is sequential and is designed to work on a single processing unit. This algorithm forms the backbone of our method along with the split method, which aims to reduce communication between workers and increase parallelism.

FFA has significantly influenced neural network research, leading to innovative integrations and modifications. For example, Ororbia et al. [14] combined FFA with predictive coding, while Scodellaro et al. [19] demonstrated that CNNs trained using FFA can achieve up to 99.16% accuracy, approaching the performance of backpropagation. In parallel, Zhao et al. [20] developed CaFo, an algorithm that constructs cascaded neural blocks with independently trainable layers suitable for parallelization, and [17] proposed a variant of FFA Contrastive Learning that replaces later training stages with dual local updates employing separate loss functions.

Additional studies have extended FFA for various architectures and training paradigms. Gautham et al. [4] investigated the application of FFA in convolutional and recurrent models for multiclass classification and regression tasks, while Hwang et al. [7] introduced a Local Back-Propagation (LBP) algorithm that leverages standard unsupervised models, such as autoencoders, for independent layerwise training in distributed environments. Furthermore, Krutsylo [8] proposed a scalable hybrid blockwise approach that integrates backpropagation within blocks for modern architectures such as ResNet18 and MobileNetV3, and Papachristodoulou et al. [15] addressed FFA 甕洒 limitations by introducing a novel convolutional design with channel-wise competitive learning via CFSE blocks, which achieved a testing error as low as 0.58% on MNIST.

Distributed Forward-Forward (DFF) [3] is an example of the use of FFA in distributed training system. DFF aims to create a decentralized and distributed training system to allow multiple low-performance devices to train a large model. DFF creates a cluster with one master node and multiple server nodes. Each server is assigned a layer(s) by the master node. These server nodes train their assigned layers using FFA and send their output to other layers.

Park et al. [16] propose FedFwd, a federated learning algorithm that replaces traditional backpropagation with FFA to perform layer-wise updates, thus reducing demands on local clients. The authors aim to tackle the inherent resource constraints in distributed training by eliminating the need to store all intermediate activations during training. Experimental results on datasets such as MNIST and CIFAR-10 show that FedFwd achieves competitive test accuracies and comparable training times. These findings suggest that FFA-based approaches offer a promising alternative for efficient distributed training.

While PipeDream and GPipe aim to parallelize backpropagation, DFF [3] is closest to our work, as it also tries to integrate the FFA into a distributed setting. However, in terms of accuracy, our implementation achieves better results than DFF because our implementation updates the weights more frequently, using minibatches, generates the negative samples adaptively, and uses an additional classifier which all contribute to the performance of the network.

3 Forward-Forward Algorithm

The FFA, proposed by Geoffrey Hinton [5], presents a novel approach to train neural networks that does not involve backpropagation, which is the standard learning algorithm used in training neural networks.

Inspired by the biological processes of the brain, the FFA trains layers individually and sequentially, utilizing two forward passes and a local backward pass to update the layer weights. Those passes are called the positive pass and the negative pass. The positive pass adjusts the weights to increase the "goodness" of the positive or real data, while the negative pass does the opposite for negative data, as defined below.

Negative Data. Negative data are obtained by giving incorrect labels to the samples provided as positive data. In [5], the MNIST dataset is used for the evaluation of the FFA. The existence of black borders in this image data set enabled encoding labels in the top-left corner of the input images (a 10-pixel area on the border denotes the label where a 1-of-C encoding is used). A positive sample is generated by adding the correct label of the digit in the image, whereas a negative sample is produced by encoding an incorrect digit as the label. Other alternatives for creating negative data, including unsupervised methods, are also possible and explored in [5].

Goodness Function. The goodness of a layer explored in [5] is the sum of the squares of the activities of the rectified linear neurons in that layer, and the aim during the learning period is to raise it above some threshold value for positive (real) data and below the threshold for negative data. The goodness function p can be captured by applying the logistic function σ to the sum of squared activities y_j^2 minus a threshold θ:

$$p(data) = \sigma(\sum_j y_j^2 - \theta) \tag{1}$$

Prediction. Two methods have been proposed to predict the label of an input image. In the *Goodness* prediction, the input is run through the network with all possible labels encoded in 1-of-C format so that the label vector consists of all 0s except a single 1 placed in the index representing this class. Then, the activations from all but the first hidden layer of the network are accumulated and the label yielding the maximum goodness is selected as the predicted class.

In the *Softmax* prediction, the raw input image is labeled with a neutral vector consisting of 0.1 values for each class and the activity vectors collected from all except the first hidden layer are fed into a Softmax layer which is trained to predict the class. The softmax layer is trained using backpropagation at the end of the training or during the training. As a remark, the softmax layer is a separate single-layer network, and it does not perform backpropagation to the FF layers. Hence, it can also be trained independently like an FF layer. This prediction approach is faster for inference since it is sufficient to perform a single pass for each datum; on the other hand, it is sub-optimal with respect to the Goodness prediction which better corresponds to how the network was trained.

Sequential Training of the Forward-Forward Algorithm. The layers of the network are trained for several epochs where an epoch is defined as training the network for the entire training dataset once. Since FF does not involve backpropagation, layers can be trained independently, each layer can be trained for more than one epoch waiting the upper layers to finish the previous epochs. For instance, assuming that the network will be trained for 60 epochs, we can train

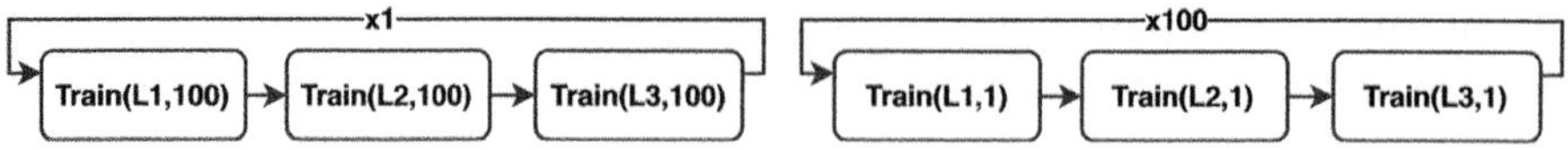

Fig. 3. Comparison of the FFA with split counts 1 (left) and 100 (right) across 3 layers. $Train(L, E)$ in a block denotes training the layer L for E epochs before passing its output to the next layer.

the first layer for 30 epochs, and use this half-trained layer-1 for training the second layer for its 30 epochs and so on.

Moreover, training a layer for the total number of epochs and providing its output to the next layer is not good for accuracy. Training each layer for a small number of epochs allows fine-grained adjustments on this layer and yields better results. So, we divide the training process of each layer into splits, basically the number of consecutive epochs passed from a layer before giving its output to the next layer. Figure 3 shows the difference between the 1 and 100 split values.

4 PipelineFF: A Pipeline Forward-Forward Algorithm

In this section, we propose three parallel Pipeline Forward Forward (PFF) algorithms: Single-Layer PFF (Sect. 4.1), All-Layers PFF (Sect. 4.2), Federated PFF (Sect. 4.3) and Performance-Optimized Network PFF (Sect. 4.4).

The Single-Layer PFF employs an architecture in which each node is dedicated to training only one layer, while All-Layers and Federated PFF algorithms distribute the training load more evenly, by asking every node to train all network layers in turn. All models enjoy model and pipeline parallelism, while the federated PFF also takes advantage of data parallelism.

In all proposed PFF models, we divide the total number of E epochs into S splits to facilitate distributed training. The sequential training periods of layers are called chapters, and each chapter takes $C = E/S$ training epochs. Consequently, each node has to process S chapters to complete the training for E epochs. The variable N denotes the number of nodes in the distributed system. The input data set is abstracted as x, which consists of positive and negative samples. $L_i(x)$ is used to denote the output of the ith layer of the neural network after a forward pass with the input data x. Finally, $Train(L_i, n)$ is an abstraction for training the layer L_i for n epochs.

4.1 Single-Layer PFF Algorithm

Single-Layer PFF employs an architecture in which each node is dedicated to training only one layer, as shown in Fig. 4. This procedure ensures that while node i is training the layer L_i for the jth split, the previous node can train the layer L_{i-1} concurrently on the split number $j' > j$. Already with this simple architecture, we achieve parallelism among the nodes, unlike the sequential FFA.

The distributed training example provided in Fig. 4 illustrates a scenario with three compute nodes and a three-layer neural network. The number of nodes,

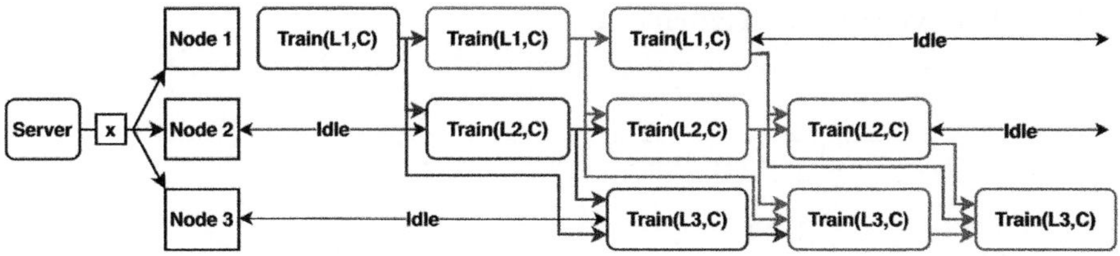

Fig. 4. Single-Layer PFF Algorithm example with three layers and three splits.

N, is selected to be equal to the number of layers L and each node trains the corresponding layer of the network. In the following, we detail the algorithm with a pseudo code and the training process.

Node Initialization: Each node $i \in [1, N]$ is initialized with training data and layer parameters and hyperparameters.

Initialization and Training of Node 1: Node 1 initializes neurons of L_1 randomly and trains this layer for C epochs. Then, it sends L_1's weight and biases to Node $i' > 1$ and starts training L_1 for C more epochs and repeats.

Other Nodes: To train L_i for the jth split, Node i needs to prepare the output of L_{i-1} (trained for $j' > j$ splits). This is done by getting the layers L_k where $k < i$ and doing a forward pass until L_i. Then, it trains L_i for C epochs and sends its weight and bias values to each Node $i' > i$ and repeats.

Termination: Each node iterates for S chapters and E epochs in total. After each iteration, a node might update the negative examples based on a protocol.

Transferring large layer outputs, which grow with dataset size, between computing nodes leads to a communication bottleneck. To enhance time efficiency, our approach prioritizes the transmission of layer parameters over output tensors. By sending the parameters and executing the forward pass on each node, we drastically reduce the amount of data transferred, resulting in a faster overall process. This optimization is represented in Fig. 4 and the loop within Algorithm 1, Lines 3–5.

Algorithm 1. Single-Layer Training Procedure

1: **for** *chapter* = 1 to *split* **do**
2: $\quad x_{pos}, x_{neg} \leftarrow X_{POS}, X_{NEG}$
3: $\quad$ **for** *layerIndex* = 1 to *currentClientIndex* **do**
4: $\quad\quad layer \leftarrow getLayer(layerIndex, chapter)$
5: $\quad\quad x_{pos}, x_{neg} \leftarrow layer(x_{pos}, x_{neg})$
6: $\quad$ **for** *miniEpoch* = 1 to *epochs/split* **do**
7: $\quad\quad learningRateCooldown(chapter, miniEpoch)$
8: $\quad\quad$ **for each** *batch* in x_{pos}, x_{neg} **do**
9: $\quad\quad\quad trainLayer(currentClientIndex, batch)$
10: $\quad PublishLayer(chapter, layerIndex)$
11: $\quad UpdateXNEG(publish = False)$

4.2 All-Layers PFF Algorithm

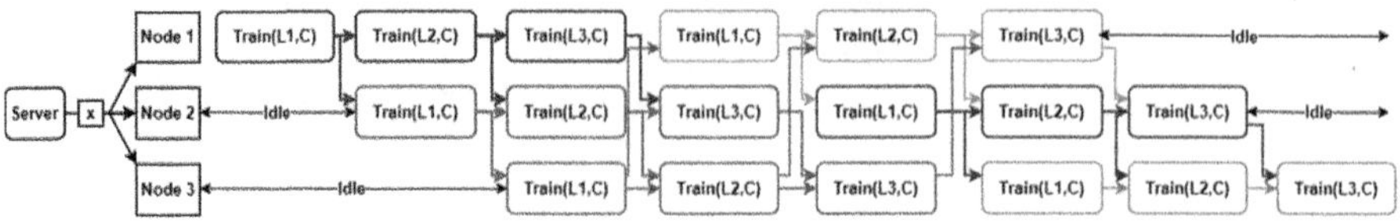

Fig. 5. All-Layers PFF Algorithm example with three layers and two splits.

The All-Layers PFF model builds upon the Single-Layer approach by allowing each compute node to train the entire network, affording a more balanced load among the nodes.

Figure 5 illustrates the approach in the context of a system with three compute nodes and a three-layer neural network, but with two splits for clarity.

Node Initialization: Each node is initialized with the dataset and the required hyperparameters.

Initial Training: $Node_1$ trains the entire network with randomly initialized layers for C epochs.

Rest of the training: Concurrently, each $Node_i$ trains the layer L_{k-1} immediately after $Node_{i-1}$ has completed its C epochs of training for the layer L_{k-2}. Each $Node_i$ sends its last trained layer to $Node_{i+1(mod(N))}$ and receives the layer to be trained from $Node_{i-1(mod(N))}$.

Iteration and Convergence: The process repeats for S/N splits but not S since in this approach every node trains each layer. The algorithm converges when the entire network has been trained for a total of E epochs.

Algorithm 2. All-Layers Training Procedure

for $chapter = 1$ to $split$ **do**
  $x_{pos}, x_{neg} \leftarrow X_{POS}, X_{NEG}$
  for $layerIndex = 1$ to $numLayers$ **do**
    if not $(firstClient$ and $chapter = 0)$ **then**
      $getLayer(layerIndex, chapter)$
    for $miniEpoch = 1$ to $epochs/split$ **do**
      $learningRateCooldown(chapter, miniEpoch)$
      for each $batch$ in x_{pos}, x_{neg} **do**
        $trainLayer(layerIndex, batch)$
    $PublishLayer(chapter, layerIndex)$
    $x_{pos}, x_{neg} \leftarrow layer(x_{pos}, x_{neg})$
  $UpdateXNEG(publish = False)$

4.3 Federated PFF Algorithm

In contrast to the All-Layers PFF Algorithm, the Federated PFF Algorithm employs the same training procedure but differentiates in the data it utilizes for training. Each node trains on its own local dataset rather than a shared one. This preserves data privacy, as there is no need to share raw data with other nodes or a centralized server. While the data remain localized, the nodes exchange model updates. This allows nodes to benefit from learning carried out by their counterparts, which iteratively improves the global model that benefits from diverse data without central aggregation. This federated structure is crucial not only for scenarios requiring data privacy but also enables distributed training over networks where central data aggregation is impractical or undesired.

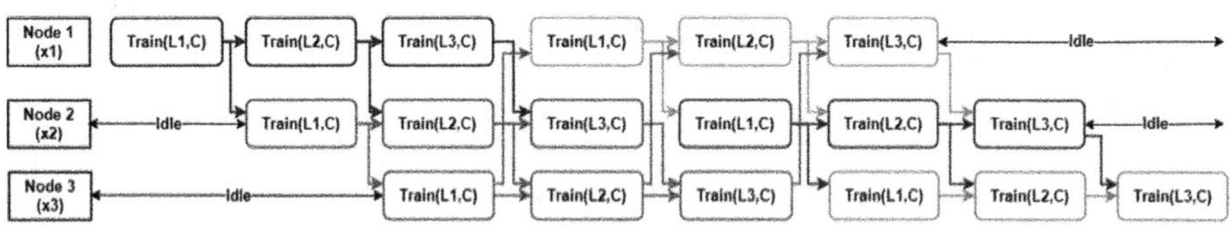

Fig. 6. Federated PFF Algorithm example with 3 layers and 6 split.

4.4 PFF with A New Goodness Function

The FFA [5] states that different goodness functions can be used while training each layer individually. In this section, we propose a new PFF algorithm called Performance-Optimized Network (PON) that uses a goodness function based on classification accuracy. Specifically, we add a softmax activated layer to each network layer and update only the weights of these two layers via backpropagation (as illustrated in Fig. 7b), training each layer to maximize classification accuracy and thereby making this approach suitable only for supervised learning problems. Furthermore, the rest of the training is performed exactly in accordance with the FFA except that there are no negative data.

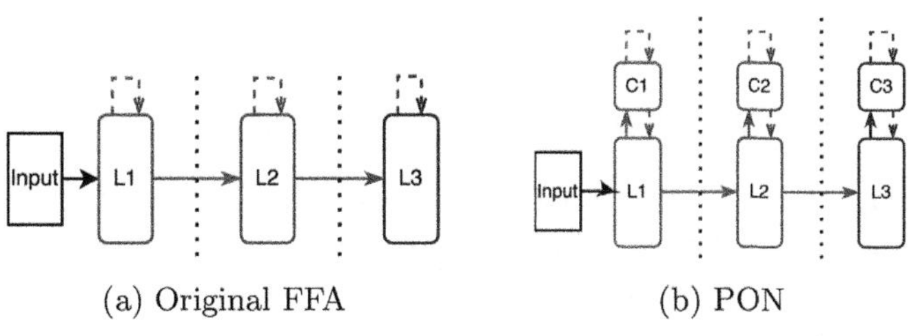

Fig. 7. Comparison of forward and backward passes between FFA and PON.

5 Experimental Evaluation

We obtain and compare several models by modifying the distributed model (Single-Layer or All-Layers), negative data selection (Adaptive, Fixed, or Random), classification strategies (Goodness and Softmax) and goodness function.

The two variants of the PFF (Single-Layer and All-Layers models, as explained in Sects. 4.1 and 4.2, respectively) are compared with the sequential implementation (node count $N = 1$), which is equivalent to the original FFA and can be used to compare models using the same code base.

To select negative samples, we implemented AdaptiveNEG, the method proposed in [5], which selects the most predicted incorrect label as the negative label. The second approach is FixedNEG, which involves choosing random incorrect labels for each instance in the beginning of the training. The third approach, called RandomNEG, selects the random incorrect labels at the end of each chapter. The last two are proposed to speed up the training.

For the classification approach, we implemented both approaches explained in Sect. 3 proposed by Hinton in [5]. In the Goodness based approach, a sample is classified into the class that results in the highest goodness score (considering all but the first layer). In the Softmax approach, a single layer classification head is added to the network with softmax activation.

Finally, we evaluated the PON proposed in 4.4 in supervised learning scenarios.

5.1 Implementation Details

Our chosen architecture is the same feedforward neural network as in [5]. Its configuration is [784, 2000, 2000, 2000, 2000], where the numbers indicate the number of nodes in each layer. Thus, the input, which is 784-dimensional, is followed by four hidden layers with 2000 nodes each. Each of these layers employs the ReLU activation function.

The network is trained and tested using the MNIST dataset, using 60,000 training instances with mini-batches of size 64 and testing on a separate test set comprising 10,000 instances for 100 epochs and 100 splits. The Adam optimizer is used for both the FF Layers and the Softmax layer (trained using Backpropagation) is set initially at 0.01 and 0.0001 respectively and cooldowns after the 50th epoch. The threshold coefficient θ in Eq. 1 is set to 0.01, as in [5].

5.2 Comparison of FF, DFF and PFF Models

We first compare the accuracy and speed of the PFF variants using the Goodness approach with the Matlab implementation of the original Forward-Forward paper's results [5] and another distributed implementation [3] of the Forward-Forward algorithm. The results are given in Table 1.

The AdaptiveNEG approach, which selects negative data based on the network's performance at each chapter, outperforms both RandomNEG and FixedNEG models in terms of accuracy. Remarkably, despite shorter training times

(7,178 vs 11,190 s), RandomNEG performs close to AdaptiveNEG in terms of accuracy (98.33 vs 98.52 in Sequential), making these models more accurate than FixedNEG in every implementation.

The AdaptiveNEG Goodness model with Sequential implementation is basically the same as [5] and it indeed achieves almost the same accuracy as Hinton's Matlab implementation [11]. It enables us to compare the training time of the model with our Python implementation.

Furthermore, AdaptiveNEG with All-Layers implementation matches the highest accuracy of its sequential version (98.51% vs. 98.52%) but in about a quarter of the time (2,980 vs. 11,190 s), using four compute nodes. This finding showcases the PFF Algorithm's efficiency in distributing the training, achieving 94% utilization (3.75/4), significantly speeding up the process. The All-Layers method speeds up training for AdaptiveNEG by efficiently distributing tasks between nodes, allowing each to compute its own negative samples after every chapter, unlike the Single-Layer approach, where the last node generates and publishes the generated labels.

Table 1. Original, DFF and PFF comparison. Baseline is highlighted as bold.

Model	Setup	Training Time (s)	Test Accuracy (%)
Hinton's Matlab Code [11]			98.53
DFF (1000 epochs) [3]			93.15
AdaptiveNEG-Goodness	Sequential	**11,190.72**	**98.52**
	Single-Layer	5,254.87	98.43
	All-Layers	2,980.76	98.51
RandomNEG-Goodness	Sequential	7,178.71	98.33
	Single-Layer	1,974.10	98.26
	All-Layers	2,008.25	98.17
FixedNEG-Goodness	Sequential	7,143.28	97.95
	Single-Layer	1,920.80	97.94
	All-Layers	1,978.21	97.89

5.3 Classifier Mode Comparison for AdaptiveNEG

In the first evaluation, we compared PFF variants that used the Goodness approach for classification and established the AdaptiveNEG Goodness model as the proposed baseline. The second experiment compares the performance of this model with that using the Softmax approach. As mentioned before, the goodness method is the first method provided in [5] and uses only the FF layers. The Softmax method on the other hand, is presented as a faster alternative, predicting the output using a Softmax layer that gets the activations of the hidden FF layers (except the first). The corresponding results can be found in Table 2.

The results show that the AdaptiveNEG Softmax model trains faster than the AdaptiveNEG-Goodness model, for all different implementations (e.g. 1,886 versus 2,980 secs). This accelerated training is due to the single-step prediction in the softmax approach, rather than predicting across 10 different classes. However, the accuracies all slightly decrease compared to comparable Goodness models.

The advantage of the All-Layers PFF Algorithm on the AdaptiveNEG explained in Sect. 5.2 is still very observable for the Softmax methods.

Table 2. Classification mode comparison for AdaptiveNEG. The first three row results indicated in italic denote the baseline model from Table 1. Bold results indicate suggested models for each classification mode.

Model	Setup	Training Time (s)	Test Accuracy (%)
	Sequential	11,190.72	98.52
AdaptiveNEG-Goodness	Single-Layer	5,254.87	98.43
	All-Layers	**2,980.76**	**98.51**
	Sequential	8,365.96	98.38
AdaptiveNEG-Softmax	Single-Layer	2,471.27	98.31
	All-Layers	**1,886.42**	**98.30**

5.4 Classifier Mode Comparison for RandomNEG

Based on the previous findings in Sect. 5.2, we observed that RandomNEG closely rivals AdaptiveNEG in accuracy, while significantly reducing training time. This observation leads us to further investigate the impact of employing softmax within the RandomNEG framework. This section thus compares the effects of softmax and Goodness prediction on both FixedNEG and RandomNEG strategies. The results of this comparison are detailed in Table 3, providing insight into how these elements influence the effectiveness and efficiency of the methods under review.

In terms of accuracy, the Softmax approach outperforms the Goodness approach for prediction. For instance, while the Sequential RandomNEG Goodness model performed 98.33 the softmax version performed 98.48. This level of accuracy of the softmax version is very close to the performance of our baseline model (98.51 Accuracy using AdaptiveNEG Goodness). Although the accuracy levels are very close, we observe that there is a significant speed-up using RandomNEG (8,104 versus 11,190).

In terms of training speed, on the other hand, training a model with the additional Softmax layer takes longer in the Sequential model as expected. However, Single-Layer implementation is not affected by this additional complexity. This is due to the fact that Softmax Layer is easier/faster to train than the FF Layers, and due to the pipeline architecture this only adds a small delay.

Surprisingly, Softmax models give faster results compared to same Goodness models for All-Layers implementation. This again stems from the fact that training Softmax is faster than training FF Layers, and distributing this job between 5 nodes speeds up the overall training.

Table 3. Classification mode comparison for RandomNEG. The first three row results indicated in italic are from Table 1. Bold text shows the proposed RandomNEG model balancing accuracy and speed.

Model	Setup	Training Time (s)	Test Accuracy (%)
	Sequential	7,178.71	98.33
RandomNEG-Goodness	Single-Layer	1,974.15	98.26
	All-Layers	2,008.25	98.17
	Sequential	8,104.96	98.48
RandomNEG-Softmax	Single-Layer	1,891.86	98.31
	All-Layers	**1,786.30**	**98.33**

5.5 Evaluation of the Performance-Optimized Network

This section explores the evaluation of our Performance-Optimized Network (PON) that is created by incorporating a new goodness function into the Forward-Forward algorithm. Our analysis shows that while the Performance-Optimized Model performs slightly worse than the best-performing AdaptiveNEG Goodness model, there is a notable reduction in training times, indicating a significant step towards efficient computing without significantly sacrificing performance.

In the MNIST dataset, the results presented in Table 4 highlight the effectiveness of the new goodness function proposed when integrated with the Forward-Forward algorithm. The highest test accuracy is achieved by the AdaptiveNEG Goodness model, reaching 98.52%, which is slightly superior to the 98.48% accuracy of the RandomNEG Softmax model. It should be noted that the Performance-Optimized Network, whether using only the last layer or all layers, shows a small decrease in accuracy. Specifically, using all layers slightly improves the accuracy to 98.38% compared to 98.30% when only the last layer is used. These results underscore the robustness of the proposed goodness function, particularly when all layers are optimized, despite a considerable reduction in training time (4219.97 s) compared to the AdaptiveNEG Goodness model (11190.72 s).

5.6 Experiments with CIFAR-10

To extend our analysis to a more complex scenario, we replicated the experiments described in Sects. 5.2 through 5.5 using the CIFAR-10 dataset. CIFAR-10, known for its higher variability and complexity compared to MNIST, serves

Table 4. MNIST evaluation of PON with the baseline models from Table 1.

Model	Training Time (s)	Test Accuracy (%)
AdaptiveNEG-Goodness	11,190.72	98.52
RandomNEG-Softmax	8,104.96	98.48
PON (only last layer)	4,219.97	98.30
PON (using all layers)	4,219.97	98.38

as a challenging benchmark to test the robustness and effectiveness of our models.

Table 5 presents the detailed results of these experiments. Performance-Optimized Network (PON), whether it uses only the last layer or all layers, demonstrated a superior ability to handle the complexities of CIFAR-10, with the prediction using all of the layers achieving the highest accuracy of 53.50%. This was closely followed by the RandomNEG Softmax model, which achieved 52.18% accuracy. Furthermore, the PON models show relatively efficient training durations compared to the other sequential PFF Models. Surprisingly, the AdaptiveNEG Goodness model, which performed exceptionally well in MNIST, significantly underperformed in CIFAR-10, with an accuracy of only 11.10%. This difference suggests a potential mismatch between the model's capabilities and the dataset's requirements.

It should be noted that while state-of-the-art models have achieved above 99% accuracy on CIFAR-10, the performance of our models is similar to Hinton's original FFA, which reported an accuracy of 56% using CNNs [5].

Table 5. CIFAR-10 Results

Model	Training Time (s)	Test Accuracy (%)
PON (using all layers)	**4,920.97**	**53.50**
PON (only last layer)	4,920.97	53.11
FixedNEG-Softmax	8,021.15	50.89
RandomNEG-Softmax	7,636.99	52.18
AdaptiveNEG-Goodness	10,148.23	11.10

6 Conclusion and Future Work

Our work in this paper presents Pipeline Forward-Forward Algorithm (PFF), a novel way to train distributed neural networks using Forward-Forward Algorithm. Compared to the classic implementations with backpropagation and pipeline parallelism [6,13], PFF is inherently different as it does not enforce backpropagation dependency on the system, thus achieving higher utilization of computational units with fewer bubbles and idle time. Experiments done with PFF show that the PFF Algorithm achieves the same accuracy as the standard FF implementation [5] with a 4x speed up. Comparison of PFF with an existing distributed implementation of Forward-Forward (DFF [3]) shows even greater improvements, as PFF achieves %5 more accuracy in 10 times less epochs. This improvement in accuracy is mainly because PFF splits the data into batches and feeds them to the network batch by batch, unlike DFF which feeds the data as a whole. In addition, the data that are exchanged between layers in PFF is a lot less than DFF since PFF sends the layer information (weights and biases), whereas DFF sends the whole output of the data. This results in less communication overhead compared to DFF.

Besides the exciting results that PFF produced, we believe that our work paves the way for a brand new path in the area of Distributed training of Neural Networks. Thus, there are plenty of different ways that can improve PFF, with some of these approaches outlined below.

- **Exchanging parameters after each batch:** In the current implementation of PFF, the exchange of parameters between different layers takes place after each chapter. Making this exchange after each batch is worth trying since it could better tune the weights and produce higher accuracy. However, it could potentially increase the communication overhead.
- **Different Setups:** In the experiments of this work, we used sockets to establish communication between different nodes. This brings additional communication overhead, as the data is sent through the network. In a setup where computational units of the PFF are closer and can access to a shared resource (Multi GPU architectures) the time of training networks can decrease drastically.
- **Generating Negative Samples Differently:** The way negative samples are generated is a very important aspect of the Forward-Forward Algorithm as it directly affects the learning of the network. Thus, discovering new and better ways to generate negative samples would definitely result in a better performing system.
- **Forming an Innovative Framework:** A general and efficient framework can be implemented for training large neural networks following and improving the novel ideas presented in this work.

References

1. Ben-Nun, T., Hoefler, T.: Demystifying parallel and distributed deep learning: an in-depth concurrency analysis. ACM Comput. Surv. **52**(4), Article 65 (2019). https://doi.org/10.1145/3320060
2. Beutel, D.J., et al.: Flower: a friendly federated learning research framework (2022). https://arxiv.org/abs/2007.14390

3. Deng, Q., et al.: Dff: Distributed forward-forward algorithm for large-scale model in low-performance devices. In: 2023 IEEE 6th International Conference on Pattern Recognition and Artificial Intelligence (PRAI). IEEE (2023)
4. Gautham, S.R., Nair, S., Jamadagni, S., Khurana, M., Assadi, M.: Exploring the feasibility of forward forward algorithm in neural networks. In: 2024 International Conference on Advances in Modern Age Technologies for Health and Engineering Science (AMATHE), pp. 1–6 (2024). https://doi.org/10.1109/AMATHE61652.2024.10582053
5. Hinton, G.: The forward-forward algorithm: Some preliminary investigations. arXiv preprint arXiv:2212.13345 (2022)
6. Huang, Y., et al.: Gpipe: Efficient training of giant neural networks using pipeline parallelism. In: Advances in Neural Information Processing Systems, vol. 32 (2019)
7. Hwang, T., Seo, H., Jung, S.: Local back-propagation: layer-wise unsupervised learning in forward-forward algorithms (12 2024). https://doi.org/10.21203/rs.3.rs-5695830/v1
8. Krutsylo, A.: Scalable forward-forward algorithm (2025). https://arxiv.org/abs/2501.03176
9. Laskin, M., et al.: Parallel training of deep networks with local updates (2021)
10. Li, S., et al.: Pytorch distributed: experiences on accelerating data parallel training (2020). https://arxiv.org/abs/2006.15704
11. Löwe, S., Baichuan: Forward-forward. https://github.com/loeweX/Forward-Forward (2023)
12. Mayer, R., et al.: Scalable deep learning on distributed infrastructures: challenges, techniques, and tools. ACM Comput. Surv. **53**(1), Article 3 (2020https://doi.org/10.1145/3363554
13. Narayanan, D., Harlap, A., et al.: Pipedream: generalized pipeline parallelism for DNN training. In: Proceedings of the 27th ACM Symposium on Operating Systems Principles. pp. 1–15. SOSP '19, New York, NY, USA (2019). https://doi.org/10.1145/3341301.3359646
14. Ororbia, A., Mali, A.: The predictive forward-forward algorithm (2023)
15. Papachristodoulou, A., Kyrkou, C., Timotheou, S., Theocharides, T.: Convolutional channel-wise competitive learning for the forward-forward algorithm. In: Proceedings of the AAAI Conference on Artificial Intelligence, vol. 38(13), pp. 14536–14544 (2024). https://doi.org/10.1609/aaai.v38i13.29369
16. Park, S., Shin, D., Chung, J., Lee, N.: Fedfwd: federated learning without backpropagation (2023). https://arxiv.org/abs/2309.01150
17. R, G.: Improved forward-forward contrastive learning (2024). https://arxiv.org/abs/2405.03432
18. Rumelhart, D.E., Hinton, G.E., Williams, R.J.: Learning representations by backpropagating errors. Nature **323**(6088), 533–536 (1986). https://doi.org/10.1038/323533a0
19. Scodellaro, R., et al.: Training convolutional neural networks with the forward-forward algorithm. arXiv preprint arXiv:2312.14924 (2023)
20. Zhao, G., et al.: The cascaded forward algorithm for neural network training (2023)

An Ensemble Model for 30-Minute Blood Glucose Prediction in Type 1 Diabetes: Balancing Accuracy and Simplicity

Khadija Tlemçani(✉), Kebira Azbeg, Wafaa Wakrim, Laila Fetjah, Ouail Ouchetto, and Said Jai Andaloussi

Laboratory of Data Engineering and Intelligent Systems (LIDSI), Department of Mathematics and Computer Science, Faculty of Sciences Ain Chock, University Hassan II of Casablanca, Casablanca, Morocco
khadija.tlemcani-etu@etu.univh2c.ma

Abstract. Precise short-term blood glucose forecasting is critical for managing type 1 diabetes (T1D), enabling timely interventions to prevent complications. Complex deep learning models often rely on intricate architectures, increasing computational demands. We propose an ensemble model integrating XGBoost and LSTM, evaluated on the OhioT1DM dataset. Our preprocessing pipeline employs Kalman Filter smoothing, oversampling of high-glucose events, and feature engineering to extract lagged, rolling, and interaction features. The ensemble achieves an RMSE of 19.89 mg/dL, an MAE of 10.37 mg/dL, and 99.20% of predictions in Clarke Error Grid (CEG) Zones A and B, outperforming individual models and competing with state-of-the-art methods. Its simple architecture and fast inference time of 1.33 s for 3738 samples support real-time deployment on constrained devices such as smartphones. Feature importance and uncertainty estimation (85.58% coverage for 90% prediction intervals) enhance clinical usability, while future work will explore generalization to diverse cohorts and longer prediction horizons.

Keywords: Blood Glucose Prediction · Type 1 Diabetes · Ensemble Learning · Continuous Glucose Monitoring · Clinical Accuracy

1 Introduction

Diabetes is a metabolic condition characterized by chronically elevated blood glucose levels resulting from a total or partial deficiency of insulin [4]. Diabetes is typically categorized into two types: Type 1 diabetes involves an autoimmune response that eliminates beta cells, resulting in decreasing insulin levels, whereas Type 2 diabetes is marked by insulin resistance despite ongoing insulin production [17].

Unregulated blood glucose levels can precipitate severe health complications, including cardiovascular disease, kidney failure, neuropathy, and sight loss, all

S. Lahlou and M. Mukund (Eds.): NETYS 2025, LNCS 15736, pp. 187–201, 2026.
https://doi.org/10.1007/978-3-032-00347-8_12

of which markedly reduce quality of life and shorten life expectancy [24]. Consequently, sustaining optimal blood glucose levels is essential for effective diabetes management [11].

Recent technological advancements have revolutionized diabetes management. The extensive utilization of smartphones, IoT devices, wearables, and sensors today allows patients to effortlessly document and track health-related occurrences in real time [18,19]. Furthermore, the networked, real-time data environment enabled by these technologies has transformed diabetes management by allowing continuous glucose monitoring and the integration of connected insulin pumps, hence improving glycemic control [12,15].

Precise short-term blood glucose forecasting is essential for the management of type 1 diabetes, as even minor fluctuations can precipitate serious complications—including hypoglycemia, hyperglycemia, renal failure, and loss of consciousness–that adversely affect patient health and quality of life [2,22]. Recent studies have shown that sophisticated deep learning models, including the VAE-GRU framework [1], autonomous channel networks [22], BGformer [20], and PBGTAM [21], can effectively capture intricate temporal dynamics in continuous glucose monitoring (CGM) data, yielding competitive predictive outcomes. Nonetheless, these advanced models generally depend on intricate architectures and comprehensive preprocessing methods—spanning latent space imputation to multi-head attention mechanisms—which elevate computational requirements and hinder real-time implementation, particularly on resource-limited devices [10,23].

Although continuous monitoring and closed-loop insulin delivery systems demonstrate promising clinical accuracy [5,7], their dependence on intricate techniques constrains practical implementation in everyday settings [16]. An interesting approach would be to harmonize high prediction accuracy with architectural simplicity to enable practical implementation. Our research presents an ensemble paradigm that integrates XGBoost and LSTM, augmented by data-driven weight optimization. This method seeks to get accurate 30-minute glucose predictions with less complexity, hence lowering the risk of severe consequences while providing a viable alternative for real-time Type 1 Diabetes treatment.

2 Related Work

Recent deep learning methodologies utilizing CGM data have enhanced predicted accuracy, however sometimes accompanied with significant computing complexity [14], hence restricting their implementation on resource-limited devices. This section evaluates cutting-edge methodologies for T1D glucose prediction, emphasizing their strategies, datasets, and constraints, to underscore the necessity for more straightforward, resource-efficient alternatives.

Abusaleh and Rahim (2024) proposed a multitask VAE-GRU model for preprocessing and predicting glucose levels on the OhioT1DM dataset, achieving moderate accuracy but with high computational demands due to internal preprocessing [1]. Yang et al. (2022) introduced an autonomous channel deep learning framework with LSTM layers to handle time-dependent scale discrepancies in OhioT1DM data, offering high accuracy at the expense of high computational cost [22]. Van Smeden et al. (2021) developed an LSTM model, initially trained on a non-T1D cohort and adapted to OhioT1DM, achieving excellent short-term accuracy but requiring extensive training [7]. Zhu et al. (2022) presented the FCNN, a bidirectional GRU with attention, evaluated on multiple datasets, delivering strong performance but hindered by computational overhead [23]. Yang et al. (2023) proposed PBGTAM, a temporal multi-head attention model with BiLSTM, which performs well on OhioT1DM but is limited by its complex architecture [21]. Alvarado et al. (2023) introduced the WTG Prediction system using wavelet transforms and CNNs for long-term hypoglycemia prediction, achieving high accuracy at the cost of computational complexity [2]. Rodríguez-Rodríguez et al. (2023) explored lightweight algorithms like Random Forest for glycemia forecasting on IoT devices, offering efficiency but facing scalability challenges [16]. Cheng et al. (2024) developed TimeGlu, a Bi-LSTM encoder-decoder, focusing on CGM data, with good accuracy but high processing demands [5]. Xue et al. (2024) proposed BGformer, an enhanced Informer model, for longer-term predictions, limited by its transformer-based computational cost [20].

These studies, summarized in Table 1, demonstrate that while advanced deep learning models achieve high predictive accuracy, their computational complexity—due to extensive preprocessing, long training times, and resource demands—often makes them impractical for real-time T1D management on resource-constrained devices [14]. Our work addresses this gap with a simple ensemble of XGBoost and basic LSTM, optimized for accuracy and deployability on limited hardware.

Table 1. Summary of Related Work on Blood Glucose Prediction for T1D

Study	Dataset	Model	Horizon	Limitation
[1]	OhioT1DM	VAE-GRU	30 min	High computational demand
[22]	OhioT1DM	Autonomous LSTM	30 min	Complex preprocessing
[7]	OhioT1DM	LSTM	15 min	Extensive training needs
[23]	OhioT1DM	FCNN (GRU)	30 min	High computational overhead
[21]	OhioT1DM	PBGTAM (BiLSTM)	30 min	Complex architecture
[2]	Private (20 patients)	WTG (CNN)	24 hr	High computational cost
[16]	Private (40 patients)	RF	15 min	Scalability issues
[5]	CGM Glucose	TimeGlu (Bi-LSTM)	Short-term	High processing demands
[20]	DirecNet	BGformer	60 min	Transformer-based cost

3 Materials and Methods

3.1 Dataset

We use the OhioT1DM dataset [13], a widely adopted benchmark in T1D research. The dataset contains CGM data, recorded at 5-minute intervals, from

12 T1D patients over an 8-week period. In addition to CGM measurements, the dataset includes basal and bolus insulin doses, self-reported meal events with carbohydrate estimates (`meals`), and activity data from fitness wristbands. Time-related features such as hour and day-of-week are derived during preprocessing. For each patient, the first 38 days of data are used for training, and the final 10 days are reserved for testing. The `meals` column is relabeled as `carbs` during preprocessing to reflect carbohydrate intake in the feature set.

3.2 Data Preprocessing and Feature Engineering

A series of preprocessing steps and feature engineering routines were implemented to align the raw data on a 5-minute interval grid, smooth CGM data, impute missing values, and extract predictive features. We used Python libraries including `pandas`, `numpy`, `scikit-learn`, `tensorflow`, `pykalman`, and `xgboost`.

Data Alignment and Imputation. Raw data from multiple patients were initially processed from raw grid CSV files using a custom preprocessing pipeline. The raw data, including CGM readings (`glucose`), basal insulin (`basal`), bolus insulin (`bolus`), and carbohydrate intake (`carbs`), was aligned to a 5-minute interval grid. Missing values in `glucose` were imputed using linear interpolation followed by forward-fill, and for `basal`, backward-fill was also applied in the main modeling stage. The `bolus` and `carbs` columns were filled with zeros to reflect the absence of events. The imputation for `glucose` is formalized as:

$$G(t_i) = G(t_{i-1}) + \frac{(t_i - t_{i-1})}{(t_{i+1} - t_{i-1})} \cdot \Big(G(t_{i+1}) - G(t_{i-1})\Big) \tag{1}$$

Additionally, `glucose_smoothed` was created from `glucose` using a Kalman Filter during preprocessing, and its missing values were imputed using the same method to ensure consistency.

Kalman Filter Smoothing. To reduce noise and artifacts in the raw glucose readings from the Enlite CGM device, we applied a linear Kalman Filter for smoothing [9]. The filter employs the standard state transition and observation models:

$$x_t = x_{t-1} + w_t, \quad w_t \sim \mathcal{N}(0, Q) \tag{2}$$

$$z_t = x_t + v_t, \quad v_t \sim \mathcal{N}(0, R) \tag{3}$$

where w_t and v_t denote the process and observation noise, respectively. The algorithm recursively predicts the current state and updates it when new measurements become available.

Target Creation. A target variable representing the glucose level 30 min ahead was created by shifting the `glucose_smoothed` time series by 6 steps:

$$G(t + 30) = \texttt{glucose\_smoothed}(t + 6) \tag{4}$$

Rows with missing target values were subsequently dropped to ensure a complete dataset.

Feature Extraction. To capture both short- and medium-term glucose dynamics, we engineered several features:

- **Lagged Features:** Two sets of lag features were generated:
  - Short lags for 1, 2, 3, and 4 min:

$$G_{\text{lag},k}(t) = \texttt{glucose\_smoothed}(t - k), \quad k \in \{1, 2, 3, 4\} \tag{5}$$

  - Longer lags for 5, 10, 15, 20, 25, and 30 min, with integer shifts based on 5-minute intervals:

$$G_{\text{lag},\ell}(t) = \texttt{glucose\_smoothed}(t - \lfloor \ell/5 \rfloor), \quad \ell \in \{5, 10, 15, 20, 25, 30\} \tag{6}$$

- **Rolling Statistics:** A 30-minute rolling mean and standard deviation (over 6 time steps) were computed:

$$\text{mean}_{30}(t) = \frac{1}{6} \sum_{i=0}^{5} \texttt{glucose\_smoothed}(t - i) \tag{7}$$

$$\text{std}_{30}(t) = \sqrt{\frac{1}{6} \sum_{i=0}^{5} \left(\texttt{glucose\_smoothed}(t - i) - \text{mean}_{30}(t)\right)^2} \tag{8}$$

- **Insulin, Meal, and Temporal Features:** Current values of `basal`, `bolus`, and `carbs` are included, along with the hour and day-of-week extracted from the timestamp.
- **Interaction Terms:** Interaction features such as `bolus_carbs_interaction` (product of `bolus` and `carbs`), `bolus_hour_interaction`, and `carbs_hour_interaction` were computed.

The final feature vector, denoted by X, is composed of 20 features:

$$\begin{aligned} X = \Big[& \texttt{glucose\_smoothed}, \{\, G_{\text{lag},k} \,\}_{k \in \{1,2,3,4,5,10,15,20,25,30\}}, \texttt{mean}_{30}, \texttt{std}_{30}, \\ & \texttt{basal}, \texttt{bolus}, \texttt{hour}, \texttt{day\_of\_week}, \\ & \texttt{bolus\_carbs\_interaction}, \texttt{bolus\_hour\_interaction}, \texttt{carbs\_hour\_interaction} \Big] \end{aligned} \tag{9}$$

Oversampling and Scaling. To mitigate the imbalance in high-glucose instances (values > 190 mg/dL), samples with `glucose_smoothed` exceeding 190 mg/dL were oversampled by a factor of 20, with 10 additional noisy copies generated using Gaussian noise $\mathcal{N}(0, 5)$. All features were then scaled using a RobustScaler, applied to the combined training and testing feature set after oversampling:

$$X_{\text{scaled}} = \frac{X - \text{median}(X)}{IQR(X)} \tag{10}$$

For the LSTM model, the target y was scaled to the range [0,1] using a MinMaxScaler.

3.3 Modeling

We adopt an ensemble framework that combines the strengths of XGBoost (for tabular data) and LSTM (for temporal sequences), along with a hybrid model integrating LSTM features with XGBoost. Detailed architectures and training procedures are described below.

XGBoost Model. The XGBoost model is trained on the 20-dimensional feature vectors using the following hyperparameters:

- Maximum tree depth: 3
- Learning rate (η): 0.05
- Subsample ratio: 0.6
- Column sampling ratio: 0.8
- Regularization: $\lambda = 5.0$ and $\alpha = 2.0$
- Number of boosting rounds: 200 with early stopping after 30 rounds

It minimizes the squared error loss:

$$L_{\text{XGB}} = \sum_{i=1}^{N} (y_i - \hat{y}_i)^2 \tag{11}$$

The model was trained using a dedicated validation set for early stopping.

LSTM Model. The LSTM model processes sequences of 6 time steps (representing 30 min) where each time step is a 20-dimensional vector. Its architecture is:

- **Input:** $(6, 20)$
- **Layers:** Three LSTM layers with 128, 64, and 32 units, respectively; the first two layers return sequences, each followed by a Dropout layer (rate 0.2).
- **Output:** A Dense layer producing a single output.

The model is compiled using the Adam optimizer (learning rate = 0.0005, with gradient clipping at 1.0) and is trained using mean squared error (MSE) loss over 50 epochs with a batch size of 64, utilizing a 10% validation split for monitoring.

Ensemble and Hybrid Models *Ensemble Model:* The predictions from XGBoost and LSTM are combined using a weighted ensemble:

$$\hat{y}_{\text{ensemble}} = w_{\text{XGB}} \cdot \hat{y}_{\text{XGB}} + w_{\text{LSTM}} \cdot \hat{y}_{\text{LSTM}} \tag{12}$$

Weights were optimized via a grid search on a validation set, testing combinations $\{(0.7, 0.3), (0.8, 0.2), (0.9, 0.1), (0.6, 0.4), (0.5, 0.5)\}$. The optimal weights ($w_{\text{XGB}} = 0.9$, $w_{\text{LSTM}} = 0.1$) achieved the lowest validation RMSE of 9.75 mg/dL.

Hybrid Model: In addition, a hybrid model was developed by extracting features from the third LSTM layer and concatenating these with the original tabular features for XGBoost training. An ablation study was conducted to investigate its underperformance (Sect. 4).

3.4 Evaluation Metrics

The models are evaluated using:

- **Root Mean Squared Error (RMSE)** [8]:

$$\text{RMSE} = \sqrt{\frac{1}{N}\sum_{i=1}^{N}(y_i - \hat{y}_i)^2} \tag{13}$$

- **Mean Absolute Error (MAE)** [8]:

$$\text{MAE} = \frac{1}{N}\sum_{i=1}^{N}|y_i - \hat{y}_i| \tag{14}$$

- **Clarke Error Grid Analysis:** Predictions are evaluated clinically using Clarke Error Grid Analysis [6], classifying predictions into zones A–E based on their clinical impact.
- **Prediction Interval Coverage:** To enhance clinical usability, we compute 90% prediction intervals using quantile regression, measuring the percentage of true glucose values falling within these intervals. This quantifies prediction uncertainty [2], aiding clinicians in assessing forecast reliability for T1D management decisions.
- **Additional Metrics:** Inference time, memory usage, and feature importance are reported to assess clinical and practical utility.

4 Results

This section presents the performance of the proposed models for 30-minute-ahead blood glucose prediction on the OhioT1DM test set, evaluated using RMSE, MAE, CEG analysis, computational efficiency, uncertainty estimation, feature importance, and an ablation study for the hybrid model.

Performance of Individual Models. The standalone XGBoost and LSTM models were evaluated on the test set to establish a baseline. The XGBoost model, trained on the 20-dimensional tabular feature vectors, achieved an RMSE of 20.25 mg/dL, an MAE of 10.65 mg/dL, and 99.01% of predictions in CEG Zones A and B (93.47% in Zone A, 5.54% in Zone B). The LSTM model, processing sequences of 6 time steps, recorded an RMSE of 22.03 mg/dL, an MAE of 11.94 mg/dL, and 98.45% in Zones A and B (92.80% in Zone A, 5.64% in Zone B). These results indicate that XGBoost outperforms LSTM, likely due to its effective handling of static features, with both models demonstrating strong clinical accuracy.

Performance of the Ensemble Model. The weighted ensemble model, combining XGBoost and LSTM predictions with optimized weights ($w_{\text{XGB}} = 0.9$, $w_{\text{LSTM}} = 0.1$) determined via grid search (Sect. 3.3), achieved the best overall performance. On the test set, it obtained an RMSE of 19.89 mg/dL, an MAE of 10.37 mg/dL, and 99.20% of predictions in CEG Zones A and B (94.06% in Zone A, 5.14% in Zone B). This represents an improvement over the standalone XGBoost (RMSE reduced by 0.36 mg/dL) and LSTM (RMSE reduced by 2.14 mg/dL), leveraging XGBoost's dominance due to its higher weight. A comparison with state-of-the-art models using the OhioT1DM dataset is provided in Table 2.

Table 2. Comparison with State-of-the-Art Models on OhioT1DM (30-min Horizon)

Study	RMSE (mg/dL)	MAE (mg/dL)	CEG A (%)	CEG B (%)
Abusaleh and Rahim (2024) [1]	28.26 ± 6.53	-	83.55	14.19
Yang et al. (2022) [22]	18.930 ± 2.155	-	89.21	9.47
Zhu et al. (2022) [23]	18.64 ± 2.60	13.25	89.80	8.96
Yang et al. (2023) [21]	20.57	-	85.18	14.36
Ensemble (Ours)	19.89	10.37	94.06	5.14

Performance of the Hybrid Model. The hybrid model, integrating features from the third LSTM layer with tabular features for XGBoost training, achieved an RMSE of 21.27 mg/dL, an MAE of 11.30 mg/dL, and 98.39% of predictions in CEG Zones A and B (92.94% in Zone A, 5.46% in Zone B). The hybrid model underperformed compared to the ensemble (RMSE increased by 1.38 mg/dL) and the standalone XGBoost (RMSE increased by 1.02 mg/dL). An ablation study (Sect. 4) investigates this underperformance.

Ablation Study for Hybrid Model. To investigate the hybrid model's underperformance, we conducted an ablation study training XGBoost on: (1) original tabular features, achieving an RMSE of 20.28 mg/dL, MAE of 10.84 mg/dL, and CEG A+B of 99.01%; (2) LSTM-extracted features, achieving an RMSE of 21.47 mg/dL, MAE of 11.56 mg/dL, and CEG A+B of 98.39%; and (3) combined features (hybrid model, RMSE 21.27 mg/dL). The results suggest that LSTM-extracted features introduce noise, reducing performance compared to tabular features alone, potentially due to misalignment with XGBoost's decision-tree learning.

Computational Efficiency. To assess suitability for real-time T1D management on resource-constrained devices, we evaluated the ensemble model's computational efficiency on a Google Colab environment with a Tesla T4 GPU. The model processed 3738 test samples in 1.33 s ($\approx$ 0.36 ms/sample) with a memory footprint of 1257.94 MB. The fast inference time supports real-time deployment, though the memory usage suggests optimization needs for constrained devices like wearables. Energy consumption was not measured, as it requires specialized hardware testing.

Uncertainty Estimation. To enhance clinical usability, we implemented quantile regression with XGBoost to estimate 90% prediction intervals, achieving 85.58% coverage on the test set. This quantifies prediction uncertainty, aiding clinical decision-making by providing confidence bounds for glucose forecasts.

Feature Importance Analysis. XGBoost's gain metric identified `glucose_smoothed`, `glucose_lag_5min`, and `glucose_rolling_mean_30min` as the most influential features, highlighting the importance of recent glucose trends. Insulin-related features (`basal`, `bolus`) and interaction terms (e.g., `bolus_carbs_interaction`) also contributed significantly, as shown in Fig. 1. This analysis enhances interpretability, guiding clinical and system design decisions.

Clinical Implications. The high percentages of predictions in CEG Zones A and B (99.01% for XGBoost, 98.45% for LSTM, 99.20% for ensemble, 98.39% for hybrid) indicate excellent clinical reliability, with Zone A (e.g., 94.06% for the ensemble) representing accurate predictions and Zone B (e.g., 5.14% for the ensemble) indicating benign errors. The uncertainty estimation (Sect. 4) further supports clinical trust, while feature importance (Sect. 4) enhances interpretability. The oversampling of high-glucose instances (`glucose_smoothed` > 190 mg/dL) enhanced performance during hyperglycemic events, critical for T1D management. However, minor errors in Zones C (0.37% for ensemble) and D (0.43% for ensemble) suggest limitations in predicting rapid fluctuations, warranting further study.

Summary of Performance Metrics. Table 3 summarizes the performance of all models on the test set, highlighting the ensemble model's superiority over individual and hybrid approaches (Fig. 2).

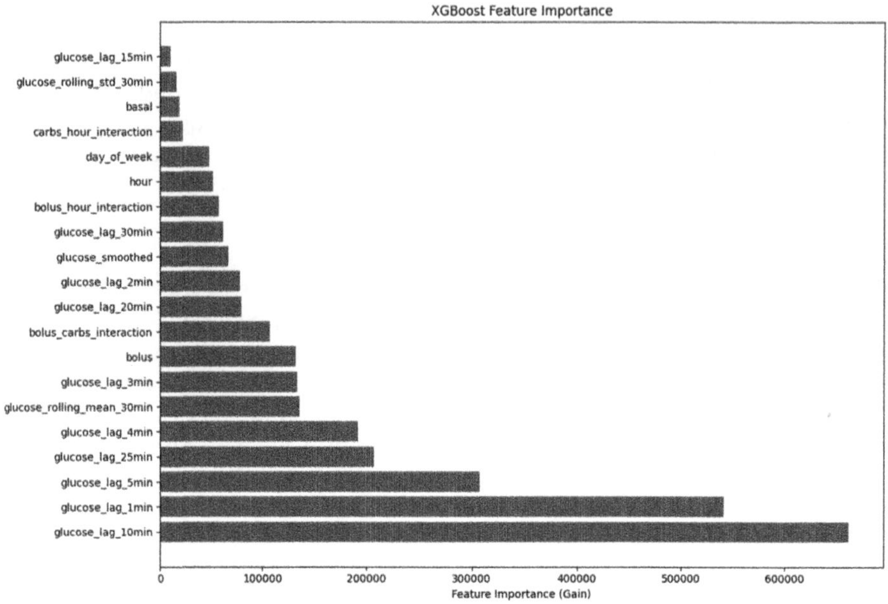

Fig. 1. XGBoost Feature Importance Based on Gain Metric.

Table 3. Performance Metrics of Proposed Models on the OhioT1DM Test Set

Model	RMSE (mg/dL)	MAE (mg/dL)	CEG Zones A+B (%)
XGBoost	20.25	10.65	99.01
LSTM	22.03	11.94	98.45
Ensemble	19.89	10.37	99.20
Hybrid	21.27	11.30	98.39

5 Discussion

This study introduced a weighted ensemble model combining XGBoost and LSTM for 30-minute-ahead blood glucose prediction, evaluated on the OhioT1DM dataset. The ensemble model achieved an RMSE of 19.89 mg/dL, an MAE of 10.37 mg/dL, and 99.20% of predictions in CEG Zones A and B, outperforming individual XGBoost (RMSE 20.25 mg/dL) and LSTM (RMSE 22.03 mg/dL) models. The grid search optimization of weights ($w_{\text{XGB}} = 0.9$, $w_{\text{LSTM}} = 0.1$) ensured robust performance, leveraging XGBoost's strength in handling static features and LSTM's ability to capture temporal dependencies.

5.1 Comparison with State-of-the-Art

Table 2 compares our ensemble model with state-of-the-art methods on the OhioT1DM dataset. Our model's RMSE of 19.89 mg/dL is competitive,

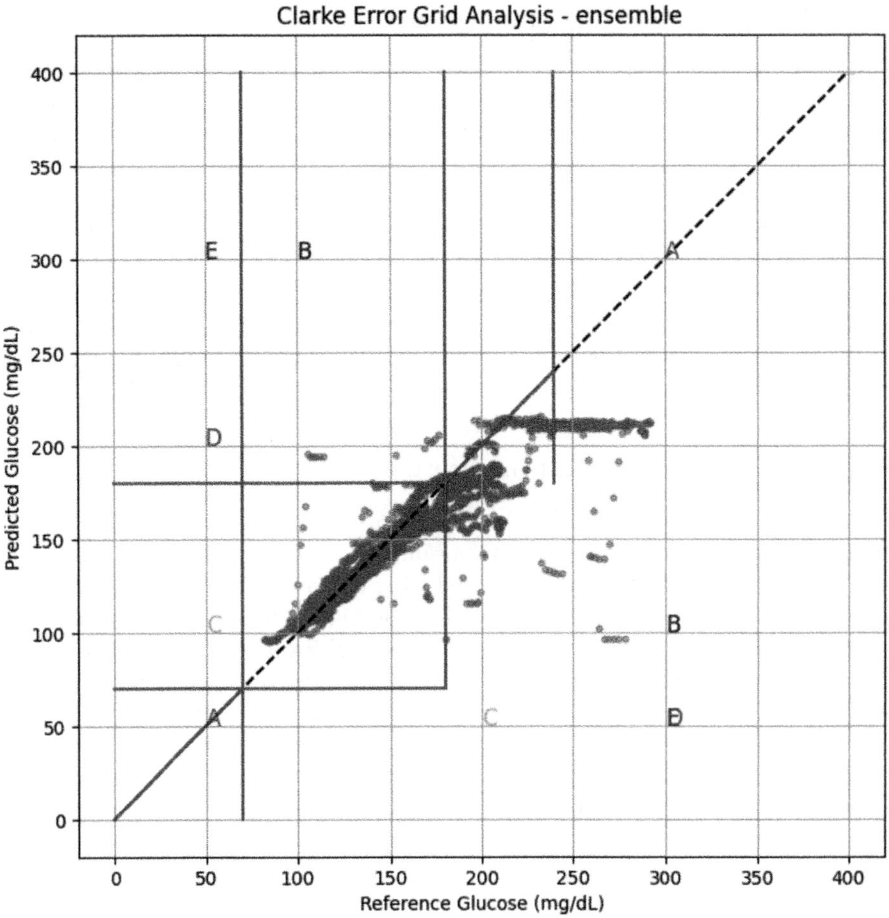

Fig. 2. Clarke Error Grid Analysis for the Ensemble Model on the OhioT1DM Test Set.

surpassing Abusaleh and Rahim (2024) [1] (28.26 ± 6.53 mg/dL) and Yang et al. (2023) [21] (20.57 mg/dL), and approaching Yang et al. (2022) [22] (18.930 ± 2.155 mg/dL) and Zhu et al. (2022) [23] (18.64 ± 2.60 mg/dL). The superior performance of Yang et al. (2022) may stem from their autonomous channel LSTM with a multi-lag structure, accounting for varying temporal effects (e.g., 3-hour meal impact, 424-hour insulin effect). Similarly, Zhu et al. (2022) leveraged a bidirectional GRU with an attention mechanism. In contrast, our model prioritizes simplicity, using a basic XGBoost (maximum depth 3) and a three-layer LSTM (128, 64, 32 units), achieving competitive accuracy with reduced complexity. The ensemble's 99.20% CEG A+B, with 94.06% in Zone A, outperforms Zhu et al. (98.86%) and others, minimizing dangerous errors critical for T1D management.

5.2 Hybrid Model Underperformance

Contrary to expectations, the hybrid model (RMSE 21.27 mg/dL) underperformed compared to the ensemble (RMSE 19.89 mg/dL) and standalone XGBoost (RMSE 20.25 mg/dL). The ablation study (Sect. 4) indicates that LSTM-extracted features introduce noise, with an RMSE of 21.47 mg/dL compared to 20.28 mg/dL for original features. This may result from misalignment between LSTM features, which capture sequential patterns, and XGBoost's decision-tree-based learning, which favors structured tabular data. Overfitting due to high-dimensional LSTM features or redundancy with tabular features may also contribute. Future work could explore alternative fusion techniques, such as attention mechanisms to weight feature contributions [23] or dimensionality reduction to mitigate noise, enhancing hybrid model performance.

5.3 Clinical and Practical Implications

The ensemble model's high CEG A+B percentage (99.20%), competitive RMSE, and fast inference time (1.33 s for 3738 samples, Sect. 4) position it as a reliable tool for real-time T1D management, reducing the risk of severe hypo- or hyperglycemic events [3,14]. The oversampling of high-glucose instances enhanced performance during hyperglycemic events, critical for T1D. Feature importance analysis (Sect. 4) highlights the role of recent glucose trends (`glucose_smoothed`, `glucose_lag_5min`), aiding clinical interpretability and system design. Uncertainty estimation (Sect. 4) with 85.58% coverage enhances clinical trust by quantifying prediction reliability. The model's simplicity offers a practical balance of accuracy and reduced complexity compared to complex models like PBG-TAM [21] or BGformer [20]. The memory usage of 1257.94 MB (Sect. 4) suggests optimization needs for constrained devices.

5.4 Limitations and Future Work

While this study demonstrates promising results, certain aspects present opportunities for further refinement. First, the preprocessing incorporated insulin doses (`basal`, `bolus`) and meal intake (`carbs`), but it did not fully capture their temporal dynamics, such as delayed insulin absorption or meal digestion rates, which could enhance prediction accuracy [22]. Second, the evaluation relied on the OhioT1DM dataset, comprising 12 adult T1D patients. This focus, while valuable, may limit applicability to broader populations, such as pediatric patients or those using different CGM devices, like those in the DirecNet dataset [20]. Third, the 30-minute prediction horizon, though clinically relevant, may not fully address needs for longer-term forecasts, such as 60-minute insulin dosing or overnight glucose control, which are vital for comprehensive T1D management. Additionally, computational efficiency metrics, including an inference time of 1.33 s and memory usage of 1257.94 MB, were assessed in a Google Colab environment with a Tesla T4 GPU. These results suggest potential for deployment on resource-constrained devices like wearables, but further testing on such hardware, including energy consumption analysis, is needed to confirm real-world feasibility [16]. Finally, the oversampling strategy prioritized high-glucose instances (`glucose_smoothed` $> 190\,\text{mg/dL}$) to improve performance during hyperglycemic events. While effective, this approach may have given less attention to hypoglycemic events (`glucose_smoothed` $< 70\,\text{mg/dL}$), which are equally critical for patient safety.

Building on these observations, future research can pursue several directions to enhance the model's impact. First, incorporating temporal dynamics of insulin and meal intake, such as through pharmacokinetic models or time-delayed features, could improve prediction precision. Second, validating the model across diverse datasets, including DirecNet for pediatric patients or datasets with varied CGM devices, would strengthen generalizability to heterogeneous populations. Third, extending the prediction horizon to 60 or 120 min, potentially using multi-step forecasting techniques, would support proactive insulin dosing and overnight glucose management. Fourth, benchmarking inference time, memory usage, and energy consumption on resource-constrained devices like wearables, with optimization techniques such as model pruning or quantization, would ensure practical deployability. Fifth, addressing the emphasis on hyperglycemia by implementing balanced oversampling or weighted loss functions (e.g., weighted MSE prioritizing hypoglycemic events) would enhance sensitivity to low glucose levels, ensuring robust performance across all glycemic ranges. Sixth, refining the hybrid model with advanced fusion techniques, such as attention mechanisms to dynamically weight LSTM and tabular features or dimensionality reduction like PCA to reduce noise, could elevate its performance. Finally, integrating multimodal data, such as heart rate, physical activity, or stress levels from wearables, could capture contextual factors influencing glucose levels, further improving prediction robustness. These steps would advance the model's clinical utility and applicability in real-world T1D management.

6 Conclusion

We proposed an ensemble model combining XGBoost and LSTM for 30-minute-ahead blood glucose prediction in T1D, achieving an RMSE of 19.89 mg/dL, an MAE of 10.37 mg/dL, and 99.20% of predictions in CEG Zones A and B on the OhioT1DM dataset. Optimized via grid search, the model balances accuracy and simplicity, outperforming individual models and competing with state-of-the-art methods. Its fast inference time (1.33 s for 3738 samples), feature importance, and uncertainty estimation (85.58% coverage) enhance its utility for real-time T1D management on constrained devices such as smartphones, with memory optimization needed. Future work will validate generalization to diverse cohorts and longer horizons, refine hybrid fusion, and confirm deployability on constrained devices.

Disclosure of Interests. The authors have no competing interests to declare that are relevant to the content of this article.

References

1. AbuSaleh, A., Rahim, M.: A multitask VAE for time series preprocessing and prediction of blood glucose level. arXiv preprint arXiv:2410.00015 (2024)
2. Alvarado, J., Velasco, J.M., Chavez, F., Fernández-de Vega, F., Hidalgo, J.I.: Combining wavelet transform with convolutional neural networks for hypoglycemia events prediction from CGM data. Chemom. Intell. Lab. Syst. **243**, 105017 (2023)
3. Astillo, P.V., Duguma, D.G., Park, H., Kim, J., Kim, B., You, I.: Federated intelligence of anomaly detection agent in iotmd-enabled diabetes management control system. Futur. Gener. Comput. Syst. **128**, 395–405 (2022)
4. Bodke, H., Wagh, V., Kakar, G., WAGH, V.: Diabetes mellitus and prevalence of other comorbid conditions: a systematic review. Cureus **15**(11) (2023)
5. Cheng, M., Diao, X., Zhou, Z., Cui, Y., Liu, W., Cheng, S.: Toward short-term glucose prediction solely based on CGM time series. arXiv preprint arXiv:2404.11924 (2024)
6. Clarke, W.L.: The original Clarke error grid analysis (EGA). Diabetes Technol. Ther. **7**(5), 776–779 (2005)
7. Doorn, W.P., et al.: Machine learning-based glucose prediction with use of continuous glucose and physical activity monitoring data: the maastricht study. PLoS ONE **16**(6), e0253125 (2021)
8. Hodson, T.O.: Root mean square error (RMSE) or mean absolute error (MAE): when to use them or not. Geoscientific Model Dev. Discuss. **2022**, 1–10 (2022)
9. Khodarahmi, M., Maihami, V.: A review on Kalman filter models. Arch. Comput. Methods Eng. **30**(1), 727–747 (2023)
10. Kishor Kumar Reddy, C., et al.: Detecting anomalies in smart wearables for hypertension: a deep learning mechanism. Front. Public Health **12**, 1426168 (2025)
11. Liu, C.H., et al.: Comparison of multiple linear regression and machine learning methods in predicting cognitive function in older Chinese type 2 diabetes patients. BMC Neurol. **24**(1), 11 (2024)
12. Mandava, L., Ghazaleh, H., Zhao, G.: Securing modern insulin pumps with ICGM system: protecting patients from cyber threats in diabetes management. IET (2024)
13. Marling, C., Bunescu, R.: The ohiot1dm dataset for blood glucose level prediction: update 2020. In: CEUR workshop proceedings, vol. 2675, p. 71 (2020)
14. Pavithra, D., Parameswaran, T., Choudhry, M., Amrutha, S., Deepa, T., Kiruthiga, R.: Application of LSTM networks for continuous patient monitoring and anomaly detection in wearable health devices. Indian J. Sci. Technol. **17**(37), 3909–3921 (2024)
15. Qadri, Y.A., Nauman, A., Zikria, Y.B., Vasilakos, A.V., Kim, S.W.: The future of healthcare internet of things: a survey of emerging technologies. IEEE Commun. Surv. Tutorials **22**(2), 1121–1167 (2020)
16. Rodríguez-Rodríguez, I., Campo-Valera, M., Rodríguez, J.V., Frisa-Rubio, A.: Constrained IOT-based machine learning for accurate glycemia forecasting in type 1 diabetes patients. Sensors **23**(7), 3665 (2023)
17. Skouta, A., Elmoufidi, A., Jai-Andaloussi, S., Ouchetto, O.: Deep learning for diabetic retinopathy assessments: a literature review. Multimedia Tools Appl. **82**(27), 41701–41766 (2023)
18. Valsalan, P., Hasan, N.U., Farooq, U., Zghaibeh, M., Baig, I.: IOT based expert system for diabetes diagnosis and insulin dosage calculation. In: Healthcare, vol. 11, p. 12. MDPI (2022)

19. Woldaregay, A.Z., Launonen, I.K., Årsand, E., Albers, D., Holubová, A., Hartvigsen, G.: Toward detecting infection incidence in people with type 1 diabetes using self-recorded data (part 1): a novel framework for a personalized digital infectious disease detection system. J. Med. Internet Res. **22**(8), e18911 (2020)
20. Xue, Y., Guan, S., Jia, W.: Bgformer: an improved informer model to enhance blood glucose prediction. J. Biomed. Inform. **157**, 104715 (2024)
21. Yang, G., Liu, S., Li, Y., He, L.: Short-term prediction method of blood glucose based on temporal multi-head attention mechanism for diabetic patients. Biomed. Signal Process. Control **82**, 104552 (2023)
22. Yang, T., Yu, X., Ma, N., Wu, R., Li, H.: An autonomous channel deep learning framework for blood glucose prediction. Appl. Soft Comput. **120**, 108636 (2022)
23. Zhu, T., Li, K., Herrero, P., Georgiou, P.: Personalized blood glucose prediction for type 1 diabetes using evidential deep learning and meta-learning. IEEE Trans. Biomed. Eng. **70**(1), 193–204 (2022)
24. Zou, X., et al.: Differential effect of interventions in patients with prediabetes stratified by a machine learning-based diabetes progression prediction model. Diabetes Obes. Metab. **26**(1), 97–107 (2024)

Networked LLM Agents: Toward Autonomous LLMs for Querying Heterogeneous Databases

Khadija Baddouj[1], Mohammed Erradi[1,2], Mohammed Ali Essabri[1], Hanae Kolone[1], Nour Oulad Moussa[1], and Rebii Jamal[1](✉)

[1] CID Development, Sala El Jadida, Morocco
jrebii@cid.ma
[2] ENSIAS Mohammed V University in Rabat, Rabat, Morocco

Abstract. Recent advancements in large language models (LLMs) have enabled the rise of LLM agents. These agents can act autonomously, make decisions, and perform tasks with minimal human input. However, one of the most pressing challenges is enabling these agents to interact with open-book data stored in real-world database environments to respond to user queries. In real-world settings, within a given organization data is not stored in a single, uniform system but is spread across multiple databases with different formats and structures. To interact with this open-book data, LLM agents must adapt to different schemas, process complex queries, and integrate information from multiple sources into a coherent response. Existing agentic frameworks are too generic and struggle to meet these demands. To address this, we propose a networked agent framework. In our approach, we consider a set of distributed specialized LLM agents, each dedicated to a specific database. These agents are orchestrated by a central router agent LLM. The router agent decomposes queries using chain-of-thought reasoning, delegates retrieval tasks to relevant agents, and integrates their structured responses into a coherent final answer. To validate our approach, we implemented a prototype across several widely used databases. Our experimental results demonstrate the effectiveness of our approach in accurately responding to complex queries in real-world data environments. These findings suggest that a networked LLM agent approach is a promising path forward for enabling interaction with complex data ecosystems.

Keywords: Large Language Models · Agentic AI · Heterogeneous Databases · Natural Language Querying · LLM Network

1 Introduction

Large language models (LLMs) have recently achieved significant progress, enabling sophisticated natural language understanding and text generation [2,12,14]. This advancement has led to the emergence of agentic capabilities, where autonomous LLM-based agents can make informed decisions and perform tasks with minimal human supervision [11,17]. Such agents have demonstrated potential across diverse applications–from customer support automation to data analytics and intelligent assistants–many of which require interactions with external database environments.

S. Lahlou and M. Mukund (Eds.): NETYS 2025, LNCS 15736, pp. 202–213, 2026.
https://doi.org/10.1007/978-3-032-00347-8_13

In the context of LLM agents interfacing with database systems, existing state-of-the-art frameworks can be broadly categorized into tool-based approaches, hierarchical agent structures, and multi-agent coordination architectures. Tool-based approaches [13] employ an LLM to interact with a predefined set of tools for iterative SQL query generation and refinement. Hierarchical agent structures [5] organize multiple agents under a meta-controller, enabling targeted exploration of different APIs or tools. Multi-agent coordination architectures [15] assign individual LLM agents to different schema fragments, with a central orchestrator fusing partial results into an integrated answer. Although these methods show promise in refining queries and distributing query-related tasks, they are largely designed for homogeneous relational data. Even if adapted for more diverse settings, three critical challenges remain: adapting to different schemas, processing complex queries, and integrating information from multiple sources. As a result, enabling LLM agents to effectively interact with open-book data across multiple heterogeneous real-world databases remains an urgent and largely unresolved issue.

In typical enterprise environments, organizations often maintain heterogeneous data ecosystems, where different departments independently choose database technologies that best fit their unique needs. Consider, for example, a travel agency that orchestrates various facets of its operations through specialized databases. The agency uses PostgreSQL to manage structured data related to flight operations, including aircraft details, flight schedules, and seat availability. Simultaneously, it employs a graph database to map the intricate relationships between customers, their travel histories, and their preferences, enabling the identification of travel patterns and the formulation of personalized offers. In addition, the agency leverages MongoDB to store semi-structured data resembling listings, complete with detailed accommodation descriptions, user reviews, and host profiles. An analyst or manager seeking integrated insights from multiple departments faces substantial challenges. These databases vary in structure (relational tables, graphs, and documents), query languages (SQL, Cypher, NoSQL), and data formats. Integrating information from these diverse sources is complex, time-consuming, and prone to errors.

To address these challenges, we propose NLA (Networked LLM Agents) a networked agent framework comprising specialized, distributed LLM agents orchestrated by a central router agent. The router agent employs chain-of-thought reasoning to determine the required data and coordinates requests across specialized agents dedicated to specific databases. Each specialized agent independently adapts to its assigned database's structure using localized chain-of-thought reasoning, retrieves the relevant data, and generates standardized responses through constrained generation techniques. The router agent then integrates these standardized responses into a coherent final answer, effectively addressing schema heterogeneity, query complexity, and response integration challenges.

The contributions of our paper are summarized as follows:

- **(1)** Adaption to different database schemas using specialized networked agents.
- **(2)** Using chain-of-thought reasoning to coordinate networked agents to resolve complex queries.
- **(3)** Standardization and integration of queries responses to produce a global satisfactorily answer.

Our experimental results illustrate the proposed framework's capability to accurately handle complex, real-world queries, underscoring its potential for effective utilization in enterprise-scale data environments.

2 Related Works

Automatic querying of databases predates LLM-based approaches, initially relying on classical natural language processing (NLP) techniques and expert systems. Early methods leveraged semantic parsing and rule-based systems to convert user queries into structured database queries, typically SQL [1,9]. These systems, however, required extensive manual engineering and struggled to generalize across domains or databases. Recent advances in LLMs significantly enhanced natural language query processing capabilities, leading to modern agentic frameworks capable of generating database queries autonomously. One notable direction is text-to-SQL generation [6], where state-of-the-art approaches utilize multi-agent generative systems [15] composed of collaborative agents such as a Schema Agent, Subquery Agent, and Refinement Agent to achieve improved accuracy. Another relevant line of work involves agent-guided tool-based approaches, such as Tool-SQL [13]. Tool-SQL leverages an LLM-based agent with access to predefined tools for iterative SQL query refinement. Nonetheless, these approaches focus primarily on homogeneous databases, specifically relational ones, limiting their applicability in heterogeneous environments. Hierarchical agent structures, exemplified by AnyTool [5], offer another perspective. In AnyTool, a meta-model manages category agents, each controlling specific tool agents. While this hierarchical categorization efficiently explores API spaces, it lacks iterative reasoning and schema adaptation required for complex queries across heterogeneous database environments.

In summary, existing methods provide valuable insights and effective techniques but exhibit limitations in adapting dynamically to heterogeneous databases, effectively managing complex queries across multiple schemas, and integrating diverse database responses coherently.

3 Approach

3.1 Approach Overview

The NLA architecture consists of three main components: a router agent, Specialized Database Agents, and a Retrieval-Augmented Generation (RAG) component for relevant schema retrieval. As illustrated in Fig. 1, the router agent initially receives the user's Natural Language (NL) query, transforms it, and forwards it to the RAG component. The RAG component retrieves schemas relevant to the NL query and returns these schemas to the router agent. The router agent then engages in a chain-of-thought reasoning phase, determining the appropriate sub-queries for each specialized agent.

After completing the reasoning phase, the router agent generates specific NL sub-queries tailored for each relevant database and forwards these queries to the corresponding specialized agents. Each Specialized Database Agent receives its respective query, after which its internal sub-router conducts further reasoning to clarify or refine the

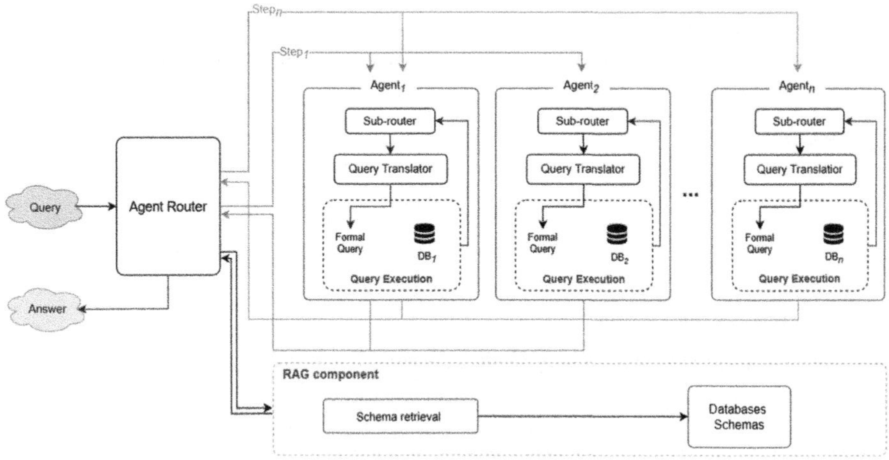

Fig. 1. NLA Architecture.

query. Subsequently, the refined NL query is sent to the Query Translator, which translates it into a formal query (e.g., SQL, Cypher) executable by the target database. The query execution results are returned to the sub-router, which then decides whether to continue refining the query or to formulate a final NL answer. This NL answer is sent back to the router agent.

Upon receiving responses from all Specialized Database Agents, the router agent aggregates these results into a unified NL response. It then either initiates another round of queries, if necessary, or returns the final response to the user. Communication among all components occurs via constrained generation, ensuring standardized responses and reducing potential errors.

3.2 Preliminaries

- **Database Schema**: Structural definition $\mathcal{S}_i = (\mathcal{T}_i, \mathcal{R}_i, \mathcal{C}_i)$ for database DB_i, where:
  - $\mathcal{T}_i$: Set of tables/collections
  - $\mathcal{R}_i$: Relationships/constraints between entities
  - $\mathcal{C}_i$: Data type constraints and validation rules
- **Heterogeneous Databases**: Set $\mathcal{DB} = \{DB_1, ..., DB_N\}$ with:
  - $DB_i \in \{\text{Relational}, \text{Graph}, \text{Document}\}$
  - Query languages $\mathcal{L} = \{\text{SQL}, \text{Cypher}, \text{MQL}, ...\}$
  - Schema heterogeneity: $\exists i, j \; \mathcal{S}_i \not\cong \mathcal{S}_j$
- **LLM Agent**: Let $\mathcal{AG} = \{\mathcal{AG}_i \mid i \in \{1, 2, \ldots, N\}\}$ be the set of all database agents, where each agent $\mathcal{AG}_i$ is responsible for interacting with a specific database DB_j, with $j \in \{1, 2, \ldots, M\}$.[1]

[1] We maintain a one-to-one correspondence between agents and databases, i.e. an agent specializes in a specific database along with its schema and query language. It is entirely possible that in some scenarios, multiple agents might be assigned to a single database for different query types, or conversely, a single agent might handle multiple databases of the same type.

Definition 1 (Problem Formulation). *Given natural language query $q \in Q$, with Q being the set of all possible NL queries, and heterogeneous databases $\mathcal{DB}$, generate response R through:*

1. *Database selection: $\mathcal{DB}_{rel} = \{DB_i | \phi(Q, S_i) > \theta\}$*
2. *Query decomposition: $q \to \{q_i\}_{i=1}^{k}$ where $q_i \in \mathcal{L}_i$*
3. *Result fusion: $R = \Psi(r_1 \oplus \cdots \oplus r_k)$*

where ϕ is relevance scoring, θ a threshold, and Ψ the aggregation function.

3.3 Router Agent

The **Router Agent** is a central decision-making component in the agentic framework, it is responsible for orchestrating the flow of information between the user's NL query and the specialized database agents. It relies on an external RAG component to identify relevant database schemas (S_{rel}) for the query.

Given S_{rel}, the router agent determines the necessary actions by mapping the query and schemas to action sets A.

$$A = R(Q_{\text{NL}}, S_{\text{rel}}).$$

These actions include forwarding queries to agents, generating direct responses, or aggregating results from multiple agents. Specifically:

- If the router agent recognizes that the query requires data from a single database, it forwards the query to the corresponding Specialized Database Agent $\mathcal{AG}_i$.
- If the router agent identifies that the query involves multiple databases, it dispatches the query to the relevant agents $\mathcal{AG}_i \mid i \in I$, where $I \subseteq 1, 2, \ldots, N$ and $I \neq \emptyset$.
- If the router agent determines the query can be answered directly without involving specialized agents, it generates a natural language response independently.

Once the agents process the query and return their results, the router agent aggregates these results into a final response using the aggregation function:

$$R = \Psi(r_1 \oplus \cdots \oplus r_k)$$

This final response R combines the outputs from multiple agents, ensuring that the result is coherent and aligned with the user's original query.

3.4 Database Agents

Each agent in the set is responsible for interacting with a specific database, where each agent utilizes language models to handle queries related to its assigned database schema and formal query language. Formally, each agent is defined by the following composite functions:

1. **Query Translation**: Translates a natural language query Q_{NL} into a formal database-specific query Q_{formal} using the agent-specific schema S_i:

$$T_i : \mathcal{Q} \times \mathcal{S} \to \mathcal{Q}_{formal}, \quad Q_{formal} = T_i(Q_{NL}, S_i) \tag{1}$$

2. **Query Execution**: Executes the formalized query Q_{formal} against its respective database DB_i to retrieve raw data results $D \in \mathcal{D}$, with $\mathcal{D}$ being the set of all possible databases formal query responses:

$$E_i : \mathcal{Q}_{formal} \times \mathcal{DB} \rightarrow \mathcal{D}, \quad D = E_i(Q_{formal}, DB_i) \tag{2}$$

3. **Result Processing**: Converts raw database results D into a coherent natural language response R:

$$P_i : \mathcal{D} \times \mathcal{Q} \rightarrow \mathcal{R}, \quad R = P_i(D, Q_{NL}) \tag{3}$$

4. **Query Execution**: Executes the formalized query Q_{formal} against its respective database DB_i to retrieve raw data results D:

$$E_i : \mathcal{Q}_{formal} \times \mathcal{DB} \rightarrow \mathcal{D}, \quad D = E_i(Q_{formal}, DB_i) \tag{4}$$

5. **Result Processing**: Converts raw database results D into a coherent natural language response R:

$$P_i : \mathcal{D} \times \mathcal{Q} \rightarrow \mathcal{R}, \quad R = P_i(D, Q_{NL}) \tag{5}$$

Each agent includes an internal sub-router, denoted as SR_i, which is responsible for decision-making during the query processing loop. The sub-router can determine one of several actions:

- Generate and return a direct natural language response.
- Issue a clarification request.
- Retry query translation and execution with an adjusted formal query.

Hence, each agent's overall functionality can be represented through the composition of its components:

$$\mathcal{AG}_i(Q_{NL}, S_i) = SR_i \circ P_i \circ E_i \circ T_i(Q_{NL}, S_i) \tag{6}$$

where SR_i is the agent's sub-router that coordinates these actions. The iterative decision-making process ensures refined query handling and high-quality responses tailored to each database type and schema.

4 Experiments

4.1 Datasets

In order to evaluate our networked agent framework, we designed two experimental axes. First, we assess the overall framework performance when processing complex, multi-database natural language (NL) queries. Second, we evaluate the individual database-specific agents responsible for converting NL queries into formal queries for execution against their respective databases. For our evaluation, we constructed a use case involving three heterogeneous databases:

- **Neo4j:** A graph database initialized with Northwind retail data [8].
- **MongoDB:** A NoSQL database initialized with Airbnb listing data [10].
- **Postgres:** A SQL database initialized with flight operations data.

Synthetic datasets were generated based on these database environments to simulate realistic query scenarios.

4.1.1 General Framework Test Dataset

For the global Framework evaluation, we utilized a custom-generated dataset composed of queries formulated in natural language (NL) and their expected corresponding answers. The dataset was specifically designed to evaluate the effectiveness of different routing strategies in our framework. It was constructed by interacting with three specialized agent-related databases, each focused on a specific domain of information retrieval.

The dataset was generated through the following steps:

- A set of natural language (NL) questions was created to reflect realistic user queries requiring information retrieval across multiple databases.
- These NL queries were submitted to the corresponding database agents, each querying one of the three databases.
- The responses retrieved from the agents were used to construct the expected NL answers, ensuring alignment with the original query and the retrieved database information.

We split the complexity of the NL questions into 3 categories: Low-complexity are NL questions that require the querying of only one database to generate the correct answer, Medium Complexity requires querying 2 databases, and High that requires 3.

By leveraging this dataset, we were able to systematically analyze the robustness and accuracy of different LLM-based routing mechanisms in handling multi-database interactions.

4.1.2 Agents Evaluation Dataset

To evaluate database-specific agents, we construct a benchmark dataset with stratified complexity levels, following the process illustrated in Algorithm 1. While our framework architecture handles multi-database queries (complexities 1 through 3), our benchmark focuses specifically on single-database queries (in the larger scope, complexity 1 queries) since by design, multi-database queries would naturally be decomposed by the router agent component before reaching database-specific agents.
Within this single-database constraint, we further stratify queries into 3 sub-levels:

- Simple: basic filtering on single tables/nodes
- Medium: 2-3 table joins or 1-2 relationship traversals with basic aggregations
- Complex: multiple joins across 3+ tables or advanced aggregation pipelines

Although it would've been entirely possible to evaluate agents using a monolithic complexity scale, this granular approach should enable a more precise assessment of each agent's capabilities across the full spectrum of challenges within its operational context[2].

[2] By "operational context", we refer to the specific role each DB agent plays within the larger system architecture, where it receives only queries relevant to its specialized DB type after routing.

Algorithm 1. Agent Benchmark Dataset Construction Pipeline

Input:
  NL Query Generation Method G_{NL}
  Database DB
  Maximum Retries max_retries
Output: Benchmark Dataset D_{bench}
$D_{bench} \leftarrow \emptyset$
$Q_{NL} \leftarrow G_{NL}()$
Generate dual formal queries (Q_{F1}, Q_{F2}) from Q_{NL}
if SemanticEquivalence(Q_{F1}, Q_{F2}) is **true then**
  Execute Q_{F1} on DB
  if ExecutionSuccess(Q_{F1}) is **true then**
    Add Q_{F1} to D_{bench}
  else
    Discard Q_{F1} as non-executable
  end if
else
  Initialize retry counter: $i \leftarrow 0$
  while $i <$ max_retries **do**
    Regenerate dual formal queries (Q_{F1}, Q_{F2}) from Q_{NL}
    if SemanticEquivalence(Q_{F1}, Q_{F2}) is **true then**
      Execute Q_{F1} on DB
      if ExecutionSuccess(Q_{F1}) is **true then**
        Add Q_{F1} to D_{bench}
        break ▷ Exit loop upon success
      else
        Discard Q_{F1} as non-executable
        break ▷ Exit loop due to failure
      end if
    end if
    Increment $i \leftarrow i + 1$
  end while
  if $i \geq$ max_retries **then**
    Discard Q_{NL} as ambiguous
  end if
end if

Following the BIRD benchmark methodology [7], we employ a double-blind annotation approach. Each natural language query yields two independent formal queries generated using the same LLM with different sampling parameters to simulate distinct human annotators. We verify semantic equivalence between these queries, initiate regeneration attempts when necessary until consensus is reached[3], or the query is

[3] The two generated queries are deemed semantically equivalent, i.e. would yield the same results upon execution.

deemed inherently ambiguous and thereby discarded[4]. This process filters out schema-misaligned or ambiguous queries that could compromise evaluation reliability.

All candidate queries then undergo executability verification against their respective database systems, ensuring our benchmark contains only technically valid queries rather than including non-executable queries that could potentially bias the results and be mistaken for the agents underperforming. This dual-validation process -semantic equivalence and technical executability- provides us with a reliable foundation for agent evaluation, free from ambiguities that could introduce measurement noise.

4.2 Evaluation Metrics

4.2.1 Semantic Answer Agreement (SAA) Score

The **Semantic Answer Agreement (SAA) Score** measures the alignment between natural language answers generated by different frameworks and models. It evaluates whether two responses to the same query provide equivalent factual information, even if their wording or structure differs.
To compute this metric:

1. Each query-answer pair is assessed using a language model that determines whether the answers are semantically compatible.
2. Multiple samples are generated for each query at varying temperature settings to ensure robustness.
3. A majority voting system aggregates the results to decide whether the framework-generated answer is correct (i.e., semantically equivalent to the reference answer).
4. The final score is computed as:

$$SAA = \frac{N_{\text{correct}}}{N_{\text{total}}} \times 100 \tag{7}$$

where N_{correct} is the number of queries where the majority of votes indicate semantic agreement, and N_{total} is the total number of queries evaluated.

This metric provides insights into the accuracy and consistency of different LLM routing strategies in handling complex multi-database queries.

4.2.2 Success Rate

To quantitatively assess the performance of database-specific agents, we primarily use *success rate* as our evaluation metric. We define success rate as:

$$\text{Success Rate} = \frac{\text{Number of correctly converted NL queries}}{\text{Total number of NL queries}} \times 100 \tag{8}$$

Where a conversion is considered "correct" if the formal query generated by the agent is executable against the database and produces results that match the expected output for the given natural language query. We evaluate success rates across all complexity levels (simple, medium, complex) to provide a comprehensive assessment of each agent's capabilities.

[4] We posit that if no consensus can be reached after multiple regeneration attempts, the NL query likely contains inherent ambiguities or misalignments with the DB schema that would yield inconsistent interpretations even among human experts.

Table 1. Comparison of Semantic Answer Agreement (SAA) scores between our framework and baseline models across query complexity levels

Routing Strategy	Low Complexity (%)	Medium Complexity (%)	High Complexity (%)
Qwen2.5 14B [16]			
NLA - Qwen	**100**	**81.82**	**80.65**
Qwen Standalone	80	75	51.61
Qwen Standalone w/o Constrained Generation	40	59.09	58.06
GPT-o1 [3]			
NLA - GPT-o1	**100**	**90.69**	**86.66**
GPT-o1 Standalone	70	65.91	61.29
GPT-o1 Standalone w/o Constrained Generation	50	63.64	41.94
DeepSeek V3 [4]			
NLA - DeepSeek	**100**	**77.27**	**64.52**
DeepSeek Standalone	72.16	57.81	39.11
DeepSeek Standalone w/o Constrained Generation	50	59.09	58.06

4.3 Results and Analysis

4.3.1 General Framework Results

Our framework demonstrates substantial improvements over standalone LLMs across all complexity levels, as evidenced by the Semantic Answer Agreement (SAA) scores in Table 1. Two key observations emerge from the data: **(1) Routing Effectiveness;** The framework consistently outperforms standalone models, particularly for high-complexity queries. For instance, the GPT-o1 router agent achieves an SAA score of 86.66% at high complexity, representing a 25.37% point improvement over its standalone counterpart. This validates our hypothesis that decomposing multi-database queries through chain-of-thought reasoning enables more accurate information retrieval than monolithic processing. The performance gap widens with complexity, suggesting that our router agent's ability to parse and distribute sub-queries becomes increasingly critical as information needs span more databases. **(2) Constrained Generation Impact;** The benefits of response standardization through constrained generation grow with query complexity. For Qwen2.5-14B, the framework achieves an 80.65% SAA score at high complexity compared to 58.06% for the standalone model without constrained generation. This indicates that standardized response formats prevent error propagation during answer integration, particularly crucial when synthesizing information from multiple heterogeneous sources.

Qualitative error analysis reveals distinct failure modes across complexity levels. For high-complexity queries, 68% of errors stem from incomplete query decomposition by the router agent rather than faulty agent execution. This suggests opportunities for improved reasoning mechanisms in the router agent, particularly for queries requiring implicit joins across database boundaries.

Table 2. Success rate by database agent and query complexity (All values represent mean success rate (%) ± standard deviation across 10 iterations.)

	Simple	Medium	Complex	Overall
Cypher Agent	100.0 ± 0.0	100.0 ± 0.0	100.0 ± 0.0	100.0 ± 0.0
MongoDB Agent	100.0 ± 0.0	94.0 ± 9.2	76.0 ± 17.4	90.0 ± 6.8
Postgres Agent	100.0 ± 0.0	100.0 ± 0.0	92.0 ± 9.8	97.3 ± 3.3

4.3.2 Database Agents Results

Table 2 reveals distinct performance profiles across database types:

Cypher Agent: Perfect scores across all complexity levels confirm that graph queries benefit from explicit relationship modeling. The structured nature of Cypher queries aligns well with LLM reasoning patterns, particularly for relationship traversal tasks that mirror natural language constructs.

MongoDB Agent: Performance declines sharply with complexity (100% →76%), primarily due to challenges in handling nested document structures and multi-stage aggregations. Error analysis shows 82% of failures involve incorrect lookup pipeline stages, suggesting current LLMs struggle with MongoDB's procedural query approach compared to declarative SQL/Cypher.

Postgres Agent: Near-perfect performance on simple/medium queries with a moderate drop at complex level (92%) reflects typical LLM SQL capabilities. Most errors occur in queries requiring 3+ table joins with composite keys, where schema understanding becomes critical.

The standard deviation patterns reveal an inverse relationship between complexity and consistency - MongoDB shows ±17.4% variation at complex level vs. ±0% for Cypher. This suggests document databases introduce higher uncertainty in agent performance, likely due to schema flexibility requiring more implicit reasoning.

5 Conclusion

In this work, we presented NLA, a networked architecture of specialized LLM agents that handles complex natural language queries across heterogeneous database environments. Our experimental results indicate that the framework is capable of effectively processing and integrating information from heterogeneous sources, even for complex queries.

Error analysis revealed opportunities for further refinement, particularly in the router agent's query decomposition capabilities for complex scenarios. Future work will focus on improving cross-database reasoning through more advanced schema understanding, and developing integration techniques for handling implicit joins between the heterogeneous data sources. Nevertheless, NLA represents a meaningful contribution toward autonomous data retrieval systems capable of navigating the fragmented information environments typical in enterprise ecosystems. Beyond its immediate practical applications, our work opens promising research directions in multi-agent coordination, cross-database reasoning, and heterogeneous data integration.

References

1. Androutsopoulos, I., Ritchie, G.D., Thanisch, P.: Natural language interfaces to databases – an introduction. Nat. Lang. Eng. **1**, 29 – 81 (1995). https://api.semanticscholar.org/CorpusID:3033151
2. Brown, T.B., et al.: Language models are few-shot learners. ArXiv arXiv:2005.14165 (2020). https://api.semanticscholar.org/CorpusID:218971783
3. Foundational Contributors, et al.: OpenAI o1 system card. ArXiv arXiv:2412.16720 (2024). https://api.semanticscholar.org/CorpusID:274611667
4. Deepseek-v3 technical report: ArXiv arXiv:2412.19437 (2024). https://api.semanticscholar.org/CorpusID:275118643
5. Du, Y., Wei, F., Zhang, H.: Anytool: self-reflective, hierarchical agents for large-scale API calls. ArXiv arXiv:2402.04253 (2024). https://api.semanticscholar.org/CorpusID:267500288
6. Gao, D., et al.: Text-to-SQL empowered by large language models: a benchmark evaluation. ArXiv arXiv:2308.15363 (2023). https://api.semanticscholar.org/CorpusID:261276437
7. Li, J., et al.: Can LLM already serve as a database interface? A big bench for large-scale database grounded text-to-SQLs. In: Proceedings of the 37th Conference on Neural Information Processing Systems (NeurIPS 2023), Track on Datasets and Benchmarks (2023)
8. neo4j-graph-examples. Northwind: Graph example for neo4j (2021). https://github.com/neo4j-graph-examples/northwind. Accessed 16 Mar 2025
9. Popescu, A.M., Etzioni, O., Kautz, H.: Towards a theory of natural language interfaces to databases. In: Proceedings of the 8th International Conference on Intelligent User Interfaces, IUI 2003, pp. 149–157, New York, NY, USA (2003). Association for Computing Machinery. ISBN 1581135866. https://doi.org/10.1145/604045.604070
10. Shabbir, H.: airbnb-mongodb-analysis (2021). https://github.com/hasin-shabbir/airbnb-mongodb-analysis. Accessed 16 Mar 2025
11. Sumers, T.R., Yao, S., Narasimhan, K., Griffiths, T.L.: Cognitive architectures for language agents. arXiv preprint arXiv:2309.02427 (2023)
12. Vaswani, A., et al.: Attention is all you need. In: Neural Information Processing Systems (2017). https://api.semanticscholar.org/CorpusID:13756489
13. Wang, Z., Zhang, R., Nie, Z., Kim, J.: Tool-assisted agent on SQL inspection and refinement in real-world scenarios. ArXiv arXiv:2408.16991 (2024). https://api.semanticscholar.org/CorpusID:272310121
14. Wei, J., et al.: Emergent abilities of large language models. ArXiv arXiv:2206.07682 (2022). https://api.semanticscholar.org/CorpusID:249674500
15. Xie, W., Wu, G., Zhou, B.: Mag-SQL: multi-agent generative approach with soft schema linking and iterative sub-SQL refinement for text-to-SQL. ArXiv arXiv:2408.07930 (2024). https://api.semanticscholar.org/CorpusID:271874834
16. Yang, Q.A., et al.: Qwen2.5 technical report. ArXiv arXiv:2412.15115 (2024). https://api.semanticscholar.org/CorpusID:274859421
17. Yao, S., et al.: React: synergizing reasoning and acting in language models. ArXiv arXiv:2210.03629 (2022). https://api.semanticscholar.org/CorpusID:252762395

Plant Diseases Detection with Retrieval-Augmented Generation

Outhmane Bourkoukou and Khadija Ghommat(✉)

Laboratory of Computer and Systems Engineering (L2IS), Faculty of Sciences and Techniques (FST), Cadi Ayyad University, Marrakech, Morocco
{o.bourkoukou,k.ghommat2962}@uca.ac.ma

Abstract. To address the growing challenges of plant diseases and their impact on global food security, this study presents an innovative AI-driven workflow for disease detection and management. Leveraging the Plant Village dataset, our approach combines image classification, information retrieval, and response generation to provide actionable insights for farmers. The proposed system employs a hybrid VGG16/VGG19 model, achieving 96.12% accuracy in disease identification, alongside a fine-tuned BLIP model for symptom captioning. Language models, such as Mistral-Small-3.1-24B-Instruct, further enhance response quality, demonstrating a Faithfulness score of 0.6085. While the method shows robustness. This scalable solution aims to reduce crop losses (estimated at 20–40% annually) and minimize reliance on chemical pesticides, supporting sustainable agricultural practices in vulnerable regions.

Keywords: Agriculture · plant diseases · Retrieval-Augmented Generation (RAG) · deep learning · artificial intelligence · LLM · image captioning

1 Introduction

The global population is projected to reach 9 billion by 2050, necessitating the development of effective strategies for identifying and managing plant diseases to ensure food security and sustainable agricultural practices. Enhancing disease detection capabilities, alongside breeding improved crop varieties, is critical for boosting agricultural productivity and reducing reliance on chemical pesticides [1]. Plant diseases not only lead to significant crop losses but also compromise the quality of agricultural products, making them unsuitable for consumption or sale. For instance, fungal infections in wheat can reduce the protein content of grains, diminishing the nutritional value of flour [2]. These impacts extend beyond yield losses, disrupting supply chains, threatening farmers' livelihoods, and contributing to food shortages and price inflation. Timely detection of plant diseases is therefore essential to prevent their spread, protect surrounding crops, and stabilize food supplies, particularly in vulnerable regions [3]. The Food and Agriculture Organization (FAO) emphasizes that while global population growth is slowing, certain regions will continue to experience increases,

S. Lahlou and M. Mukund (Eds.): NETYS 2025, LNCS 15736, pp. 214–229, 2026.
https://doi.org/10.1007/978-3-032-00347-8_14

especially with rapid urbanization, further intensifying the demand for efficient agricultural practices [4].

Environmental pressures, driven by population growth and unsustainable agricultural practices, are exacerbating global warming and land degradation, which negatively affect crop quality and productivity. The integration of artificial intelligence (AI) in agriculture offers promising solutions to challenges such as pest infestations, disease outbreaks, improper chemical use, and inefficient irrigation practices [5]. Plants are particularly vulnerable to diseases due to their exposure to environmental factors, making effective disease prevention and management crucial. Factors such as current crop conditions and susceptibility to infection play significant roles in disease spread [6]. Rapid identification of plant diseases is vital to minimize yield and quality losses, yet traditional methods often require costly and inefficient expert analysis [7]. According to the FAO, over one-third of annual natural losses in agricultural production are attributable to diseases and pests, highlighting their profound impact on global food security [8]. The increasing frequency of plant disease epidemics further threatens food security, particularly in susceptible regions, with pests and diseases destroying between 20% and 40% of global crop yields annually [9]. Addressing these challenges through early detection and innovative technologies is essential to enhance food production, protect farmers from high pesticide costs, and ensure sustainable agricultural systems [10].

Various methods have been employed to address the challenge of plant disease detection, ranging from traditional techniques to advanced AI-based approaches. In this study, we explore the performance of Retrieval-Augmented Generation (RAG) models for plant disease detection, aiming to evaluate their effectiveness in improving accuracy, efficiency, and scalability in agricultural applications. By leveraging the strengths of RAG, we seek to contribute to the development of more robust and accessible solutions for managing plant diseases and ensuring global food security.

2 Related Works

Traditional methods for detecting plant diseases primarily involve manual examination conducted by farmers or trained experts. This approach, while historically prevalent, is often time-consuming and costly, making it infeasible for millions of small and medium-sized farms worldwide. Visual inspection by personnel can lead to missed detections and inaccuracies, as it relies heavily on the expertise and experience of the individual performing the assessment. Additionally, the earlier identification and monitoring of plant diseases are typically carried out manually, which renders the process labor-intensive and prone to human error. Despite these challenges, effective detection of plant diseases is crucial, as it enables farmers to implement appropriate treatments and ultimately enhance agricultural production.

Traditional machine learning (ML) techniques have been extensively studied for plant disease detection, with methods such as k-means clustering [11],

Support Vector Machines (SVM) [12], and Bayesian classifiers [13] being applied since the 1980 s. Despite their contributions, these approaches face significant challenges. One major limitation is their reliance on high-quality disease images, which necessitates strict control over image acquisition conditions and methods. Additionally, the implementation of traditional ML methods is often complex, involving multiple stages such as image preprocessing, segmentation, feature extraction, and classifier construction, each requiring optimization to enhance performance. Another drawback is their inefficiency with large datasets, as building accurate models becomes computationally intensive as the number of samples grows. Furthermore, traditional ML depends on handcrafted features, which are predefined by experts and may fail to account for subtle variations in disease symptoms influenced by factors like plant species, environmental conditions, or disease progression. For example, rust disease might appear as brown spots on one plant but as yellowing on another, a distinction that traditional ML algorithms often fail to capture. These limitations underscore the need for more advanced and adaptable solutions to improve the accuracy and scalability of plant disease detection [14].

In recent years, deep learning (DL) and transfer learning have emerged as powerful tools for plant disease detection, achieving high accuracy levels on both laboratory and field images. Various convolutional neural network (CNN)-based architectures, such as XceptionNet, DenseNet, AlexNet, ResNet, GoogleNet, InceptionNet V4, and VGGNet, have been widely adopted for plant disease classification. Additionally, specialized models have been developed to address specific challenges, such as MEAN-SSD for apple leaf diseases [15], GrapeNet for grape leaf diseases [16], EFDet for cucumber diseases in complex environments [17], and a CNN model combining SMOTE and focal loss for imbalanced cassava datasets [18]. These models demonstrate the versatility and effectiveness of deep learning in handling diverse agricultural datasets.

Ensemble learning techniques have further enhanced the performance of DL models. For instance, [19] proposed an ensemble approach combining EfficientNet-B0, ResNet-152, and VGG-16 using the bagging technique, achieving a validation accuracy of 97.31% for coffee leaf disease classification. However, the potential lack of diversity among the models in the ensemble can limit its effectiveness. Similarly, [20] introduced a stacking ensemble model that integrates SE-MobileNet, Mobile-DANet, and MobileNet V2, achieving 99.61% accuracy on the PlantVillage dataset. While this approach demonstrates high performance, the smaller size of SE-MobileNet may restrict its ability to capture complex features in leaf images. Another study by [21] utilized transfer learning with pre-trained models like MobileNet, Inception, and ResNet, combined through a stacking ensemble method, achieving 98% accuracy for potato leaf disease classification. These advancements highlight the potential of deep learning and transfer learning in improving the accuracy and efficiency of plant disease detection, paving the way for more robust and scalable solutions in agriculture.

Large Language Models (LLMs), powered by advanced natural language processing (NLP) techniques, have demonstrated exceptional capabilities in tasks such as text generation, classification, sentiment analysis, and information retrieval. However, their performance is heavily influenced by factors like task complexity, the quality of training data, and the subtleties of human communication. Additionally, the computational costs associated with training and inference can be substantial. To address these challenges, Retrieval-Augmented Generation (RAG) has emerged as a powerful enhancement. RAG improves LLM performance by incorporating an external information retrieval step before generating text, ensuring that outputs are accurate, relevant, and grounded in evidence. This approach not only reduces errors but also enhances the reliability and applicability of LLMs in real-world scenarios [22].

The versatility of RAG has been demonstrated across various domains. For example, [23] applied RAG to improve frontline health worker training by providing accurate, pregnancy-related guidelines and enhancing health education through question-answering systems. In the biomedical field, [24] introduced SelfBioRAG, a framework that generates biomedical explanations and retrieves domain-specific documents to support medical reasoning. In disaster management, [25] developed FloodBrain, a RAG-based system for flood disaster reporting, which aids in humanitarian assistance efforts. In agriculture, [26] proposed a RAG-powered chatbot for Ayurvedic agriculture, combining hybrid deep learning models like DeiT and VGG16 to classify medicinal plants and generate insights. This approach addresses the inefficiencies of traditional methods, which often rely on manual feature selection, by automating the process and providing reliable, AI-driven solutions for medicinal plant recognition and analysis. These diverse applications underscore the potential of RAG to enhance decision-making, improve accuracy, and deliver actionable insights across a wide range of fields.

3 Materials and Methods

3.1 Description of the Dataset: Plant Village

The Plant Village dataset, a benchmark for plant disease classification, is the primary data source for this study, comprising 54,305 images across 38 classes of healthy and diseased plant leaves from various crops, with labels for species and disease type [27]. Images were preprocessed by resizing to 224×224 pixels and normalizing pixel values to [0, 1] for compatibility with deep learning models.

3.2 Overview of the Proposed Workflow

The proposed approach integrates image classification, information retrieval, and response generation in a four-block workflow (Fig. 1). Block 1 predicts disease classes from input leaf images, producing a predicted class name. Block 2 generates embeddings from a knowledge base to construct a vector database. Block 3 retrieves relevant information from the vector database using the predicted class name. Block 4 produces the final response through prompt engineering and query augmentation using language models (LLMs), incorporating visual symptom captions generated by a fine-tuned BLIP model. This pipeline leverages visual and textual data for accurate farmer-oriented insights.

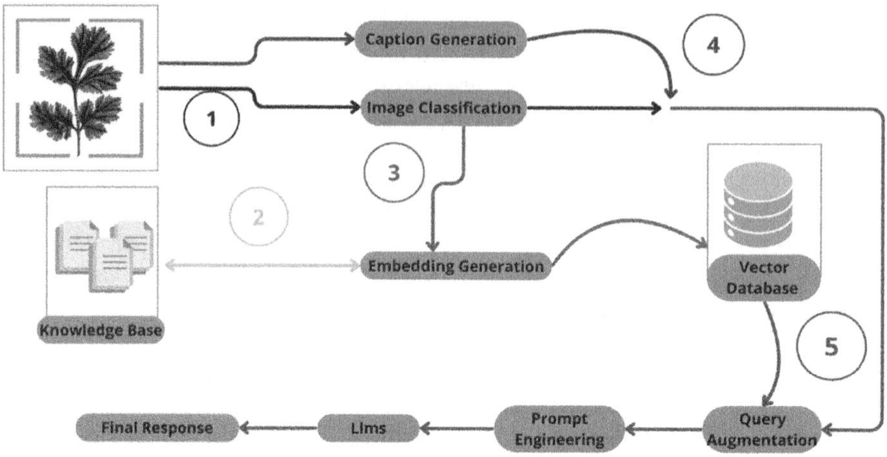

Fig. 1. Schematic of the proposed workflow, illustrating the four main blocks: (1) Image classification to identify plant diseases, producing a predicted class name, (2) Embedding generation from a knowledge base, (3) Retrieval of relevant information from a vector database using the predicted class name, and (4) Final response generation through prompt engineering and query augmentation using LLMs, incorporating visual symptom captions.

3.3 Block 1: Input Data Preparation

Classification Model. A hybrid VGG16/VGG19 model, enhanced with an attention layer, was trained and fine-tuned on the Plant Village dataset (38 classes) for plant disease classification. The model achieved a test accuracy of 96.12%, with training loss decreasing from 1.0 to 0.2 over 20 epochs, and training accuracy improving from 0.75 to 0.95. The training process utilized 224×224 pixel images, and the confusion matrix revealed high accuracy overall, with some confusion between similar classes. Class-specific metrics, such as precision, recall, and F1 scores, ranged from 0.6522 to 1.0000, reflecting robust performance across most categories.

The evolution of the model's loss and accuracy over the training epochs is illustrated in Fig. 2. This figure shows the convergence of the training and validation metrics, demonstrating the model's ability to learn effectively from the dataset.

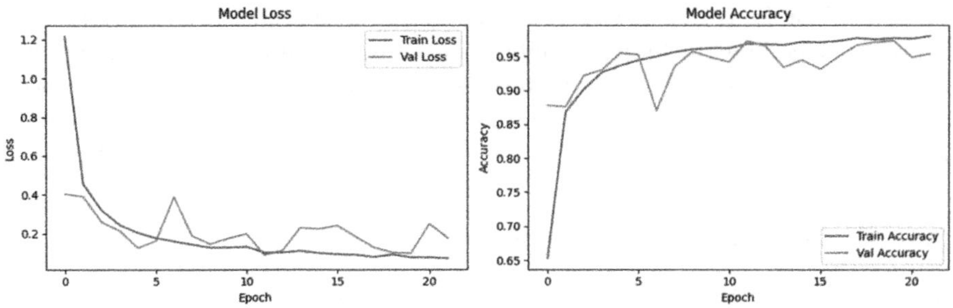

Fig. 2. Model Loss and Accuracy over 20 epochs.

3.4 Block 2: Construction and Storage of the Vector Database

Gathering Information on Diseases. A knowledge base was constructed by aggregating textual data on plant diseases from multiple sources. The data included detailed information on disease names, scientific names, host plants, symptoms, favorable conditions, management strategies, and additional details such as related diseases and resistant varieties. The sources encompassed academic institutions like Cornell University, University of Florida IFAS Extension, North Carolina State University Extension, and gardening platforms like Epic Gardening.

Transformation Into Numerical Maps. The textual data from the knowledge base was transformed into vector representations, or embeddings, using the SentenceTransformer model (all-MiniLM-L6-v2). Each text entry, such as a disease description, was encoded into a 384-dimensional semantic vector. These embeddings were normalized using L2 normalization to ensure compatibility with cosine similarity computations in the subsequent retrieval step.

Storage in an Organized Map. The generated embeddings were stored in a vector database using FAISS (Facebook AI Similarity Search) with the HNSW (Hierarchical Navigable Small World) indexing method.

3.5 Block 3: Retrieval of Relevant Information

The initial query, based on the predicted disease class, was converted into a vector representation using the SentenceTransformer model (all-MiniLM-L6-v2). The query was encoded into a 384-dimensional embedding and normalized with L2 normalization to ensure compatibility with the vector database. This query embedding was then used to search the FAISS HNSW vector database via approximate nearest neighbor search, employing cosine similarity as the metric. The search returned the top-5 most similar entry from the knowledge base, identifying the closest match in terms of semantic content.

Retrieval of Details. The retrieved entry provided detailed information from the knowledge base, including specific symptoms, favorable conditions, and management strategies. These details were used to enrich the query for the response generation phase, ensuring that the final output was informed by both visual and textual data.

3.6 Block 4: Image Captioning

The BLIP (Bootstrapping Language-Image Pre-training) model [28], developed by Salesforce, is a vision-language model that leverages pre-trained representations to generate textual descriptions from images. Without fine-tuning, BLIP produces generic captions that lack specificity, failing to provide detailed descriptions of plant leaf disease symptoms, such as lesion color, texture, or distribution. To address this, we fine-tuned the BLIP model on a custom dataset comprising paired plant leaf images and their corresponding detailed captions, focusing on disease-specific visual features.

The fine-tuning pipeline involved adapting the model to a dataset derived from the PlantVillage dataset, augmented with manually curated captions that detailed symptoms across 38 disease classes (e.g., spot color, size, and leaf condition). Data augmentation, including random flipping and contrast adjustments, was applied to enhance model robustness. The model was optimized with the AdamW optimizer at a learning rate of 5e-5 over 30 epochs, using a batch size of 8. A custom collate function ensured proper handling of image-caption pairs, and metrics such as BLEU, ROUGE (1, 2, L) [29], METEOR, precision, recall, and F1 were computed to evaluate performance.

The fine-tuning results are illustrated in the following figures, which depict the evolution of training and validation metrics over 30 epochs. Figure 3 shows the training and validation scores for text metrics (BLEU, ROUGE1, ROUGE2, ROUGEL, METEOR), indicating consistent improvement with scores stabilizing around 0.8–0.9 by epoch 30. Figure 4 presents accuracy metrics (precision, recall, F1), with training precision and recall reaching approximately 0.9. These results demonstrate that the fine-tuned BLIP model effectively captures detailed disease symptoms, as evidenced by the high text metric scores.

The fine-tuned BLIP model, leveraging this dataset, successfully generates detailed captions that enhance the downstream query construction process by providing precise symptom descriptions.

3.7 Block 5: Generation of the Final Response

Query Augmentation Using Retrieved Information. The initial query was augmented by incorporating relevant chunks retrieved from the knowledge base in step 3, as well as captions describing visual symptoms from images, generated using the fine-tuned BLIP model. This query augmentation process involved appending detailed information, such as disease symptoms and visual characteristics, to the query, creating a more comprehensive input for response generation.

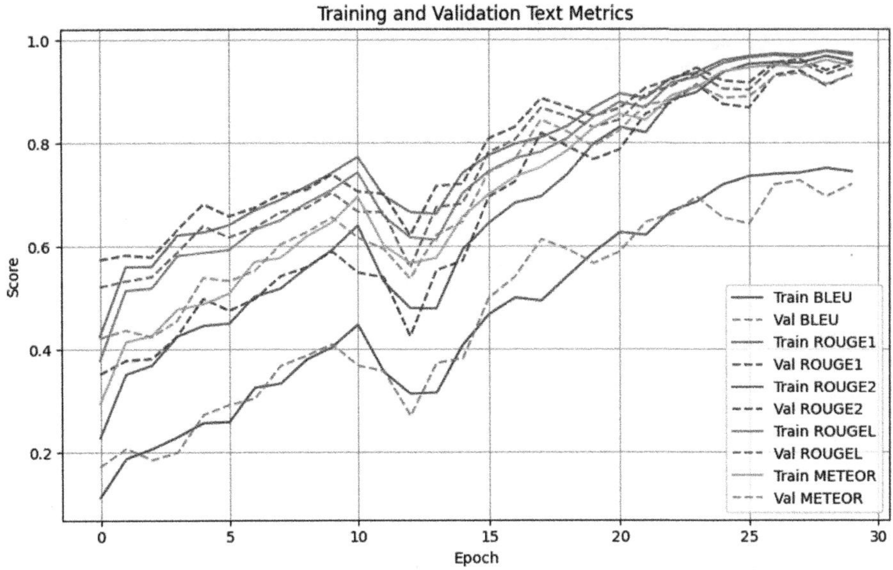

Fig. 3. Training and Validation Text Metrics (BLEU, ROUGE1, ROUGE2, ROUGEL, METEOR) over 30 epochs.

Prompt Engineering. The augmented query was structured into a prompt suitable for a language model, following prompt engineering techniques to ensure clarity and specificity. The prompt was formatted to instruct the model to act as an agricultural expert and provide a concise response, covering aspects like disease definition, symptoms, causes, immediate solutions, and prevention tips for farmers.

Language Models. The prompt was submitted to four language models designed for natural language generation tasks: LLaMA-3.1, Gemma, Mistral, and DeepSeek-R1. All models were evaluated to assess their performance in generating concise and contextually relevant responses.

Production of the Final Response. The language models generated detailed responses tailored for farmers, covering the disease definition, symptoms, causes, immediate solutions, and prevention tips.

4 Results and Discussion

To evaluate the proposed approach, we selected four images representing distinct diseases across different plants: an apple leaf (Image 1), a pepper leaf (Image 2), a tomato leaf (Image 3), and a potato leaf (Image 4). These images were

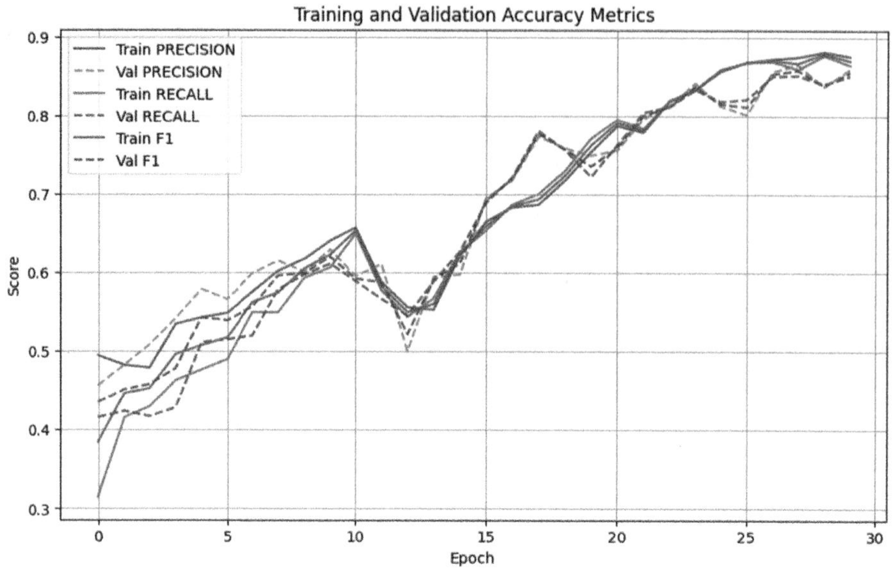

Fig. 4. Training and Validation Accuracy Metrics (Precision, Recall, F1) over 30 epochs.

processed through our five-block workflow, including image classification, information retrieval, caption generation using the fine-tuned BLIP model, and final response generation. The predicted classes for these images, generated in Block 1, are Cedar Apple Rust (Image 1), Bacterial Spot (Image 2), Tomato Yellow Leaf Curl Virus (Image 3), and Early Blight (Image 4). The fine-tuned BLIP model generated detailed captions for these images, as shown in Fig. 5, which also displays the predicted classes. Examples include "numerous rust-colored circular spots" for the apple leaf (Image 1) and "numerous small, irregularly shaped reddish-brown to dark brown spots" for the pepper leaf (Image 2). The responses were generated by four language models: Gemma-3-27B-IT, DeepSeek-R1, Mistral-Small-3.1-24B-Instruct, and LLaMA-3.2-3B-Instruct. The performance of these models was assessed using three metrics: Faithfulness, Answer Relevancy, and Context Precision. The results are summarized in Table 1, followed by an analysis of the obtained measures and a presentation of the ground truth data.

4.1 Ground Truth

Below, we present the ground truth data for the four test images, which includes detailed information about each disease, such as identification, definition, symptoms, causes, control and management strategies, and prevention methods.

Image 1 (Apple leaf):

- **Disease**: Cedar Apple Rust

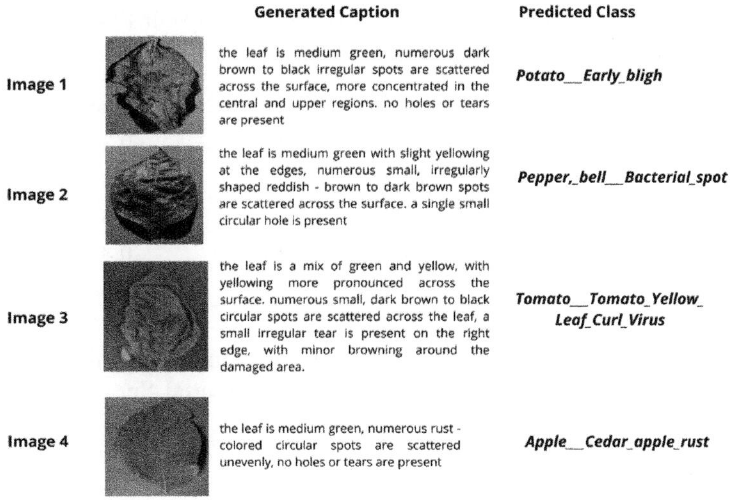

Fig. 5. Four plant leaves with predicted classes and captions generated by the fine-tuned BLIP model: (a) Image 1: Apple leaf, Predicted Class: Cedar Apple Rust ("the leaf is medium green, numerous rust-colored circular spots are scattered unevenly, no holes or tears are present"), (b) Image 2: Pepper leaf, Predicted Class: Bacterial Spot ("the leaf is medium green with slight yellowing at the edges, numerous small, irregularly shaped reddish-brown to dark brown spots are scattered across the surface, a single small circular hole is present"), (c) Image 3: Tomato leaf, Predicted Class: Tomato Yellow Leaf Curl Virus ("the leaf is medium green with slight yellowing along the edges, exhibiting upward curling"), and (d) Image 4: Potato leaf, Predicted Class: Early Blight ("the leaf is medium green, with circular dark brown spots featuring concentric rings and yellow margins, no holes or tears are present"). (Color figure online)

- **Identification**: The image shows a leaf with brown spots and lesions, which are characteristic of Cedar Apple Rust caused by *Gymnosporangium juniperi-virginianae.*
- **Causes**: The disease is caused by the fungus *Gymnosporangium juniperi-virginianae*, which requires both apple trees and Eastern red cedar as hosts to complete its life cycle. High humidity and wet conditions favor spore production and spread. Proximity to Eastern red cedar trees increases the risk of infection.
- **Control and Management**: 1. Remove infected plant material to prevent further spread. 2. Apply fungicides containing sulfur, copper, or modern systemic fungicides during early spring before bud break. 3. Separate apple trees from Eastern red cedar trees if possible to disrupt the disease cycle. 4. Practice regular sanitation and remove fallen leaves promptly.

Image 2 (Pepper leaf):

- **Disease**: Bacterial Spot

Table 1. Performance Metrics of Language Models Across Four Plant Disease Images

Model	Faithfulness	Answer Relevancy	Context Precision
Gemma-3-27B-IT	0.4717	1.0000	0.3222
DeepSeek-R1	0.4644	0.8333	0.3222
Mistral-Small-3.1-24B-Instruct	0.6085	1.0000	0.3222
LLaMA-3.2-3B-Instruct	0.4712	0.9167	0.3222

- **Identification**: The image shows a leaf with small, irregular brown spots scattered across its surface, characteristic of Bacterial Spot caused by *Xanthomonas campestris* pv. *vesicatoria*.
- **Causes**: The disease is caused by *Xanthomonas campestris* pv. *vesicatoria*, which enters plants through natural openings or wounds. Warm temperatures (75–85 °F/24–29 °C) and high humidity favor bacterial growth and spread. Infected plant debris and contaminated tools can contribute to reinfection.
- **Control and Management**: 1. Prune and destroy infected leaves and fruits to prevent further spread. 2. Apply copper-based bactericides as a preventive measure early in the growing season. 3. Clean pruning tools between cuts using alcohol or bleach to avoid spreading the bacteria. 4. Remove and destroy all plant debris at the end of the growing season.

Image 3 (Tomato leaf):

- **Disease**: Tomato Yellow Leaf Curl Virus (TYLCV)
- **Identification**: The image shows a tomato leaf with upward curling and yellowing between the veins, which are characteristic symptoms of Tomato Yellow Leaf Curl Virus (TYLCV) caused by *Xanthomonas campestris* pv. *vesicatoria*.
- **Causes**: The disease is caused by the begomovirus *Tomato yellow leaf curl virus*, which is transmitted primarily by whiteflies (*Bemisia tabaci*). Warm temperatures (70–85 °F/21–29 °C) favor the development of both the virus and its vector, whiteflies. High humidity can increase whitefly populations and facilitate virus transmission.
- **Control and Management**: 1. Control whiteflies using insecticidal soaps or neem oil. 2. Remove and destroy infected plants to prevent further spread. 3. Use resistant tomato varieties such as 'Beaufort' or 'Florida 47'. 4. Grow tomatoes in screened greenhouses to exclude whiteflies. 5. Rotate crops to reduce soil-borne pathogens and break the life cycle of whiteflies.

Image 4 (Potato leaf):

- **Disease**: Early Blight
- **Identification**: The image shows a potato leaf with brown, circular lesions that have concentric rings and yellow margins, characteristic of Early Blight caused by *Alternaria solani*.

- **Causes**: The disease is caused by the fungus *Alternaria solani*, which produces spores that spread via wind, rain, or irrigation water. Warm temperatures (70–85 °F/21–29 °C) and high humidity favor fungal growth and spread. Poor sanitation and stressed plants increase susceptibility.
- **Control and Management**: 1. Rotate crops with non-host crops. 2. Apply fungicides containing copper, chlorothalonil, or mancozeb at the first sign of infection. 3. Remove and destroy infected plant material. 4. Avoid overhead irrigation to keep foliage dry.

4.2 Analysis and Interpretation

The results demonstrate the effectiveness of our proposed five-block workflow in delivering accurate plant disease identification and practical, farmer-oriented advice, highlighting the robustness of integrating image classification, information retrieval, and language model-based response generation. The image classification model in Block 1, a hybrid VGG16/VGG19 with an attention layer, achieved a test accuracy of 96.12% on the Plant Village dataset, as detailed in the Materials and Methods section. This high accuracy is reflected in the correct prediction of disease classes for all four test images: Cedar Apple Rust (Image 1), Bacterial Spot (Image 2), Tomato Yellow Leaf Curl Virus (Image 3), and Early Blight (Image 4), as shown in Fig. 5. These predictions align perfectly with the ground truth data, underscoring the reliability of our classification approach in real-world scenarios.

The fine-tuned BLIP model in Block 4 further enhances the workflow by generating precise captions that capture disease-specific visual symptoms, such as "numerous rust-colored circular spots" for Image 1 and "circular dark brown spots featuring concentric rings" for Image 4. These captions, trained on a custom dataset with high text metric scores (BLEU, ROUGE, METEOR reaching 0.8–0.9) and accuracy metrics (precision and recall at 0.9), as shown in Figs. 3 and 4, provide detailed symptom descriptions that significantly improve query augmentation in Block 5. This visual-to-textual translation ensures that the language models receive comprehensive inputs, bridging the gap between image-based data and textual knowledge.

The performance metrics of the language models, presented in Table 1, further validate the efficacy of our approach. Mistral-Small-3.1-24B-Instruct achieved the highest Faithfulness score of 0.6085, indicating its superior ability to generate responses that remain true to the retrieved information. Both Mistral and Gemma-3-27B-IT scored a perfect Answer Relevancy of 1.0000, demonstrating their capability to produce highly relevant advice for farmers. For instance, the outputs for Image 1 from Gemma-3-27B-IT and Mistral-Small-3.1-24B-Instruct, although misidentifying the disease as Early Blight instead of the ground truth Cedar Apple Rust, still provide actionable management strategies, such as applying fungicides and practicing crop rotation, which are broadly applicable and useful. This adaptability highlights the robustness of our prompt engineering in Block 5, which ensures that even in cases of misidentification, the responses remain practical and relevant.

However, the consistent Context Precision score of 0.3222 across all models indicates a limitation in the retrieval step (Block 3). Despite this, the high Answer Relevancy scores demonstrate that our query augmentation strategy, incorporating BLIP-generated captions and retrieved knowledge, effectively compensates for retrieval limitations by providing the language models with sufficient context to generate relevant responses.

Overall, our approach excels in integrating multimodal data–visual inputs from images and textual knowledge from a vector database–to produce actionable insights for farmers. The high classification accuracy, detailed BLIP captions, and relevant language model responses collectively demonstrate the potential of our pipeline for real-world agricultural applications. To further enhance performance, future work should focus on improving the retrieval mechanism, possibly by increasing the number of retrieved entries or using a more specialized embedding model, and fine-tuning larger language models to better differentiate between similar diseases. Expanding the dataset to include more diverse plant images and exploring lightweight models for deployment in resource-constrained environments will also strengthen the practical utility of this approach.

Gemma-3-27B-IT Output for Image 1 **1. Identification**

The plant disease is confirmed as **Early Blight of Potato** (*Alternaria solani*), a fungal pathogen. The observed symptoms align with early-stage infection, though some classic signs (e.g., target-like rings) may not yet be fully developed.

2. Definition

Early Blight is a **fungal disease** caused by *Alternaria solani.* It primarily affects potatoes and tomatoes, leading to leaf blight, stem lesions, and tuber damage.

4. Causes

- **Pathogen**: Spread via fungal spores (conidia) from infected debris, soil, or wind.
- **Environmental**: Warm (24–30 ° C/75–86 ° F), humid conditions, frequent rain, or overhead irrigation.
- **Cultural**: Poor air circulation, dense planting, or nutrient-deficient soil (especially low nitrogen).

5. Control and Management

- **Immediate Actions**:
  - Remove and destroy infected leaves/stems to reduce spore spread.
  - Apply **fungicides** (e.g., chlorothalonil, copper-based products) at 7–10-day intervals.

    - Avoid overhead watering; irrigate at the base.
- **Long-term**:
    - Rotate crops (3+ years) with non-solanaceous plants (e.g., corn, beans).
    - Use resistant potato varieties (e.g., 'Defender', 'Elba').

Mistral-Small-3.1-24B-Instruct Output for Image 1. **1. Identification**

Based on the provided information, the disease observed appears to be **Early Blight of Potato**. The dark brown to black irregular spots on the leaf, more concentrated in the central and upper regions, align with the symptoms of Early Blight.

2. Definition

Early Blight, scientifically known as *Alternaria solani*, is a **fungal** disease. This disease affects potatoes as well as tomatoes and other solanaceous plants. The fungus infects leaves, stems, and tubers, causing significant damage if left untreated.

4. Causes

- **Pathogen**: The primary cause is the fungus *Alternaria solani*.
- **Environmental Factors**: High humidity, warm temperatures, and prolonged foliar wetness favor the spread and development of the disease.
- **Care Practices**: Poor sanitation, including not removing infected plant debris, and insufficient plant spacing can exacerbate the problem.

5. Control and Management

- **Immediate Actions**:
    - **Remove Infected Material**: Immediately remove and destroy infected leaves and plants to prevent the spread of the fungus.
    - **Fungicides**: Apply fungicides containing active ingredients like chlorothalonil, mancozeb, or metiram. Follow the manufacturer's instructions for application rates and frequencies.
    - **Crop Rotation**: Implement a 3–4 year rotation with non-host crops to reduce the fungal population in the soil.

5 Conclusion

This study successfully integrated Retrieval-Augmented Generation (RAG) with deep learning to enhance plant disease detection. Our five-block workflow, combining image classification, information retrieval, and response generation, achieved a 96.12% accuracy in identifying diseases from leaf images. The fine-tuned BLIP model provided detailed symptom descriptions, improving the relevance of responses generated by language models like Mistral and Gemma.

While effective, the approach highlighted areas for improvement, particularly in retrieval mechanisms and language model reasoning. Future work will focus on refining these aspects and expanding the dataset to include more diverse plant images, aiming to further enhance the practical utility and accuracy of this approach in agricultural diagnostics.

References

1. Sharma, P., Berwal, Y.P.S., Ghai, W.: Performance analysis of deep learning cnn models for disease detection in plants using image segmentation. Inf. Process. Agric. **7**(4), 566–574 (2020)
2. Balaska, V., Adamidou, Z., Vryzas, Z., Gasteratos, A.: Sustainable crop protection via robotics and artificial intelligence solutions. Machines (2023)
3. Raval, H., Chaki, J.: Ensemble transfer learning meets explainable ai: a deep learning approach for leaf disease detection. Ecol. Inf. **84**, 102925 (2024)
4. Food and Agriculture Organization of the United Nations (FAO). The Future of Food and Agriculture: Trends and Challenges (2017)
5. Bannerjee, G., Sarkar, U., Das, S., Ghosh, I.: Artificial intelligence in agriculture: a literature survey. Int. J. Sci. Res. Comput. Sci. Appl. Manage. Stud. **7**(3), 1–6 (2018)
6. Lucas, G.B., Campbell, C.L., Lucas, L.T.: Introduction to plant diseases: Identification and management (1991)
7. Khirade, S.D., Patil, A.B.: Plant disease detection using image processing. In: 2015 International Conference on Computing Communication Control and Automation, pp. 768–771 (2015)
8. Wan, H., Lu, Z., Qi, W., Chen, Y.: Plant disease classification using deep learning methods. In: Proceedings of the 4th International Conference on Machine Learning and Soft Computing (2020)
9. Dwivedi, R., Dutta, T., Yu-Chen, H.: A leaf disease detection mechanism based on l1-norm minimization extreme learning machine. IEEE Geosci. Remote Sens. Lett. **19**, 1–5 (2022)
10. Ristaino, J.B., et al.: The persistent threat of emerging plant disease pandemics to global food security. In: Proceedings of the National Academy of Sciences, vol. 118 (2021)
11. Al, M., et al.: Detection of plant diseases using k-means clustering. J. Plant Dis. **1**, 1–10 (2011)
12. Zhou, L., et al.: Early detection of plant diseases using svm. Agric. Syst. **2**, 11–20 (2013)
13. Bi, X., et al.: Bayesian classifiers for plant disease detection. Plant. Pathol. **3**, 21–30 (2011)
14. Simhadri, V., et al.: Deep learning for plant disease detection. Artif. Intell. Agric. **4**, 31–40 (2024)
15. Sun, Y., et al.: Mean-ssd for apple leaf disease detection. Comput. Electron. Agric. **5**, 41–50 (2021)
16. Lin, H., et al.: Grapenet for grape leaf disease detection. Precision Agric. **6**, 51–60 (2022)
17. Liu, J., et al.: Efdet for cucumber disease detection in complex environments. Biosys. Eng. **7**, 61–70 (2021)
18. Sambasivam, P., et al.: Predictive modeling of cassava diseases using cnn and smote. Agric. Syst. **8**, 71–80 (2021)
19. Novtahaning, T., et al.: Deep ensemble learning for coffee leaf disease classification. Comput. Electron. Agric. **9**, 81–90 (2022)
20. Chen, W., et al.: Stacking ensemble model for plant disease detection. Precision Agric. **10**, 91–100 (2023)
21. Jha, R., et al.: Deep transfer learning for potato leaf disease classification. Biosys. Eng. **11**, 101–110 (2024)

22. Lewis, P., et al.: Retrieval-augmented generation for knowledge-intensive nlp tasks. *arXiv preprint* arXiv:2005.11401 (2020)
23. Alghadban, A., et al.: Transforming frontline health worker training with rag. J. Health Educ. **12**, 111–120 (2023)
24. Jeong, J., et al.: Selfbiorag: improving biomedical explanations with retrieval-augmented generation. Biomed. Inf. **13**, 121–130 (2024)
25. Colverd, M., et al.: Floodbrain: a rag-based system for flood disaster reporting. Disaster Manage. J. **14**, 131–140 (2023)
26. Paneru, S., et al.: Leveraging rag for ayurvedic agriculture: a hybrid deep learning approach. Agric. Technol. **15**, 141–150 (2024)
27. Hughes, D.P., Salathé, M.: An open access repository of images on plant health to enable the development of mobile disease diagnostics through machine learning and crowdsourcing. CoRR, arXiv:1511.08060
28. Li, J., Li, D., Xiong, C., Hoi, S. Blip: Bootstrapping language-image pre-training for unified vision-language understanding and generation. In: International Conference on Machine Learning (2022)
29. Lin, C.-Y.: Rouge: a package for automatic evaluation of summaries. In: Text Summarization Branches Out, pp. 74–81 (2004)

Impact of Sparsification and Quantization on Energy Consumption in Federated Learning

Ouiame Marnissi(✉), Karim Boubouh, Hajar EL Hammouti, El Houcine Bergou, and Robert Basmadjian

College of Computing, Mohammed VI Polytechnic University (UM6P), Ben Guerir, Morocco
{ouiame.marnissi,karim.boubouh,hajar.elhammouti,elhoucine.bergou, robert.basmadjian}@um6p.ma

Abstract. Federated learning (FL) is a distributed machine learning (ML) scheme that enables collaborative model training without compromising data privacy. In the TinyML community, communication is often prioritized over computation due to the limited bandwidth of the client devices. This paper aims to explore the rationale behind this perception by focusing on small models with approximately 1M parameters and investigating the effects of quantization and sparsification techniques for computation and communication purposes. We introduce mathematical models essential for estimating the time and energy consumption of computation and communication in an FL setup. Our research explores various configurations that impact FL efficiency, including model quantization and sparsification, processor frequency, batch sizes, and ML architecture. Notably, we demonstrate that for small models, communication energy can be negligible compared to computational energy. Consequently, contrary to existing literature, we propose that sparsification for communication may not be necessary as it introduces additional computational effort and energy consumption to achieve a target accuracy without significant gains in communication energy. This research enhances our understanding of the trade-offs between communication and computation in FL, particularly for small models like in TinyML. By emphasizing the importance of computational energy, our findings provide valuable insights for the design and optimization of FL systems.

Keywords: Sparsification · Quantization · Federated Learning

1 Introduction

Machine learning (ML) algorithms contribute significantly to the rising energy consumption of data centers [2,13] due to their inherent computation and communication steps. In the computation step, these algorithms perform a sequence

S. Lahlou and M. Mukund (Eds.): NETYS 2025, LNCS 15736, pp. 230–240, 2026.
https://doi.org/10.1007/978-3-032-00347-8_15

of mathematical calculations (e.g., subtraction, multiplication, gradient) utilizing the provided dataset. On the other hand, the communication step involves the transmission and reception of pertinent information, such as data or models.

To address data privacy concerns associated with centralized learning, a federated learning (FL) scheme has emerged. In this scheme, the clients independently execute an ML algorithm and train a model (computation step) using their local datasets. Subsequently, they send (communication step) their respective models to the central server. Upon receiving the models from each client, the server aggregates them into a unified model and returns it to the clients (communication step) [22].

In the domain of TinyML [5,15,17], where IoT devices having limited resources are used to train an ML model, it is often assumed that communication takes precedence over computation due to limited client device bandwidth. Additionally, compression methods including quantization [23] and sparsification [6] have been suggested to lessen the computation and communication overheads of these ML algorithms running on the client devices (e.g., IoT or mobile devices having limited resources).

In this paper, we aim to investigate and validate this perception by assessing the effectiveness of both quantization and sparsification techniques. To achieve this, we initially present mathematical models for calculating the time and energy required for both the computation and communication steps. To this end, we identify the key factors impacting the time required to carry out the ML algorithm for training purposes (e.g., the computation step). Furthermore, we empirically analyze the theoretical models by implementing an FL setup and applying ML algorithms, such as DNN and CNN, to two distinct datasets: MNIST and CIFAR-10 [20]. Our experimental findings indicate that for models with fewer than 10^6 parameters (e.g., small models like TinyML), the communication energy is negligible compared to the computation one. Consequently, unlike the literature, we conclude that employing sparsification for such small models offers no added value from an energy consumption standpoint. Therefore, one of our key findings is not to utilize sparsification for small models as it places additional strain on the computational aspect to attain a certain level of accuracy, with negligible benefits for communication.

Our key contributions can be summarized as:

- We investigate, in an FL scheme, the pertinent factors impacting the ML algorithm's execution time and energy consumption for computation, including the quantization level (e.g., number of bits), processor's frequency (e.g., GHz), chosen architecture (e.g., DNN, CNN), batch size, and dataset size. Furthermore, for communication, we consider sparsification and analyze the impact of various configurations on the execution time and energy consumption.
- We demonstrate that computation energy is a crucial factor in achieving efficient FL, often overlooked in the literature. In particular, we reveal that for small models (e.g., less than 10^6 parameters), transmission energy is indeed negligible compared to computational energy.

– We shed a light that sparsification results in negligible communication energy gains for small ML models. However, achieving a target accuracy may require more iterations and result in additional computational overhead.

The rest of this paper is organized as: In Sect. 2, contributions in the literature related to the ML algorithms in the FL scheme are presented. Our considered FL setup, as well as the mathematical models for calculating time and energy of computation and communication steps, are presented in Sect. 3. The methodology adopted in calculating the energy consumed by the computation and communication steps for our experiments is given in Sect. 4. Experimental results and conclusion as well as future work are presented in Sects. 5 and 6, respectively.

2 Related Work

Prior literature has studied compression methods to alleviate the computation bottleneck in FL. One effective strategy is quantization [7,19], where the number of bits used to encode the gradient vector is reduced. Various quantization techniques have been proposed. One approach is probabilistic quantization, where an element in the ML vector is randomly mapped to one of the closest predefined quantized values. Another technique, dense quantization, requires devices to reduce their gradients' values to a single bit representing the sign of the gradient. To reduce the FL costs, authors in [1] present an adaptive model quantization that aims to homogenize the computing resources of the clients. In the same context, the work in [8] formulates a multi-objective problem that controls the optimal quantization level for training to minimize the energy consumption and the number of communication rounds simultaneously.

In contrast, there has been a significant focus on reducing communication overhead in FL, particularly for edge devices with constrained bandwidth. Various techniques have emerged to address this challenge, including local iterations, sparsification, and quantization. One effective strategy to reduce communication overhead, as proposed by Lin et al. [11] and McMahan et al. [14], is to alternate between several local computations at edge devices, followed by a model averaging at the server. The authors show that performing computational steps locally reduces the number of communication rounds required to train an ML model, which results in a reduction of the overall communication overhead. Moreover, fine-tuning the number of local updates also contributes to improved performance in multi-task settings, as shown in [3].

While performing local iterations reduces the frequency of communications, the size of the transmitted ML vectors remains considerable. To address this challenge, compression techniques such as sparsification and quantization have been proposed [4,12,21]. Sparsification aims to send a sparse vector of weights containing only selected elements of the vector. One sparsification method involves retaining the most impactful values of the gradient while discarding the others [6,9,10,21]. To further reduce communication expenses, sparsification is often combined with quantization [4,12,16].

3 System Model

We consider an FL setup where K clients communicate with a distant server over the wireless network. Each client k has a local dataset D_k with $|D_k|$ data samples. At each global communication round, three steps are repeated in FL: i) local computation at each client, ii) uplink communication, and iii) aggregation at the server side and downlink communication with the client. The computation and communication steps incur energy consumption, which we describe next.

3.1 Computation Model

Let g_k and f_k be the available number and computation speed (measured in GHz) of the processor for client k, respectively. Then, the time it takes to train locally an ML model can be calculated as:

$$T_k^c = \frac{S}{g_k\, f_k} = \frac{o\, i\, e\, b\, d}{g_k\, f_k}, \tag{1}$$

where S denotes the amount of work to be realized due to running a specific ML algorithm. Rationally, S can be further decomposed into the number of iterations i of the ML algorithm, the number of epochs e, the batch size b, the number of model parameters d, as well as the number of floating-point operations o required to complete the computation for training purposes. Note that the value of o in Eq. (1) is processor dependent, with smaller values on powerful CPUs, and larger values for ARM-based processors like for IoT and mobile devices (see Fig. 2).

To quantify the computations required by a given ML algorithm (e.g., the value of o), let us first draw our attention to the mathematics involved in these computational steps:

$$y_t = y_{t-1} - \frac{\eta}{b} \sum_{j \in \mathcal{B}_t} \nabla F_j(y_{t-1}), \tag{2}$$

where y_t is the output at the tth iteration, η is the learning rate, $\mathcal{B}_t$ is the used mini-batch at the tth iteration, and ∇F_j is the gradient of the loss function F_j. It can be noticed from Eq. (2) that there are basic operations such as subtraction, addition, division, and multiplication, whereas a complex set of operations to calculate the stochastic gradient, where the dataset size has the highest impact. In this paper, we studied different dataset sizes, frequencies of the CPU, quantization levels, as well as ML algorithms such as simple DNN and more complex CNN, to find out which among those have an impact on the value of o.

The power demand of CMOS circuits such as CPUs and GPUs can be approximated as:

$$P_k^c \approx \epsilon_k f_k^3, \tag{3}$$

where ϵ_k is a hardware intrinsic constant of the device k. Thus, the energy consumption for computation is given by:

$$E_k^c = P_k^c T_k^c, \tag{4}$$

where T_k^c and P_k^c are given in Eqs. (1) and (3), respectively.

3.2 Transmission Model

After i local computation rounds, the clients upload their local updates to the server using orthogonal frequency domain multiple access channels. The achievable rate of client k is given as [18]:

$$r_k = w_k log_2 \left(1 + \frac{h_k P_k^t}{\sigma^2}\right), \tag{5}$$

where w_k is the bandwidth allocated to client k, P_k^t is the transmission power, h_k is the channel gain and σ^2 is power spectral density of the Gaussian noise. To reduce the amount of transmitted data from clients to the server and therefore optimize the energy consumption, we assume that, before transmission, the update is quantized with a precision level q (in bits) and sparsified with a sparsity ration γ. Hence, the size of the transmitted data is $\gamma q d$ and the time needed for transmission is given as follows:

$$T_k^t = \frac{\gamma q d}{r_k}. \tag{6}$$

Accordingly, the energy consumption for the uplink transmission is:

$$E_k^t = P_k^t T_k^t = P_k^t \frac{\gamma q d}{r_k} \tag{7}$$

where P_k^t is the power used to transmit the machine learning vector. Note that in this paper, we consider that the transmission takes place through a wireless communication medium such as Wi-Fi.

4 Methodology

To empirically evaluate Eqs. (1) and (4), we conducted experiments on a server with a quad-core CPU. Each core of the CPU had minimum, middle, and maximum frequencies of 1.2, 1.9, and 3.6 GHz respectively.

Initially, we determined the average power demand of the CPU when the server was in an idle state. Subsequently, we set all the cores to the minimum, middle, and maximum frequencies and allowed the server to remain idle in each case for 10 min. During this time, we monitored the CPU's power demand for each of the aforementioned three cases using the *powerstat* tool. As the next step, we utilized Linux's *shield* command to isolate one of the CPU cores. We then assigned our ML algorithms to this shielded core, ensuring that no other applications or operating system routines would be executed on it. This approach guarantees that the execution time of our algorithm should closely align with the theoretical value stated in Eq. (1). Note that this methodology leads to having an overall average minimum, middle, and maximum frequencies of 1.2, 1.37, and 1.8[1] GHz.

[1] Average of 1 core running at 3.6 GHz and 3 other cores running at 1.2 GHz.

To assess the impact of CPU frequency on quantization and sparsification techniques, we conducted experiments where we set the frequency to the minimum, middle, and maximum values. As mentioned earlier, we calculated the average power demand of the CPU in an idle state for each of these three cases. By subtracting the overall power demand of the CPU from the idle power demand, we derived the power demanded specifically by our ML algorithm (referred to as Eq. (3)). It is important to note that the overall power demand values were obtained using the *powerstat* tool.

To empirically assess the power demanded during message transmission from devices to the server, we have created a customized application on an Android-based phone. The primary purpose of this mobile application is to send messages to a cloud server using the phone's Wi-Fi interface. To measure the power used during transmission (referred to as P_k^t in Eq. (7)), we have utilized a custom-made Android-based *Power Profiler*. This tool is designed to monitor power-related key performance indicators (KPIs) such as voltage, current, battery temperature, and more, specifically for the selected application.

5 Evaluation

In this section, we present the findings from our experiments aimed at quantifying the energy consumption for computation and communication. To conduct these experiments, we utilized two distinct datasets, namely MNIST and CIFAR-10, each consisting of 60k sample points. Our FL setup involved 100 client devices, with each node assigned 600 sample points arbitrarily, where 500 points were used for training and the rest for testing. Within this setup, each client device independently executed two ML models: Deep Neural Network (DNN) and Convolutional Neural Network (CNN), utilizing their respective local datasets.

For the MNIST dataset, the DNN model had a total of about 200k parameters, while the CNN model had 694k parameters. On the other hand, for the CIFAR-10 dataset, the DNN model had 657k parameters, and the CNN model had 924k parameters. Both the DNN and CNN models shared a similar architecture, consisting of two hidden dense layers with 200 neurons, a convolution layer with 32 filters using a 3-by-3 kernel size, and a dense hidden layer with 128 neurons respectively. For the quantization levels, we considered 32, 16, and 8 bits, and for sparsification, the considered values were 1, 0.26, and 0.13. The client devices are equipped with a quad-core processor having an average minimum, middle, and maximum frequencies of 1.2, 1.37, and 1.8 GHz respectively.

The source code of our experiments is available at the following GitHub repository: https://anonymous.4open.science/r/SQFL-39F0. To measure the energy consumption on Android mobile devices, we utilized the Power Profiler tool, available at https://anonymous.4open.science/r/PowerManager-7CB3.

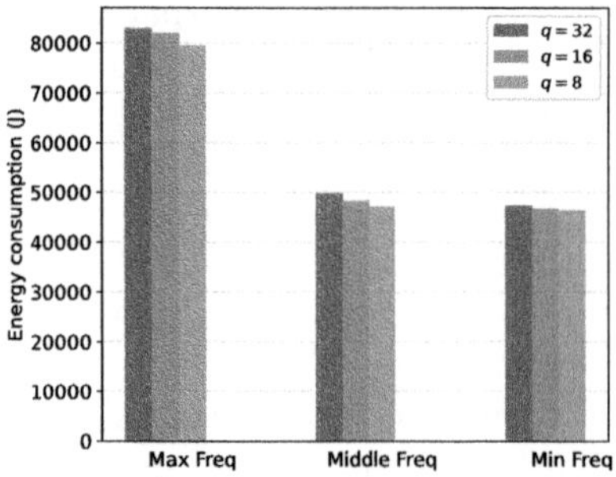

(a) Training a CNN on CIFAR-10 with different CPU frequencies and quantization levels.

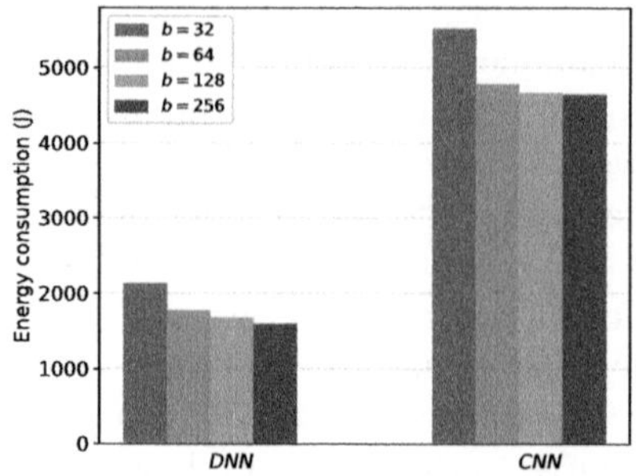

(b) Training a DNN and CNN on CIFAR-10 with different batch sizes.

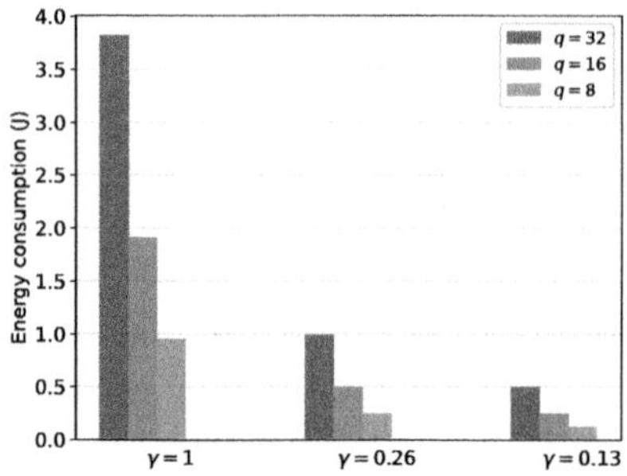

(c) Uplink transmission of CNN on CIFAR-10 using sparsification and quantization.

Fig. 1. Computation and communication energy required for training DNN and CNN models on CIFAR-10 under different configurations, including varying CPU frequencies, sparsification and quantization levels, and batch sizes. The experiments demonstrate a direct influence of these configurations on the energy consumption of ML training.

5.1 Computation Energy

The energy consumption of the computation step in training DNN and CNN models using the MNIST and CIFAR-10 datasets is depicted in Fig. 1. The analysis considers different processor frequencies (f), quantization levels (q), and batch sizes (b). From Fig. 1a, it is evident that selecting the maximum frequency is inefficient and results in excessive energy consumption (almost double compared to the other frequencies). On the other hand, both the middle and minimum frequencies exhibit comparable energy consumption, with the advantage of faster training completion for the former. Hence, the second conclusion is that executing ML algorithms using the middle frequency is a sensible choice. Furthermore, those figures demonstrate that a quantization level of 32 bits consumes the highest energy across all three frequencies for both DNN and CNN models. However, the energy consumption difference between quantization levels of 16 and 8 bits is not significant. This leads us to the third conclusion that a quantization level of 16 bits is reasonable for small models like in TinyML, as further reduction in quantization may result in accuracy degradation.

Figure 1b showcases the energy consumption comparison between DNN and CNN models using the CIFAR-10 dataset. Regardless of the batch size, it is evident that the CNN, with its intricate architecture, consumes nearly 2.5 times more energy than the DNN. When examining each model individually, we observe that increasing the batch size leads to a reduction in energy consumption. However, it is important to note that larger batch sizes necessitate additional hardware resources, such as increased RAM capacity.

5.2 Communication Energy

Figure 1c, we plot the communication energy consumed during the training of CNN model for CIFAR-10 with various quantization and sparsification levels. The figure depicts a clear trend: the total communication energy consumed during training decreases as the number of bits used for quantization decreases. Additionally, the energy consumption is reduced with increased sparsification. More precisely, a reduction of 50% in communication energy is achieved when the number of bits used to encode ML vectors is decreased from 32 to 16 bits. Moreover, when the number of bits is further reduced to 8 bits, a significant saving of 70% in communication energy is realized as compared to the case of 32 bits.

Table 1. Energy consumption to achieve a 90% accuracy for the MNIST dataset using a DNN model (in Joules).

	Computation energy	Communication energy
Without sparsification	363	0.24
With sparsification	413	0.07

Furthermore, we perform the training with and without sparsification. As depicted in the figure, when we drop 74% of the weight vector during communication, the corresponding energy decreases by approximately 70%. With a higher sparsification ratio, where only 13% of the vector is transmitted, the communication energy is reduced by 87% compared to the case without sparsification. These results are in line with Eq. (7) which demonstrates the dependency of communication energy on the size of the transmitted vector. It is important to note that as we decrease the number of quantization bits and increase sparsification, the communication energy per round decreases. However, quantization and sparsification may increase the total number of iterations required for the training to achieve a target accuracy. Our results shown in Table 1 demonstrate that despite the increase in iterations, the total communication energy needed for training remains reduced. However, the computation energy is increased with sparsification which incurs a considerable increase in the total energy consumption.

5.3 Impact of Processor Architecture

In Fig. 2, we present the impact of processor architecture on the reliability of the value o in Eq. (1) during the execution of ML algorithms. To investigate this, we conducted experiments using two different processor architectures: x86 and ARM. Our experiments focused on the MNIST dataset and utilized the DNN model. For more information regarding the dataset and model parameters, please refer to Sect. 5.

Within the x86 architecture, we observed a clear relationship between processor frequency and the number of required floating-point operations for the ML algorithm. Higher processor frequencies resulted in fewer floating-point operations. On the other hand, when comparing similar frequencies between x86 (e.g., 1.9 GHz) and ARM (e.g., 2.2 GHz), we found that the ARM architecture required more floating point operations compared to x86. This leads us to the conclusion that the value of o depends primarily on the architecture of the underlying processor.

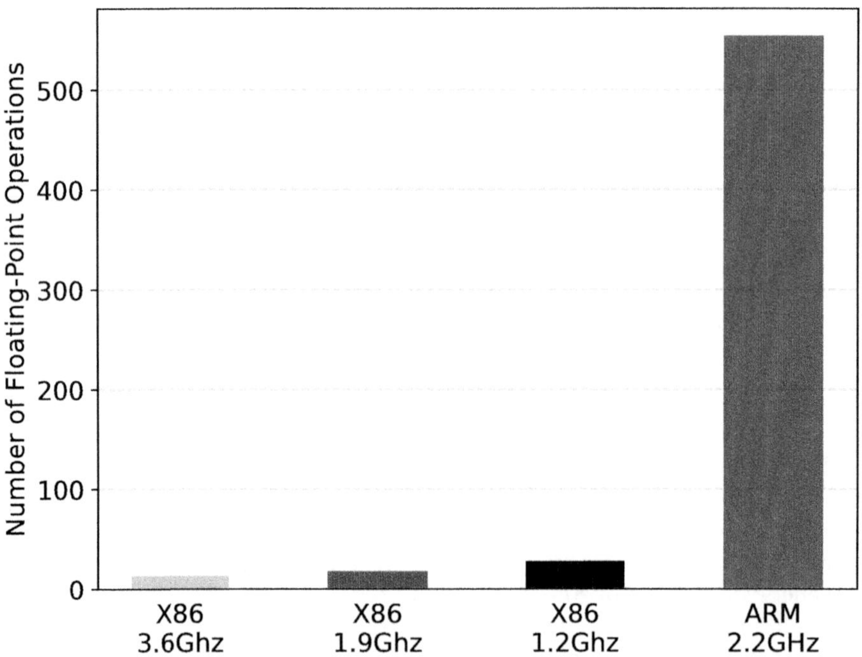

Fig. 2. Number of Floating Point Operations o required by an X86 CPU (e.g., workstation) and ARM CPU (e.g., mobile device) under different CPU frequency configurations.

6 Conclusion and Future Work

In this paper, we explored various factors affecting FL efficiency, including model quantization and sparsification, processor frequency, batch sizes, and ML architecture. Specifically, we showed that for small models like in TinyML, communication energy can be negligible compared to computational energy. As a result, sparsification for communication might not be necessary, as it may introduce additional computational effort and energy consumption without yielding substantial benefits in communication energy. Furthermore, our findings show the importance of choosing the appropriate frequency to minimize computation energy while attaining the desired accuracy. They also highlight the importance of selecting the right batch size and quantization level which significantly impact the computation energy.

In this paper, our primary focus is on the critical aspect of energy consumption in federated learning. However, in certain scenarios, it is equally crucial to ensure that the training process respects time constraints while minimizing energy consumption. As such, in our future work, we will investigate the optimization of total energy expenditure within FL framework under time constraints. We will also expand our analysis to larger ML models and propose adapted training approaches to enhance the energy efficiency.

Acknowledgments. This document has been produced with the financial assistance of the European Union (Grant no. DCIPANAF/2020/420-028), through the African Research Initiative for Scientific Excellence (ARISE), pilot programme. ARISE is implemented by the African Academy of Sciences with support from the European Commission and the African Union Commission. The contents of this document are the sole responsibility of the author(s) and can under no circumstances be regarded as reflecting the position of the European Union, the African Academy of Sciences, and the African Union Commission.

References

1. Abdelmoniem, A.M., Canini, M.: Towards mitigating device heterogeneity in federated learning via adaptive model quantization. In: Proceedings of the 1st Workshop on Machine Learning and Systems, pp. 96–103 (2021)
2. Avgerinou, M., Bertoldi, P., Castellazzi, L.: Trends in data centre energy consumption under the european code of conduct for data centre energy efficiency. Energies **10**(10), 1470 (2017)
3. Collins, L., Hassani, H., Mokhtari, A., Shakkottai, S.: Fedavg with fine tuning: local updates lead to representation learning. Adv. Neural. Inf. Process. Syst. **35**, 10572–10586 (2022)
4. Cui, L., Su, X., Zhou, Y., Liu, J.: Optimal rate adaption in federated learning with compressed communications. In: IEEE INFOCOM 2022-IEEE Conference on Computer Communications, pp. 1459–1468. IEEE (2022)
5. Dutta, L., Bharali, S.: Tinyml meets iot: a comprehensive survey. Internet Things **16**, 100461 (2021)

6. Han, P., Wang, S., Leung, K.K.: Adaptive gradient sparsification for efficient federated learning: An online learning approach. In: 2020 IEEE 40th International Conference on Distributed Computing Systems (ICDCS), pp. 300–310. IEEE (2020)
7. Ji, Y., Chen, L.: Fedqnn: a computation-communication-efficient federated learning framework for iot with low-bitwidth neural network quantization. IEEE Internet Things J. **10**(3), 2494–2507 (2022)
8. Kim, M., Saad, W., Mozaffari, M., Debbah, M.: Green, quantized federated learning over wireless networks: an energy-efficient design. IEEE Trans. Wirel. Commun. (2023)
9. Li, L., Shi, D., Hou, R., Li, H., Pan, M., Han, Z.: To talk or to work: flexible communication compression for energy efficient federated learning over heterogeneous mobile edge devices. In: IEEE INFOCOM 2021-IEEE Conference on Computer Communications, pp. 1–10. IEEE (2021)
10. Li, S., Qi, Q., Wang, J., Sun, H., Li, Y., Yu, F.R.: Ggs: general gradient sparsification for federated learning in edge computing. In: ICC 2020-2020 IEEE International Conference on Communications (ICC), pp. 1–7. IEEE (2020)
11. Lin, T., Stich, S.U., Patel, K.K., Jaggi, M.: Don't use large mini-batches, use local sgd. arXiv preprint arXiv:1808.07217 (2018)
12. Liu, H., He, F., Cao, G.: Communication-efficient federated learning for heterogeneous edge devices based on adaptive gradient quantization. In: IEEE INFOCOM 2023-IEEE Conference on Computer Communications, pp. 1–10. IEEE (2023)
13. Liu, Y., Wei, X., Xiao, J., Liu, Z., Xu, Y., Tian, Y.: Energy consumption and emission mitigation prediction based on data center traffic and PUE for global data centers. Global Energy Interconnection **3**(3), 272–282 (2020)
14. McMahan, B., Moore, E., Ramage, D., Hampson, S., y Arcas, B.A.: Communication-efficient learning of deep networks from decentralized data. In: Artificial Intelligence and Statistics, pp. 1273–1282. PMLR (2017)
15. Ray, P.P.: A review on tinyml: State-of-the-art and prospects. J. King Saud Univ.-Comput. Inf. Sci. **34**(4), 1595–1623 (2022)
16. Reisizadeh, A., Mokhtari, A., Hassani, H., Jadbabaie, A., Pedarsani, R.: Fedpaq: a communication-efficient federated learning method with periodic averaging and quantization. In: International Conference on Artificial Intelligence and Statistics, pp. 2021–2031. PMLR (2020)
17. Sanchez-Iborra, R., Skarmeta, A.F.: Tinyml-enabled frugal smart objects: challenges and opportunities. IEEE Circuits Syst. Mag. **20**(3), 4–18 (2020)
18. Shi, W., Zhou, S., Niu, Z.: Device scheduling with fast convergence for wireless federated learning. In: ICC 2020-2020 IEEE International Conference on Communications (ICC), pp. 1–6. IEEE (2020)
19. Wang, S., Chen, M., Brinton, C.G., Yin, C., Saad, W., Cui, S.: Performance optimization for variable bitwidth federated learning in wireless networks. IEEE Trans. Wirel. Commun. (2023)
20. Xiao, H., Rasul, K., Vollgraf, R.: Fashion-mnist: a novel image dataset for benchmarking machine learning algorithms. arXiv preprint arXiv:1708.07747 (2017)
21. Xu, H., Kostopoulou, K., Dutta, A., Li, X., Ntoulas, A., Kalnis, P.: Deepreduce: a sparse-tensor communication framework for federated deep learning. Adv. Neural. Inf. Process. Syst. **34**, 21150–21163 (2021)
22. Zhang, C., Xie, Y., Bai, H., Yu, B., Li, W., Gao, Y.: A survey on federated learning. Knowl.-Based Syst. **216**, 106775 (2021)
23. Zhou, D., et al.: Dataset quantization. In: Proceedings of the IEEE/CVF International Conference on Computer Vision, pp. 17205–17216 (2023)

Vgg-ViT: A Framework for Deepfakes Images Detection

Achraf Ibnouzaher(✉) and Noureddine Moumkine

Team Data Science and Artificial Intelligence, Laboratory LIM, Faculty of Science and Technology, Hassan II University of Casablanca, Mohammedia, Morocco
achraf.ibn19@gmail.com, noureddine.moumkine@fstm.ac.ma

Abstract. Deepfake videos have been getting increasingly prevalent in recent years due to the presence of mobile apps and tools that can create highly realistic deepfake images/videos without any technical expertise. With the evolution of this domain of technology in the future, the quality and quantity of deepfake videos are expected to increase while making deepfake media a likely tool for disseminating misinformation. Due to these concerns, the deepfake video identification techniques are becoming essential. In this paper, we present a novel hybrid deep-learning model that combines two different models for deepfake identification. Our network employs Vgg-16 as a feature extractor and a Vision Transformer as the feature classifier. We train the Vision Transformer, as well as the feature extractors end to end manner, on the CelebDF and Faceforensics benchmarks. Notwithstanding a comparatively straightforward architecture, our network performs better than previous methods when evaluated on Faceforensics and CelebDF benchmark. Additionally, we introduce a novel random erasing image augmentation technique for training our network. We demonstrate that the proposed image augmentation technique improves the network's identification performance and reduces overfitting. Finally, we demonstrate that our network is able to learn from a substantially smaller amount of data.

Keywords: Deepfake Detection · Random Erasing · Vision Transformer

1 Introduction

A deepfake is an alteration of videos/images or audio using machine-learning algorithms and techniques to generate deceptive synthetic media [1]. Technologies such as Voice-Cloning, face-swapping, and Body-swapping are commonly employed to generate synthetic videos/images, and speech [2–4]. This technological progress has led to a notable increase in the production of synthetic audio or images/videos [2]. According to recent research [5] around ninety-five thousand deepfake videos were detected in 2022 with 97% of these videos being of a pornographic nature where the visages of celebrities were placed onto pornographic content. These fabricated videos may target celebrities to tarnish their reputation causing severe harm. For instance, fabricated media can damage a political candidate's public perception by making them say or do things that never truly transpired.

S. Lahlou and M. Mukund (Eds.): NETYS 2025, LNCS 15736, pp. 241–252, 2026.
https://doi.org/10.1007/978-3-032-00347-8_16

The progress in deepfake methods raises concerns among individuals as these methods can create fraudulent content that appears identical to reality. The most alarming deepfakes involve methods that are able to manipulate facial characteristics in pictures or videos. There are 4 types of facial manipulation [6]: Face Replacement, Face Reanimation, Face Modification, and Face Generation. This research concentrates on the identification of synthetic media created through face replacement and face reanimation methodologies.

Employing fusion or ensemble-based networks tends to yield better performance relative to individual networks [7, 8]. We therefore suggest utilizing two deep learning models Vgg-16 for deep feature extraction and a Vision Transformer (ViT) framework as a classifier [9]. We expect that by extracting features using a CNN model will capture important spatial patterns and hierarchical representations [10] allowing the ViT framework to acquire richer contextual relationships and improve feature discrimination. The ViT framework is able to concurrently capture meaningful dependencies across lengthy input sequences. We therefore opt for the ViT framework [9] to learn features rather than the traditional approach of utilizing a fully-connected (FC) layer for classification after deep feature extraction. Moreover hybrid (utilizes CNN as a feature extractor rather than employing basic patch embeddings) ViT encoder tends to yield excellent findings.

We chose Vgg-16 as one of the feature extractors because it has the ability to capture subtle features even in the presence of variations in image quality (e.g., differences in noise, lighting, and resolution). Additionally since Vgg-16 is pretrained on large image sets like ImageNet it already has some human face knowledge allowing it to leverage pretrained knowledge and extract meaningful features without requiring substantial retraining. We train ViT model and the feature extractor together in an end to end manner utilizing a single-loss function.

The key contributions of this research are threefold (1) we introduce Vgg-ViT deep-learning architecture that learns from the deep features extracted by Vgg-16 model (2) we demonstrate that the image augmentation method applied increases effectiveness of identification network and minimizes over-fitting (3) we demonstrate that even though the proposed network has an easy and simple architecture our network achieves excellent findings when compared with previous approaches although it is trained on a smaller dataset.

The rest of this research is organized as follows; Section "Related Work" discusses the related works. Section "Methods and Materials" describes the dataset, data augmentation technique, and Vgg-ViT model. Section "Results" presents the findings of Vgg-ViT model and comparisons with existing approaches. Section "Conclusion" summarizes the findings and suggests directions for future research.

2 Related Works

Recent research on deepfake video identification has focused on single or individual networks (e.g., CNN networks, recurrent networks, etc.) the ensemble model approaches have not been well investigated. Unlike previous research, this work introduces an innovative approach that utilizes CNN as features extracted and Vision Transformer as a classifier to identify deepfake.

Ashok et al. [11] introduced a deepfake identification method using the Xception CNN network pretrained on the CIFAR-100 dataset. Researchers adapted Xception to their Faceforensics++ benchmark and reported perfect results on the 4 Faceforensics++ manipulations set: Face2Face (F2F), Neural-Textures (NT), FaceSwap (FS), and Deep-Fakes (DF) [12]. The proposed network achieved perfect findings on uncompressed images, but its effectiveness declined when assessed on compressed images.

Fei et al. [13] suggest using three-dimensional facial features to identify fake videos. Researchers find that fusing direct light and the three-dimensional identity texture is significantly beneficial in identifying fake video. They use the Xception CNN network for deep feature extraction. A face-cropped picture and its three-dimensional details are utilized to train the classifier network. They also conduct an in-depth study of several different deep feature merging techniques. The proposed network was trained on CelebDF dataset and assessed on Faceforensics++ datasets. Researchers report promising findings on three datasets alongside enhanced generalization capability compared to the previously suggested method.

Guo et al. [14] suggest a new deepfake identification method which they name, DeepRhythm. The suggested method operates by analyzing the heartbeat rhythm of an individual in a video clip. They use remote Photoplethysmography (rPPG) to examine minute variations in skin color associated with the blood flow visible on the facial skin. Researchers assess the suggested method on DFDC and Faceforensics datasets and report outstanding performance findings.

Dong et al. [15] suggest a fake video identification method by applying image augmentation techniques, such as Gaussian noise and Gaussian blur, to preprocess video frames in order to eliminate low-level high-frequency GAN artifacts present inside the manipulated frames. They then trained a forensic-CNN model on the preprocessed frames. They found that by employing the augmentation technique on both fake and real frames, it eliminates the low-level noise signals while forcing the backbone to capture significant deep feature. Through their results, researchers establish the efficacy of their presented method on synthetic video identification.

Chintha et al. in [16] presented a recurrent neural architecture for synthetic video identification. Recurrent neural network (RNN) was used in conjunction with DenseNet CNN model to exploit temporal discrepancies present between images of a fake video. The suggested approach was assessed on the face-forensics dataset exhibiting promising performance.

Delp and Guera [17] suggested using a long short-term memory (LSTM) model along with CNN model for fake video identification. Researchers attempted to exploit inter-image inconsistencies inherent in fake videos. The convolutional neural network was assigned with extracting image-level features, which were subsequently passed to LSTM module to capture temporal dependencies. Researchers assessed the network on their custom dataset exhibiting outstanding performance.

Yamagishi et al. [18] suggest a capsule-based deep-learning network to identify synthetic video. The suggested network was assessed on three different forgery datasets comprising a wide variety of manipulated videos and pictures. The suggested network achieved outstanding results compared to other approaches on all three datasets.

Again Yamagishi et al. [19] suggest a distinct technique utilizing a Y-shaped decoder/encoder network. Researchers trained the network by following a multitask learning-based strategy, which was capable of generating and classifying a partitioning mask for the modified regions within altered videos or images. The suggested network was assessed on the CelebDF and Faceforensics datasets achieving excellent findings even when fine-tuned on a limited number of frames.

Demir et al. [20] suggest an innovative deepfake identification method by employing biological signal (i.e., PPG signals or photoplethysmography) to train a support-vector-machine (SVM) and CNN model. The predictions from the SVM and CNN were combined to obtain final label. The suggested network achieved excellent findings when assessed on two different forgery datasets, CelebDF and Faceforensics datasets.

Nozick et al. [21] suggest two distinct CNN networks, which they named MesoInception-4 and Meso-4, both having a limited number of blocks concentrating on mesoscopic frame features. The suggested network was evaluated on a CelebDF dataset and a data collected by the researchers. The network achieved outstanding findings on two deepfake datasets.

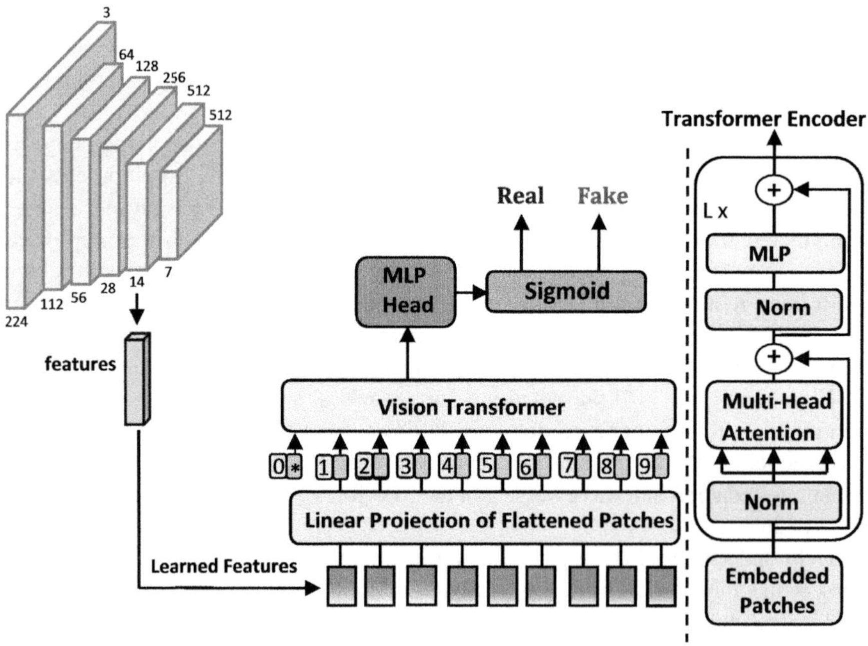

Fig. 1. The architecture of our hybrid model comprises two deep learning networks, Vgg-16 and Vision Transformer (ViT). The pre-trained CNN model serves as a feature extractor while the ViT encoder which includes a perceptron multilayer (MLP Block) and multi-head self-attention mechanism is used for deepfake accurate detection.

Khan et al. [22] presented an innovative video transformer (VT) model for deepfake identification, designed to learn through new data in a progressive way. The introduced video transformer (VT) network was trained on multi-modal data (i.e., UV texture map, and face-cropped frames). The proposed network achieved outstanding results on various deepfake identification benchmarks.

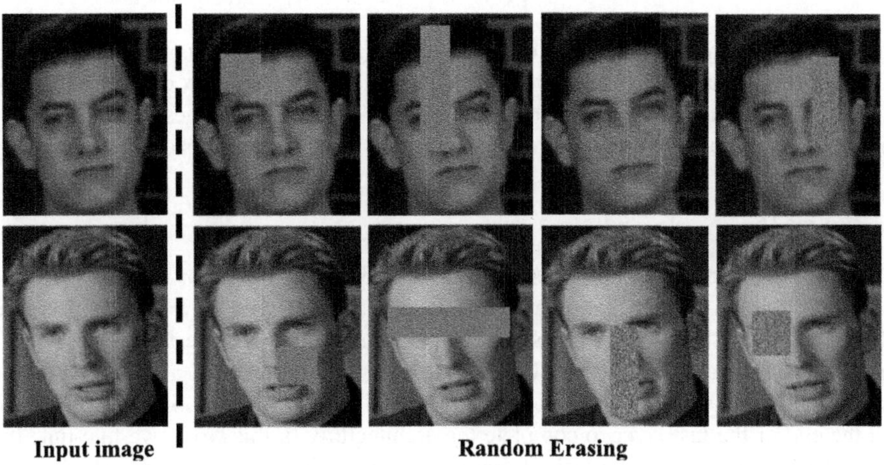

Fig. 2. Example of the Random Erasing technique.

3 Methods and Materials

In this part, we present a concise overview of the following: (1) random erasing augmentation technique employed to train the Vgg-ViT model, (2) the Vgg-16 network architecture utilized for deep feature extraction, and (3) the Vgg-ViT architecture model.

3.1 Random Erasing

Random Erasing (RE) [23] is an augmentation technique that employs regional dropout methods [24] to improve the robustness and generalization performance of Vgg-ViT network by encouraging the network to focus on the whole object area rather than only the most distinctive parts. The regional dropout methods remove random areas in input images. Random Erasing is similar to other techniques, such as Cut-Out [25] and MixUp [26], that modify the training images by masking or removing segments of the image. However, the main distinction of Random Erasing is that the removed regions are replaced with random pixels or noise, rather than simply being replaced with a fixed value as shown in Fig. 2. This allows the network to learn more robust deep feature representations during the training process.

Given training images I and their corresponding labels L, the Random Erasing generates augmented training image by randomly selecting a rectangular section of the image and replacing the pixels in that region with a matrix R of random values, which can be sampled from a uniform distribution $R \sim Uniform(0,255)$, a Gaussian distribution

$R \sim N(\mu, \sigma^2)$, or the image itself. The augmented image I_{aug} is defined as:

$$I_{aug}(y : y + h, x : x + w, :) = \begin{cases} R & (random\ values) \\ I(y : y + h, x : x + w, :) & (original\ image) \end{cases} \quad (1)$$

Where w, h are width and height of rectangular region respectively, and (x, y) is coordinates of the top-left corner of the rectangular region. R is a matrix of random values. The Vgg-ViT network is then trained on the newly augmented images, with the goal of introducing a broader variety of training sets to enhance the model's efficacy.

3.2 Vgg-16

Vgg-16 [27]: Vgg-16 comprises sixteen layers, following the preprocessing stage the extracted values are fed into a series convolutional layer with $(3 * 3)$ receptive-field filters and a constant stride of 1. Subsequently, spatial pooling is performed by 5 max-pooling of several convolutional layers. The max-pooling layer of a $(2 * 2)$ kernel is performed with a stride of 2. Two fully-connected (FC) layers and Sigmoid are added at the end of the last layer to complete the architecture. In this work, we fine-tune the Vgg-16 architecture for the task of feature extraction. The first top layer which is the classification layer of network is removed while the deep features were extracted from the last block convolution layer. After removing the classification layer, the output of the Vgg-16 architecture was (None, 7,7, 512), which was then passed into a Vision Transformer for classification.

3.3 Architecture Proposed Model

Figure 1 shows the framework of our network. The Vgg-ViT network works in two phases. Firstly, we employ Vgg-16 model to extract features from the frames. Next, we use Vision Transformer [9] to learn the deep features obtained from Vgg-16. Given that Vision Transformer framework has demonstrated effectiveness in capturing meaningful correlations from input sequences simultaneously, so we use this network to learn deep feature obtained from Vgg-16 model. We believe that applying a Vision Transformer (ViT) to learn the deep features, instead of using a feature followed by a dense layer will achieve excellent findings. In addition, we can infer from the image classification challenge [28] that transformers utilizing CNN-features show excellent results compared to individual transformers. The highest rankings in the challenge were obtained by network utilizing CNN as a feature extractor [28].

In our approach, we use a pretrained ViT framework to classify features extracted from the Vgg-16 model, as mentioned above. After extracting features from Vgg-16, we apply a convolutional layer to reduce the spatial dimensions from (7×7) to (3×3), to align with the ViT's tokenization process. These reduced features are then flattened into a sequence of tokens, resulting in a tensor of shape (None, 9, 512). A learnable classification token (CLS) is added to the sequence which makes the size of the vector (None, 10, 512). Following this, positional embeddings are added to these deep features through element-wise addition and we input the final features into the transformer. The Vision Transformer encoder consists of two components: Multi-head Self-Attention

(MSA) and Multi-Layer Perceptron (MLP), and two normalization layers, as shown in Fig. 1. The transformer uses eight attention heads. The model is trained using single-loss function. The output of the transformer is a sequence of feature representations with the first token (corresponding to the CLS token) serving as the aggregated representation of the entire input sequence. This CLS token is passed through an MLP head consists of a Feed Forward Network (FFN) with ReLU nonlinearity and a few additional layers. The final MLP head applies sigmoid activation function for label prediction.

3.4 Dataset

The proposed neural network was validated, assessed and trained utilizing two distinct deepfake datasets: Faceforensics [29] and CelebDF [30] datasets. The CelebDF dataset comprises 580 authentic videos of famous individuals sourced from YouTube that vary in gender, age, and ethnic groups, and 5639 generated Deepfake videos. It also comprises 300 additional real videos of random topics gathered from YouTube [30]. The Faceforensics dataset [29] includes 1K real videos that have been modified with four face manipulation techniques: Face2Face, NeuralTextures, FaceSwap, and Deepfakes. It is produced with three compression levels: raw (H.264) [26], light (c23), and high (c40) [31].

The Faceforensics dataset is split following the guidelines in the paper [29], with 720 videos chosen for training, 140 for testing and 140 for validation. For the CelebDF dataset, 400 fake and real videos are utilized for testing and 8K videos are utilized for training the proposed network. We extract 40 pictures from forged videos and 145 pictures from authentic videos to balance the authentic test sets and the forged test sets. The exact number of pictures from the two datasets, Faceforensics and CelebDF, employed to validate, train, and test the Vgg-ViT network is presented in Tables 2 and 4, respectively. To assess the proposed network, we extracted 10 pictures from each test video. To determine the class label to test video we extract 10 pictures and input them individually into the proposed network. The final prediction is obtained by averaging the predictions for all frames.

3.5 Experimental Setup

Neural networks acquire knowledge from datasets; thus, the data must be carefully prepared for higher prediction accuracy. Therefore, we preprocess the dataset so that the model acquires all relevant information accurately. We utilize the OpenCV tool for facial detection and cropping, which is recognized for its efficient and rapid handling of large numbers of frames. The cropped frames are saved in JPEG format and resized to 224∗224 pixels. We use Roman Solovyev's GitHub repository to download the pretrained weights of the Vgg-16 trained on the ImageNet data. Additionally, the pretrained weights of the ViT network trained on ImageNet-21k are obtained from the following repository: https://huggingface.co/google/vit-base-patch16-224.

To train the Vgg-ViT network, we use the Adam optimizer with β_1 fixed at 9e-1, β_2 fixed at 99e-2, epsilon fixed at 10^{-8}, and learning rate fixed at 10^{-3}. We train the Vgg-16 network and ViT model in an end to end manner and fine-tune them using the cross-entropy loss function. After extracting frame features from the Vgg-16 network, we obtain a feature vector with dimensions [7,7,512]. We then use a convolutional layer to reduce dimensionality. Afterward, we add positional embeddings and a learnable classification token. The final vector with a size of (None, 10, 512) is then passed to Vit model.

4 Results and Discussion

In this part, we compare and discuss the findings achieved by the proposed network on the CelebDF and Faceforensics datasets. We trained the Vgg-ViT network on the Faceforensics dataset using three different configurations (i.e., without image augmentation technique, with traditional augmentation techniques, and with random erasing augmentation technique). The results show that the network trained utilizing the random erasing technique outperformed the other two configurations, thus we decided to train our backbone with the same configuration on the CelebDF dataset. A performance evaluation of our backbone using two augmentation techniques is reported in Table 1. We attribute the reason behind such excellent results of random erasing augmentation to its ability to randomly erase segments of the input frame during training, forcing the backbone to learn meaningful and relevant features from the frame.

It should also be highlighted that the proposed network trained on a limited number of instances from the Faceforensics dataset, in contrast to other approaches. The number of training frames is reported in Table 2; for example, Verdoliva et al. [12] trained their network on around 387*K* frames, Fei et al. [13] trained their networks on around 359*K* frames. We compare the Vgg-ViT network with the reference performance findings presented in Faceforensics research paper [12], because they provide performance results of all network on the four subsets of the Faceforensics data. We also showcase the outcomes achieved by the proposed network on the CelebDF dataset in Table 4.

Table 3 provides a comprehensive comparison of the performance achieved on each subset of the Faceforensics dataset. The proposed network trained utilizing image augmentation techniques achieves excellent results compared to the baseline methods presented in Table 3 and other previous forged media identification approaches [13, 14]. The reason for opting for the methods in Table 3 for comparison is that these approaches are also assessed in the Faceforensics paper and follow the same training configurations as applied in this research. Testing is conducted in a different manner than these methods i.e., we test proposed network on 10 face images for each video while these methods test their networks on 50 face images for each video. For validation, the methods in Faceforensics paper utilize 50 face images for each video while we divide the validation and train set in 20:80 ratio i.e., 41K frames for validation and 200K frames for training.

Table 4 presents the performance comparison with previous approaches on the CelebDF dataset. Despite being trained on a limited training set the proposed network achieves superior performance scores compared to previous approaches. For instance, Yamagishi et al. [18] trained their network on 415 videos (or 112k frames) since they utilized 270 frames from every video for training while we only utilize 23k real frames and 23k fake frames. This demonstrates that our network even when trained on limited set achieves better classification accuracy.

Table 1. Classification performance of Vgg-ViT with and without data augmentation.

Network	Face2Face	Deepfake	NeuralTextures	FaceSwap
Vgg-ViT	85.50%	84.14%	82.70%	85.43%
Vgg-ViT+Tra	86.02%	84.80%	83.03%	86.29%
Vgg-ViT+RE	*93.80%*	93.24%	80.45%	91.85%

Table 2. Number of validation and training frames used by Vgg-ViT model and other methods on the FaceForensic dataset.

Method	Training	Validation	Testing
Verdoliva et al. [12]	387K	71K	71K
Fei et al. [13]	359K	71K	71K
Vgg-ViT	200K	41K	11K

Table 3. Performance comparison with previous approaches on the FaceForensic dataset

Approach	NT		FS		F2F		DF	
	AUC	ACC	AUC	ACC	AUC	ACC	AUC	ACC
Verdoliva et al. [12]	–	60.97%	–	56.21%	–	64.13%	–	85.45%
Fei et al. [13]	–	63.23%	–	68.83%	–	73.62%	–	73.54%
Guo et al. [14]	79.10%	67.70%	65.50%	58.10%	81.30%	68.20%	94.00%	86.20%
Peng et al. [15]	–	–	–	92.69%	–	90.26%	–	92.07%
Yamagishi et al. [19]	87.47%	79.35%	92.14%	90.01%	92.71%	86.38%	90.52%	93.01%
Demir et al. [20]	90.10%	80.04%	93.80%	85.17%	94.20%	86.38%	95.01%	92.24%
Nozick et al. [21]	–	40.57%	–	61.07%	–	56.10%	–	87.17%
Vgg-ViT+RE	**87.55%**	**80.45%**	**93.10%**	**91.85%**	**94.48%**	**93.80%**	**95.24%**	**93.24%**

5 Conclusion

In this research, we proposed a robust backbone to identify deepfake videos using two deep-learning models. The proposed network used a Vgg-16 model as a feature extractor and the Vision Transformer as a classifier. We tested our proposed network on the Face-forensics and CelebDF datasets and achieved remarkable results compared to previous

Table 4. Performance comparison with previous approaches on the CelebDF dataset

Approach	Training size	Accuracy	
		AUC	ACC
Rao et al. [16]	–	86.95%	80.64%
Echizen et al. [18]	112K	94.31%	93.54%
Demir et al. [20]	100K	90.10%	80.04%
Nozick et al. [21]	–	–	90.85%
Vgg-ViT+RE	46K	95.74%	94.45%

methods. We improved the effectiveness of the Vgg-ViT network by using the Random Erasing image augmentation method. The Vgg-ViT network with the Random Erasing technique showed the highest performance in identifying manipulated videos on two benchmark datasets. In future work, we will evaluate the proposed network on some different DeepFake datasets and apply some different augmentation methods in order to improve its performance.

References

1. Westerlund, M.: The emergence of deepfake technology: a review (2019). https://doi.org/10.22215/TIMREVIEW/1282
2. Rao, S., Verma, A.K., Bhatia, T.: A review on social spam detection: challenges, open issues, and future directions (2021). https://doi.org/10.1016/j.eswa.2021.115742
3. Nguyen, T.T., et al.: Deep learning for deepfakes creation and detection: a survey. Comput. Vis. Image Understand. **223** (2022). https://doi.org/10.1016/j.cviu.2022.103525
4. Masood, M., Nawaz, M., Malik, K.M., Javed, A., Irtaza, A., Malik, H.: Deepfakes generation and detection: state-of-the-art, open challenges, countermeasures, and way forward. Appl. Intell. **53**(4) (2023). https://doi.org/10.1007/s10489-022-03766-z
5. Zheng, L., Zhang, Y., Thing, V.L.L.: A survey on image tampering and its detection in real-world photos. J. Vis. Commun. Image Represent **58** (2019). https://doi.org/10.1016/j.jvcir.2018.12.022
6. Tolosana, R., Vera-Rodriguez, R., Fierrez, J., Morales, A., Ortega-Garcia, J.: Deepfakes and beyond: a Survey of face manipulation and fake detection. Inform. Fus. **64** (2020). https://doi.org/10.1016/j.inffus.2020.06.014
7. Lucas, T.J., et al.: A comprehensive survey on ensemble learning-based intrusion detection approaches in computer networks. IEEE Access **11** (2023). https://doi.org/10.1109/ACCESS.2023.3328535
8. Liu, H., Liu, Z., Hou, Q., Xiao, L., Li, M.: Deep fusion network based ensemble learning approach for detection intensive classification. In: International Conference on Wavelet Analysis and Pattern Recognition (2022). https://doi.org/10.1109/ICWAPR56446.2022.9947146
9. Han, K., et al.: A survey on vision transformer. IEEE Trans. Pattern Anal. Mach. Intell. **45**(1) (2023). https://doi.org/10.1109/TPAMI.2022.3152247
10. Chen, Y., Jiang, H., Li, C., Jia, X., Ghamisi, P.: Deep feature extraction and classification of hyperspectral images based on convolutional neural networks. IEEE Trans. Geosci. Remote Sens. **54**(10) (2016). https://doi.org/10.1109/TGRS.2016.2584107

11. Ashok, V., Joy, P.T.: Deepfake detection using XceptionNet. In: RASSE 2023 - IEEE International Conference on Recent Advances in Systems Science and Engineering, Proceedings (2023). https://doi.org/10.1109/RASSE60029.2023.10363477
12. Cozzolino, D., Rossler, A., Verdoliva, L., Riess, C., Thies, J., Niessner, M.: Faceforensics++: learning to detect manipulated facial images. In: Proceedings of the IEEE International Conference on Computer Vision (2019). https://doi.org/10.1109/ICCV.2019.00009
13. Fei, H., et al.: Face forgery detection by 3D decomposition and composition search. IEEE Trans. Pattern. Anal. Mach. Intell. **45**(7) (2023). https://doi.org/10.1109/TPAMI.2022.3233586
14. Guo, Q., et al.: DeepRhythm: exposing DeepFakes with attentional visual heartbeat rhythms. In: MM 2020 - Proceedings of the 28th ACM International Conference on Multimedia (2020). https://doi.org/10.1145/3394171.3413707
15. Xuan, X., Peng, B., Wang, W., Dong, J.: On the generalization of GAN image forensics. In: Sun, Z., He, R., Feng, J., Shan, S., Guo, Z. (eds.) CCBR 2019. LNCS, vol. 11818, pp. 134–141. Springer, Cham (2019). https://doi.org/10.1007/978-3-030-31456-9_15
16. Chintha, A., Rao, A., Sohrawardi, S., Bhatt, K., Wright, M., Ptucha, R.: Leveraging edges and optical flow on faces for deepfake detection. In: IJCB 2020 - IEEE/IAPR International Joint Conference on Biometrics (2020). https://doi.org/10.1109/IJCB48548.2020.9304936
17. Delp, E.J., Guera, D.: Deepfake video detection using recurrent neural networks. In: Proceedings of AVSS 2018 - 2018 15th IEEE International Conference on Advanced Video and Signal-Based Surveillance (2018). https://doi.org/10.1109/AVSS.2018.8639163
18. Nguyen, H.H., Yamagishi, J., Echizen, I.: Capsule-forensics: using capsule networks to detect forged images and videos. In: ICASSP, IEEE International Conference on Acoustics, Speech and Signal Processing - Proceedings (2019). https://doi.org/10.1109/ICASSP.2019.8682602
19. Yamagishi, J., Fang, F., Nguyen, H.H., Echizen, I.: Multi-task learning for detecting and segmenting manipulated facial images and videos. In: 2019 IEEE 10th International Conference on Biometrics Theory, Applications and Systems, BTAS 2019 (2019). https://doi.org/10.1109/BTAS46853.2019.9185974
20. Demir, I., Ciftci, U.A., Yin, L.: FakeCatcher: detection of synthetic portrait videos using biological signals. IEEE Trans. Pattern Anal. Mach. Intell. (2023). https://doi.org/10.1109/TPAMI.2020.3009287
21. Afchar, D., Nozick, V., Yamagishi, J., Echizen, I.: MesoNet: a compact facial video forgery detection network. In: 10th IEEE International Workshop on Information Forensics and Security, WIFS 2018 (2018). https://doi.org/10.1109/WIFS.2018.8630761
22. Khan, S.A., Dai, H.: Video transformer for deepfake detection with incremental learning. In: MM 2021 - Proceedings of the 29th ACM International Conference on Multimedia (2021). https://doi.org/10.1145/3474085.3475332
23. Zhong, Z., Zheng, L., Kang, G., Li, S., Yang, Y.: Random erasing data augmentation. In: AAAI 2020 - 34th AAAI Conference on Artificial Intelligence (2020). https://doi.org/10.1609/aaai.v34i07.7000
24. Xu, M., Yoon, S., Fuentes, A., Park, D.S.: A comprehensive survey of image augmentation techniques for deep learning. Pattern Recognit. **137** (2023). https://doi.org/10.1016/j.patcog.2023.109347
25. DeVries, T., Taylor, G.W.: Improved regularization of convolutional neural networks with cutout (2017). http://arxiv.org/abs/1708.04552
26. Wang, Z., et al.: enhance image classification via inter-class image mixup with diffusion model (2024). http://arxiv.org/abs/2403.19600
27. Liu, S., Deng, W.: Very deep convolutional neural network based image classification using small training sample size. In: Proceedings - 3rd IAPR Asian Conference on Pattern Recognition, ACPR 2015 (2016). https://doi.org/10.1109/ACPR.2015.7486599

28. Dolhansky, B., et al.: The DeepFake Detection Challenge (DFDC) Dataset (2020). http://arxiv.org/abs/2006.07397
29. Rössler, A., Cozzolino, D., Verdoliva, L., Riess, C., Thies, J., Nießner, M.: Faceforensics: a large-scale video dataset for forgery detection in human faces (2018). http://arxiv.org/abs/1803.09179
30. Li, Y., Yang, X., Sun, P., Qi, H., Lyu, S.: Celeb-DF: a large-scale challenging dataset for DeepFake forensics. In: Proceedings of the IEEE Computer Society Conference on Computer Vision and Pattern Recognition (2020). https://doi.org/10.1109/CVPR42600.2020.00327
31. Yu, G.: Emotion monitoring for preschool children based on face recognition and emotion recognition algorithms. Complexity **2021** (2021). https://doi.org/10.1155/2021/6654455

Heterogeneous Graph Neural Network Based Arabic Coreference Resolution

Rihab EL Yousfi[1(✉)], Mounir Ourekouch[1,2], and Mohammed Erradi[3]

[1] CID-Developpement, Rabat, Morocco
rihabelyousfi1@gmail.com
[2] College of Computing, Mohammed VI Polytechnic University, Ben Guerir, Morocco
[3] ENSIAS, Mohammed V University in Rabat, Rabat, Morocco

Abstract. Coreference resolution aims to identify and link mentions that refer to a same entity in a text. However, Arabic coreference resolution remains under-explored due to data scarcity and linguistic complexity. Previous work has primarily relied on pre-trained language models, multilingual transformers, and cross-lingual transfer learning. Yet, these approaches often overlook syntactic and semantic structures, which are essential for capturing richer contextual representations. In this work, we focus on considering syntactic and semantic information to improve mentions linking for the Arabic language. We propose a heterogeneous graph-based model that jointly leverages these features to enhance Arabic coreference resolution. The suggested model encodes syntactic structure via dependency trees, using the Arabic parser, Camel-Parser 2.0. This model refines contextual representations by incorporating semantic role labeling (SRL), leading to a deeper semantic understanding. We conduct an analysis of our approach, comparing its performance with BERT-based methods and sequence-to-sequence models. Experiments on Arabic CoNLL-2012 shared task show that the suggested model outperforms BERT-based approaches in terms of F1 score and achieves competitive results against state-of-the-art sequence-to-sequence models.

Keywords: Arabic coreference resolution · Heterogeneous graph neural network · Dependency parsing · Semantic role labeling (SRL)

1 Introduction

Coreference Resolution is a fundamental task in Natural Language Processing (NLP) that aims to cluster mentions referring to the same real-world entities in a text. It enables a coherent understanding of discourse by linking pronouns, noun phrases, and other referring expressions to their corresponding antecedents or postcedents. For example, in a sentence like "وُلِدَ الخوارزمي في أوزبكستان، من أشهر مؤلفات العلامة كتاب المختصر في حساب الجبر والمقابلة" [Al-Khwarizmi was born in Uzbekistan; among the most famous works of the scholar is the book 'The Compendious Book on Calculation by Completion and Balancing']. The mention "العلامة" (the scholar)

S. Lahlou and M. Mukund (Eds.): NETYS 2025, LNCS 15736, pp. 253–270, 2026.
https://doi.org/10.1007/978-3-032-00347-8_17

refers back to "الخوارزمي" (Al-Khwarizmi) (the person named Al-Khwarizmi). They form a coreference chain (Fig. 1). Identifying such coreferences is essential for achieving a deeper understanding of the text, making it a fundamental step in many advanced NLP applications, such as information extraction, question answering, and text summarization. However, coreference resolution is considered a challenging task and has several difficulties including handling ambiguous references, resolving long-distance dependencies, and dealing with domain-specific or context-dependent entities.

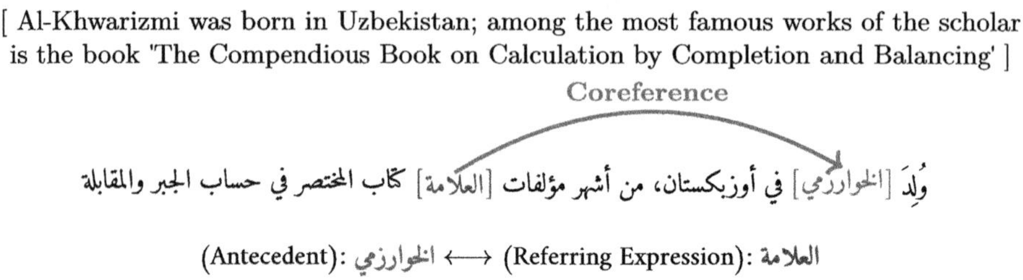

Fig. 1. Example of Arabic Coreference Resolution

Coreference resolution has evolved significantly over time, from rule-based approaches that relied on handcrafted linguistic rules to machine learning models that use annotated corpora to train feature-based classifiers. Although rule-based methods leveraged syntactic constraints such as gender and number agreement, they struggled with complex cases and required extensive manual effort. The introduction of supervised machine learning improved generalization by training classifiers on hand-engineered features, such as lexical similarity and syntactic dependencies. However, these methods still faced limitations in handling ambiguous or context-dependent references due to their reliance on manual feature extraction. The emergence of deep learning further transformed coreference resolution. Neural models, particularly Recurrent Neural Networks (RNNs) and Long Short-Term Memory networks (LSTMs), demonstrated superior ability in capturing contextual dependencies. Bidirectional LSTMs, in particular, have proven effective in modeling long-range dependencies, making them well-suited for modern end-to-end coreference resolution models, where the models jointly learn to detect mentions and link coreferent mentions [13, 14].

The introduction of transformer-based models, such as BERT and its variants, has revolutionized the field by enabling the capture of long-range dependencies [6, 7, 10, 11]. These models provide contextualized word representations, enhancing the ability to understand word meanings in different contexts. These advancements have significantly improved the accuracy and robustness of coreference resolution models, especially in handling challenging cases such as ambiguous pronouns, long-distance dependencies, and domain-specific texts.

For Arabic, several techniques have been introduced to handle its unique challenges posed by the language's rich morphology and syntactic structure. Unlike

English, Arabic lacks abundant annotated datasets and linguistic resources, making the development of robust coreference resolution models more difficult. To address these limitations, researchers have explored various techniques, including transfer learning, which leverages knowledge from high-resource languages to improve performance in Arabic [16]. Another approach involves replacing English-only pre-trained models with those trained on Arabic corpora while maintaining the same end-to-end coreference resolution architecture [2]. These models are specifically tailored to Arabic linguistic characteristics, improving performance by capturing language-specific features more effectively.

Despite advancements in leveraging pre-trained models and transfer learning techniques, Arabic coreference resolution still faces significant challenges due to the language's intricate morphology. These challenges often result in models that are less accurate and generalized compared to their English counterparts.

In this work, we address the existing challenges in Arabic language by introducing a neural coreference resolution model that integrates external syntactic and semantic information. This is achieved through the incorporation of dependency parsing and Semantic Role Labeling (SRL).

Consider the example in Fig. 2, syntactically, "وُلِدَ" (was born) is the main verb, with "الخوارزمي" (Al-Khwarizmi) as the subject and "في أوزبكستان" (in Uzbekistan) as a locative modifier. In the second clause, "العلامة" (the scholar) appears in a possessive structure linked to "مؤلفات" (works) but lacks an explicit antecedent, requiring coreference resolution. Semantically, semantic role labeling (SRL) assigns "الخوارزمي" the Patient or Theme, as it is the entity undergoing the action of being born. "كتاب المختصر" (The Compendious Book) takes the Theme role, as it is the entity being described. "العلامة" is assigned the Possessor role, indicating ownership or authorship of "كتاب المختصر". Since the only candidate for "العلامة" within the sentence is "الخوارزمي", coreference resolution links them.

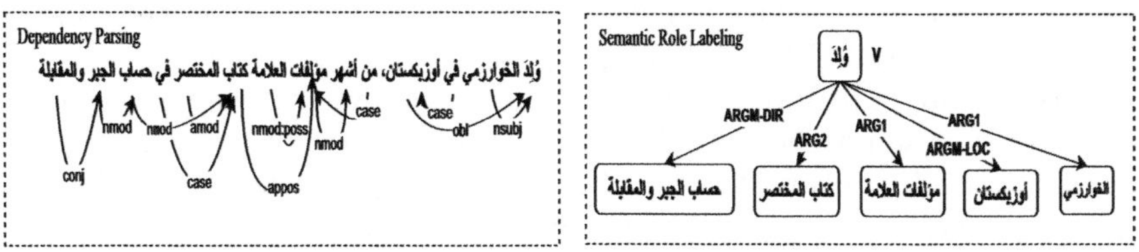

Fig. 2. Example of Syntactic and Semantic Annotation

The paper makes the following main contributions:

- **Enriched Semantic and Syntactic Architecture for Arabic.** Propose an enhanced architecture for Arabic coreference resolution by integrating

dependency parsing and Semantic Role Labeling (SRL), leveraging the best-performing Arabic pre-trained language model (PLM) to capture rich syntactic and semantic information.
- **Benchmarking and analysis of Arabic parsers.** Conduct a benchmarking analysis of existing Arabic parsers to assess their performance and identify the most effective one, providing a solid foundation for our work.
- **Empirical validation.** Validate the proposed approach through experiments on the Arabic CoNLL-2012 shared task dataset.

2 Related Work

Non-arabic Coreference Resolution. Coreference resolution for English is an active area of research. The first end-to-end coreference resolution system was introduced by Lee et al., 2017 [13], that performs span extraction and coreference classification in a single end to end model. It consider all possible text spans as potential mentions and learns to score them using a neural network. This model enhances a simple feed-forward neural network by incorporating LSTMs for contextualized representations and attention mechanisms to refine mention spans. It then scores mention pairs using a feedforward network. c2f-coref model [14] is an extended version of the previous system. The authors introduced a second order inference model, which leverages global features to mitigate errors stemming from independent decisions. Additionally, the model benefited from Coarse-to fine Inference, which integrates a coarse factor into the pairwise scoring function, facilitating further pruning and computational reduction. Later, the model was further improved [11] by replacing the Bi-LSTM text encoder with BERT allowing the model to leverage contextualized word representations and better capture long-range dependencies. This was further refined with SpanBERT [10], which is specifically trained to improve span-level representations, making it more effective for tasks like coreference resolution that involve identifying and linking spans of text. Dobrovolskii (2021) [6] considers coreference links between words instead of spans which reduces the complexity to O(n2) of the coreference models and uses RoBERTa as a language model.

Recent state-of-the-art Coreference Resolution systems employ autoregressive generative approaches, the Seq2seq model [4] was implemented as a transition system and uses multilingual T5 as the underlying language model; it is a text-to-text paradigm to predict mentions and links jointly. The current state-of-the-art system on the OntoNotes benchmark is held by maverick system [15]. The new approach identifies potential mentions by first detecting probable start positions and then determining their corresponding end positions. To further streamline the processing, it employs an end-of-sentence (EOS) regularization strategy. Following extraction and regularization, Maverick significantly reduces the number of candidate mentions by filtering out those with low confidence scores.

Arabic Coreference Resolution. Several approaches have been proposed for Arabic coreference resolution, including early rule-based methods, machine learning-based techniques, and hybrid approaches. However, these methods often require significant human effort in designing rules or features.

Aloraini et al. (2020) [2] introduced the first Arabic neural coreference system, based on Lee et al.'s end-to-end architecture [13], using Arabert as an encoder and an external mention detector. This approach was the first that specifically aimed to solve Arabic coreference resolution by adapting existing methodologies to the unique linguistic features of Arabic. Bonan Min [16] developed a new model that uses bilingual transfer learning approaches to improve Arabic coreference resolution by leveraging additional English annotation via bilingual or multilingual pre-trained transformers. By utilizing cross-lingual transfer, this model effectively enhances performance by incorporating knowledge from English language, thereby addressing data scarcity challenges in Arabic. Seq2seq model [4] based on multilingual T5 was also applied to the Arabic OntoNotes 5.0 dataset with the same settings as English and achieved state-of-the-art results. This model benefits from sequence-to-sequence learning, allowing it to capture long-range dependencies and contextual information more effectively.

Pre-trained Transformers. Pre-trained transformers based language model have shown good results for many Arabic NLP tasks, such as sentiment analysis, named entity recognition and question answering. The widely used models are Multilingual BERT [5], AraBERT [3], MARBERT [1], and GigaBert [12]. mBert [5] is a single language model pre-trained from monolingual corpora in 104 languages, it has shown good results at zero-shot cross-lingual model transfer, in which task-specific annotations in one language are used to fine-tune the model for evaluation in another language. AraBERT [3] is a Bert-based model pre-trained specifically for the Arabic language. GigaBert [12] a customized BERT for English-to-Arabic cross-lingual transfer that is trained on newswire text in the Gigaword corpus in addition to Wikipedia and web crawl data (Table 1).

Table 1. Model configurations for the Arabic pre-trained transformers

Model	Training source	Training tokens	Model parameters
AraBERT	newswire	2.5B	136M
ARBERT	Several (6 sources)	6.2B	163M
MARBERT	Arabic Twitter	15.6B	163M
mBert	Wikipedia	1.5B	110M
Gigabert	Gigaword, Wiki, Oscar	0.4B-10.4B	125M
XLM-Roberta	CommonCrawl	295B	B: 270M, L: 550M

3 Methodology

The proposed approach is an extension of the coref-HGAT [9] work to the Arabic language. The model consists of four main layers; the first layer generates word embeddings from the preprocessed data using the AraBERT pre-trained language model as an encoder. The second layer, the graph attention layer, learns the syntactic and semantic information and uses a Graph Attention Network to propagate this information to the basic token nodes. The third layer is the Attentive Integration layer, which selectively incorporates the syntactic and semantic information. Finally, the coreference layer, which takes the augmented token representation and computes pairwise coreference score. Figure 3 shows the model architecture.

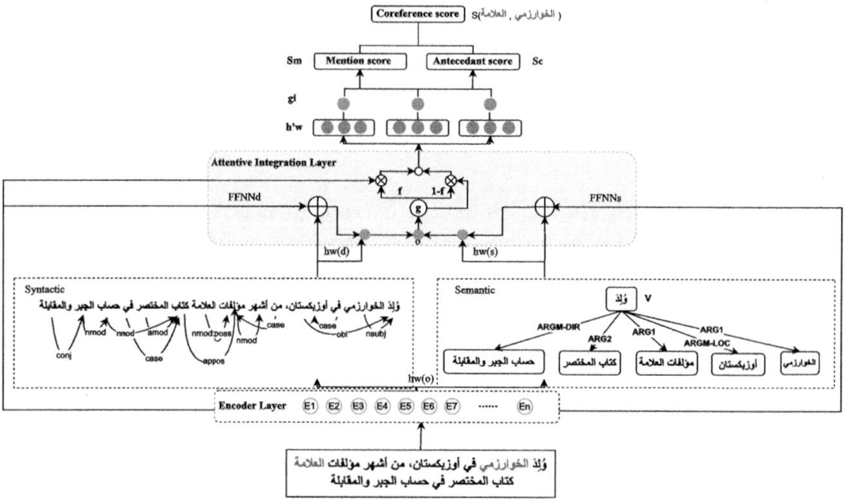

Fig. 3. The architecture of the proposed model

3.1 Data Pre-processing

The CoNLL-2012 shared task dataset used for training, in its original format, requires additional preprocessing to be properly resolved. It contains words in various forms, including commonly misspelled versions, such as different representations of the letter "alif" (إ ,أ ,آ) and inconsistencies in diacritic placement. To ensure that the encoder processes the data correctly, we implemented a series of steps to prepare the data.

- **Standardizing Alif Variants:** All instances of إ ,أ, and آ are replaced with the standard form ا.

- **Removing Incorrect Backticks:** The backtick (‘) character, which is sometimes mistakenly inserted between Arabic letters, is removed to correct distorted word forms. Example: - Incorrect: ال`له → Correct: الله- Incorrect: ه`ذين → Correct: هذين
- **Applying the AraBERT Preprocessor:** It further performs a series of text normalization and cleaning tasks, including:
  - *Removing diacritics*, such as ً ٌ ٍ َ ُ ِ ّ ْ
  - *Inserting whitespace* where necessary for proper tokenization.
  - *Eliminating excessive repetition* of non-digit characters.
  - *Applying word segmentation* when required.

These steps ensure that the Arabic text is properly formatted and ready for processing by the AraBERT model, ensuring consistency and reducing noise in the input data (Table 2).

Table 2. Example of Arabic Word Preprocessing

Before Processing	**After Processing**
إِسْتَطَاعَةُ	استطاعة

3.2 Parsing

In our pipeline, parsing is the initial step, a fundamental process in natural language processing that involves analyzing sentences to extract their underlying grammatical structures and relationships. Since our approach relies on dependency parsing structures, which reveal the grammatical and semantic relationships between words in a sentence by uncovering the dependencies between them, we used CamelParser2.0 [8] for this task. CamelParser2.0 is an open-source, Python-based Arabic dependency parser that supports two widely used Arabic dependency formalisms: the Columbia Arabic Treebank (CATiB) and Universal Dependencies (UD). It provides flexibility in disambiguation methods, allowing users to choose between a BERT unfactored disambiguator or a lighter Maximum Likelihood Estimation (MLE) disambiguator. By leveraging the advanced capabilities of CamelParser2.0, we ensure accurate parsing and processing of Arabic text, providing a robust foundation for subsequent stages of our pipeline. Further details about the parser and its implementation are discussed in Sect. 5.4.

3.3 Encoder Layer

The encoder layer is based on AraBERT [3], a pretrained Arabic language model developed to address the unique linguistic characteristics of Arabic. Similar to

BERT, it employs a bidirectional Transformer architecture, capturing contextual information from both directions for a deeper understanding of Arabic text. AraBERT comes in two versions AraBERTv2 and AraBERTv0.2, the first one requires segmentation while the latter does not, offering flexibility depending on the specific needs of the task at hand. In the proposed approach, we exploit AraBERTv0.2 as the encoder, because empirically it proved more compatible with the coreference resolution system. The choice of AraBERTv0.2 as the pre-trained model is discussed in detail in Sect. 5.1.

The preprocessed input sentences is first tokenized using the AraBERT tokenizer, which converts the raw Arabic text into token IDs. These tokens are then fed into the AraBERT model, which consists of multiple layers of self-attention mechanisms. This allows the model to learn rich contextual embeddings by focusing on different parts of the input sequence at each layer. The encoder processes the input and generates dense vector representations. The output of the encoder is a sequence of token embeddings, which are passed to the Graph Attention Layer in order to enhance those embeddings with syntactic and semantic information.

3.4 Graph Attention Layer

Following the encoder layer, the Graph Attention Layer constructs both syntactic and semantic graphs. The syntactic graph represents grammatical relationships between tokens, using dependency parsing to capture how words in a sentence relate to each other. Meanwhile, the semantic graph represents predicate-argument structures, highlighting the roles of entities within actions or states. This layer uses an iterative attention mechanism to refine these graphs, ensuring that the most relevant information is emphasized during processing. For a node i, the attention mechanism allows it to selectively incorporate information from its neighbor nodes:

$$\alpha_{ij} = \text{softmax}\left(\sigma\left(\mathbf{a}^T[\mathbf{W}\mathbf{h}_i; \mathbf{W}\mathbf{h}_j; \mathbf{e}_{ij}]\right)\right) \tag{1}$$

$$\mathbf{h}_i' = \|_{k=1}^{K} \text{ReLU}\left(\sum_j \alpha_{ij}^k \mathbf{W}^k \mathbf{h}_j\right) \tag{2}$$

where $\mathbf{h}_i$ and $\mathbf{h}_j$ are embeddings of node i and j, $\mathbf{a}^T$, $\mathbf{W}$ and $\mathbf{W}^k$ are trainable parameters. $\mathbf{e}_{ij}$ is the embedding of edge label type between node i and j based on graph structures, σ is the **LeakyReLU** activation function. $\|$ and $[;]$ represent the concatenation operation. The embedding of target node is then updated as :

$$\mathbf{h}_i' = \text{GAT}(\mathbf{h}_i, \mathbf{h}_j) \tag{3}$$

Initially, token nodes are updated using neighboring token nodes connected by syntactic dependency edges. In parallel, arguments are updated using token representations, followed by updating predicates with the new argument features.

Predicate nodes then propagate information back to their connected argument nodes, which in turn update the token nodes. Both the syntactic and semantic update processes are repeated for multiple iterations, resulting in final token representations enriched with syntactic and semantic information, denoted as $\mathbf{h}_w^d$ and $\mathbf{h}_w^s$, respectively.

3.5 Attentive Integration Layer

The next step is the Attentive Integration Layer, which integrates the information from the graph attention layer. This layer employs feed-forward neural networks (FFNN) combined with attention mechanisms. The attention weights (α_d for syntactic and α_s for semantic) computed from the concatenation of these features with the initial token representation h_w^0, guide the construction of a more comprehensive representation of the input data.

$$\alpha_d = \text{softmax}(\text{FFNN}_d([h_w^0; h_w^d])) \tag{4}$$

$$\alpha_s = \text{softmax}(\text{FFNN}_s([h_w^0; h_w^s])) \tag{5}$$

Since the extra syntactic and semantic information is not always useful, the model employs a fusion mechanism to leverage such information dynamically. This fusion is achieved using a learnable fusion gate that outputs a scalar value between 0 and 1. The fusion gate then applies a sigmoid activation function to compute a weight, which determines the contribution of each embedding to the final representation. The resulting token embeddings are a weighted combination of both the initial and enriched embeddings, ensuring that the most relevant information is retained while minimizing the impact of less useful features.

$$o = \sum_{c \in \{d,s\}} \alpha_c \mathbf{h}_w^c \tag{6}$$

$$f = \sigma(W_g \cdot [h_w^0, o] + b_g) \tag{7}$$

$$h'_w = f \odot h_w^0 + (1 - f) \odot o \tag{8}$$

where $h_c^w \in \{h_d^w, h_s^w\}$, $\mathbf{W}_g$ and $\mathbf{b}_g$ are trainable parameters, $\odot$ represents element-wise multiplication and σ is the logistic sigmoid function.

3.6 Coreference Layer

Finally, the augmented token representation is then used to form span representation and compute pairwise coreference score in the same way as in c2f-coref model [14]. For each mention i, the model learns a distribution over its possible antecedents :

$$P(y) = \frac{e^{s(i,y)}}{\sum_{y' \in \mathcal{Y}(i)} e^{s(i,y')}} \tag{9}$$

Here the scoring function s(i, j) measures how likely span i and j comprise valid mentions and corefer to one another.
The model is trained using a cross-entropy loss function, which minimizes the negative log-likelihood of the correct antecedent for each mention:

$$\mathcal{L} = -\sum_{i} \log P(y_i^*) \tag{10}$$

where y_i^* is the ground-truth antecedent for mention i. This loss function ensures that the model learns to assign higher probabilities to correct antecedents during training.

4 Experiments

4.1 DataSet

We train our model on the OntoNotes dataset, a large corpus that includes various genres of text (news, conversational telephone speech, weblogs, Usenet newsgroups, broadcast, and talk shows) in three languages (English, Chinese, and Arabic). The dataset provides rich annotations, including structural information (syntax and predicate-argument structure) and shallow semantics (word sense linked to an ontology and coreference). For our experiments, we use the official train/dev/test splits defined by the CoNLL-2012 shared task on multilingual coreference resolution, which standardizes the evaluation of coreference systems on the OntoNotes 5.0 dataset [17]. For arabic, the dataset has 359 document for training, 44 for development, and 44 for test (Tables 3 and 4).

Table 3. Number of documents in the train, dev and test sections of the English and Arabic CoNLL-2012 shared task datasets.

Language	Train	Development	Test
Arabic	359	44	44
English	2,802	343	348

Table 4. Number of entities, links, and mentions in the Arabic CoNLL-2012 shared task dataset.

Language	Type	Train	Development	Test
Arabic	Entities/Chains	8,330	936	980
	Links	19,260	2,381	2,255
	Mentions	27,590	3,313	3,235

4.2 Baseline

To establish a reference performance with minimal and standard architecture, we employ baselines that allow us to assess how our approach enhances the standard way of addressing Arabic coreference resolution. Specifically, we reimplement the c2f-Coref [11] baseline by replacing the original BERT encoder with an Arabic pretrained language model, evaluating its performance on the Arabic OntoNotes dataset. Additionally, we explore another baseline based on the approach proposed by Xu and Choi [18], which uses cluster merging as a higher-order inference technique to improve coreference resolution by consolidating clusters of mentions referring to the same entity. Each baseline model is trained using its official implementation configuration to ensure consistency and comparability.

4.3 Results

The primary evaluation metric is the average F1 score computed across three key metrics—MUC, B^3, and CEAFϕ_4—on the test set, using the official CoNLL-2012 evaluation scripts. Table 5 shows the result of the proposed model compared to previous work. The new approach demonstrates superior performance compared to the re-implemented baseline models across all three evaluation metrics achieving an average F1-score of 66.2. Furthermore, the proposed method outperforms previous works, including Aracoref and studies on Transfer Learning for Arabic Coreference Resolution, in terms of these same metrics. This improvement highlights the effectiveness of our approach in addressing the challenges of Arabic coreference resolution, showcasing its ability to better capture and resolve coreference relationships in Arabic text.

Table 5. Performance comparison of coreference resolution models on the test set on the Arabic data from the CoNLL-2012 shared task. * indicates our re-implemented baselines. † indicates the official implementation. The averaged F1 of MUC, B^3, CEAFϕ_4 is the main evaluation metric.

	MUC			**B^3**			**CEAF$_{\phi_4}$**			**Avg. F1**
	P	R	F1	P	R	F1	P	R	F1	
Encoder-Only (BERT-Based) Models										
c2f-Coref (Baseline)*	71.27	67.94	66.79	66.5	57.02	61.28	65.89	58.96	62.17	**63.41(±0.59)**
coref-hoi (Baseline)*	72.20	61.96	66.69	68.01	55.25	60.97	66.06	57.44	61.44	**63.03(±0.44)**
aracoref†	70.9	63.2	66.8	66.3	57.1	61.3	65.5	61.6	63.5	63.9
GigaBert (pipeline)†	71.46	63.19	67.07	66.93	57.62	61.92	65	61.48	63.19	64.06
GigaBert (Joint)†	73.63	61.81	67.21	70.74	55.92	62.46	66.07	62.03	63.99	64.55
Our Model (ArCo-HGNN)	71.71	67.34	69.46	66.78	61.84	64.21	66.18	63.75	64.94	**66.2(±0.44)**
Encoder-Decoder (Seq2Seq) Models										
seq2seq†	71.0	70.9	70.9	66.5	66.7	66.6	68.3	68.6	68.4	**68.7**

4.4 Ablation Study

In this study, we conduct an ablation analysis to evaluate the contributions of different components in the proposed approach with results shown in Table 6.

We compare a baseline model against variants incorporating semantic features (Semantic Role Labeling) and syntactic features (dependency parsing). Results show that the syntactic-only variant, which incorporates dependency parsing, improves accuracy by 1.69% over the baseline (63.41% to 65.1%), while the semantic-only variant, using Semantic Role Labeling (SRL), provides a 1.19% gain (63.41% to 64.6%). The full model, combining both semantic and syntactic components achieves the highest accuracy (66.2%), demonstrating their complementary roles.

Table 6. The Avg. F1 of the Baseline model by adding different features

	Avg.F1	ΔF_1
Baseline	63.41	-
+Dep	64.53	+1.12
+SRL	64.6	+1.19
+Dep+SRL	66.2	+2.79

5 Discussion and Analysis

5.1 Comparative Analysis of Arabic Pre-trained Encoders

To gain deeper insights into the performance of the proposed approach, we conduct an extensive evaluation by assessing the Avg-F1 score using different Arabic pre-trained language models as text encoders. By comparing multiple encoders, we aim to assess their effectiveness in capturing linguistic nuances, handling morphological complexity, and improving overall model accuracy.

As shown in Table 7, the performance of different pre-trained models varies significantly. Among them, AraBertv02$_{base}$ demonstrates the highest effectiveness, achieving the best results in terms of F1-score. This indicates that AraBertv02$_{base}$ is better suited for our approach compared to the other evaluated models.

Table 7. Performance of different Arabic pre-trained models on the test set

Model	Avg.F1
ArCo-HGNN with ARBERTv2	63.51
ArCo-HGNN with AraBertv02$_{base}$	66.2
ArCo-HGNN with AraBertv02$_{large}$	65.40

5.2 The Impact of Document Length on Model Performance

As shown in Fig. 4, we compare our model's performance against the baseline across document length on the test set. Our model consistently outperforms the baseline across all document lengths, with particularly significant gains for documents exceeding 786 tokens (+3.18 F1 in the 1194–1397 token range). This improvement validates that the integration of semantic role labeling (SRL) and dependency parsing enhances long-range dependency modeling. However, both models shows a performance decline as document length increases, with our model showing a smaller degradation (–5.1 Avg.F1 from peak vs. baseline's –7.0 Avg.F1). This decline suggests that, while syntactic-semantic features help mitigate long-context challenges, coreference resolution remains inherently harder for long Arabic documents.

5.3 Semantic Role Labeling

The Semantic Role Labeling (SRL) information used in our approach is derived from the CoNLL-2012 dataset, which provides rich annotations for predicate-argument structures. Specifically, the CoNLL-2012 Arabic dataset employs PropBank style semantic role labeling (SRL). In this framework, predicates (typically verbs) are annotated along with their associated arguments, which are labeled with roles such as Arg0, Arg1, and so on. While this approach is based on the English PropBank guidelines, it has been adapted to account for the unique linguistic phenomena of Arabic.

Unlike more theory-driven frameworks such as FrameNet, which organizes predicates and arguments around semantic frames and their associated roles, PropBank is designed to be simpler and more consistent across different types of predicates. This consistency has made PropBank a widely adopted resource for training and evaluating automatic SRL systems across various languages and corpora. By leveraging PropBank-style annotations, our approach benefits from a well-established and standardized framework while addressing the specific challenges of Arabic text.

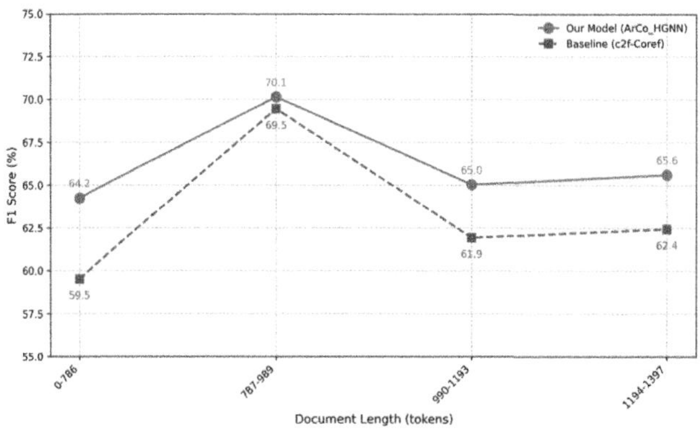

Fig. 4. Coreference Resolution Performance by Document Length

5.4 Arabic Dependency Parsing

In this approach, the selection of the CamelParser2.0 for Arabic dependency parsing is motivated by its architectural advantages, linguistic adaptability, and performance in handling the morphological and syntactic complexities of Arabic. CamelParser2.0 has demonstrated state-of-the-art performance across diverse Arabic genres, achieving superior accuracy in both the Columbia Arabic Treebank (CATiB) and Universal Dependencies (UD) formalisms compared to rule-based and classical statistical parsers as shown in Table 8.

In contrast, while parsers like Farasa and the Stanford Parser have been instrumental in advancing Arabic natural language processing, they may not offer the same level of specialization or performance in dependency parsing as CamelParser2.0. Farasa, although efficient in segmentation and POS tagging, primarily employs traditional machine learning models that lack the contextual sensitivity of neural approaches, which are critical for resolving Arabic's rich morphology and ambiguous dependency relations. Similarly, the Stanford Parser, while widely adopted, relies on transition-based algorithms optimized for English-like structures, leading to suboptimal performance on free-word-order languages like Arabic. Moreover, there is no typed dependencies (grammatical relations) analysis available for Arabic language.

Therefore, the selection of CamelParser2.0 aligns with our objectives of achieving high accuracy, maintaining processing efficiency, and leveraging a tool specifically tailored for Arabic dependency parsing.

Table 8. Scores of various dependency parsing systems trained on the PATB-CATiB and evaluated on the test set of PATB-CATiB [8].

	LAS	UAS	LS
MaltParser	80.7	83.0	93.4
Kankanampati et al. (2020)	86.2	88.1	-
CamelParser1.0	83.8	86.4	93.2
CamelParser2.0	**91.3**	**92.4**	**97.0**

5.5 LLM-Based Dependency Parsing

As an extension of this work, we explored the possibility of using Large Language Models (LLMs), specifically Qwen, as a Generative Parser. The process frames parsing as a zero-shot text generation task, where the model takes a raw sentence as input and generates a structured output representing syntactic relationships. This method eliminates the need for a dedicated parser, enhancing flexibility across diverse linguistic structures and proving efficient for low-resource languages like Arabic. To evaluate this approach, we compared our model's performance in two different settings: one using CamelParser, which was already integrated into the approach, and the other leveraging generative parsing with Qwen. Our experimental evaluation assesses the feasibility of using LLMs as generative parsers for dependency parsing, particularly in a coreference setting where a PLM with HGNN is used for resolving coreferences, while parsers provide semantic and syntactic structures. The results indicate that LLMs can effectively capture syntactic structures and maintain model performance, as shown in Table 9. These findings confirm their utility for dependency parsing and highlight their potential for broader applications in semantic-syntactic analysis.

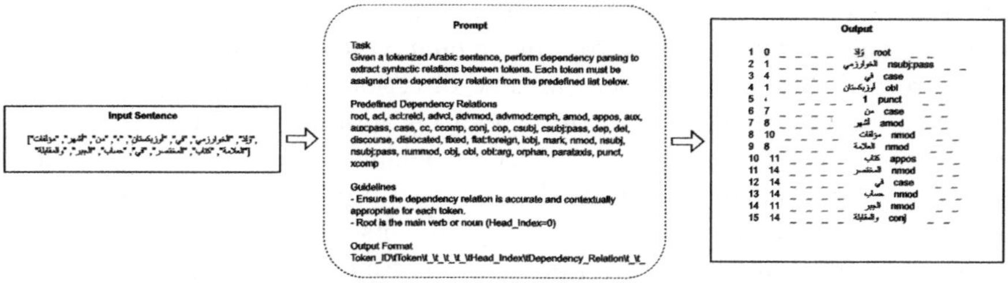

Fig. 5. Example of Zero-Shot Prompting for Dependency Parsing

Building on these insights, our analysis further demonstrates that LLMs can rival state-of-the-art parsers like CamelParser2.0, offering a flexible and adaptable solution across diverse contexts. Their ability to process complex syntactic and semantic structures suggests their potential as general-purpose parsers, reducing reliance on multiple specialized models. This adaptability streamlines data annotation, a persistent challenge for PLMs and earlier architectures.

Despite higher computational costs, LLMs remain a strong alternative to traditional parsers. In zero-shot settings, they facilitate the adoption of HGNN-based approaches by generating syntactic and semantic representations in the required format without additional fine-tuning. This capability simplifies integration into existing NLP pipelines, enhancing both research and real-world applications.

Table 9. Performance comparison of coreference resolution models.

	MUC			B^3			$CEAF_{\phi_4}$			Avg. F1
	P	R	F1	P	R	F1	P	R	F1	
ArCo-HGNN (CamelParser2.0)	71.71	67.34	69.46	66.78	61.84	64.21	66.18	63.75	64.94	**66.2**(**±0.44**)
ArCo-HGNN (LLM Parser)	71.80	67.15	69.39	66.93	61.63	64.17	66.18	63.50	64.81	**66.12**(**±0.42**)

6 Conclusion

In this work, we present a new approach for Arabic coreference resolution that incorporates both syntactic and semantic information to enrich word representations. By employing a heterogeneous graph neural network, our method effectively integrates multiple layers of linguistic cues, enabling a deeper understanding of complex coreferential relationships inherent in Arabic texts. Experiments on the Arabic OntoNotes shared task dataset show that the proposed approach outperforms traditional BERT-based models and also achieves competitive performance with current state-of-the-art methods. These promising results underscore the benefits of combining diverse linguistic features within a graph-based framework, highlighting its potential to capture nuanced contextual dependencies.

Moreover, our findings open up new directions for future research. First, refining the graph architecture by incorporating additional linguistic features and cross-lingual transfer learning may further enhance performance. Additionally, integrating large language models (LLMs) with pre-trained language models in a hybrid approach, given our initial experiments using LLMs for dependency parsing, could yield significant improvements. Finally, applying this framework to other morphologically rich languages could demonstrate its versatility and broader impact.

References

1. Abdul-Mageed, M., Elmadany, A., Nagoudi, E.M.B.: ARBERT & MARBERT: deep bidirectional transformers for Arabic. In: Zong, C., Xia, F., Li, W., Navigli, R. (eds.) Proceedings of the 59th Annual Meeting of the Association for Computational Linguistics and the 11th International Joint Conference on Natural Language Processing (Volume 1: Long Papers), pp. 7088–7105. Association for Computational Linguistics, Online (2021). https://doi.org/10.18653/v1/2021.acl-long.551
2. Aloraini, A., Yu, J., Poesio, M.: Neural coreference resolution for Arabic. In: Ogrodniczuk, M., Ng, V., Grishina, Y., Pradhan, S. (eds.) Proceedings of the Third Workshop on Computational Models of Reference, Anaphora and Coreference, pp. 99–110. Association for Computational Linguistics, Barcelona, Spain (online) (2020). https://aclanthology.org/2020.crac-1.11/
3. Antoun, W., Baly, F., Hajj, H.: AraBERT: transformer-based model for Arabic language understanding. In: Al-Khalifa, H., Magdy, W., Darwish, K., Elsayed, T., Mubarak, H. (eds.) Proceedings of the 4th Workshop on Open-Source Arabic Corpora and Processing Tools, with a Shared Task on Offensive Language Detection, pp. 9–15. European Language Resource Association, Marseille, France (2020). https://aclanthology.org/2020.osact-1.2/
4. Bohnet, B., Alberti, C., Collins, M.: Coreference resolution through a seq2seq transition-based system (2022). https://arxiv.org/abs/2211.12142
5. Devlin, J., Chang, M.W., Lee, K., Toutanova, K.: BERT: pre-training of deep bidirectional transformers for language understanding. In: Burstein, J., Doran, C., Solorio, T. (eds.) Proceedings of the 2019 Conference of the North American Chapter of the Association for Computational Linguistics: Human Language Technologies, Volume 1 (Long and Short Papers), pp. 4171–4186. Association for Computational Linguistics, Minneapolis, Minnesota (2019). https://doi.org/10.18653/v1/N19-1423, https://aclanthology.org/N19-1423/

6. Dobrovolskii, V.: Word-level coreference resolution. In: Moens, M.F., Huang, X., Specia, L., Yih, S.W.t. (eds.) Proceedings of the 2021 Conference on Empirical Methods in Natural Language Processing, pp. 7670–7675. Association for Computational Linguistics, Online and Punta Cana, Dominican Republic (2021). https://doi.org/10.18653/v1/2021.emnlp-main.605
7. D'Oosterlinck, K., Bitew, S.K., Papineau, B., Potts, C., Demeester, T., Develder, C.: CAW-coref: conjunction-aware word-level coreference resolution. In: Ogrodniczuk, M., Ng, V., Pradhan, S., Poesio, M. (eds.) Proceedings of The Sixth Workshop on Computational Models of Reference, Anaphora and Coreference (CRAC 2023), pp. 8–14. Association for Computational Linguistics, Singapore (2023). https://doi.org/10.18653/v1/2023.crac-main.2, https://aclanthology.org/2023.crac-main.2/
8. Elshabrawy, A., AbuOdeh, M., Inoue, G., Habash, N.: CamelParser2.0: a state-of-the-art dependency parser for Arabic. In: Sawaf, H., et al. (eds.) Proceedings of ArabicNLP 2023, pp. 170–180. Association for Computational Linguistics, Singapore (Hybrid) (2023). https://doi.org/10.18653/v1/2023.arabicnlp-1.15
9. Jiang, F., Cohn, T.: Incorporating syntax and semantics in coreference resolution with heterogeneous graph attention network. In: Toutanova, K., Rumshisky, A., Zettlemoyer, L., Hakkani-Tur, D., Beltagy, I., Bethard, S., Cotterell, R., Chakraborty, T., Zhou, Y. (eds.) Proceedings of the 2021 Conference of the North American Chapter of the Association for Computational Linguistics: Human Language Technologies, pp. 1584–1591. Association for Computational Linguistics, Online (2021). https://doi.org/10.18653/v1/2021.naacl-main.125
10. Joshi, M., Chen, D., Liu, Y., Weld, D.S., Zettlemoyer, L., Levy, O.: SpanBERT: Improving pre-training by representing and predicting spans (2020). https://arxiv.org/abs/1907.10529
11. Joshi, M., Levy, O., Zettlemoyer, L., Weld, D.: BERT for coreference resolution: Baselines and analysis. In: Inui, K., Jiang, J., Ng, V., Wan, X. (eds.) Proceedings of the 2019 Conference on Empirical Methods in Natural Language Processing and the 9th International Joint Conference on Natural Language Processing (EMNLP-IJCNLP), pp. 5803–5808. Association for Computational Linguistics, Hong Kong, China (Nov 2019). https://doi.org/10.18653/v1/D19-1588, https://aclanthology.org/D19-1588/
12. Lan, W., Chen, Y., Xu, W., Ritter, A.: An empirical study of pre-trained transformers for Arabic information extraction. In: Webber, B., Cohn, T., He, Y., Liu, Y. (eds.) Proceedings of the 2020 Conference on Empirical Methods in Natural Language Processing (EMNLP), pp. 4727–4734. Association for Computational Linguistics, Online (2020). https://doi.org/10.18653/v1/2020.emnlp-main.382, https://aclanthology.org/2020.emnlp-main.382/
13. Lee, K., He, L., Lewis, M., Zettlemoyer, L.: End-to-end neural coreference resolution. In: Palmer, M., Hwa, R., Riedel, S. (eds.) Proceedings of the 2017 Conference on Empirical Methods in Natural Language Processing, pp. 188–197. Association for Computational Linguistics, Copenhagen, Denmark (2017). https://doi.org/10.18653/v1/D17-1018
14. Lee, K., He, L., Zettlemoyer, L.: Higher-order coreference resolution with coarse-to-fine inference. In: Walker, M., Ji, H., Stent, A. (eds.) Proceedings of the 2018 Conference of the North American Chapter of the Association for Computational Linguistics: Human Language Technologies, Volume 2 (Short Papers), pp. 687–692. Association for Computational Linguistics, New Orleans, Louisiana (2018). https://doi.org/10.18653/v1/N18-2108, https://aclanthology.org/N18-2108/

15. Martinelli, G., Barba, E., Navigli, R.: Maverick: Efficient and accurate coreference resolution defying recent trends. In: Ku, L.W., Martins, A., Srikumar, V. (eds.) Proceedings of the 62nd Annual Meeting of the Association for Computational Linguistics (Volume 1: Long Papers), pp. 13380–13394. Association for Computational Linguistics, Bangkok, Thailand (2024). https://doi.org/10.18653/v1/2024.acl-long.722
16. Min, B.: Exploring pre-trained transformers and bilingual transfer learning for Arabic coreference resolution. In: Ogrodniczuk, M., Pradhan, S., Poesio, M., Grishina, Y., Ng, V. (eds.) Proceedings of the Fourth Workshop on Computational Models of Reference, Anaphora and Coreference, pp. 94–99. Association for Computational Linguistics, Punta Cana, Dominican Republic (2021). https://doi.org/10.18653/v1/2021.crac-1.10
17. Pradhan, S., Moschitti, A., Xue, N., Uryupina, O., Zhang, Y.: CoNLL-2012 shared task: modeling multilingual unrestricted coreference in OntoNotes. In: Pradhan, S., Moschitti, A., Xue, N. (eds.) Joint Conference on EMNLP and CoNLL - Shared Task, pp. 1–40. Association for Computational Linguistics, Jeju Island, Korea (2012). https://aclanthology.org/W12-4501/
18. Xu, L., Choi, J.D.: Revealing the myth of higher-order inference in coreference resolution. In: Webber, B., Cohn, T., He, Y., Liu, Y. (eds.) Proceedings of the 2020 Conference on Empirical Methods in Natural Language Processing (EMNLP), pp. 8527–8533. Association for Computational Linguistics, Online (2020). https://doi.org/10.18653/v1/2020.emnlp-main.686

Author Index

A
Aktemur, Ege 171
Azbeg, Kebira 187
Azerouk, Lina 39

B
Baddouj, Khadija 202
Basmadjian, Robert 230
Bergou, El Houcine 230
Bilgili, Kaan 171
Bök, Tacettin Emre 171
Bouajjani, Ahmed 19
Boubouh, Karim 230
Bourkoukou, Outhmane 214
Boutglay, Wael-Amine 19
Bramas, Quentin 163
Bui-Xuan, Binh-Minh 39

D
D'Souza, Meenakshi 3

E
Erradi, Mohammed 202, 253
Essabri, Mohammed Ali 202

F
Fetjah, Laila 187

G
Ghommat, Khadija 214

H
Habermehl, Peter 19
Hammouti, Hajar EL 230

I
Ibnouzaher, Achraf 241
Iosif, Radu 57

J
Jai Andaloussi, Said 187
Jamal, Rebii 202

K
Kakugawa, Hirotsugu 114
Kamei, Sayaka 114
Keerthan, R 129
Kolone, Hanae 202

L
Liu, Shuo 97

M
Marnissi, Ouiame 230
Moumkine, Noureddine 241
Moussa, Nour Oulad 202
Mutluergil, Süha Orhun 171

N
Nagalakshmi, S. R. 3
Nesterenko, Mikhail 146

O
Oglio, Joseph 146
Ooshita, Fukuhito 114
Ouchetto, Ouail 187
Ourekouch, Mounir 253

P
Palisoc, Camille 39
Potop-Butucaru, Maria 39, 81

S. Lahlou and M. Mukund (Eds.): NETYS 2025, LNCS 15736, pp. 271–272, 2026.
https://doi.org/10.1007/978-3-032-00347-8

S

Sangnier, Arnaud 57
Sharma, Gokarna 146
Shibata, Masahiro 114
Srivathsan, B 129

T

Tighilt, Massinissa 39
Tixeuil, Sébastien 163
Tlemçani, Khadija 187

V

Vaidya, Nitin H. 97
Venkatesh, R 129
Villani, Neven 57

W

Wakrim, Wafaa 187

Y

Yanikoglu, Berrin 171
Yousfi, Rihab EL 253

Z

Zaghdoudi, Bilel 81
Zorlutuna, Ege 171

GPSR Compliance

The European Union's (EU) General Product Safety Regulation (GPSR) is a set of rules that requires consumer products to be safe and our obligations to ensure this.

If you have any concerns about our products, you can contact us on ProductSafety@springernature.com

In case Publisher is established outside the EU, the EU authorized representative is:

Springer Nature Customer Service Center GmbH
Europaplatz 3
69115 Heidelberg, Germany

Batch number: 09013048

Printed by Printforce, the Netherlands